A History of
The Southern Confederacy

BY CLEMENT EATON

Freedom of Thought in the Old South
A History of the Old South
A History of the Southern Confederacy

A History of
The Southern Confederacy

CLEMENT EATON

⌒◄ (►⌒

THE MACMILLAN COMPANY   New York
COLLIER-MACMILLAN LTD., LONDON

Ninth Printing 1966

PRINTED IN THE UNITED STATES OF AMERICA

The Macmillan Company, New York
Collier-Macmillan Canada Ltd., Toronto, Ontario

TO

ALLIS, BILL, and CLIFTON,

who belong both to the North and to the South

Preface

IN THE SOUTH so many things are dated from the Civil War. Like the French Revolution, this conflict destroyed the old regime, affecting most drastically the life of the extremes of Southern society—the planters and the Negroes. While it destroyed a fragile type of society, it contributed greatly toward creating a glamorous legend—a legend of the Old South when the Southern people enjoyed leisure and serenity because they had attained a harmony with nature, with their fellow men (except the Yankees), and with God. All this was brushed away by the Civil War and its aftermath, the dark period of Reconstruction, and particularly by the irresistible advance of industrialization. Those days "befo' the war" which seem so splendid were splendid, of course, for the small privileged class, but not so splendid for the large middle class of Southern society—the "dirt farmers," who drank few mint juleps, and their wives, who washed the dishes—or for the field slaves, who in contrast to the house slaves did not enjoy the good food and the cast-off clothes of their masters in "the big house."

Into this world of the Old South during its final struggle I have entered as a historian trained at the University of North Carolina and in the graduate school of Harvard University. Although I have tried to be objective, I may have been influenced at times by the ordinary man's sympathy for the underdog in a fight and by my Southern birth. One of the pleasures of doing the research for this volume has been reading the letters of private soldiers and officers to their mothers, fathers, and sweethearts. These letters were never intended for the eye of a stranger of the 1950's, and at times I have felt almost a sense of shame in invading the privacy of their lives. I can still smell the incense of musty diaries, some of them with a dried flower or sprig placed between their pages in the 1860's, of yellowed newspapers, and of relics of Civil War days, preserved in Confederate depositories. I once knew an old gentleman who lived

vii

in my home town, Winston-Salem, North Carolina, who carefully cherished a few strands from the tail of Lee's war horse, "Traveller," as a medieval man would have treasured the relic of a saint or a splinter from the true cross. I have gone into the shrines of the Confederacy, attended at times by gentle old ladies who felt that the officers and privates of the Confederacy were like knights of old, *sans peur et sans reproche,* and not composed of that curious mixture of weakness and hedonism and magnanimity that we recognize as forming human nature today. Undoubtedly few Southerners can contemplate the faded gray uniforms, the swords, the dresses of Southern belles of 1860, the bearded portraits of the generals, and, above all, the tattered flags of the Confederate regiments, or read of the charges of Pickett at Gettysburg or of Cleburne at Franklin unmoved, but I have tried in these pages to tell the truth and to be fair to both sides in the struggle between the Blue and the Gray.

Interest in the Civil War has shifted in our age from military history to the life of the people during the four years of war. Here I have sought to achieve a balance between the social, political, and military history of the Southern Confederacy. Instead of giving a detailed, technical account of battles, I have sought to portray the human drama and the significance of the military campaigns. Despite the numerous books about the Civil War, many broad areas even in the military history of the period have been neglected— notably logistics, strategy, and Western campaigns. This volume is concerned with some of the neglected fields. It seems to me that the morale of the people and the army was tremendously important, and therefore I have tried to present that aspect of Confederate life. Also the operation of the Confederate government in wartime, its diplomacy, the personalities of the leaders, the common soldiers, the role of women and the attitude of the Negroes presented an absorbing side of human nature in a crisis. Above all, I have attempted to delineate the changes which occurred in the society of the Old South under the impact of war.

During 1951–1952, while I was teaching as a Fulbright Visiting Professor at the University of Manchester, I had the opportunity to view the American Civil War from the vantage point of a foreign country and to discover that, of all the periods of American history, the British universities had the strongest interest in the origins of Secession and the Civil War.

I have been fortunate in having the rough drafts of the military chapters read by such competent students of the Civil War as Kenneth P. Williams, Robert S. Henry, Branch Spalding, Wendell H. Stephenson, and T. Harry Williams. I am also grateful to Professors Albert D. Kirwan and Will D. Gilliam, Jr., of the University of Kentucky for their critical comment, and to Mrs. Monroe Billington, secretary of the history department of the University of Kentucky, for her skill and patience in typing the manuscript. The manuscript has been revised and modified a number of times between readings, but it will always be in the nature of historical writing that it is never finished or definitive.

C. E.

LEXINGTON, KENTUCKY

Contents

A History of

The Southern Confederacy

I

The Conservative Revolt

ON DECEMBER 22, 1859, a special train arrived at Richmond bringing more than two hundred medical students from Philadelphia. It was the hegira of Southern students from the North following the excitement of John Brown's raid. The faculty and students of the Richmond Medical College, the town council, and the Southern Rights Association exultantly welcomed them. All formed in procession and marched, behind the armory band, past the beautiful capitol designed by Jefferson to the governor's mansion. Here Governor Henry A. Wise, standing on his porch, delivered a tirade of incandescent Southern oratory. One of the students gracefully responded. Then they retired to the Columbian Hotel, where the hospitality of the Old South had prepared "a beautiful collation" for them.[1]

Governor Wise, fond of magniloquent phrases, said, "Let Virginia call home her children!" He assured the students that they had acted wisely in leaving a hostile community to build up Southern schools and rebuke the North for its fanaticism. Thus the reproach so often made against the South that Negro slavery paralyzed learning and science would be proved untrue. In that perfervid way of his, he said:

"Let us employ our own teachers [applause], especially that they may teach our own doctrines, Let us dress in the wool raised on our own pastures. Let us eat the flour from our own mills, and if we can't get that, why let us go back to our old accustomed corn bread." [Loud applause.][2]

The John Brown raid threw the Southern people off balance emotionally and gave them a sense of crisis. Instead of assessing the raid as the isolated act of a little band of fanatics, they attributed it to a conspiracy of the Northern abolitionists to instigate servile insurrections in various places in the South. The sympathy for John Brown which was widely manifested in the North made Southerners feel that Northerners hated their section. Out of this jittery state of mind, or popular hysteria, arose numerous vigilance committees to ferret out the emissaries of servile insurrection. As a result, Northern travelers, schoolteachers, peddlers, and workmen in the South were in constant danger of being brought before vigilance committees, flogged, and expelled from the country on the basis of unfounded suspicions.[3] Such a flagrant violation of civil liberties, moreover, was sanctioned by the legal authorities and by public opinion in general.

One of the most unfortunate consequences of the John Brown raid was that it nipped in the bud the revival of a promising Opposition or Old Whig party in the Upper South.[4] This group, led by John J. Crittenden and Joshua F. Bell in Kentucky, Congressmen Alexander R. Boteler and A. H. H. Stuart in Virginia, John Bell and John Netherland in Tennessee, and William A. Graham and George Badger in North Carolina, was seeking moderate solutions of sectional problems. The John Brown raid played into the hands of the fire-eaters in the South, the men who were determined to destroy Stephen A. Douglas's chance to be the Democratic candidate for President in 1860. To achieve this aim, as well as to unite the South by agitation, they had introduced a new and indefensible demand upon the North; namely, the passage by Congress of a slave code protecting slavery in the Federal territories.[5]

The high state of emotionalism in the South induced by the John Brown raid was further stimulated in the summer and autumn of 1860 by a prolonged scare, or panic, over rumors of the insurrection of slaves. Beginning in Texas, the fear of servile insurrection spread from state to state as newspapers reported the discovery of slave plots.[6] In December, 1860, when the secession convention met in South Carolina, many Southerners were still alarmed over the danger of slave revolts inspired by Northern emissaries. It was at this time that Major J. M. McCue of Augusta County, Virginia, arrived in Columbia to sell a rifle which he had designed to the South Carolina Convention. The model of the weapon was being fashioned in the Federal armory at Harpers Ferry, and the enterprising Major (of Virginia Militia), who directed that he be addressed as Colonel, planned to begin production of it in a plant to be located in the Shenandoah Valley. Four days after South Carolina seceded, he met Professor Charles S. Venable of South Carolina College on the street and heard a remarkable story of the dread of slave uprisings in the low country.

The professor of mathematics explained to him the excited state of the public mind which had preceded the decision to secede. If South Carolina had not taken things entirely into her own hands and withdrawn from the Union, Venable observed, "she was to be St. Domingois'd." [7] During the convention he had offered the hospitality of his home for the night to a delegate from one of the lower parishes; but the delegate had politely declined, saying that it was imperative for him to return home because, just before he left for the convention, his overseer had found some barrels of gunpowder hidden by his slaves. Venable also had heard from his sister in Alabama of her fear of the Negroes as a result of a recent discovery of an insurrection plot below Montgomery, and he mentioned the discovery of another plot in the vicinity of Wilmington which had alarmed members of the North Carolina legislature. McCue commented on these recent instances of danger to the Southern people: "The insidious means used by those wretches of the North who apotheosize Jno. Brown will leave no step of this kind unaccomplished to carry out their malignant purposes—This whole country [the South] will find, I am inclined to believe, that this Virginia rifle will be the surest defence." [8]

All over the South volunteer military companies were organized as a result of excitement over the John Brown raid. On "Looking Glass Plantation," in a placid little community in eastern North Carolina, Catherine Ann Edmondston kept a diary which reflected the emotional disturbance of many Southerners caused by the Harpers Ferry affair. On June 6, 1860, she recorded that her husband Patrick, who was a South Carolina aristocrat, had been out all day drilling his troop in the hot sun—"so much for John Brown and Northern philanthropy." Two weeks later he went with his troop to Enfield by invitation of the Enfield Blues to witness the presentation of a flag by the ladies of that community to the company. On July 16 he attended a military convention at Goldsboro to draw up a code for the organization of militia of the state. Mrs. Edmondston's father, Thomas Pollock Devereux, a prominent Whig planter, scoffed at all this military activity as folly—"no need of preparation for war," he would declare, and "he always winds up with abuse of South Carolina for her extreme views." Catherine Ann, who was a spirited sectional patriot, did not share his moderate views. "I do not see how in the present attitude of the North, [the] sample they have given us in the John Brown Raid," she wrote, "he can be so indifferent to our preparation for a future one"; her husband, however, "is on the other extreme, he is like the War Horse in the Bible who 'sniffs it afar.' He is sure that Abraham Lincoln will be elected and we plunged into a civil war before the year is ended. God arrest it!" [9]

In this inflamed state of Southern feeling the election of Lincoln on November 6, 1860, by a completely sectional vote, representing only 39.9 per cent of the popular vote, acted as the detonator of a secession movement. Lincoln, we now know, was disposed to follow a moderate course; but Southerners in 1860 had a distorted view of his personality and policies. The President-elect was regarded as an uncouth countryman who would be a figurehead in an administration controlled by Seward and the radical antislavery wing of the party. It was widely rumored among the ignorant classes of the South that Hannibal Hamlin, the Republican Vice President, was a mulatto. Southerners believed that Lincoln's real intention was to use his power of office to destroy slavery within the Southern states.

Some of the old Whig leaders and moderate newspapers in the South pointed out that Lincoln would be powerless to destroy slavery in the Southern states even if he had such a design. [10] The Supreme Court, under the lead of Taney, they argued, would shield Southern interests. Moreover, in the Thirty-seventh Congress elected in November, 1860, the Republicans would have twenty-nine Senators while the opposition would have thirty-seven; in the House of Representatives the opposition could defeat the Republicans by a vote of one hundred and twenty to one hundred and eight. Yet there was no guarantee that the Northern Democrats would vote for the preservation of slave interests, and the victorious Republican party would necessarily exclude the South from all share in the administration of the national government, for no representative Southerners would accept office from a "Black Republican." Thus the South had come to the end of a long period of control over the Federal government, which had been maintained by the mastery of the Democratic party, by the domination of the Supreme Court, and by the election of "doughfaces" such as Pierce and Buchanan to the Presidency.

The political crisis came at a time when the South was enjoying a period of great prosperity. The approach of the Presidential election broke this spell of economic euphoria. On September 26, 1860, a Kentucky mule trader wrote that "money matters are tighter in Kentucky than I ever saw them," for the planters of the lower South were not buying the Kentucky exports of Negroes, mules, and horses. One Kentucky slave trader, he reported, had recently taken forty-one slaves to Natchez but had been unable to sell a single one. The price range at the time of writing was $1,200 to $1,300 for No. 1 male slaves, and $1,000 for prime girls. In the summer the range had been $100 to $150 higher. "Politics," he declared, "is the cause of all the trouble." [11] After Lincoln was elected, business came virtually to a standstill in the South. A stock breeder of Paris, Kentucky, who was trying to sell mules in Virginia, found such a miserable market that he wrote to his wife on February 6, 1861, "It makes me sick to look at a mule." [12]

Certain that Lincoln would be elected President, Governor W. H. Gist of South Carolina on October 5 asked the governors of the cotton states what action they would take in the approaching crisis. He wrote that South Carolina preferred that some other state should take the lead in a secession movement, for the Palmetto State had a reputation for ultraism. As to the course of South Carolina, he predicted: "If a single state secedes she will follow her. If no other state takes the lead South Carolina will secede (in my opinion) alone if she has any assurance that she will be followed by another or other states; otherwise it is doubtful." The governors of Georgia, North Carolina, Alabama, Louisiana, Florida, and Mississippi replied that none of these states would take the lead in seceding. Three of the governors were of the opinion that a Southern convention should or would be called. Governor Thomas Moore of Louisiana, whose sugar planters were opposed to separation from a Union which granted them favorable tariff protection, flatly said: "I shall not advise secession of Louisiana if Lincoln is elected. . . . I do not think that the people of Louisiana will ultimately decide in favor of that course. . . . Louisiana is totally unprepared for any warlike measures. Her arsenals are empty." North Carolina's governor,

John W. Ellis, himself a secessionist, said that the majority of the people of his state would not regard the election of Lincoln as a justification for secession. Governor Joseph E. Brown of Georgia wrote that Georgia would not go out of the Union simply on account of the election of Lincoln but would wait for an overt act. The most encouraging replies for secession came from the governors of Mississippi, Alabama, and Florida, who declared that, although their states would not secede alone, they would follow if some other state seceded.[13]

There was a considerable difference of opinion in South Carolina whether she should take the lead in the secession movement. The informed leaders knew she was distrusted as hot-headed and arrogant among the more conservative Southern states. North Carolinians especially had a profound jealousy and dislike of their southern neighbor. The Raleigh *Register* declared on November 20, 1860, that South Carolina in her zeal for free trade and cheap Negroes ignored the welfare of other Southern states.[14] Consequently, one of the most talented of South Carolina's sons, William Henry Trescot, Assistant Secretary of State in the Buchanan administration, wrote to a leading fire-eater of the state, Representative William Porcher Miles, that every effort should be made to induce Georgia to take the lead in the secession movement: "Give her all the glory, take her men and her measures" to secure joint action of the Southern states. In order to accomplish this concert, with Georgia leading, he observed, "we must cut up by the roots some home ambitions and much home selfishness." [15]

On the other hand, the youthful Congressman Lawrence Keitt, most enthusiastic of the South Carolina firebrands, believed that his state must take the lead in the secession movement. "If we wait for Alabama," he wrote to Miles, "we will wait eternally." He thought William Lowndes Yancey, the foremost secession leader in that state, lacked the elements of real leadership. Keitt gave a most interesting reason for secession by South Carolina after the election of Lincoln, in the need to preserve conservatism in the South against the modern spirit of radicalism. "If we submit," he wrote, "the South is done. The concentration of absolute power in the hands of the North will develop the wildest democracy ever seen on this earth—unless it should have been matched in Paris in 1789. What of conservatism? What of order? What of social security or financial prosperity

can withstand Northern Republican license?" [16] Keitt was undoubtedly thinking of the disruptive influence on Southern society which
he believed the antislavery policy of the victorious Republican party
would have. Furthermore, he equated a Union party at the South
with an abolition party—"not at first it may be, but through quick
transitions."

By recent experience South Carolina had learned that it was impossible to get the Southern states to cooperate in a resistance movement through an All-Southern Convention. In the previous December after the John Brown raid, she had issued a call for a Southern
Convention to meet at Atlanta, and early in 1860 she had sent
Christopher Memminger, a Charleston lawyer and banker, as a
commissioner to persuade Virginia to send delegates; but the leader
of the upper South turned a cold shoulder and the movement
toward cooperation failed.[17] But after the election of Lincoln South
Carolina received assurances from commissioners sent by Mississippi
and Alabama that those states would follow her lead in seceding
from the Union. South Carolina resolved now to put into practice
the doctrine long advocated by Robert Barnwell Rhett and the
Charleston *Mercury*, edited by his son, that the secession movement
of the Southern states could be accomplished only by the bold action
of a single state withdrawing from the Union.

Disunion sentiment was strongest in the parishes of the coastal
plain containing a large slave population, but the fear of all classes
that Republican rule would destroy the control of the whites over
the Negroes, or the maintenance of white supremacy, was the dominant motive behind secession.[18] In the parishes the planters were
haunted by the fear expressed in the diary of the wealthy J. B.
Grimball (Dec. 17): "The prospect before us in regard to our
Slave Property, if we continue to remain in the Union, is nothing
less than utter ruin." [19] By December 1860 there was not a Unionist newspaper in the state. The Charleston *Daily Courier*, edited by
Aaron Willington, formerly of Massachusetts, had abandoned its
earlier opposition to a headlong movement into secession. The few
prominent men who dared to oppose the strongly flowing current,
James Louis Petigru of Charleston and Benjamin F. Perry and
Chief Justice John B. O'Neall of the upcountry, had virtually no
following. Justice O'Neall's plea to wait to see whether Lincoln
would injure Southern interests did not suit the inflamed Caroli-

nians.[20] Yet undoubtedly there were citizens, publicly mute, like the German artisan Jacob F. Schirmer of Charleston, who shared the belief confided to his diary that the state had acted hastily in "the dissolution of our glorious Union" and who feared that a civil war would follow.[20a]

The quality of the South Carolina mind in 1860 explains much in the enactment of the drama of secession. The institution of slavery had engendered in the master class a fierce and quixotic pride. The evolution of their society had nourished a romantic spirit, which placed honor and prestige high among human values and developed perhaps the most uncompromising sense of localism in America. For a generation the Carolinians had felt power slipping from them—a fact which made them ready for desperate measures. The Chesnut diary records a conversation in Columbia in which the Hampton family, who owned fifteen hundred Negroes on Lake Washington, Mississippi, were reported to hate slavery. Some one commented: "Then what are they fighting for? 'For Southern rights,' whatever that is! And they do not want to be understrappers forever to those nasty Yankees." [21] The temper of the lowland aristocracy is also reflected by Catherine Ann Edmondston, who on November 16, 1860, noted the remark of her sister Frances: "You slaveholders have lived so long on your plantations with no one to gainsay you and the negroes only look up and worship you that you expect to govern everybody & have it all your own way—I can see it in Father—in brother John—in Brother Patrick and in you." [22] The South Carolina mind was eminently conservative, believing in class distinctions, the right of gentlemen to rule, and the sacredness of property. The witty Columbia Jewess Miriam Cohen observed: "All good Carolinians are entitled to take the rank of Colonel if they have property enough. In Alabama, if the boat takes a hundred bales from a man's plantation, he is a Colonel. Before the war it required from three hundred to a thousand bales to make him a general." [23] South Carolinians had talked so long about seceding and not submitting to Yankee rule that in 1860 their pride would not permit them to walk humbly down the hill.

Aristocratic South Carolina was the only state in the Union in 1860 whose Presidential electors still were chosen by the legislature instead of by popular vote. After casting the state's vote unanimously for Breckinridge, the legislature remained in session to learn the outcome of the election. On November 9, shortly after the news of Lincoln's victory was received, the Senate passed a bill calling a convention to meet on January 15. Thus those who wished the state to cooperate with other Southern states before making a decision as to leaving the Union won a temporary victory. The delay would give the people of South Carolina time to learn the will of other slave states and also provide more opportunity for the compromisers to work.[24]

But fate played into the hands of the extremists. Two days prior to this vote the Federal district judge, Andrew G. Magrath, son of an Irish exile, had heightened the secession sentiment by impulsively resigning. Mrs. Chesnut noted in her famous diary that after his resignation pictures of the judge "in the frightfullest signpost style of painting" were suspended across various streets in Charleston. "The happy moment seized by the painter to depict him," she wrote, "was while Magrath was in the act of dramatically tearing off his robes of office in rage and disgust at Lincoln's election. . . . He is depicted with a countenance flaming with contending emotions—rage, disgust and disdain." [25] On November 10 Senator James Chesnut resigned from his Federal office and the next day Senator James H. Hammond, who had previously opposed secession, did likewise.

The resignation of Hammond is a remarkable example of popular pressure in a hitherto aristocratic state. For years Hammond had been foremost in advocating Southern independence; but in 1860 he was very conservative in supporting such a movement. When a committee requested his views on the crisis produced by Lincoln's election he replied in a thirty-four-page letter in which he said that the constitutional election of Lincoln should not be a cause of withdrawing from the Union by a people who had always prided themselves on being constitutionalists. He feared that the Southern states could not be unified until they had suffered two defeats at the hands of the Black Republicans in Presidential elections. This letter was so far "behind the times" that the committee prudently suppressed it. On November 11, three days later, Hammond reversed his position and resigned his seat in the Senate. To a relative he apologized for this dramatic act by writing: "I thought Magrath and all those fellows were great apes for resigning and have done it myself. It is an epidemic and very foolish. It reminds me of the

Japanese who when insulted rip open their own bowels. . . . People are wild. The scenes of the French Revolution are being enacted." [25a]

South Carolina indeed surrendered to a wave of fanaticism. Minute Men of Columbia and the Association of 1860 agitated for quick action in calling a convention. An inflammatory telegram was received in Charleston on November 9, stating that the governor of Georgia had recommended the immediate summoning of a convention and Robert Toombs had resigned from the Senate. The latter item was false, but the telegram touched off a wild demonstration of secession sentiment in the hitherto conservative city of Charleston. Under such excitement the legislature, without a dissenting vote, called a convention, advancing the date of its assembly from January 15 to December 17.

So strong was the emotionalism of the hour that thousands wore the blue cockade in their hats and formed companies of "Minute Men." The upcountry Congressman John D. Ashmore, who had formerly opposed the fire-eaters, now embraced their views, declaring that Southerners would never permit "Abe Lincoln's banner"— inscribed with such slogans as "The higher law," "Negro equality," "Irrepressible conflict," and "Final emancipation" to wave over them nor submit to the logical results of this victory, "amalgamation." [26]

The campaign for the election of delegates to the convention was conducted with great fervor by the secessionists. On November 12, 1860, William Gilmore Simms the novelist urged that the secession party should place on their ticket candidates of old Revolutionary lineage, a Rutledge, a Middleton, a Heyward, or "a Gadsden if one can be found of the right lineage and decent ability." He wrote to Porcher Miles that the excitement of the time was difficult for him to forbear: "We shall carry the South, I trust, through what the Germans call the Landsturm. It will be a popular rush, as I always predicted as soon as the national party should perish. The momentum given to the people being such as no popular leader or politician would venture to head, or heading which would be sure to run over him." [27]

The secessionists organized a great demonstration at Pendleton in extreme western South Carolina, at which some of the most prominent leaders of the state were invited to make speeches. The object, wrote Ashmore, was to carry Pickens, the adjoining county, "where we have more tender-footed voters than anywhere else & make the State a unit." [28] A week later he wrote of the tie between the ambitions of certain politicians and their support of the secession movement. "Already," he observed, "have some of the most violent and ultra men seized upon the movement to ride rough shod into power and my task is and has been no small one to have to encounter their folly on the one side and Perry's course on the other. Throughout the summer I have labored incessantly to get our people up to the right mark." [29]

In the election of delegates to the convention the secessionists of South Carolina won an overwhelming victory. Even in the extreme west where Unionism had been strongest, under the leadership of Benjamin F. Perry, the opponents of secession were badly defeated. The old Cooperationists, or Unionists, of 1850–1851 now voted for secessionist delegates. Nevertheless, it is interesting to note that a majority of the people of the state did not vote in this critical election for delegates, and it is reasonable to conclude that some of them stayed away from the polls because they were afraid to vote in the negative and thus be branded as "Submissionists." The convention, composed predominantly of elderly men, met first at the capital, Columbia, but adjourned because of smallpox to Charleston, where on December 20, 1860, it passed an ordinance of secession by a unanimous vote.

Beyond the wave of emotionalism that took South Carolina and later the other cotton states out of the Union lay a great glacier of conservative thought. From being the most liberal section of the nation in the period of Jefferson and Madison the Southern states had become one of the most conservative areas of civilized life in the world.[30] Moreover, the leaders of the South regarded this conservatism with pride as an evidence of a superior civilization, forming a balance wheel of the nation, a counterpoise to Northern radicalism. The American Revolution and the French Revolution of 1789 were led by radicals and opposed by conservatives. The secession movement in the South, on the other hand, was truly a conservative revolt in that the South would not accept the nineteenth century.

By 1860–1861 many invisible bonds which held the Union together had snapped—one by one. The division of the Methodist and Baptist churches in 1844–1845 over the slavery question was prophetic of a political split. The great Whig party which had upheld the national idea so strongly had disintegrated; Southern students attending Northern colleges had returned home; and Northern magazines and newspapers were being boycotted in the South. As Carl Russell Fish has observed, "The Democratic party, the Roman Catholic Church, the Episcopal Church, the American Medical Association, and the Constitution were among the few ties that had not snapped." [31]

The tensions between the North and the South had become so great that the admirable art of compromise, which had hitherto preserved the American experiment of democratic government, failed to function in 1860–1861. Neither the victorious Republicans, with the exception of the business interests in the party, nor the leaders of the lower South were in any mood for compromise. Only in the border states was there a strong movement for conciliation. Too often had the Republicans heard Southerners threaten secession to be alarmed for the safety of the Union. The evidence indicates that Lincoln and the Republican party leaders entertained serious misconceptions about the strength and nature of Union sentiment in the South. They were not disposed therefore to appeasement.

The leaders of secession in the lower South also were in no mood for compromise. Indeed, they were determined to rush the secession movement through before the excitement over the recent presidential election subsided. Representative David Clopton of Alabama, for example, wrote to Senator Clement C. Clay of that state on December 13 strongly opposing compromise. "Many and various efforts," he reported from Washington, "are being made to compromise existing difficulties and patch up the rotten concern. They will all be futile." He and several Alabama colleagues, Curry, Pugh, Moore, as well as some other secessionist congressmen had declined to vote on certain issues, "believing that we ought to keep ourselves clean of all compromises." He declared that the general impression in Congress among all parties was that a dissolution of the Union was inevitable. As for himself, he was determined to die a freeman rather than live a slave to Black Republicanism. "I would be an equal, or a corpse," he wrote. "The argument is exhausted, further remonstrance is dishonorable, hesitation is dangerous, delay is submission, 'to your tents O! Israel!' and let the God of battles decide the issue." [32]

Shortly before the Georgia Convention Howell Cobb, Secretary of the Treasury under Buchanan and one of the most influential leaders of the lower South, revealed his uncompromising spirit in a letter to William Porcher Miles. Referring to rumors of coercion, he attributed much of this talk to "the false position of southern men at Washington struggling for an adjustment in *the Union*. We ought to let it be distinctly understood that we will accept no settlement and if that position had been firmly taken at Washington from the beginning the trouble would now be all over." [33]

Nevertheless, there was much conservative sentiment in the lower South as well as in the border states which would have welcomed a compromise designed to preserve the Union and at the same time give guarantees for the safety of slavery. In the election of 1860 Georgia and Louisiana, as well as the states of the upper South, had given a majority of their popular vote to Bell and Douglas, the Union candidates—a fact which indicated that the people of these states had no desire to follow the lead of the fire-eaters. Breckinridge had polled only 44.7 per cent of the vote of the slave states. Undoubtedly many of those who voted for Breckinridge, the candidate of the Southern extremists although he himself was a Unionist, desired to remain in the Union if a settlement protecting Southern rights could be secured.

Whatever chance there may have been for a compromise was frustrated by late timing. South Carolina had already seceded when the Senate Committee of Thirteen met on December 22 and considered the Crittenden Compromise presented by the venerable Senator from Kentucky, the successor of Henry Clay. The crucial issue in Crittenden's proposals was the restoration of the Missouri Compromise line in the federal territories. The Republican members voted against this concession, which would have meant a surrender of one of the main planks of the Republican platform. The representatives on the committee from the lower South, Robert Toombs and Jefferson Davis, also voted in the negative because the Republicans had done so. Consequently, on December 31, nine days after its first meeting, the committee reported to the Senate that it was unable to agree on any plan of adjustment. When the Crittenden Compromise was presented directly to the Senate, it was brushed aside by the Clark substitute, affirming that there was no need for new amendments to the Constitution or new guarantees to the South.[34] The vote on the Clark resolution was 25 to 23, with six Senators from the lower South abstaining from voting.[35] Thus these Southern Senators contributed to the defeat of the plan of adjustment that had the best chance of acceptance.

Other last-minute efforts for an acceptable compromise that would prevent the disruption of the Union were also failures. The House of Representatives Committee of Thirty-three appointed by the Republican Speaker Pennington to bring about a solution of the sectional crisis revealed only the partisanship and disharmony of Congress. When the Washington Peace Conference met on February 4 at the call of the Virginia legislature representatives from the states of the lower South and from Arkansas, Michigan, Wisconsin, Minnesota, California, and Oregon absented themselves. It recommended an amendment to the Constitution that would have met Lincoln's main objection to the Crittenden Compromise—a fear of Southern efforts to acquire additional slave territory south of the Missouri Compromise line—by requiring that the addition of any new territory to the United States must obtain the sanction of a majority of the Senators from the free and a majority of the Senators from the slave states. Perhaps the best avenue toward a compromise would have been a national convention, which was proposed by President Buchanan and others; but it was not seriously considered.

While moderates in Congress were desperately fighting to save the Union by compromise, the states of the lower South were assembling in conventions and hastily passing secession ordinances.[36] Had they delayed action until Lincoln and his party had come into power and actually hurt them, secession might not have occurred. Mississippi, on January 9, was the second state to leave the Union; Florida seceded the following day; Alabama, January 11; Georgia, January 19; Louisiana, January 26; and Texas, February 1. The secessionists were in favor of quick measures in precipitating a revolution. They wished to take advantage of the emotional reaction of the people toward the election of Lincoln. Consequently, they were more active and better organized than their opponents, whom they branded as "submissionists." They promised that secession would be peaceful, and that it would bring the South freedom from economic vassalage to the North, and prosperity. The secession movement, moreover, was accelerated by interstate commissioners who acted as ambassadors to urge sister states to secede.

In every state there was a group known as cooperationists, who were opposed to immediate secession. They wished to call a Southern convention to discuss grievances; and, if secession became necessary, they proposed cooperation instead of separate state action in seceding and forming a new nation. They advocated, moreover, submitting the question of secession to popular vote.[37] Some cooperationists hoped by these tactics to produce delay, so that compromise and sober second thought would prevent the dissolution of the Union. Most of these moderates admitted the legal right of secession, but questioned its expediency. They were strong in the Piedmont and mountainous sections of the South, where slavery was relatively weak.

In northern Alabama, for example, the opposition to secession was strenuous, with violent threats of separating from the rest of the state and creating the state of "Nickajack," to be called after the old Indian name for this region. Hugh Lawson Clay wrote to his brother, Senator Clement C. Clay, about a protest meeting in Huntsville on the day before the secession of the state which passed resolutions instructing the delegates from northern Alabama to retire from the convention if the ordinance of secession was not submitted to the vote of the people. "The people have been so aroused by Red republican harangues," Clay wrote, "that they are in *advance of their leaders* and prepared for anything." He feared that an attempt would be made "to excite the people of N. Ala. to rebellion vs. the State and that we will have a civil war in our midst. *'The State of Nickajack'* looms grandly in the future in the imaginations of some of the leaders of the Union party." [38]

Although it seems probable that a majority of the people of the lower South were opposed to secession in November, 1860, the desire to leave the Union developed strongly during the next two months. Such an accentuation of the secession fever was not the result of a conspiracy of a few leaders, but was brought on by emotionalism, the failure to obtain a reasonable compromise, and the contagious example of the more extremist states. Nevertheless, large minorities in Alabama, Georgia, Louisiana, and Texas were opposed to immediate secession. Only in Texas did the people have the opportunity to vote directly on the issue of separating from the Union, and here the vote was 46,129 affirmative and 14,697 negative. Secession was rushed through its last stages without a thorough canvass. Yet the Southern people had contemplated dissolving the Union for ten years and had discussed the pros and cons in countless debates. The wave of rejoicing throughout the lower South which followed the passage of the secession ordinances indicated a deep popular approval. The common people of the South, except in the mountain and hill area which jutted down from Pennsylvania, agreed with the aristocrats that the victory of the Republican party was a danger to Southern society which must be met by secession. Rejecting the sagacious advice of the little statesman Alexander H. Stephens, "Let us not anticipate a threatened evil," six states of the lower South dissolved their connection with the Union and sent delegates to a convention at Montgomery, Alabama, February 4, 1861, which created the Southern Confederacy.[39]

The rise of this new nation was a part of that romantic nationalism of the mid-nineteenth century which was agitating Europe. At last the dream of Southern nationality which the fire-eaters had cherished seemed to be realized—the romantic vision expressed by Langdon Cheves ten years earlier at the Nashville Convention: "Unite and you shall form one of the most splendid empires on which the sun ever shone." [40] The decline of the tradition of American nationality below the Mason and Dixon line which began in the decade of the 1830's was one of the great tragedies of our history. Loyalty to the Union, however, survived in the upper South until Fort Sumter was fired upon, and the states of this border belt were forced to decide whether to fight for or against the Confederacy.

Secession was carried out in a wave of emotionalism. The secessionist leaders used various devices to appeal to the emotions of the rural folk of the South, such as alarming telegrams from Washington, misrepresentations of Lincoln and his party, parades, cockades, the mustering of "Minute Men," and, above all, the branding of cool, sensible persons who opposed their designs as "submissionists." Fiery orators inflamed the electorate, and even the pulpit was employed to bring people over to the secession cause. John Brown's raid and the slave insurrection scare of 1860 so upset the emotional balance of the Southern people that they could not view the election of Lincoln with common sense and reasonable perspective.

The role of agitators in the break-up of the Union was made possible by real grievances and anxieties in both sections. Agitators are powerless unless the tinder is ready for the spark, although they can contribute toward accumulating the tinder. In the North editors like Horace Greeley of the New York *Tribune,* writers such as Harriet Beecher Stowe, antislavery ministers, and demagogic politicians as well as sincere but fanatical Congressmen, such as Joshua R. Giddings of Ohio, emotionalized the problem of dealing with Southern slavery and created pernicious stereotypes of the Southern people.[41] Below the Mason and Dixon line the fire-eaters aroused acrimonious feelings in the Southern people, fears of the future, and propagated misconceptions of "the Yankees" which contributed to the creation of an emotional chasm between the two sections. Because the United States was a land of frequent elections and of multiple state parties, the politicians had abundant opportunities to arouse the passions of the electorate for their personal aggrandizement and the victory of the party.[42] The indiscriminating indictment of Southern society by the abolitionists stirred up so much ill will between the sections that there is some truth in the exaggerated remark of Mrs. Mary Boykin Chesnut of South Carolina on the psychological reason for the secession movement: "We separated from the North because of incompatibility of temper; we are divorced, North from South, because we have hated each other so."[43]

Some modern students of the Civil War have emphasized economic factors as the most important reason for secession and the subsequent outbreak of war. Charles A. Beard minimizes slavery as a cause of the conflict and interprets the Civil War as produced by the struggle between rival industrial and agricultural societies to control the Federal government for their selfish economic ends.[44] But the Beard thesis neglects the role of the agricultural West in the sectional controversy and fails to explain the behavior of the Northern businessmen during the secession movement. It also does not take account of the determination of the South to keep the South a "white man's country."[45]

At the beginning of the secession crisis a severe financial panic in Wall Street frightened businessmen. Consequently, they and their mouthpiece, the *Journal of Commerce* of New York, favored compromise on the slavery issue, and huge Union-saving conventions were held by the businessmen in New York, Boston, and Philadelphia. Southern merchants owed to Northern suppliers and bankers, it has been estimated, approximately one hundred and fifty million dollars, which might become a total loss in case of war.[46] It is notable, however, that the businessmen stoutly opposed any compromise on economic matters that affected their profits. They refused to yield on the question of abolishing the Northern monopoly of the coastal trade by repeal of the laws excluding foreign competition, they declined to give up the Federal subsidy to New England fishermen, and they insisted on raising the tariff by the Morrill Act.[47]

The South had a strong sense of being exploited by the Northern merchants, shippers, and factors. Southern commercial conventions had on numerous occasions protested against this exploitation, and in the last few years of the ante-bellum period a movement had developed to boycott Northern goods and Northern universities, textbooks, and magazines. Resentment over such economic grievances, both real and imagined, was an incalculable element in Southern nationalism—a desire to be free from economic vassalage. Although the South was not suffering from a high-tariff policy in 1860, the victory of the Republican party presaged the adoption of such a policy.

Most writers on this period of American history have overlooked the importance of sectional pride or "Southern honor" in motivating the secession movement. Because of pride men at times deliberately act against their own economic interest or comfort. As a matter of self-respect Southerners with few exceptions insisted on "equality in the Union," which they interpreted to mean the right to take their slaves into Federal territory purchased by common blood and common treasure. In 1857 the Supreme Court adopted the Southern point of view in the Dred Scott decision by declaring that neither the Federal government nor a territorial legislature could exclude slaves from the Federal territories. It was only a logical step for the proslavery interest to demand a Congressional slave code to protect slavery in the national territories.

Such a demand did not represent a real pressure of slavery expansion, for it was recognized by many leaders in the South that the territory remaining unoccupied in 1860 was economically not suited to slavery. How far the common people, with their ignorance of geography, realized this fact is, of course, impossible to determine.

If slavery expansion into the Federal territories in 1860 was largely an abstract question, why then did the Southern leaders insist on it? The answer, at least partly, was Southern pride, for the Republican program of excluding slavery from the Federal territories placed a stigma on slave-holding in the Southern states. Such a program also struck a blow at Southern political prestige and power.

On the other hand, to many Northern voters in 1860 the South as a section seemed to be acting in an aggressive fashion to advance proslavery interests. George Fitzhugh and some of his fellow extremists were predicting the enslavement of the white masses of the North, following a collapse of free industrial society.[48] A small minority of Southerners also were advocating the opening of the African slave trade, and the pro-Southern Buchanan administration was favorable to the acquisition of Cuba and other territory from which slave states could be created. At the same time the leaders of the Cotton Kingdom made serious mistakes in opposing the adoption of a free homestead law, in trying to force the proslavery Lecompton constitution on Kansas, and in demanding a Congressional slave code for the Federal territories.

Consequently the masses of voters in the North were stirred to take a stand against the extension of slavery into the territories as a moral duty, as "a principle." They could not have had the benefit of reading Professor Ramsdell's essay "The Natural Limits of Slavery Expansion" and thereby realize that they were contending for an abstraction.[49] Certainly a tremendous moral force was generated, particularly in New England and the Northwest, by the antislavery crusade which implemented the program of the Republican party and a coercion policy. A philosopher might observe, however, that this moral fervor on the part of Northerners did not involve great sacrifices such as a prospective loss of property, a serious disturbance of race adjustments, or the deprivation of dominant political power. It should also be remembered that a large segment of Northern public opinion, the Northern Democrats, did not succumb to this moral zeal.

To the South the real issue which the victory of the Republicans in 1860 raised was the safety of the institution of slavery within the old states. Although the Republican platform and Lincoln clearly renounced any intention to disturb this archaic institution within the states, Southerners as a whole were skeptical, knowing how often platforms were forgotten after elections. Regarding the race problem in the South as a strictly local concern they violently resented Northern attempts to interfere, as a minority of their descendants did in the Dixiecrat movement of 1948.

How could the election of a Republican President endanger the security of slavery within the old states of the South? In the first place the President could force the free circulation of abolition literature through the Federal mails below the Mason and Dixon line. From 1835 to 1860 the Presidents, who were either Southerners or Northern "doughfaces," had sanctioned the Southern censorship of the mails. If this censorship were removed, Southerners believed, inflammatory literature might instigate a servile insurrection and also might eventually affect the white non-slaveholders.[50] The victory of the Republicans threatened to lead to the abolition of slavery in the District of Columbia and eventually to the repeal of the fugitive slave laws. The President could use the patronage to appoint violent antislavery men to Federal offices in the South. In many indirect ways the Federal power could be used by the Republicans to weaken the institution of slavery. Southerners in 1860–1861 did not know that Lincoln was a moderate; they believed that the administration would be controlled by Seward, whom they erroneously regarded as a dangerous fanatic.[51]

Today we can see that the dominant public opinion in the North in 1860–1861 was based on something deeper than preventing the extension of slavery into territory where it would not naturally go anyway. The real purpose of the Northern majority was nothing less, as a recent historian has pointed out, than "the containment" of slavery geographically and politically with a view to its ultimate destruction.[52] This determination represented a part of the movement of enlightened world opinion, which had already abolished slavery in the Western hemisphere with the exception of Brazil, Cuba, and Dutch Guiana. Lincoln had clearly expressed this objective of his party in the famous House-Divided speech of 1858; namely, that the opponents of Southern slavery "will arrest the further spread of it, and place it where the public mind shall rest in the belief that it is in the course of ultimate extinction." [53]

Southerners realized the danger to their way of life in the victory of the Republican party, animated by a purpose of weakening slavery in every legal way possible. Disturbed by a profound sense of insecurity, the black belts of the South looked with fear not merely toward the loss of valuable property, but toward the social consequences of liberating the Negro in districts where black people outnumbered the whites.[54] Political rights, Southerners recognized, would eventually have to be given to the freed Negro, as was actually done in the Reconstruction period to the great temporary injury of the Southern states. They believed that emancipation would lead ultimately to the breakdown of all racial barriers and taboos and to the final degradation of amalgamation—a theme that was used widely in the campaign of emotionalism which preceded secession. These apprehensions over the future alarmed all classes of Southern society, non-slaveholders as well as masters, and seemed to justify secession and in the last extremity a resort to war.

II

The Decision for War

B Y APRIL 1, 1861, the Confederate flag was flying over all the Federal forts in the Confederacy except Fort Sumter at Charleston, and three Florida forts: Taylor at Key West, Jefferson and Pickens commanding the entrance to Pensacola Bay. In Texas the commanding officer, General David E. Twiggs, a native of Georgia, surrendered nineteen Federal army posts to Texan troops without a struggle. He was dismissed from the United States Army for "treachery to the flag." When South Carolina seceded she sent commissioners to Washington to arrange for the transfer of Federal property within her boundaries, particularly the Charleston forts. Although President Buchanan would not recognize the commissioners officially, he did grant them an informal interview. A gentleman's agreement was arrived at between the President and the South Carolina commissioners (at least they understood that Buchanan had given his pledge) temporarily to preserve the status quo in regard to the forts in Charleston harbor.[1]

This understanding was upset on the night of December 26 by the decision of Major Robert Anderson to remove his command of 82 men from Fort Moultrie on Sullivan's Island, accessible to the mainland, to the much stronger Fort Sumter three miles out in the harbor. The action was taken without the direct order of the President or Secretary of War John B. Floyd, a Virginia politician. Although it greatly disturbed Buchanan, he refused to order Anderson to return to Fort Moultrie as the South Carolina commissioners demanded. Instead, on January 5, 1861, he sent from New York the *Star of the West*, an unarmed merchant steamer, with troops and supplies. This ship, flying the United States flag, was fired upon by the Confederates at Charleston and turned back. The letter informing Anderson of the dispatch of the vessel did not arrive in time to give him authority to use his guns for its protection, and he withheld his fire.

For a short while after this incident Buchanan became popular in the North, and there was a spirited uprising of the Northern people to support a firm policy in preserving the Union. When Secretary of the Interior Jacob Thompson, the last Southerner remaining in the cabinet, resigned after the sending of the *Star of the West,* the cabinet, now dominated by Secretary of State Jeremiah S. Black, became completely Unionist in sentiment. Buchanan, nearly seventy years of age at this time, had long been associated with Southern politicians, and he rightly believed that the wisest policy for him to pursue was not to force the issue but to transmit a free hand to the incoming President. Likewise, Major Anderson dreaded the outbreak of a civil war and neither asked for reinforcements nor informed the government of his need of supplies until the morning of Lincoln's inauguration. He then advised the evacuation of the fort on the ground of military necessity, estimating that it would take twenty thousand soldiers to relieve the fort.[2]

The North and the South tensely awaited the inaugural address of Lincoln for omens of peace or war. In this message he announced that he would administer the government on the theory that the Union was unbroken and perpetual. Asserting the pacific disposition of his administration, he declared that he would not interfere with slavery in the states. In the noble closing passage, suggested by Secretary of State Seward, he pleaded with the Southern people not to oppose the Federal government in its necessary duty of enforcing the laws. The address was regarded as ominous in the South, for it announced that the President would execute the Federal laws in the seceded states, hold and occupy the Federal property, and collect the customs duties.

One of the most urgent decisions which Lincoln had to make following the inauguration concerned the government's policy toward Fort Sumter and Fort Pickens. Major Anderson, General in Chief Winfield Scott, and General Joseph Totten of the army engineers agreed that Sumter could not be reenforced without a powerful fleet and a large military force, which were not available. Yet Gustavus V. Fox, shortly to become Assistant Secretary of the Navy, presented to Lincoln on March 13 a plan for sending troops to Fort Sumter by running tugboats past the Confederate batteries. Two days later Lincoln requested written opinions from his cabinet as to the course for the government to pursue in regard to Fort Sumter. Only Postmaster General Montgomery Blair, son of the old Jacksonian editor, Frank Blair, unqualifiedly advocated reenforcing Major Anderson's beleaguered garrison.

On March 12 the Confederate commissioners in Washington, Martin J. Crawford of Georgia, A. B. Roman of Louisiana, and John Forsyth of Alabama, requested an unofficial interview with Secretary Seward. They sought to negotiate for peaceful relationships between their government and the United States. It is significant that the provisional Confederate Congress had taken an important step in this direction as early as February 25, 1861, by freely opening the navigation of the lower Mississippi River to the Northern states. The most pressing objective of the commissioners was to secure the evacuation of Fort Sumter and the Florida forts. But Seward flatly refused to see them, although he did have conversations with an intermediary—Associate Justice of the Supreme Court John A. Campbell, of Alabama. In the conversations the Secretary gave the distinct impression that Fort Sumter would be evacuated. Such was Seward's actual policy, and he believed that he could carry it out.[3] But Lincoln proved to be master of the cabinet, and his policy toward the Confederacy and the controversial forts was different from that of his Secretary of State.[4]

The Robert Todd Lincoln Papers in the Library of Congress reveal the tremendous pressure put upon the President by Northern men to hold Fort Sumter. Against this policy are a few letters, particularly one of March 13, 1861, from Neal Dow, the famous prohibition champion of Maine, assuring the President that "the evacuation of Fort Sumter will be fully approved by the entire body of Republicans in this State," if such an action arises from "a military necessity," but expressing the hope that Fort Pickens will be held.[5] Most of the letters relating to this crisis which have been preserved in the Lincoln collection urge a firm course, not only from motives of patriotism and honor but also from fear that a policy of appeasement would ruin the Republican party. Recent Democratic victories in local and state elections had alarmed the Republicans. Carl Schurz, a leader of the radical wing of the party, urged Lincoln on April 5 to take firm action to reenforce the forts, declaring that the Republicans were disheartened by his indecisive action and warning him of the loss of the fall elections by the Republicans if he failed to do so.[6]

The mounting sense that war was inevitable is reflected in a letter of Captain (later, General) Abner Doubleday to his wife, April 2, 1861. From the garrison of Fort Sumter he wrote, "How we can get along without fighting in the midst of all this lawlessness is impossible for me to see." [7] Such a pessimistic outlook was a definite handicap to the prevention of war. Whether it affected Lincoln's action, it is impossible to fathom. Besides pragmatic considerations in favor of coercion Lincoln believed that the United States had a mission to prove the capability of the people to govern themselves, and that this noble experiment would fail if any disgruntled minority were permitted to break up the government at will.

Before Lincoln was inaugurated, the evidence indicates, he had resolved to "enforce the laws" and hold the Federal forts. But after he faced the grave responsibilities of office, he appeared to waver over the expediency of surrendering Fort Sumter. The Lincoln Papers establish the fact that shortly before the firing on Fort Sumter he invited John B. Baldwin of Augusta County, Virginia, to a conference at the White House with the object of holding Virginia in the Union. Baldwin is described by John Tyler in a letter to his wife as "the ablest man on the North side" of the Convention, to whom, after he had made a three-day speech opposing secession, the Union ladies of Richmond presented a wreath of flowers accompanied by "some silly verse." [8] To this Unionist, Lincoln proposed that if the Virginia convention would pass resolutions of adherence to the Union and adjourn *sine die* he would take the responsibility of evacuating Fort Sumter. But Baldwin did not present the proposal to members of the convention, and nothing came of this effort of conciliation. Later, Lincoln desired that the offer should be kept secret.[9]

Because Major Anderson's supplies were running low and soon would be exhausted, the President had to take some decisive action. On March 28 a message from General Scott advised the abandonment of both Sumter and Pickens for *political* reasons. Shocked by the advice of the general in chief, Lincoln consulted his cabinet again (March 29) in regard to Fort Sumter, and this time only three of the seven secretaries clearly advocated holding the fort. On the following day he ordered an expedition to be prepared in New York harbor for the purpose of relieving the beleaguered garrison at Charleston, to be "used or not according to circumstances."[10]

Earlier he had ordered an expedition under Captain Vogdes to be sent to reenforce Fort Pickens at Pensacola, where tension was not so great and it was unlikely that the landing of reenforcements would lead to a clash of arms. Indeed, Secretary of State Seward advocated a policy of yielding Fort Sumter and at the same time asserting the national authority by sending reenforcements to Fort Pickens. Lincoln seriously considered this alternative, as he indicated in his message of July 4 to Congress. The Fort Pickens expedition, however, failed to carry out its mission because of an informal armistice made in Buchanan's administration with the Florida authorities. On April 6 Lincoln learned of this fiasco, which seems to have had a strong influence on his decision that day to let the Fort Sumter expedition go.[10a] On the same day, accordingly, without informing his cabinet, he sent R. S. Chew, a clerk in the State Department, to announce to the governor of South Carolina that he was sending an expedition carrying provisions to the garrison at Sumter. His note informed the governor that the troops in the expedition would not be landed unless the provisioning should be resisted or the fort fired upon.

The next move was up to the South Carolina authorities and the Confederate government. The cabinet at Montgomery held a meeting on April 9 to decide the wise course of action in this crisis. The Secretary of State, Robert Toombs, frequently impetuous and belligerent, on this occasion opposed striking the first blow. The Confederate officials feared that, if they did not act, the hotheaded South Carolinians would capture the fort by state authority. Accordingly, on April 10 President Davis ordered Beauregard, the Confederate commander at Charleston, to demand the surrender of Fort Sumter and to reduce it if the request should be refused.

On April 11 about two o'clock in the afternoon three aides-de-camp of Beauregard landed at Fort Sumter and presented a formal demand of surrender. Major Anderson, a native of Kentucky, loved both the South and the Union and had no heart for a war against his native section. Although he refused to yield, he said that lack of supplies would force him to capitulate in a few days. This information was telegraphed to Montgomery by Beauregard. The Confederate government, very reluctant to begin a civil war, now agreed to withhold bombardment if Anderson would state the time at which he would be forced to evacuate the fort and promise to fire only if attacked. When the young aides returned to the fort that night with these terms, Anderson replied that he would be forced to surrender April 15 at noon unless he received "prior to that time controlling instructions from my Government or additional supplies." [11] A. R. Chisolm, one of the aides, wrote in his diary that it was left to them to determine whether Anderson's reply was satisfactory. So delicately balanced was the tense situation at Sumter, it was unfortunate that these men were intrusted with such authority, and that the person who dictated the answer was ex-Senator James Chesnut, Jr., a South Carolina fire-eater. The aides deemed Anderson's terms unsatisfactory, and they announced that in one hour the Confederate batteries would open fire on the fort. The Major was deeply affected by this decision, and, warmly shaking the hands of the Confederates, said in the spirit of the religion of his age that "he hoped if we did not meet again in this world, we would in the better one." [12]

At 4:30 A.M., April 12, a red ball from one of the mortars of the harbor defense traversed the night sky in a semicircle and exploded above the Federal fort, the first shot in the Civil War. From their porches and rooftops the people of Charleston witnessed this historic battle. The Federal expedition, under the command of Gustavus V. Fox, arrived while the firing was in progress, but was unable to land troops through an error of Seward, who had detached from the expedition the powerful warship, *Powhatan,* to carry reenforcements to Fort Pickens and because a gale had delayed the arrival of the tugboats. On April 13 Major Anderson surrendered the fort to Beauregard, who had been a student of artillery under his instruction at West Point. The action of the Southerners in firing on Fort Sumter, it seems from the vantage point of today, was a serious mistake. It would have been a wiser policy to permit the provisioning of Fort Sumter and continue negotiations. But relatively few Southerners—including Alexander H. Stephens and Jefferson Davis—foresaw a long, civil war. Nor did Lincoln, Seward, and the Republican press expect a bloody conflict.

A study of public opinion in the North indicates that the mass of Northerners, now including the businessmen, strongly favored reenforcing Fort Sumter. Lincoln responded like a shrewd politician to this popular pressure which also coincided with his own convictions. Although he appears to have genuinely desired to avoid war, delaying the Fort Sumter expedition to the last moment for this reason, he finally reached the decision to uphold the symbol of national unity by keeping the American flag floating above both Fort Sumter and Fort Pickens. His policy was based on what has been aptly called "the strategy of defense," or making it appear that the Federal government was engaged in the peaceful act of "enforcing the laws" and preserving Federal territory.[13] If a conflict resulted therefrom the South, not the North, would be guilty of striking the first blow.

Lincoln's purpose in dispatching the Fort Sumter expedition seems to have been non-aggressive, but actually in view of the state of feeling at Charleston this act was virtually forcing the issue of peace and war.[14] One may well raise the question whether Seward's policy at this juncture, of letting the fort go as a result of military necessity and of continuing to seek a reconciliation, might not have been the wiser course. The crucial point was to prevent the seven slave states of the upper South from seceding and to give the strong Union minorities in Georgia, Alabama, and Louisiana opportunity to work for a restoration of the Union. Who can tell what pragmatic solution, what change of feeling, might have come out of time gained by refraining from pressing a decision at Charleston?

On April 15, after the Confederate attack on Fort Sumter, Lincoln called for 75,000 volunteers for ninety days' service to coerce the lower South. The summons forced the border states to decide whether they would fight for the South or the North. In the great tier of Southern border states Union sentiment seemed to be in the ascendant until Lincoln's proclamation. That document, according to Jonathan Worth, a North Carolina Unionist, "prostrated us."[15] The Unionists in this region felt that Fort Sumter and Fort Pickens should have been evacuated, and that conciliation and compromise should have had a further trial. Accordingly, not a single governor of a slave state, not even the governor of Delaware, responded affirmatively to this request for troops.

The leader of public opinion in the upper South was Virginia, and her action in regard to secession may have been a decisive influence on neighboring states. The Virginia legislature had called a convention to meet in Richmond on February 13, 1861, to determine the course of the state. During the two months it remained in session the majority of the delegates were for delay and compromise. John M. Daniel, editor of the secessionist Richmond *Examiner,* satirized their temporizing spirit in a witty allegory entitled "The Parliament of Beasts." [16] It was during this period that Professor Maximilian Schele de Vere of the University of Virginia wrote to the son of Secretary of State Seward expressing "the intense anxiety with which the loyal and Union-loving men of Virginia look for some evidence of the conciliatory spirit of the administration." [17] But the President-elect preserved a noncommittal silence.

The convention represented the divided mind of the upper South. A small radical group, led by ex-Governor Henry A. Wise, favored an ultimatum to the North setting forth the minimum terms under which Virginia would remain in the Union. The majority group advocated a border-state convention at Frankfort, Kentucky, and the adoption of constitutional amendments protecting the rights of the South. Unwilling to secede merely because Lincoln had been elected President, the people of the state, who had been greatly excited by the John Brown invasion, demanded nevertheless security in the Union.

Although a majority of Virginians believed in the right of secession, they doubted the expediency of exercising that right.[18] General George E. Pickett, a native of Richmond, wrote to his sweetheart after he had resigned from the United States Army and accepted a commission in the Confederate Army: "I, of course, have always strenuously opposed disunion, not as doubting the right of secession, which was taught in our text-book at West Point, but as gravely questioning its expediency." [19] Despite their love for the Union the Virginians were strongly opposed to coercion of the seceded states by the Federal government.

William Cabell Rives of "Castle Hill," an old Jacksonian nationalist, recognized the limited nature of Southern unionism, which Lincoln failed to perceive. While a delegate to the Washington Peace Conference he wrote to his son, W. C. Rives, Jr.: "It would be a dangerous mistake to consider any of those denominated Union men in either state [Virginia or Tennessee] as Union men *en tout prise.* They all concur in the indispensable necessity of obtaining new and sufficient constitutional guarantees for the rights of the

Southern States, under existing circumstances; and if the convention now assembled here should fail to agree upon such, they will, I fear, all, or nearly all, give up the Union in despair." [20] Ex-President John Tyler wrote that the failure of the Washington Peace Conference convinced him of the futility of trying to preserve the Union, and accordingly he voted for secession.[21]

The small group of active Virginia secessionists seems to have belonged to the same class of society that in 1775–1776 had furnished the leaders in precipitating the American Revolution. They were, according to the famous Civil War diary of J. B. Jones, the rebel war clerk, "representatives of the most ancient and respectable families of the state." [22] Among them was Thomas Jefferson's grandson George Wythe Randolph, a wealthy lawyer of Richmond, who wrote to a young man that his policy was to lead Virginia out of the Union to join the cotton states; North Carolina would follow; and thus war would be prevented. Virginia, he predicted, would become the manufacturing state of a Southern Confederacy, protected by a tariff from the competition of Northern industry, and would enjoy freedom from antislavery agitation.[23] White-haired Edmund Ruffin, the eminent agricultural reformer, had agitated for a decade the secession of the state, particularly at White Sulphur Springs and Warm Springs, where the élite and influential of Virginia gathered.[24] There were also several powerful editors, notably Roger Pryor and O. Jennings Wise of the Richmond *Enquirer*, George Bagby of the *Southern Literary Messenger*, and John M. Daniel of the Richmond *Examiner*, who were bold leaders of secession.

The secessionists used various means to inflame the convention to abandon the Union. They made eloquent speeches appealing to the honor of Virginia; they invited commissioners from the cotton states to address the convention; they read in the convention inflammatory telegrams from Washington, and they organized torchlight parades to stir up enthusiasm for secession. Notwithstanding, the majority of the convention delegates remained cold to the appeals until Lincoln called upon Governor Letcher after the firing on Fort Sumter to furnish troops to coerce the seceded states. Even then, conservative men like Rives believed that Virginia should not yield to the passion of the moment but should preserve a mediatorial position and call a border-state convention.[25]

In this crisis ex-Governor Wise summoned a Spontaneous People's Convention to meet in Richmond on April 16, in order to put pressure upon the reluctant convention.[26] Also he engineered a *coup d'état* by sending an expedition to seize the arsenal at Harpers Ferry. Under the stress of deep emotion the convention finally passed a secession ordinance on April 17 by a vote of 88 to 55, providing that it should be submitted to popular vote at an election on May 23. However, a military alliance which had been concluded on April 24 between Virginia and the Confederacy made this election a mere form.

Virginia's action in joining the Confederacy led to the creation of a new loyal state, West Virginia. When the convention voted on the secession ordinance an overwhelming majority of the delegates from the area that is now West Virginia voted against it. At this time the bitter sectionalism that had so long divided the state flared up.[27] Also the people of the western section feared that secession might result in war, in which case their area would become an easy conquest for a Federal army operating from Ohio. Accordingly, a convention met at Wheeling in June, 1861, and organized a loyal state government claiming to represent the whole of Virginia with Francis H. Pierpont as governor and its capital first at Wheeling and later at Alexandria within the Union lines.[28] This government eventually gave its consent to the division of the state, and on April 20, 1863, West Virginia, consisting of fifty counties, was admitted into the Union. The separatist movement, however, was carried out by a distinct minority of the population. Only 18,862 people, out of a normal vote of 47,000 for the region, ratified the Constitution, which significantly did not abolish slavery. Two counties, Jefferson and Berkeley, were included in the new state despite the opposition of a majority of their inhabitants.[29] The new state refused to assume its just share of the old public debt of Virginia until 1920, when it was forced to do so by the Supreme Court of the United States.

Tennessee was another state extremely reluctant to leave the Union. The eastern portion of the state was occupied chiefly by a yeomanry who held few slaves and disliked the aristocrats of the Nashville basin and the cotton district of West Tennessee. Both John Bell, among the Whigs, and Andrew Johnson, among the Democrats, were devoted Union men. The most influential editor of East Tennessee, "Parson" Brownlow of the Knoxville *Whig*, was such a violent Unionist that his paper was suppressed after Tennessee joined the Confederacy, and he was thrown in prison.[30] On February 9 the question whether a convention should be called was submitted to the vote of the people. The result was an overwhelming majority against calling such a convention. The firing on Fort Sumter and Lincoln's call for troops, however, brought about a reversal of sentiment in the western and middle sections of the state. John Bell now threw his influence on the side of secession and urged resistance to coercion of the seceded states by the Federal government. The people of Nashville were so aroused by the Fort Sumter affair that a vigilance committee expelled Supreme Court Justice John Catron from the city because he refused to resign his Federal office.

On April 25 Governor Isham G. Harris, the most prominent secessionist in the state, summoned the legislature into special session. He had refused Lincoln's call for troops, and now he urged secession. The people of East Tennessee, intensely loyal to the Union, held great rallies which were addressed by prominent Union leaders including Andrew Johnson and the Whig Congressmen, Thomas A. R. Nelson and Horace Maynard; but the legislature in secret session on May 6 passed an ordinance of secession as well as a declaration of independence to be submitted to popular vote and on the following day signed a military alliance with the Southern Confederacy which had been negotiated a few days before by the aggressive governor. From a practical point of view Tennessee had seceded; but the formal recognition of that fact did not occur until June 8, when the people voted for the secession ordinance and the declaration of independence by a majority of two to one.

The Unionists of East Tennessee presented a difficult problem in the movement for Southern independence. Most of the votes on June 8 against secession were cast in this section. On June 17 a Union convention was held at Greeneville, the old home of Andrew Johnson, which adopted a "Declaration of Grievances" drawn up by Thomas A. R. Nelson.[31] This document made a strong indictment of the secessionists for interfering with freedom of speech and the freedom of election and declared that the will of the majority had been defeated in an election in which a fair vote was denied. In East Tennessee, however, a separatist movement such as occurred in western Virginia was prevented by force: a vital railroad line to Richmond ran through this region, a line of communication which the Confederate government could not permit to fall into the hands of a hostile power. Nevertheless, many natives of Tennessee crossed through the Cumberland Gap to Camp Dick Robinson near Danville, Kentucky, where they enlisted in the Federal Army.

The neighboring state of North Carolina, a land predominantly of yeomen farmers, was also devoted to the Union. When Lincoln was elected President, the majority of her people favored giving his administration a trial; if he committed no overt act violating Southern rights, the prevailing sentiment was to accept the Republican administration. The press bitterly condemned South Carolina for her precipitate action. The pro-Union sentiment was revealed by a popular vote on February 28, when the people defeated a proposal to call a convention, by a majority of 651 votes.

The secessionists, who were largely concentrated in the eastern counties with large rice and cotton plantations where the Negroes were most numerous, began a campaign to overcome loyalty to the Union. Led by Senator Thomas L. Clingman and Governor John W. Ellis, they made eloquent speeches at secession rallies, branding the moderates as "submissionists." In the manuscript papers of B. F. Moore, a prominent Whig Unionist of Wake County, is an account of young men wearing roses in their hats to church as symbols of their secession sentiment.[32] However, in the western part of the state Union sentiment was so strong that secessionists were threatened with tar and feathers. The former Whig leaders William A. Graham, Jonathan Worth, George E. Badger, President David L. Swain of the University of North Carolina, and Zebulon B. Vance resisted the secession movement until the firing on Fort Sumter.[33]

The failure of the Washington Peace Conference had a marked effect in strengthening disunion. It was not until the call of Lincoln for troops, however, that public sentiment became largely unified. This transformation is revealed in the change of sentiment of William W. Holden, editor of the powerful Democratic *North Carolina Standard,* who has been called the Talleyrand of North Carolina politics, because he changed his political allegiance so frequently.[34] A zealous secessionist in 1850, he vigorously supported the Union cause ten years later until Lincoln's call for troops, when he reversed his position once more in an editorial entitled "We Must Fight." A special session of the legislature which assembled on May 1 called a convention to meet in Raleigh on May 20. This body passed a secession ordinance on the first day by a unanimous vote. Some of the old Whigs, like George Badger, who did not believe in the legal right of secession, wished the convention to adopt a declaration of independence; but they were overruled. Although the ordinance was not submitted to the popular vote, it undoubtedly represented the will of a large majority of the people. When the news of the secession of the state was announced, there was great rejoicing in Raleigh, Ramseur's Battery fired a salute of a hundred guns, men shook hands with each other, "women rushed into each other's arms," and "everybody congratulated everybody else." [35]

It was essential to the safety of the Confederacy that its northern border should be the strategic line of the Ohio River. From a military point of view Kentucky was, next to Virginia, the most important border state. The people of the state were in the uncomfortable position of having conflicting loyalties. The hearts of a majority probably were with the South, but their heads were with the North. Kentucky therefore stood for compromise, and throughout the secession crisis the legislature refused to summon a convention. However, the governor, Beriah Magoffin, was a secessionist, and replied to Lincoln's call for troops, "I say *emphatically* Kentucky will furnish no troops for the wicked purpose of subduing her sister Southern States." [36] The legislature expressed the divided mind of the people, proclaiming by an overwhelming majority the neutrality of the state.

During this period of indecision the state had in reality two small hostile armies.[37] The state militia had recently been reorganized under Simon Bolivar Buckner, a graduate of West Point and one of the wealthiest and most aristocratic gentlemen of Kentucky. He and the majority of the state militia favored the Confederacy. Indeed, perhaps three-fourths of this body eventually entered the Confederate army. The Unionist element, on the other hand, formed Home Guards under the leadership of Lovell H. Rousseau and William Nelson, a lieutenant in the United States Navy, who in the course of the war became a major general in the United States Army. "Bull" Nelson, as he was called, was a giant in physique, six feet four inches in height and weighing three hundred pounds. From the Federal government he secured ten thousand muskets with which he armed his followers. His dictatorial manner and hot temper resulted in a tragic death on September 29, 1862, when Brigadier General Jefferson C. Davis, incensed by a reprimand, shot him in the Galt House at Louisville.

Lincoln temporized in regard to the neutrality of Kentucky, for he hoped to win the border states to the Union side by patient diplomacy. He sent the recently promoted Brigadier General Robert Anderson, who had commanded at Fort Sumter, to his native state as his representative; and he authorized the establishment of Camp Dick Robinson near Danville. He also tried to keep Kentucky in the Union by proclaiming that the war was solely to preserve the Union and not to destroy slavery. In the August state elections, the secessionists refrained from voting, with the result that the legislature then chosen was predominantly Unionist.

The Confederacy was first seriously to violate Kentucky's neutrality. On September 3 General Leonidas Polk, fearing that the Federal Army would anticipate him, sent General Gideon J. Pillow to capture Columbus, Kentucky, which was regarded as the key to the Mississippi River. The Confederate Secretary of War strongly condemned this act and ordered him to withdraw; but Polk persuaded President Davis to allow him to remain.[38] The Kentucky legislature responded to the aggression by abandoning neutrality and declaring its allegiance to the United States. Kentucky soldiers in the Confederate Army, thereupon, summoned a convention to meet in Russellville, November 18, 1861. This body, 208 delegates from sixty-five counties, declared that the Kentucky legislature had betrayed the people by calling Federal troops into the state, by voting five million dollars for the prosecution of a war against the South, by failing to preserve the writ of *habeas corpus,* and by subjecting the property of Kentuckians who joined the Confederate Army to confiscation. Therefore, maintaining that the legislature no longer represented the people of the state, the convention proceeded to adopt both a declaration of independence and an ordinance of secession.[39]

Perhaps 35,000 Kentuckians fought in the Confederate Army while 75,000 joined the Union Army, as many as joined from Iowa or New Jersey. Families were tragically divided. Senator Crittenden had one son fighting for the Confederacy as a major general, while another son had the same rank in the Union Army. The Unionist editor of the Louisville *Journal,* George D. Prentice, had two sons in the Confederate Army. Three of Henry Clay's grandsons joined the Union Army, and four enlisted in the Confederate Army. The eminent Jewish citizen of Lexington, Benjamin Gratz, hemp manufacturer and merchant, had one son killed in Union service while another son fought in the Confederate Army. Kentucky furnished to the Confederate Army such valuable officers as Simon Bolivar Buckner, John Hunt Morgan, Albert Sidney Johnston, John B. Hood, John C. Breckinridge, and Ben Hardin Helm, whose wife was a sister of Mrs. Abraham Lincoln. Helm wrote to his wife on October 10, 1861: "I have gone in for the war and if God spares my life I expect to battle to the end of it. I feel that I am fighting for civil liberty & in that cause I feel that all men capable of bearing arms should be in the service." [40] He was mortally wounded leading his men in battle at Chickamauga.

During and after the war sentiment in Kentucky for the Confederacy increased. Kentuckians greatly resented Lincoln's Emancipation Proclamation as well as the use of the state as a recruiting ground by Northern states for Negroes to fill up their quotas of soldiers and thus avoid the application of the draft. In 1864 fourteen thousand Kentucky Negroes, most of them slaves, were enrolled in the Union army. An equally serious grievance was the oppression of Federal military commanders, particularly General Stephen G. Burbridge, military commander in the state from February, 1864, to February, 1865, who interfered with elections and violated the civil rights of citizens. Accordingly, in the Presidential election of 1864 McClellan received 61,000 civilian votes to 21,000 for Lincoln. A recent authority on the Civil War has observed concerning the change in Kentucky public opinion, "It was as if Kentucky retroactively and sentimentally joined the Confederacy after Appomattox." [41]

Maryland was strongly divided in sentiment in regard to secession. The eastern part of the state, containing many slave plantations, was pro-Southern, while the western section, inhabited largely by small farmers with few slaves, was for the Union. The governor, Thomas H. Hicks, was a Union man and refused to summon the legislature during the crisis of the secession movement, for he feared that it would call a convention, which in turn would pass a secession ordinance. After the war had started, however, he summoned the legislature to meet at Frederick instead of the state capital, Annapolis, where sympathy for the Confederacy was strong. On May 10 the legislature resolved that the President should cease the unholy war against the South and recommended that the independence of the Confederacy should be recognized.

Baltimore and its influential newspaper, *The Sun,* were pro-Southern. This fact was demonstrated when the first regiment to respond to Lincoln's call for troops, the Sixth Massachusetts, passed through the city. A mob of ten thousand citizens attacked the regiment, killing two soldiers. In retaliation, the Massachusetts regiment fired into the mob. Southern sympathizers also burned the bridges of the railroads which led to the North, and Washington was isolated for several days. Governor Hicks and the mayor of Baltimore joined in a request to President Lincoln that no more troops be sent through the city; communication between Washington and the North was restored by General Ben Butler, whose Massachusetts troops rebuilt the torn-up railroad between Annapolis and the railroad junction at Baltimore.

To retain Maryland was essential to the war effort of the Union, for this state lay athwart the routes of communication between Washington and the loyal states. Consequently, Lincoln pursued a different policy toward Maryland from the one he adopted toward Kentucky. Southern sympathizers were imprisoned in flagrant violation of their civil rights.[42] Nineteen members of the Maryland legislature as well as Mayor Brown of Baltimore were arrested and unceremoniously thrown into jail. John Merryman, a citizen of Baltimore and a Southern sympathizer, was arrested in May, 1861, by military authorities and imprisoned in Fort McHenry. Chief Justice Roger B. Taney then issued a writ of *habeas corpus,* which was ignored. In a famous opinion, Ex Parte Merryman, he ruled that the writ of *habeas corpus* could be suspended only by Congress and only for the sake of public safety. None the less, hundreds of citizens were illegally arrested under the authority of the President, and on September 18 the hall of the Maryland legislature was closed by the provost marshal. It is surprising, however, to note the quick subsidence of secession feeling under the heel of the Federal government and at the dictates of expediency. The Episcopal Church threw its support on the side of the Union, and the undecided, or the waverers, were drawn to the safer side of loyalty to the national government. "By the middle of May," James Ford Rhodes has written, "Maryland was actively on the side of the North." [43] Such a statement is a great oversimplification, for it may be argued with much reason that the eastern part of Maryland was held in the Union by force, just as East Tennessee was retained in the Confederacy against its will.[44]

The secession movement in Missouri led to a bloody internecine conflict. In this state the wild and woolly West met the South. The proslavery sentiment had been very strong, especially in the central belt of counties along the Missouri River, during the last decade before the war. Senator David R. Atchison, born at Frogtown, Kentucky, and educated at Transylvania University, was the leader of the aggressive proslavery forces, and Senator Thomas Hart Benton, although an opponent of the Northern abolitionists, was the leader of the free-soil advocates. Atchison was instrumental in the defeat of Benton ("Old Bullion") for reelection to the Senate after he opposed the Compromise of 1850. The proslavery element in the state was balanced to some extent by the Germans of the St. Louis area and by the resourceful leadership of Congressman Francis Blair, Jr. In the Presidential election of 1860 Douglas and Bell received nearly 71 per cent of the popular vote. Breckinridge carried the Ozarks, the most primitive part of the state.[45] The pro-Southern group controlled the legislature and called a convention to meet at Jefferson City on February 28 and consider Federal relations. The Unionists scored a triumph when the convention was moved from the capital to St. Louis, the Unionist stronghold. The convention adjourned March 22 without making a decision, but there was a two-thirds majority of Union men who favored compromise—the calling of a national convention or of a border-state convention. Lincoln's call for troops was violently refused by Governor Claiborne F. Jackson, a pronounced secessionist.

A struggle now began between the pro-Southern group led by Governor Jackson and the Union forces led by Congressman Blair and Captain Nathaniel Lyon.[46] The pro-Southern group established Camp Jackson in St. Louis and began to drill their troops. Opposing them were the Home Guards organized by Blair, and the Germans led by General Franz Sigel. The redheaded Nathaniel Lyon, commandant of the Federal garrison in St. Louis, was a zealot in the Union cause. His first step in thwarting the secessionists was the removal during the night of April 24 of 60,000 stand of arms from the arsenal at St. Louis to Illinois to prevent their seizure by Southern sympathizers. In order to spy on Camp Jackson he dressed as a woman and rode slowly through the camp in a carriage. Then, on May 10, he surrounded that encampment and captured its seven hundred men. Street fighting followed between the troops of Lyon and the Confederate sympathizers, in which twenty-eight persons were killed. These bloody "massacres" alienated some Unionist followers, including General Sterling Price, who soon became head of the state militia by appointment of Governor Jackson.

Guerrilla warfare now broke out. John C. Frémont was sent to St. Louis to take charge of the Department of the West; but he disgraced himself by the fraud and pomp of his regime. When he issued an emancipation proclamation August 30, 1861, on his own authority, he was recalled. During a period of civil strife two governments functioned within Missouri, each claiming to be the legal one. Claiborne F. Jackson and the Southern sympathizers were established at Neosho in the southwestern part of the state, while the Union government sat at Jefferson City with Hamilton R. Gamble as its head. Missouri elected representatives to the Confederate Congress and was accorded a star in the Southern flag. The state furnished 20,000 soldiers to the Confederate army, and more than 100,000 to the Union armies.

In Arkansas the secession faction was led by the governor, Henry M. Rector. A special war correspondent of the New York *Tribune,* Junius H. Browne, described some of the tactics of the secessionists in Arkansas: "Throughout the entire state men went as emissaries of Secession and told the people they must go out of the Union if they did not wish to be deprived of their slaves and ruled by the 'Yankees' who would compel them to perform all menial offices . . . they would exchange position with their negroes and the latter be made their masters." [47] The western counties, however, were deterred from joining the secession movement by fear of the strong Indian tribes to the west who were under Federal control. The people of the state voted for the calling of a convention, which assembled at Little Rock on March 4. It proved to be decidedly

Unionist in complexion but finally made a concession to the secessionists by providing for a popular referendum on the issue of the secession or cooperation.[48] Before the vote could be taken Lincoln called for troops to suppress the rebellion. Consequently, the convention reassembled on May 6 and quickly passed an ordinance of secession by the overwhelming vote of 69 to 1, the sole opponent being Isaac Murphy from the Ozark region.[49]

Farther west the Confederacy won the allegiance of some of the tribes of the Indian Territory. Most of these Indians had been removed from the South in 1830–1840, and they had carried their slaves with them. Also they had affiliations with Southern churches; the superintendent of Indians at Fort Smith, Arkansas, and his agents were Southerners; and Southern statesmen favored granting a territorial status to them. President Davis sent a diplomatic agent, Albert Pike, and a military commandant, General Ben McCulloch, to win the Indian tribes over to the support of the Confederacy. The Confederate government promised to continue the financial payments which the Indians had received from the Federal government, to apply the fugitive slave law to their slaves, and to grant them statehood. Albert Pike, who was a remarkable Indian diplomat, made nine treaties with the different tribes in 1861. The Cherokee at first proclaimed neutrality, but later divided into a pro-Southern faction headed by Stand Watie, and a Union group led by Chief John Ross. In the battle of Pea Ridge, Arkansas, at least 3,500 Indians participated on the Confederate side, including warriors from the Creek, Cherokee, Choctaw, Chickasaw, and Seminole nations.[50]

The Confederacy temporarily acquired two territories in the Southwest: New Mexico by force of arms, and Arizona with the cooperation of the leading inhabitants. The governor of New Mexico, Henry Connelly, skillfully rallied the Mexican population to the support of the Federal government by arousing their latent fears and hatred of the Texans, who had earlier attempted to annex a large portion of the territory. In December, 1861, the drastic slave code which had been adopted by the legislature two years before was repealed. In the same month, however, General Henry H. Sibley assumed command of some Texan troops in the service of the Confederacy and began an invasion of New Mexico that resulted in the hoisting of the Confederate flag over Albuquerque and the capital, Sante Fe. In the following March he retreated down the Rio Grande and was defeated at Glorieta Pass, twenty-eight miles from Santa Fe. New Mexico was restored to the Union by the courageous efforts of Major John M. Chivington and Colonel Edward Canby, assisted by converging Federal forces from Colorado and California.

The southern and western parts of the territory were Southern in sentiment. The leading American citizens with Sylvester Mowry, a prominent mine operator of Northern birth, at their head resented the control of the territorial government by the Mexican-dominated northern section and wished to separate from it.[51] Accordingly, when Colonel John Baylor brought Texan troops into Mesilla in July, 1861, the "white" inhabitants hailed them with joy; but the Mexican inhabitants showed no enthusiasm. On January 24, 1862, the territory of Arizona, formed from the southern part of New Mexico, was admitted into the Confederacy. Its existence was short-lived, however, for in the summer of that year Union troops recovered control of the territory. Thereafter, Confederate jurisdiction was confined to the eleven states which had seceded, but Southerners continued to claim also Missouri and Kentucky, and there were thirteen stars in the Confederate flag.[52]

Although some Southerners were hopeful that secession would lead to the reconstruction and reformation of the old Union, the great majority in the seceded states welcomed the creation of a permanent new republic. Relatively few shared the point of view of A. H. Handy, commissioner of Mississippi to his native state of Maryland, who argued that by seceding the South could make better terms for the reconstruction of the Union than by remaining within it. As the bells rang and the bonfires flared in celebration of secession the Southern people rejoiced at escaping from a "house of bondage," while the thought that war might be imminent scarcely crossed their minds. Because they were a provincial people, and because it was a Southern habit of mind to think of their relationship to the North primarily as a legal nexus, the Southern people failed to realize that their claim for legality in withdrawing from the Union was based on an unrealistic and archaic foundation. Minority groups in America almost invariably have resorted to the defense mechanism of state rights when their interests were seriously threatened. The Southern assertion of state sovereignty as the legal basis of secession is an illustration of this phenomenon, rather than the expression of a sincere philosophy of decentralization. The North, whose economic system favored the growth of nationalism, denied that secession was a legal right. Accordingly, the new nation had to fight for survival.

III

Creating a Southern Republic

ON FEBRUARY 4, 1861, delegates from six states of the lower South met in convention at Montgomery, the capital of the Black Belt, to form a Southern republic. Five weeks were devoted to choosing provisional officers and drawing up a frame of government. It is significant that Yancey was not a delegate, and that extreme Southern nationalists like Robert Barnwell Rhett feared the "dread spirit of reconstruction" of the old Union. The convention was dominated by a conservative spirit, which ex-Senator Hammond expressed when he pointed out, "In this era of demagogism a new constitution would be bad—The little great men who would seek notoriety by proposing to elect Judges, Senators and Representatives annually and perhaps by universal suffrage must be kept from putting their hands upon our Constitution." [1]

The Confederate blueprint of government drafted at Montgomery was largely a copy of the Constitution of the United States. Southerners had revered the Constitution of 1787; they were opposed only to what they believed was a distorted interpretation of it by the antislavery, industrial North. Vice President Alexander H. Stephens bent his energies to making the Confederate Constitution a close replica of the Federal document. Experience with the working of the national government during the heated slavery controversy suggested the wisdom of making plain in the new document certain points which the old Constitution left ambiguous. The Confederate Constitution, therefore, expressly recognized the sovereignty of the states; but it was silent on the right of secession. [2]

The Confederate frame of government incorporated some provisions which might be regarded as an improvement over its prototype. The President was to be elected for a single term of six years, and he received the power to veto separate items of appropriation bills. Congress was authorized to enact legislation granting Cabinet officers the right to speak on the floor of Congress (but such a law was not passed). Amendment was made easier by reducing the required number of ratifying states from a three-fourths to a two-thirds majority.

Certain innovations reflected the agrarian interests of the vast majority of the people. Protective tariffs (as distinguished from revenue tariffs), bounties, and appropriations for internal improvements were outlawed. Export duties could be levied and new states admitted only by a two-thirds vote of Congress. The Post Office was required to become self-sustaining. A two-thirds vote of each house of Congress was required for any appropriation of money, except in answer to the request of a cabinet officer who submitted an estimate through the President. The general welfare clause of the old Constitution was omitted. The progress of the rural South toward orthodoxy in religion was registered by a definite invocation of "the guidance of Almighty God." The old Constitution, drafted in a more skeptical era, omitted direct reference to God.

The framers of the Federal Constitution, who had been ashamed of slavery, had omitted inclusion of the word in the written document; unlike them, the authors of the Confederate Constitution were zealous to protect slavery by ironclad guarantees. Congress was forbidden to pass any bill impairing the right of property in slaves. In all the territories of the new republic slavery must be protected by Congressional legislation. The right of transit and of sojourn of slaves in any state of the Confederacy was guaranteed. The political power of slave-owners within the Confederacy was bolstered by the retention of the three-fifths ratio in apportioning representatives in Congress. However, the African slave trade was prohibited, and Congress received the power to forbid the importation of slaves from states outside the Confederacy.

From the beginning the Confederate States of America was a land of profound conservatism and was proud of that fact. The fiery Georgia secessionist, Thomas R. R. Cobb, proposed to name the new government the Republic of Washington because its founding represented a return to the principles of George Washington. William Gilmore Simms wrote to Porcher Miles, a member of the convention, that the new Constitution should return to the principle in the old Articles of Confederation of equality of state representation—in the House of Representatives as well as in the Senate. "The great principle of safety," he warned, "is the protection of minorities or feeble states." [3]

The most striking example of conservative reaction in constitutional theory during this period occurred in the Virginia convention that passed the secession ordinance. Conservatives in the convention agitated for a revision of the state constitution to curb democracy. On May 1, 1861, after many of the delegates from the western counties had withdrawn, Alexander H. H. Stuart, a prominent Whig from the Shenandoah Valley, proposed the appointment of a committee to revise the constitution as a whole. The old Whigs as a group, and men of property among the secessionists, favored making it more conservative. Equating full democracy with Yankee reforms and agrarianism, the conservatives condemned the democratic reforms of the constitution of 1850 and proposed to restore the aristocratic provisions of the constitution of 1776. A committee, headed by Stuart, was appointed to draft changes; but action was deferred until an adjourned session of the legislature in November, 1861. The conservatives advocated particularly limiting suffrage to taxpayers and establishing the short ballot. The western delegates in general opposed the undemocratic proposals; and many tidewater Virginians believed, with the Richmond *Enquirer,* that it was inexpedient to change the constitution in wartime, primarily because the proposed amendments would tend to alienate the western counties, and because the soldiers would not be able to vote on the measures.

Notwithstanding, a new constitution was drafted, for the people to ratify on March 13, 1862. It provided that the legislature instead of the people should elect judges, to serve during good behavior or until seventy years of age. The short ballot was to be established, notably by ending the election of sheriffs and most local officials by popular vote, and by providing for selection of state officers except the governor and lieutenant governor by the legislature. A majority of the convention voted against restricting the suffrage but submitted the matter to the people in a separate referendum. Previously an inequality had been removed from the constitution by striking out the exemption from taxation of slaves under twelve years of age. The popular vote on the constitution was extremely light, less than 30,000 as compared with a normal 160,000. The conservative constitution was rejected by the slight margin of 678 votes, although strangely the amendment limiting the franchise to taxpayers was adopted by a majority of 7,317.[4]

The antidemocratic movement was by no means confined to the Old Dominion. In July, 1863, the novelist Augusta J. Evans of Mobile suggested to Jabez L. M. Curry of the Confederate Congress, as a proper topic for a lecture, the need of restricting the suffrage. When she heard of Curry's defeat for reelection she wrote to him that his defeat was the result of a national ulcer, demagogism —that "Universal Suffrage is an effete theory of Utopian origin." [5] Later she pronounced Curry's defeat to be a disgrace to the state, an indication that the polls and the legislature were controlled by "co-operation reconstructionists." Many people in the Confederacy, she declared, were now willing to accept a military dictatorship.[6] Antidemocratic sentiment that was thus expressed by conservatives of the old South and of the Confederacy finally triumphed after the Civil War by the imposition of literacy tests and poll taxes which in the twentieth century have disfranchised many white as well as colored citizens.

In addition to establishing a new government, based on conservatism, the Southern Confederacy created a flag as an emblem of its nationality. The official flag, popularly called the "Stars and Bars," consisted of a field of three broad horizontal bars, the outer ones red, the inner one white, with a blue union in the upper left-hand corner containing a circle of thirteen stars. Because of the difficulty of distinguishing this banner from the United States flag, the War Department authorized the battle flag, which had a blue St. Andrew's cross, studded with thirteen white stars, resting on a background of red. At the very end of the war, on March 4, 1865, Congress created a new flag, either as a last gesture of defiance or, more likely, as an expression of desperate hope that the South would win its independence.[7]

Jefferson Davis was in his rose garden at "Brierfield" in Mississippi when the news arrived that he had been chosen provisional President of the Confederacy. Educated at West Point, he had been an officer in the Mexican War, and he preferred a high military command in the Confederate Army; but he accepted the executive position in the civil government as a duty. Although he had favored secession in 1850, he took a conservative position on the expediency of secession in the crisis of 1860–1861. Notwithstanding, the Montgomery Convention chose him in preference to either of the fire-eaters, William Lowndes Yancey and Robert Barnwell Rhett. Robert Toombs also was a prominent candidate; but his chances of being chosen President were lessened by his excessive drinking and by a misunderstanding among the delegates that the unpopular Howell Cobb was the candidate of Georgia. The desire to win the support of Virginia and the border states may have been decisive in the selection of Davis—the second choice of states with favorite sons. The balloting was by states, and on February 9 he received the unanimous vote of the six states represented. The Montgomery Convention was influenced in some of the decisions by "a mania for unanimity"—the desire to present a united front to the world.[3] After choosing the Mississippian for President it undertook to placate Georgia, "the Empire State," by electing Alexander H. Stephens Vice President.

The selection of Stephens was a mistake in spite of his ability, because his heart was not in the cause. The son of a poor farmer and schoolteacher, Stephens grew up in middle Georgia in an atmosphere of stern religion and hard work. After attending the University of Georgia he taught school and studied law. His whole life was shadowed by rebellion against his frail and sickly body—weighing less than a hundred pounds—and his gamecock spirit, involved him in physical fights such as the melodramatic one with Judge Francis Cone, a three-hundred-pounder who nearly killed him. Possessing a brilliant but conservative mind, and intensely ambitious, Stephens rose rapidly in the profession of law and in politics. A dyspeptic with a deeply melancholy nature, he never married; but he developed passionate and noble friendships with his half-brother Linton, whom he educated at the University of Virginia and at Harvard, and with the robust, flamboyant Robert Toombs. Stephens was an austere Southern puritan and condemned the human race with its hedonistic weaknesses, such as the love of dancing. His profound devotion to civil liberty was reflected in the name of his home, "Liberty Hall," at Crawfordville. His mind was legalistic, as demonstrated in his book *A Constitutional View of the Late War Between the States,* defending the Confederacy. It is a strange anomaly to find this representative of the yeomen, this passionate lover of liberty for white men, this kind slave master, declaring in a speech at Savannah, March 21, 1861, that the Confederacy's "cornerstone rests upon the great truth, that the negro is not equal to the white man." Yet he may have been unconsciously affected by the fact that he had become one of the large slaveholders of his county, owning in 1860 thirty-two slaves and an estate valued at $53,000.[9]

Neuralgia and rheumatism deterred Vice President Stephens in winter from the journey to Richmond, in unheated cars, so that he rarely appeared in the Capital after the first year of the war and his brilliant mind was practically lost to the Confederacy. On one occasion he wrote to Senator Thomas J. Semmes that he would make the difficult journey to Richmond if he saw the least prospect of doing any good; but "to sit and hear debates without the right or privilege to take part or to express an opinion is to me the most tantalizing or worrying position in life."[10] Pessimistic and embittered, he did incalculable harm to the Confederate cause by obstructionist tactics and violent opposition to the Davis policies. He thought in terms of state rights and civil liberties; but these luxuries of peacetime had to be suspended in order to prosecute a successful war for independence. He opposed conscription, the suspension of the writ of *habeas corpus,* the funding act, and the impressment of supplies—measures vital to the success of the military effort. His hatred of Davis became an obsession, and after 1863 he attacked the President publicly as seeking to establish a military despotism.[11]

Modern historians differ sharply in the evaluation of Jefferson Davis as leader of the Confederacy.[12] Most of them would agree, however, that he was inferior to Abraham Lincoln as a war President. By a curious coincidence both were born in Kentucky, within a hundred miles of each other. Thomas Lincoln crossed the Ohio River to settle in Indiana and Illinois, where his son split rails and educated himself by reading deeply a few great books. Samuel Davis, on the other hand, migrated down river to the undeveloped state of Mississippi and became a cotton planter and slave owner. Young Jefferson was sent to Transylvania University and to West Point. After he resigned from the army his millionaire brother Joseph gave him the plantation "Brierfield." He looked every inch the Southern aristocrat, over six feet in height, thin, erect in bearing, reserved, with the habit of command. He was free from the minor vices of tobacco chewing, and florid oratory. In contrast to Lincoln, he was sensitive to criticism, had a dangerous sense of pride, and lacked the safety valve of a keen and relaxing sense of humor. The Confederate President rarely was able to bolster the morale of his people by magnetic appeals, for he did not have the power of his rival to write great speeches—speeches whose phrases linger in the memory.

Davis's faults produced discord in the Confederacy. Like the Vice President, he was a dyspeptic and had frail health. During the war his frayed nerves, neuralgia, and an ailment which caused the loss of an eye tended to make him irritable and tense. James A. Seddon, his high-spirited Secretary of War, declared that "the President was the most difficult man to get along with that he had ever seen." [13] His quarrels with some of his leading generals, such as Joseph E. Johnston and Pierre G. T. Beauregard, and his fatal predilection for the unsuccessful Bragg, Hood, and Pemberton and the unpopular Commissary General Lucius B. Northrop influenced the course of the war. His legalistic and inflexible mind is shown in his speech in the United States Senate in 1859 opposing the Morrill land grant for agricultural colleges and in his history, *The Rise and Fall of the Confederate Government*.[14]

President Davis had the serious fault of attending to details of government which should have been entrusted to subordinates. Robert Kean in the Confederate Bureau of War wrote in his diary August 23, 1864, that the President's consumption of time on "little trash which ought to be dispatched by clerks in the Adjt. Genl's office" was almost a scandal. He attributed this waste to Davis's desire to be "personally conversant about everything" and to "the weakness of men about him who run to him for instructions." [15] Secretary George W. Randolph wrote to his brother of the failings of Davis as an administrator: "He lacks system, is very slow, does not discriminate between important and unimportant matters, has no practical knowledge of the workings of our military system in the field." [16]

Nevertheless, Jefferson Davis had many qualifications for his great responsibility as chief executive of the newborn Confederacy. As Secretary of War he had dominated the administration of Franklin Pierce and made one of the best war secretaries in United States history. A man of high honor and deep religious feeling, he was intensely devoted to the Confederacy and was a tireless worker in its service. His wife, Varina Howell Davis, wrote to Clement C. Clay, "The President hardly takes time to eat his meals and works late at night." [17] Unlike many political leaders of the period, he possessed a genuine culture of books. His admirable moral courage led him to do the thing that seemed right, regardless of popular clamor. Himself willing to make supreme sacrifices for Southern independence, he urged the people of Charleston in December, 1863, should the invader ever set foot on the soil of their city, to win the glory which he had desired for his county town, Vicksburg, of resisting until the whole city should be "one mass of rubbish." [18] Contrary to the accusations of his enemies, he had a high regard for the Confederate Constitution; but he also realized clearly the necessity of surrendering peacetime civil liberties in order to prosecute the war to a successful conclusion.

The fairest and perhaps most penetrating evaluation of the Confederate President was given by the Secretary of the Navy, Stephen Mallory, in a letter of September 27, 1865, from La Fayette prison to his son. The pen portrait reveals both the strength and the weakness of the Confederate leader. Mallory was impressed by the defensive armor which enabled Davis, despite extremely acute sensibilities, to keep his composure when he received adverse news or bitter criticism—only the compression of his lips and a slight change of color revealed his emotions. Although he was outwardly cold and exclusive, his nature was naturally genial and social, and to intimate friends he revealed a delightful sense of humor and a gift for conversing on many subjects. He was a tremendous worker who loved to deal with military affairs. His greatest fault was giving too much time to unimportant details. His cabinet meetings, which were frequent and often lasted four or five hours, accomplished little because of digressions. Mallory thought that the President needed the punctuality and efficient business habits of a merchant. He had an unyielding will and great energy, and his sense of justice and extreme conscientiousness led him to read and reply to thousands of letters from all ranks of society on all sorts of subjects, such as a widow's complaint that the Confederate cavalry had stolen her hogs, or the protest of a fearful citizen against enrolling so many men in military service from a county teeming with slaves liable to rebel.[19]

The first task of President Davis was to form a cabinet that would win the confidence of the Southern people. The Confederate cabinet consisted of six department heads. Although there was no Department of the Interior, the Attorney General headed a Department of Justice—a branch of government which the United States did not organize until 1870. It is strange that this new nation, representing agricultural states, did not establish a Department of Agriculture. In selecting his cabinet Davis was limited by the fact that some of the most forceful political leaders of the ante-bellum South, such as John C. Breckinridge, Howell Cobb, Robert Toombs, and Henry A. Wise, spent most of their careers in the Confederacy as generals. Thus their brains were scarcely used in the administration of the civil government where they would have been most useful.

So strong was state pride that political expediency required the President to choose cabinet members partly by the principle of geographical representation. He recognized the claims of Georgia by appointing Robert Toombs to the premier position, Secretary of State. In order to give South Carolina a representative he appointed Christopher G. Memminger Secretary of the Treasury. Memminger's career in South Carolina had been distinguished by an advocacy of sound money; but in his new position he was forced to operate largely by the issue of tremendous quantities of paper money. Lacking in personality, he was unsuccessful in persuading Congress to accept his financial proposals. To represent Alabama, Davis appointed Leroy Pope Walker, a tobacco-chewing aristocrat, Secretary of War. For Secretary of the Navy he chose Stephen R. Mallory of Florida, who had served as chairman of the Naval Affairs Committee of the United States Senate; Mallory was described by John L. Peyton, Agent of North Carolina to Great Britain, as a short, fat man, with a big head, leaden eye, and a heavy countenance, wearing clothes so tight that he literally seemed "too big for his breeches." [20] His nomination was the only one that caused opposition from Congress, because some of the Florida delegation believed that he had been opposed to secession and had prevented the state from seizing Fort Pickens at Pensacola. Louisiana received recognition in the cabinet by the appointment of Judah P. Benjamin as Attorney General. Benjamin became the most trusted adviser of Davis.

The Postmaster General was John H. Reagan of Texas, a self-made man of very independent mind. He was limited by a provision in the Confederate Constitution requiring the Post Office Department to be self-supporting after March 1, 1863. By discontinuing numerous small post offices, reducing the franking privilege, driving sharp bargains with railroads, and charging high postal rates, he succeeded in making a profit for his department. However, the surplus was obtained partly by the use of stamps for fractional currency and by the willingness of mail contractors to accept ridiculously low compensation in order to escape the draft. The Federal postal system continued to function within the Confederacy until June 6, 1861, four months after the rebel government was organized. It was not until eight months after Jefferson Davis was inaugurated, October 16, that the new government was able to issue its first stamps, of five-cent denomination, green in color, bearing the picture of the Confederate President. In February, 1862, the first shipment of more than two million stamps made in London was imported through the blockade.

The cabinet of Davis was constantly changing. During the four years' existence of the Confederacy, fourteen appointees held the six cabinet positions. Stephen Mallory and John Reagan were the only members who retained their original positions until the end of the war. Davis had six Secretaries of War during the period. Critics of the Confederate President who explain the instability of the cabinet on the ground that he made mere clerks of them and tolerated only complaisant yes-men as advisers, ignore the fact that changes occurred for a variety of reasons.[21] Leroy Pope Walker resigned because of ill health and the criticism of his conduct of the office by the people. Secretary of the Treasury Memminger resigned in 1864 because Congress rejected his financial proposals, and the great Charleston cotton exporter, George A. Trenholm, succeeded him. James A. Seddon, who was the Secretary of War for the longest period, was forced out of office by the hostility of Congress despite Davis's loyalty to him. Although Judah P. Benjamin was retained in the cabinet until the very end, he held three different portfolios: Attorney General, Secretary of War, and Secretary of State.

Davis was far from a dictator domineering over a rubber-stamp council. He carefully discussed important matters of policy with his cabinet and frequently took their advice. Indeed, one admirable trait in his character was his loyalty to cabinet members when they were attacked in Congress and the press. After the loss of Norfolk and the destruction of the *Virginia* (*Merrimac*) in the spring of 1862 a tremendous clamor to remove Mallory resulted in a Congressional investigation of his department. Davis stood by him, and the investigation finally approved his conduct of naval affairs. Benjamin was also bitterly criticized after the disaster of Roanoke Island in February, 1862, during his tenure as Secretary of War. Opposition in Congress prevented Davis from continuing him as Secretary of War; but he promoted him to the Secretaryship of State and made him his most trusted adviser. In cabinet meetings Davis was willing to listen to opposing opinions. Postmaster General Reagan, for example, often disagreed with the President and with the majority of the cabinet, yet he remained with Davis to the very end.

It is significant that few of the leading statesmen of the Confederacy were of aristocratic lineage. Postmaster General Reagan's father was a tanner, and he himself had been an overseer. Stephen Mallory, the son of a Connecticut Yankee, had aided his widowed mother in running a boarding house for sailors in Key West, Florida. Christopher Memminger, who represented the aristocratic state of South Carolina in the cabinet, was a German immigrant who had spent part of his youth in an orphanage. Judah P. Benjamin was the son of a small merchant; and the ablest diplomat of the Confederacy, John Slidell, was born in New York City, the son of a tallow chandler. Jefferson Davis himself was the son of a yeoman farmer and was born in a house not much better than the log cabin in which Abraham Lincoln was born. On the other hand, Secretaries of State Robert Toombs and Robert M. T. Hunter and Secretaries of War George W. Randolph, James A. Seddon, Leroy P. Walker, and John C. Breckinridge belonged to the plantation aristocracy.

The statesmen of the Confederacy worked under irritating and uncomfortable conditions in the hot, provincial capital at Montgomery. This capital in the black belt was teeming with office seekers, and was cursed with miserable hotel facilities; moreover, mosquitoes were eternally biting the statesmen and their ladies. After Virginia joined the Confederacy there was a strong desire to remove the Capital to Richmond, a city of 40,000 people; and in May, 1861, Congress, overriding a veto of the President, voted to transfer the Capital. Richmond occupied a vulnerable position, one hundred and fifteen miles from Washington, and it was accessible to Federal warships by the James River approach. Soon the city was doubled in population by government officials, army men, hangers-on, and prostitutes.[22] The hotel rates became so high ($3 a night) that poor soldiers passing through the city could not afford such luxury on a private's pay ($11 a month). Consequently they roamed the streets at night, got drunk, and created disorder. Gambling flourished, and spies and fifth columnists were active. Most dangerous of the latter was Elizabeth Van Lew, member of a wealthy local Unionist family, who ministered to Federal prisoners and gave valuable military information to the enemy but was never caught.[23] Finally martial law was proclaimed in the spring of 1862 in order to permit the military governor, General John H. Winder, to free the city from the criminal class. The Capital was alarmed by constant rumors, and the government clerks were organized into companies to defend it.

On February 22, 1862, Washington's birthday anniversary, the "permanent" government succeeded the provisional one. Jefferson Davis and Alexander H. Stephens, having been unanimously elected President and Vice President in the preceding November, were inaugurated at Richmond in a downpour of rain and in the shadow of the surrender of Fort Donelson. The keynote of Davis's inaugural speech was that the Confederate government preserved and cherished the personal liberty of its citizens while the North exercised the "tyranny of an unbridled majority." He cited as proof the suppression of civil liberties in Maryland by Lincoln's government while "there has been no act on our part to impair personal liberty or the freedom of speech, of thought, or of the press." [24]

The Confederate Congress, now a bicameral body instead of the one house of the provisional government, proved to be notably weak throughout its existence. The executive branch overshadowed it; but this subordination of the legislature in time of war is characteristic of American government. A special reason for the ineffectiveness of the Confederate Congress was that some of the ablest statesmen of the South were not elected to it. The aristocratic tradition of the place of honor being in the field was strong in the old South. Accordingly, some able and ambitious politicians preferred military glory to the pay of a Congressman, $2,760. Yancey, the great orator of secession, was sent on a diplomatic mission to Europe—for which he was unsuited—and served briefly in the Senate when he returned. In 1863, in the month of the battle of Gettysburg, he died after an encounter in the Senate with Benjamin H. Hill of Georgia, who hit him in the face with an ink bottle—a discreditable episode which the Senate tried to conceal. The failure to give Rhett a cabinet appointment, perhaps Davis's first important mistake, influenced the proud Carolinian to become a powerful opponent of the President. In 1863 he offered himself as a candidate for the lower house to "invigorate" the government, but was defeated. After this humiliation he retired from politics until the close of the war, when he wrote a forceful letter opposing the use of Negro troops.[25]

The secrecy of Congress was a factor in its ineffectiveness. After Yancey returned from Europe he fought unavailingly in the Senate to end the secret sessions. He believed that the people would cooperate better if the government and Congress would take them into their confidence. Both the President and Congress failed to realize the importance of the home front, of keeping up civilian morale.

Southerners of the ante-bellum period prided themselves on the supposition that slavery and the plantation system bred statesmen of a high quality. Varina Howell Davis wrote with warm praise of the provisional Confederate Congress at Montgomery: "They are the finest looking set of men I have ever seen collected together, grave, quiet, and thoughtful looking men with an air of refinement which makes in my mind's picture gallery a gratifying pendent to Hamlin, Durkee, Dolittle [*sic*] and Chandler"—Northern political leaders." [26] Yet by March, 1863, Alexander Stephens was reporting that Congress was a futile body, spending so much valuable time on minor details. "The mountain labors and brings forth a mouse," he commented.[27] Congress was bitterly criticized for its timidity, particularly for its reluctance to levy necessary taxes or to fashion a sensible financial policy. Robert Kean of the Confederate War Bureau sarcastically referred to "the smallness of Congress," which refused to deal courageously with finances. Although the fantastic inflation of the currency in 1863 demanded a realistic adjustment of government salaries, "Congress is *afraid* to increase salaries." [28] James H. Hammond, former United States Senator, suggested that a cause of Congressional ineptitude was the addiction of its members to alcohol, "Some malign influence," he wrote in 1863 to Senator R. M. T. Hunter, "seems to preside over your councils. Pardon me, is the majority always drunk? The People are beginning to think so." [29] Indeed, there is an untold story of the role of drunkenness in the conduct of both civil and military affairs during the Civil War.

The Confederate Congress was weakened in prestige by the fact that many of its members, as a result of the capture of large regions by Federal troops, represented only "imaginary constituencies." [30] Also the excitement over frequent rumors of attacks on Richmond was unfavorable, as Senator William A. Graham observed in 1864, to the transaction of business by Congress. The Southern people, too, may have suffered the penalty of overvaluing oratory as a qualification for office and of cherishing a sensitive pride. It was this weakness of the plantation aristocracy that led to the serious quarrel between Davis and the powerful Alabama Senator William L. Yancey. Yancey and his colleague Clement C. Clay, Jr., protested to the Confederate president on April 21, 1862, that they were "mortified" because the Alabama brigades were led by officers from other states. Yancey was further mortified and gravely insulted when Davis refused his request for a commission for his son Dalton and when, ignoring Yancey's recommendation for the appointment of the postmaster at Montgomery, had appointed instead a personal enemy of the Senator. When Yancey protested, Davis replied with asperity that he would not submit to dictation or recognize Senatorial courtesy.[31]

A weighty reason for the feebleness of Congress was that it was torn by a conflict between the Davis supporters and the opposition. The chief administration leaders in the Senate were Benjamin H. Hill and Howell Cobb of Georgia, R. M. T. Hunter of Virginia, Clement C. Clay of Alabama, and James Phelan of Mississippi; and in the House of Representatives, Ethelbert Barksdale of Mississippi and Jabez L. M. Curry of Alabama. Violently opposed to the President in the Senate were Vice President Stephens, and the imperious Louis T. Wigfall of Texas. In the House of Representatives Henry S. Foote of Tennessee, whose hatred of Davis extended back to their rivalry in Mississippi politics, was the most truculent of the opposition. These men represented a bitter criticism of the President and his policies which became prevalent throughout the Confederacy.

Stephen Mallory thought that much of the Congressional opposition arose from envy, thwarted ambition, and especially the brusqueness with which Davis treated Congressmen who besieged him with applications and requests, nine-tenths of which were for selfish objects opposed to the welfare of the country. Nevertheless, he maintained a working majority in Congress until the autumn of 1863. His strength was indicated by the fact that he vetoed thirty-nine acts of Congress during his administration, only one of which was passed over the veto.

The conflict in Congress was essentially a struggle between the realists who, in order to win the war, were willing to sacrifice temporarily some of the civil liberties enjoyed in peacetime and the doctrinaires who upheld constitutionalism and fought centralization. Military defeats strengthened the doctrinaires, and the tensions of war stirred up quarrels and petty jealousies. The bitter tirades of Henry S. Foote against Davis provoked violence in Congress in which bowie knives flashed and pistols and fists were used. Eventually he became a traitor to the Confederacy and was arrested trying to flee to the North.[32] Unorganized and unable to unite on a program, the malcontents still did untold damage in depressing the morale of the Southern people.

An intimate insight into the wrangling and ineffectiveness of the Confederate Congress can be obtained only from the private correspondence of the congressmen. The Kentucky Representative H. W. Bruce, for example, wrote to Robert McKee, Secretary of State of Kentucky in exile, expressing his "mortification and almost despair for my country" that so indifferent were congressmen to their duties, often he had seen the House of Representatives unable to transact business because of the lack of a quorum or a majority of the members present. W. B. Machen, another Kentucky congressman, wrote to McKee that although his name did not appear in the reports as an inventor of legislation, he was a faithful attendant on Congress and was a discriminating critic. Senator W. E. Simms of Kentucky, in a letter to McKee, Nov. 16, 1863, offered an explanation of the virtual paralysis of Congress: "We as Congressmen have forborne and tried to harmonize with the President. His friends have tried to get him to change his policy, give up bad generals and surrender his favorites in the army—neither they nor the pressure of public opinion have any effect—a vote of no confidence in the cabinet will not move the President—the President controls everything—he has cabinet meetings but his will prevails." One of Davis's most influential supporters, Senator Clement C. Clay, Jr., also attributed much of the discord in Congress to Davis's personality. The President, he wrote to Yancey in 1863, was a strange compound, an inscrutable man. He would not ask or receive counsel—he was predisposed to go exactly the way his friends advised him not to go. Clay lamented that he had tried hard to be friends with the President, but "he will be in a minority." [33]

The opposition in Congress was crystallized by Davis's suspension of the writ of *habeas corpus*. Lincoln suspended this writ without authority from Congress; but in the Confederacy this safeguard from arbitrary arrest was zealously guarded by the legislative branch, which first gave the President the right to suspend the writ of *habeas corpus* February 27, 1862, but only in areas threatened by invasion. After the expiration of this law Ethelbert Barksdale of Mississippi introduced a bill granting the President authority to suspend the writ in any part of the Confederacy according to his judgment. The real motive in proposing this sweeping law was to enforce conscription and suppress Unionist activity within the interior districts of the South. The Barksdale bill was defeated, and President Davis was denounced as seeking to be a despot. On February 15, 1864, however, Congress yielded to his request for a law authorizing him, the Secretary of War, and the general commanding the Trans-Mississippi Military Department to suspend the writ in order to combat peace organizations within the Confederacy, prevent unlawful trading with the enemy, and arrest deserters, persons encouraging or harboring deserters, and persons "advising or inciting others to abandon the Confederate cause"; but this authority was carefully defined and circumscribed.[34]

The weakness of the Confederate civil government was also reflected in the inadequacy of its courts. Congress established district courts which performed the major work of Confederate justice, generally on the principle of *stare decisis,* basing their decisions on previous decisions of United States courts. The Confederacy never established a Supreme Court. One reason for this remarkable omission was personal politics, particularly the fear of enemies of Davis that he would appoint Judah P. Benjamin as Chief Justice. Senator Benjamin H. Hill, chairman of the Judiciary Committee, introduced a bill for the creation of a Supreme Court; but Yancey and other senators opposed it, from fear of centralizing tendencies, and it did not pass. Another reason for the apathy of Congress toward a Supreme Court was that the higher courts of the states generally sustained the acts of the Confederate government. Thus the need was not urgent.[85]

In the autumn of 1863 there occurred a reaction against the administration of President Davis. The great military reverses of Gettysburg and Vicksburg during the summer had shaken the confidence of the people in the ultimate victory of the Confederacy. Davis did not take an active part in the fall political campaign or make stirring appeals to the people. Enough anti-Davis men were elected to deprive him of his faithful majority in Congress. His enemies tried to control his cabinet appointments. Robert Johnson of Arkansas introduced a bill into the Senate December 10, 1863, limiting the tenure of office of the cabinet members to two years, but it was finally defeated. In January, 1865, Thomas S. Bocock of Virginia, who had been Speaker of the Confederate House of Representatives, told Davis that Congress wished a reorganization of the cabinet. Ultimately a compromise was brought about by the resignation of Secretary of War Seddon. The enemies of Davis in Congress also demanded that Lee be made the commanding general of all the Confederate armies, and the Virginia legislature resolved that the appointment of Lee to such a position would reanimate the people and give them greater confidence in their cause. Davis finally surrendered to this demand by signing a bill on January 26, 1865, that created the office of Commanding General, to which he appointed Lee. One of the last attacks by a faction in Congress was a resolution of want of confidence in Judah P. Benjamin, the President's most trusted adviser, which failed, however, to secure a majority vote.

One of the ironies of Southern history was the contrast between the boast that the slave-based society of the old South produced superior statesmen and the reality of feeble or mediocre conduct of civil administration of the Confederacy. Certainly the Confederate statesmen could not compare in quality with the philosopher-statesmen of the South in its great period reaching from Washington, Jefferson, and Madison to Monroe. Was this decided decline in quality of leadership due to the democratic movement of the

Jacksonian period and the decade of the 1850's without a corresponding increase in the education of the masses? Or could the failure of the old South to produce statesmen adequate to the crisis be ascribed more reasonably to other causes, such as profound conservatism, the dominance of one economic interest, the defensive psychology of the Southern people produced by the violent attacks of the abolitionists, and the loss of freedom of thought and speech after 1835.

Although the Confederacy lacked statesmanship of a high order, it had a fair average of respectable leaders in civilian life. One test of ability of the Confederate leaders was the degree of success they had in recovering leadership in the postwar South. Professor W. B. Hesseltine has analyzed the postwar careers of 656 prominent Confederate civil and military leaders, the Who's Who of the Confederacy, and found that "only 71 failed to recover a substantial portion of the position and prestige they had enjoyed at the Confederacy's peak." [36] Of the 585 leaders who reestablished careers after Appomattox, 342 were military officers and 273 were civilian leaders. Most of these neo-Confederate architects of the new South were well educated—two-thirds of them had attended colleges, universities, or West Point—and only 26 had received little formal schooling. There was an astonishing proportion of lawyers among these leaders of the agrarian Confederacy—304 practicing lawyers out of 585 persons, far outnumbering the planters or farmers, who mustered only 134 leaders. In normal peacetimes these respectable Confederate leaders might have been adequate to the needs of a *laissez-faire* type of government. But in the great ordeal of the Confederacy they were definitely wanting in statesmanship, particularly in their failure to subordinate personal and local interests to the winning of Southern independence.

IV

Confederate Diplomacy

THE PEOPLE of the Confederate States were convinced that they occupied the ideological position of the Americans of 1776 in fighting for liberty and independence. The American colonies might not have won if they had failed to obtain valuable foreign aid, particularly the French alliance. The Confederates also had high hopes of obtaining recognition and aid from European nations, for they held some strong cards. Because the new nation was largely rural and as a whole devoted to a tradition of low tariff, it promised a much more favorable tariff policy to European exporters than the United States under Republican rule with its high protective tariff policy. The Confederacy also planned direct trade with Europe and transferring to foreign merchants the commerce which had been monopolized by Northern businessmen. Moreover a division of the United States, weakening the powerful and blatant young republic of the western hemisphere, would be particularly pleasing to John Bull. Likewise, the South's struggle for independence seemed to be a part of the spirit of nationality which was developing strongly in Europe. But the trump card in which the Southerners placed their faith was the virtual monopoly of high-grade cotton.

The effort of the Confederate government to win recognition from foreign nations has properly been described as "King Cotton diplomacy." [1] At the beginning of the war the Southern people had an illusion that cotton was king, very much like the belief of the French people prior to World War II in the impregnability of the Maginot line. More than three-fourths of the cotton used in the great textile industry of England and France was imported from the land of Dixie. It was reasonable, therefore, that the South should believe that dependence of the European governments on its main staple would force them to recognize the Confederacy and break the Federal blockade. Consequently, President Davis had strong public support in favoring an embargo on cotton which would create a cotton famine, and thus put pressure on England and France to take such action.

This fundamental assumption of Confederate diplomacy—the theory of the invincibility of King Cotton—proved to be a fallacy. Unfortunately for the South, the English mills had piled up a huge surplus of cotton goods before the outbreak of war, and they now had an opportunity to dispose of hitherto unsalable products at a good profit. By the time hostilities began, also, the bumper crop of 1860 had been sold, so that English mills had enough raw material to last into the fall of 1862. New sources of cotton were developed in Egypt and India, and approximately a million and a quarter bales of cotton were shipped through the blockade. During the early period of the war, moreover, serious failures of the wheat crop in England compelled the island people to import cereals from the Union granaries.[2] Although it is an exaggeration to say that cotton was dethroned during the war and Northern wheat became king, the shortage of wheat may have influenced in appreciable degree the English attitude towards the Confederacy; for it is a fact that Great Britain, which had imported only 90,000 quarters of wheat and flour in 1859, imported more than 3,500,000 quarters in 1861 and more than 5,000,000 in 1862.[3] Wheat could have been obtained on the continent, but its price then was higher than that of the North, whose harvest benefited from the invention of the Southerner Cyrus McCormick.

The formidable task of persuading European nations to come to the aid of the infant Confederacy was primarily the function of the President and his Secretary of State. Robert Toombs, the first holder of this post, was a man of ability; but he was very unfit for diplomacy, for he was a rough-and-tumble individual lacking in patience and given to violent and dramatic statements. The Civil War diary of J. B. Jones, the rebel war clerk, describes him as follows: "He is a portly gentleman, but with the pale face of the student and the marks of a deep thinker. To gaze at him in repose, the casual spectator would suppose, from his neglect of dress, that he was a planter in moderate circumstances, and of course not gifted with extra-ordinary powers of intellect; but let him open his mouth, and the delusion vanishes." [4] When asked where were the Confederate archives of state, Toombs replied that they were in his hat. After a few months of frustration he resigned to become an unhappy and insubordinate brigadier general. Embittered, particularly by his failure to be promoted to major general, he drank excessively and became an obstructionist and a violent enemy of President Davis. His brilliant talents were virtually lost to the Confederacy.

After Toombs, the duties of Secretary of State were briefly performed by Robert M. T. Hunter of Virginia and R. M. ("Constitution") Browne until Judah P. Benjamin received the appointment. Ultimately the most important man in the cabinet, Benjamin became known as "the brains of the Confederacy." Born in 1811 on St. Croix in the Virgin Islands, he spent his boyhood in Wilmington, North Carolina, and Charleston, where his father was an unsuccessful merchant. He attended Yale University, from which he had to leave suddenly as a result of charges of dishonesty. Going to New Orleans, he became an outstanding lawyer and Senator from Louisiana, acquired a large sugar plantation with many slaves, and married a Catholic Creole girl who lived mostly apart from her husband in Paris.[5] Benjamin was low in stature, swarthy in complexion, and decidedly Hebraic in appearance, and his enemies called him "the ever smiling Jew." By tact and brilliancy he gradually established himself as the intimate adviser of Jefferson Davis. Although he enjoyed food and delighted in gambling, he was a tremendous worker. Extremely versatile, he had the virtue of detachment and made a judicious counselor to the President, in spite of Robert Kean's description of him as "a smart lawyer, a ready, useful drawer up of papers but perhaps the least wise of our public men." [6] His main defect may have been a lack of high moral conviction. There seems to have been little prejudice in the South against Benjamin on account of his Jewish faith until his failures as War Secretary made him unpopular.

The first diplomatic agents sent by President Davis to European capitals proved to be unfit: William L. Yancey, the fire-eater; Pierre Rost, a Louisiana Creole who could speak French, and A. Dudley Mann, a Virginian who had been long in the diplomatic service of the United States. Although they were not officially received by the British government, the foreign minister, Earl Russell, granted them unofficial interviews, the first on May 3, 1861, arranged by a pro-Southern member of Parliament, W. S. Gregory. The Confederacy won its greatest diplomatic triumph at the beginning of its career when Queen Victoria, as a consequence of Lincoln's formal proclamation of a blockade of the Southern coast, recognized on May 13, 1861, the belligerency status of the Confederate States. Shortly afterwards the French Emperor Napoleon III also granted the Confederacy the rights of a belligerent.

With this exception, for which the Confederate envoys were only slightly responsible, they failed to accomplish any of the objects of their mission. Indeed, on June 14 Russell told the American minister, Charles Francis Adams, that he did not intend to have any more personal interviews with the Confederate agents. When Adams's report of his statement to Seward was published in the New York newspapers the Confederate envoys felt outraged, and Yancey wrote with scorn of the British foreign minister's "truckling" to Adams.[7] Yancey returned to the South in March, 1862, disillusioned and with a bitter prejudice against England, while Rost went to Spain and tried unsuccessfully to get that country to recognize the Confederacy.

After the failure of the first mission Davis selected James M. Mason of Virginia as Commissioner to the Court of St. James's and John Slidell of Louisiana to represent the Confederacy at the French court. They took passage at Havana on an English ship, the *Trent*; but Charles Wilkes of the United States Navy, commanding the *San Jacinto,* stopped their vessel on the high seas November 8, 1861, and removed them as prisoners to Fort Warren in Boston harbor. Captain Wilkes became a hero in the North; but Great Britain was so affronted that there was a serious threat of war with the United States, and the British ominously dispatched 8,000 troops to Canada. However, Prince Albert was able to modify the arrogant letter of Prime Minister Palmerston to the American government while President Lincoln and Secretary Seward had sense enough to disavow the act of Captain Wilkes. Accordingly, the United States released the Confederate Commissioners, and they arrived in England late in January, 1862.[8]

Mason was a strange choice to represent the Confederacy at the Court of St. James's. He was the author of the Fugitive Slave Act of 1850, so odious to liberals, and the appointment shows that the Confederate leaders had little appreciation of the strength of antislavery feeling in the world. Moreover, Mason was provincial to an absurd degree. When Mrs. Chesnut heard of the appointment of this tobacco-chewing aristocrat she wrote: "My wildest imagination will not picture Mr. Mason as a diplomat. He will say 'chaw' for 'chew,' and he will call himself 'Jeems,' and he will wear a dress coat to breakfast. Over here, whatever a Mason does is right in his own eyes. He is above law. Somebody asked him how he pronounced his wife's maiden name. She was a Miss Chew from Philadelphia." [9] Benjamin Moran, assistant secretary of the American legation in London, reported that Mason as a visitor in the House of Commons had loudly cheered some remarks favoring the South in a speech by Lindsay, the shipbuilder—a breach of decorum that "has damaged him terribly"—and had shocked the staid Britishers by chewing furiously during the debates and covering the carpet in front of him with tobacco juice. Mason's ridiculous dress also detracted from the dignity of the Confederate cause in England. [10]

The Secretary of State instructed the Confederate commissioners in Europe to base the Confederate case for the breaking of the blockade of Southern ports on the ground that it was ineffective and therefore illegal. Accordingly, Yancey, Rost, and Mann on November 29, 1861, presented a list of more than four hundred ships which had evaded the blockade, and when Mason arrived he gave a supplemental list of fifty-one additional violations. [11] Furthermore they, as well as the British consuls in those ports, reported that the blockade was not continuous but often suspended. The Confederate appeal for recognition rested on the grounds that the Southern states, like the thirteen colonies in 1776, were fighting for self-government, and that it was impossible for the North to conquer the Confederacy and for the South ever to reconstruct the Union. The Confederate agents pointed out that the North was not fighting to destroy slavery, that the South would pursue a low tariff policy in contrast to the North, that the Lincoln government, disregarding civil liberties, had established a despotism, and that the North was guilty of atrocities such as the sinking of a stone fleet to block Charleston's harbor and the infamous woman order of General Butler at New Orleans. [12]

In order to present the Confederate cause in a favorable light, the State Department commissioned Henry Hotze as propaganda agent in England. Born in Switzerland, Hotze had been on the staff of John Forsyth's Mobile *Register*.[13] He arrived in London at the close of 1861, and published a leading article in Prime Minister Palmerston's organ, the London *Morning Post*, as early as February 23, 1862. In addition to the *Morning Post*, the *Standard* and the *Herald*, organ of the Conservative leader, Lord Derby, offered their editorial columns to the Confederate agent.[14] The London *Times*, which generally supported the government in power, had been favorable to the election of Lincoln but swung over to the advocacy of the Confederate cause and published many pro-Southern articles, some of them written by James Spence, a businessman of Liverpool and paid agent of the Confederacy. In the north the powerful *Manchester Guardian* was also pro-Confederate. The British newspapers favorable to the Union cause were in a decided minority, the most important being John Bright's organ the *Morning Star*, the *Daily Telegraph*, which had the largest circulation of any newspaper in Great Britain, the *Daily News*, and the highbrow periodical *The Spectator*.

For the benefit of Secretaries of State Hunter and Benjamin, Hotze shrewdly analyzed the state of opinion in England with regard to his country. On February 28, 1862, he observed that British public opinion was cold and indifferent to the South; although the English preferred the break-up of the Union and the opening of a profitable trade with the South, there was much repugnance to slavery and "the dread of war with the United States is a national bugbear." [15] In August, however, he commented that "the Conservative party is unanimous in our favor yet its leaders, Derby, Disraeli, Walpole have carefully avoided committing themselves." [16] He noted that at least five-sixths of the House of Commons and all the peers, with two or three exceptions, were friendly to the Confederacy. Lord Campbell was so zealous for the South that he gave Hotze the privilege of writing the speech which he planned to deliver in the House of Lords advocating the recognition of the Confederacy.

On May 1, 1862, Hotze founded a Confederate organ in London: *The Index: A Weekly Journal of Politics, Literature, and News*.[17] One of the major purposes of this weekly was to provide "a means chiefly of employing the leader writers of prominent journals and bringing them into constant contact with me." [18] Thus by a small expenditure for articles in the *Index* he could

secure the unpaid services of men who wrote for the large metropolitan newspapers. The talented journalist Percy Greg, for example, contributed to the *Index* and supported the cause of the
South in the *Saturday Review*. Half of the contributors to the
Index were Englishmen.[19] Although it did not have a large circulation, it reached the influential element of British society, the editors,
Parliament, the Ministry. Hotze himself labored so zealously for its
success that he nearly ruined his eyesight.

The *Index* was an admirable propaganda paper. Prior to its
establishment the European public in general received its news of
the Civil War through Northern newspapers, whose accounts were
branded by Confederate agents as "mendacious." The London
Times, however, had two English reporters, W. H. Russell and
Charles Mackay, in America during the first year of the war.
Yancey reported on July 15, 1861, that no Southern newspapers
were received in England.[20] Accordingly, Hotze rendered a great
service to the British press and to the Confederacy by giving fair
accounts of battles and political events across the Atlantic. The
Index also contained articles on the cotton famine, statistics of
blockade running, messages of the Confederate President, notices of
the peace movement in the Northern states, Parliamentary debates
relating to the South, as well as book reviews and poetry, such as
a collection of the war poetry of the Confederacy. It was so successful that it outlasted the war, ending August 12, 1865.

The most interesting piece of propaganda published in the *Index*
appeared in the June 11, 1863, issue, entitled "Address to Christians
Throughout the World," signed by a long list of Southern ministers
arranged according to denominations. Among the signers were
Bishop James O. Andrew of Georgia, R. L. Dabney of Virginia,
Professor James Woodrow of Columbia, later the exponent of
evolution, and Braxton Craven of Trinity College, North Carolina.
These holy men justified the Confederate cause, announcing the
separation of the Confederate States from the Union to be final,
testifying that Southern slavery was not incompatible with Chris-
tianity, and that Lincoln's emancipation proclamation would lead
to a bloody tragedy. "We regard Abolitionism," they wrote, "as an
interference with the plans of Divine Providence." Citing "an
unusual proportion" of the principal men of the Confederacy,
statesmen and generals, as being Christians. they asked for the

devout prayers of all Christians for the success of Confederate arms.[21]

The ruling classes in England, France, and Spain favored the Confederacy. The English ruling class regarded Southern society as different from Northern, which was felt to be a conglomeration of many national stocks while the South was pure English. Indeed, Southern society had been profoundly influenced by the formative ideal of realizing in America the status and attractive life of the country gentleman. Although English reformers like Harriet Martineau, Charles Dickens, and Mrs. Trollope had disparaged Southern society in their travel accounts because of their antislavery bias, Englishmen of aristocratic background who had traveled in America preferred the society of the Southern planters to that of the aggressive Yankee businessmen. The South of 1860 undoubtedly represented conservative ideas and principles in contrast to the middle-class radicalism of Northern society—a fact which appealed to the European conservative classes.

The able American minister to the Court of St. James's, Charles Francis Adams, found the British official and upper class prejudiced against the United States government. On December 25, 1862, he wrote to his son in America: "The great body of the aristocracy and the wealthy commercial class are anxious to see the United States go to pieces. On the other hand the middle and lower class sympathize with us . . ." [22] He again remarked, July 31, 1863, "The privileged classes all over Europe rejoice in the thoughts of the ruin of the great experiment of popular government." [23] Henry Adams, his son and secretary, observed that whenever the Confederate armies won a victory the British aristocracy rejoiced, but when news arrived in England of the surrender of Vicksburg, the salons of London were in tears.[24]

The English people as a whole, aristocrats as well as plebians, were hostile to slavery. Yancey commented that *Uncle Tom's Cabin* had been read in England and *believed*. Yet the English people, according to Charles Francis Adams, did not at first comprehend the connection of slavery with the war, because Lincoln did not advocate emancipation but proclaimed that the war was for the preservation of the Union.[25] His preliminary emancipation proclamation issued after the battle of Antietam and the final proclamation of January 1, 1863, were regarded by the aristocracy as an

attempt to stir up a servile insurrection. The working class, however, held to the conviction that the North was fighting for the
liberation of the slaves. Henry Adams wrote to his brother, "The
Emancipation Proclamation has done more for us here than all
our former victories and all our diplomacy." [26]

The liberal and reforming element of British society was motivated in its support of the North by a belief that the issue at stake
in the Civil War was the abolition of slavery. Its leaders, such as
John Bright, Richard Cobden, George Thompson, the abolitionist,
and W. E. Forster, the magnetic leader of the movement for free
public schools, made eloquent speeches to enlist the antislavery
sentiment of the English people on the side of the North. Even the
aristocracy believed that the Confederacy would have to grant
gradual emancipation to the slaves. Spence felt it necessary to take
this point of view in winning converts to the Confederacy cause,
and, primarily because of disloyalty to slavery, he was dismissed
from his position as agent of the Confederate government in England on December 1, 1863.

The British intellectuals were divided in their sympathies toward
the combatants in the Civil War. Carlyle, Darwin, Bulwer-Lytton,
Tennyson, Lord Acton, and Matthew Arnold favored the Southern
cause.[27] On the other hand, Browning, Jowett, the translator of
Plato, Goldwin Smith, Professor of Modern History at Oxford,
Leslie Stephen, John Stuart Mill, and Sir Charles Lyell were sympathetic to the North. John E. Cairnes, an Irish economist, struck
a formidable literary blow against the Confederacy in *The Slave
Power,* portraying the great mass of Southern whites as "mean
whites," brutalized by the institution of slavery. The Southern cause
was ably defended by James Spence, in his volume *The American
Union* (1861) which was published in four large editions.

In contrast to the British aristocracy, the English working class
supported the North because they believed that the Union armies
were fighting for democracy. Henry Hotze advised Judah P. Benjamin on September 26, 1862, that extreme caution should be
exercised in agitating the Southern cause in Lancashire, the center
of the cotton textile industry: "There is only one class which as a
class continues actively inimical to us, the Lancashire operatives.
With them the unreasoning—it would perhaps be more accurate
to say instinctive—aversion to our institutions is as firmly rooted

as in any part of New England, to the population of which they bear a striking resemblance. They look upon us, and by a strange confusion of ideas, upon slavery as the author and source of their present miseries and I am convinced that the astonishing fortitude and patience with which they endure these miseries is mainly due to a consciousness that by any other course they would promote our interests, a feeling which certain supposed emissaries of the Federal Government have worked jealously to confirm." [28]

The cotton famine undoubtedly produced severe distress in Lancashire, Cheshire, and Derbyshire, where the cotton factories were concentrated. In December, 1862, approximately four hundred thousand operatives were thrown either wholly or partially out of employment.[29] Nevertheless, the workers wished for the victory of the North. Normal employment was gradually restored by other industries which were thriving on war profits, and parish relief, private charity, and gifts from the Northern states relieved the distress of the cotton-mill workers. It is interesting to observe that, of the twenty-six members of the House of Commons from Lancashire, only J. T. Hopwood ever spoke in favor of changing the British policy of neutrality; yet these members must have largely represented the "Cotton Lords." [30]

Until news of Gettysburg and Vicksburg arrived, the British on the whole believed that the North would be unable to conquer the South. Many Englishmen thought as late as the fall of 1864 that the war would result in a stalemate. The British had an astute observer at Washington in their minister, Lord Lyons, who kept Downing Street well informed on American affairs. The British consuls in the principal Confederate ports also furnished information to their government on the strength and weakness of the Confederacy. Lyons's comments in letters to the British foreign office on the low morale of the Northern people in 1863 are particularly interesting in the light of British speculations on the outcome of the war. On January 9, 1863, he wrote: "I have no hesitation in saying that all men of all parties have lost heart about the war. They are not confident of success." [31] The Democrats of New York, he thought, had given up the idea of restoring the Union by force and he judged that "the difficulty of recruiting in the North may end the war." On March 2 he reported: "But the country is growing more and more tired of the war, and unless there is something to raise the war spirit again soon the Democrats may come out as a peace party." [32]

The sympathy of the English aristocracy and of the shipping interests for the Southern cause resulted in several abortive attempts to secure the recognition of the Confederacy by Great Britain. William S. Lindsay of Liverpool, the largest shipbuilder in England, and Sir William Gregory, a member of "the gentleman ruling class," were the leaders in the House of Commons in the movement of 1862 for the recognition of the Confederacy and the breaking of the blockade. On March 7, 1862, Gregory maintained in Parliament that the blockade was illegal, citing a long list of ships that had passed through it; and he was "heartily cheered." [33] William E. Forster, the young Liberal, brilliantly replied to Gregory, showing that most of the ships which had evaded the blockade were small coastal or river vessels, not bound for Europe." [34] Sir James Fergusson as well as William Lindsay supported the Southern cause in the debate by observing that Great Britain extended her sympathy to Greeks, Italians, Poles, and Hungarians who were struggling for their liberty; likewise she should support the Southern fight for independence. [35] Neither Parliament nor the ministry took any action at this time on breaking the blockade or recognizing the Confederacy. The Southern commissioners attributed the failure to news of the Confederate defeats at Roanoke Island and Fort Donelson.

After McClellan retreated from Richmond, an excellent opportunity was presented to agitate recognition of the Confederacy. The Confederate commissioners had refrained at first from making formal demands on England and France for recognition, because they feared a rebuff. But on July 16, 1862, Slidell had an interview with the French Emperor at Vichy which elated him so that he resolved on presenting a formal demand for recognition, and he urged Mason to make a simultaneous demand on the British ministry. [36] Accordingly, on July 23 Slidell presented his note containing an able argument for the recognition of the government he represented, and on the following day Mason sent a note to the Foreign Secretary, Earl Russell, formally requesting recognition and asking for a personal interview. Russell refused the interview and said that he would submit the matter of recognition to the cabinet.

Coinciding with the formal demands of Slidell and Mason, a strong effort was made in the British Parliament to force the Ministry to intervene in the American war in behalf of the Confederacy. On July 18 Lindsay introduced a motion to offer mediation to the North and the South with a view to terminating hostilities. Lord Adolphus Vane-Tempest—whom Benjamin Moran described as "a dissipated and unprincipled young nobleman"—declared that it was an utter delusion to think that the Union could be restored; and he referred to the treatment and sympathy Great Britain had accorded to revolutionary Italy, Greece, and Belgium as an example to follow in regard to the South. He also spoke of the prohibitive tariff policy of the North and of the distress produced by the blockade in the manufacturing districts of England.[37] Another champion of the South was James Whiteside, representative of the University of Dublin in Parliament, who denied that the North was fighting for the emancipation of the slaves and pointed out the paradox of the United States government denying to the South the rights of the Declaration of Independence.[38] Prime Minister Palmerston, however, squelched the debate by requesting Parliament not to pass Lindsay's motion, which was thereupon withdrawn.

The state of British politics in 1861–1864 militated against a firm position by the British cabinet in favor of the Confederacy. The Whigs who were in power did not have a strong working majority in Parliament, so that the balance of power was held by the antislavery, pro-Northern radical group led by John Bright. The Conservatives led by Lord Derby and Disraeli were influenced by loyalty to the Queen, who was Northern in sympathy. The recognition of the Confederacy did not become a party matter, but the Southern cause had friends in both major parties.[39] The Conservatives were not deeply interested in the American struggle, and the party leaders kept a tight control over the members, restraining the Southern sympathizers.[40]

The Confederate commissioners and the *Index* believed that the Prime Minister and his Foreign Secretary, Earl Russell, were hostile to the Confederate cause, but this was not true. Prime Minister Palmerston, a jaunty and pugnacious old gentleman, proposed to Russell in August, 1862, that England and France should act as mediators to bring about an armistice and a peace on the basis of the recognition of the independence of the Confederacy. Russell favored such a course even more than Palmerston, and declared, "In case of failure, we ought ourselves to recognize the Southern

States as an independent State." [41] But Thouvenel, the French minister of foreign affairs, was opposed to action at this time, and the news that Lee had invaded Maryland caused the British to postpone a decision of the cabinet until the outcome of that campaign had been determined. Late in September the British government learned that Lee had been stopped at Antietam and had retreated into Virginia. Then the directors of British foreign policy decided to wait until the war took a more favorable turn for the Confederacy.

In this critical period on October 7, 1862, Gladstone, the Chancellor of the Exchequer, whose family had made profits from the slave trade, delivered a sensational speech at Newcastle highly favorable to the Confederacy. He expressed a kindly feeling toward the North, particularly recalling the cordial reception which the Prince of Wales had received on his visit to America, but declared: "Jefferson Davis and other leaders of the South have made an army; they are making, it appears, a navy; and they have made what is more than either—they have made a nation. . . . We may anticipate with certainty the success of the Southern States so far as regards their separation from the North." [42] His speech caused the price of cotton to fall in the British market and may have injured the Southern cause by stirring the Northern sympathizers to greater activity.

On October 22, however, Palmerston wrote to Russell, "We must continue merely to be lookers-on till the war shall have taken a more decided turn." [43] The best opportunity that the Confederacy ever had to win foreign recognition and perhaps success in the war was destroyed by the decisive battle of Antietam. Ephraim D. Adams, an expert on British-American relations during the Civil War, has observed that Russell's mediation plan of 1862 marked the most dangerous crisis in diplomacy for the United States. It came close to adoption, and it seems probable that war between Great Britain and the United States would have followed, with a strong possibility of Southern victory. But the cabinet rejected it, and, according to Adams, "Never again was there serious governmental consideration of meddling in American affairs." [44]

A paramount factor preventing British recognition of the Confederacy was the military failure of the South at critical times. In 1863 another move in England to secure the recognition of the

South was wrecked by the defeat of Southern armies. In the summer of that year Southern Independence Associations were founded in Manchester, London, and other cities to support the cause and memorialize Parliament to recognize the independence of the Confederacy; and funds were provided by Southern sympathizers, particularly Alexander Collie of Glasgow, who had made immense profits from blockade running. The leader of the Parliamentary group urging recognition was John A. Roebuck, a member from the industrial city of Sheffield. One of the most eccentric men in England, he was perhaps the worst representative that could have been chosen to champion the Southern cause in Parliament. On June 30, 1863, he introduced his resolution in favor of negotiating with the great powers of Europe for recognition of the Confederacy.[45] Indiscreetly he revealed some confidences he had received in an interview with the French Emperor, who supported joint recognition of the Confederacy by England and France. He so mismanaged the movement that it degenerated into a farce, and on July 13 he withdrew his motion. The double defeat of the Confederacy at Gettysburg and Vicksburg in early July, 1863, virtually ended the prospects of foreign intervention.

In addition to the military disasters of the Confederacy, many subsidiary influences kept England neutral. The able United States Minister, Charles Francis Adams, warned the British government that recognition of the Confederacy might lead to war with his country. Furthermore, Great Britain was making lucrative profits out of the continuation of the war, and the destruction of the American merchant marine by Confederate warships was very pleasant. Finally, the Northern practices in regard to blockade and contraband supported the historic position of Great Britain, which was therefore unimpressed by the Confederate arguments that the blockade was contrary to international law.

After the summer of 1863 the official sympathy toward the South cooled rapidly. The defeat of the South in diplomacy was signalized by the change of the British policy toward Confederate purchase of warships from English shipbuilders. The hopelessness of winning concessions from England caused Secretary of State Benjamin on August 4, 1863, to order Mason to terminate his mission.[46] This formal rupture of relations, which was hailed with glee by Henry Adams as a blunder of President Davis, came right after the American minister had prevented the delivery to the Confederacy of two powerful ironclad rams built near Liverpool—an achievement which the two Adamses regarded as a diplomatic Gettysburg.[47] Furthermore on October 7, 1864, a decision of the cabinet presided over by Benjamin in the absence of President Davis expelled the British consuls from Southern cities. They were accused of obstructing the draft by shielding individuals from conscription.[48]

The attitude of France to the Confederacy began with a certain coolness and aloofness, but, because of interest, changed to a strong wish for Confederate success. Hotze thought that French public opinion was "faintly sympathetic" to the North, desiring to preserve a strong America as a counterpoise to England.[49] When Rost went to France in the spring of 1861 he had an interview with Duc de Morny, the half-brother and adviser of the Emperor, who told him that France and England had agreed to pursue the same course toward the Confederacy and advised him that it was unwise at this time to press for recognition. Rost was encouraged, however, to find that the antislavery feeling was not strong or active in Paris.[50] Yancey and Rost sent a dispatch from Paris, October 5, 1861, to the Confederate government in which they reported that the distress among the laboring poor arising from the blockade of the Confederacy was greater in France than in England, that textile manufacturers were working little more than half-time, and that the stoppage of tobacco importations had thrown many people out of employment. The chief opponents of the Confederacy in France, they thought, were the Orleanists and the Red Republicans.[51] Also the French foreign minister, Thouvenel, seemed to be indifferent or hostile.

To influence the French press the State Department sent over Edwin De Leon, a former consul general in Egypt. De Leon was a member of a distinguished Jewish family of South Carolina and was a personal friend of President Davis, to whom he had presented a splendid white Arabian horse. In contrast to the meager financial support given to Hotze, De Leon was provided with ample funds; and great things were expected from him. But on the way to his assignment he read the confidential dispatches directed to the Confederate commissioner in Paris, John Slidell, which had been entrusted to him. In one of these dispatches he learned that Benjamin authorized Slidell to offer a huge bribe of 100,000 bales of cotton and free trade for a certain period to the Emperor if he would break the blockade. Slidell was enraged at De Leon for breaking the seals of the dispatches and treated him with hostility, refusing to introduce him to influential people or to advance his propaganda. The *Constitutionelle* and the *Patrie,* organs of the imperial party, were already advocates of the Confederacy, but De Leon bought French writers on other newspapers for the manufacture of a favorable public opinion. He developed a strong antipathy for Slidell, criticizing him at first privately in letters to Davis and then at the close of 1863 in a dispatch to the State Department which described the French as a "far more mercenary race than the English." His dispatches were intercepted and published in the New York *Daily Tribune*. They produced "painful surprise" in the mind of Benjamin, which was increased when Slidell informed him about the breaking of the seals.[52]

Early in February, 1864, De Leon was dismissed, and Hotze took charge of manipulating the French press. Hotze had a rare piece of good fortune in being able to persuade the Havas agency, the great agency for distributing news to Western Europe, to accept him as the supplier of reliable news from the South and concerning the American war, which it published without excessive *abonnements*.[53]

On April 15, 1862, Count Mercier, the French Minister at Washington, startled Benjamin by asking permission to visit Richmond. Apparently the purpose of his mission, which had the approval of Seward, was to judge of "the temper and spirit" of the Southern people and ascertain whether there was a likelihood of the reconstruction of the Union.[54] To the Emperor and his advisers, Mercier sent a report very favorable to the Confederacy, expressing the opinion that the people were determined to maintain their independence and had the ability to do it. Of all the European governments that of Napoleon III was most sympathetic to the Confederacy. In April he granted an interview to Lindsay, the Southern advocate (who had crossed the Channel to secure Napoleon's support), in which he said that he had twice made overtures to England for joint action to aid the Confederacy but had received no response. Actually the overtures were informal and were not made through the French ambassador in London; consequently the British ministry denied receiving any representations from the French ruler.

On July 16 the Emperor granted his first interview to Slidell at Vichy, lasting seventy minutes. The diplomat reported that the Emperor regretted that he had respected the blockade of the Confederacy and spoke of the probability of his Mexican policy bringing France into collision with the United States. He gave Slidell the impression that if England continued to procrastinate in recognizing the Confederacy he would act alone.[55] At this conference the diplomat brought forward the bribery plan of Benjamin contained in the dispatches which De Leon had opened. Both the Emperor and Thouvenel were so pleased at this proposition that Slidell concluded the time had arrived to make a formal demand for French recognition of the Confederate States. His note requesting recognition pointed out that it would strengthen the peace party in the North and thus have great moral weight in bringing the war to an end.

Napoleon had the support of French public opinion in his pro-Confederate policy. An able study of French public opinion, based on reports of the district attorneys rather than on corrupt and censored French newspapers, indicates that after the first year of the war there was "an almost unanimous expression of sympathy for the South." [56] But the Emperor's Mexican adventure, his main reason for supporting the South, was not popular in France. Slidell intimated that the Confederacy would acquiesce in this violation of the Monroe Doctrine. Yet Napoleon was unwilling to act alone in recognizing the Confederacy because he faced trouble in Europe, particularly in Italy, and feared provoking a war with the United States. Only with the support of England and its powerful fleet would he venture to antagonize the United States. Accordingly French policy toward the Confederacy hinged upon the action of Great Britain.

Slidell had a second interview with Napoleon at Saint-Cloud on October 24, 1862, soon after the receipt of a letter from his minister at Washington.[57] Mercier, whose advice on American affairs had great weight with him, urged the French government to intervene. Napoleon was very cordial and told Slidell that he planned to propose to England and Russia mediation in which the combatants would be urged to grant an armistice for six months, with the blockaded ports open. Such a proposal was made to Russia, which rejected it, and on November 10, Napoleon made a formal submission of the plan to England. The British cabinet held a debate on this form of intervention, which was strongly supported by Russell and Gladstone, and finally rejected it on the grounds that Russia had refused to join, and that the proposal was so unequal that the North would certainly reject it and declare war. Thus was frustrated Slidell's greatest opportunity of bringing France firmly to the Confederate side. From this time to the end of the war his principal successes were in negotiating the Erlanger loan and in getting Napoleon's consent for the Confederacy to build warships in French shipyards.

The Confederacy made little effort to win friends in central Europe. In August, 1861, Poland, with sympathy for a nation fighting for liberty and independence, sent a commission to Richmond; but nothing practical came of this gesture. On June 18, 1864, Hotze wrote to Samuel Ricker, late United States Consul General at Frankfort—who seems to have offered to act as Confederate agent —that he had often thought of attempting to influence the German press but had been deterred because (1) there was no metropolitan center upon which the effort might be concentrated; (2) the effort was apparently hopeless in view of "the instinctive antipathy between the Germans and us" (over slavery), and (3) a suitable agent would be hard to find. Moreover, in 1864 he had no money to pay such an agent.[58]

Belgium was a small country; but Leopold, King of the Belgians, had so strong an influence over Queen Victoria that it was highly desirable for the Confederacy to secure Belgian support. In September, 1861, A. Dudley Mann was appointed commissioner to Belgium. He found that Leopold was very favorable to the Confederacy. Indeed, in the autumn of 1862 the King strongly urged the French Emperor to propose mediation in the struggle between the Union and the Confederacy with a view to the recognition of the independence of the Confederacy. But the Belgian Parliament, almost evenly balanced in parties, would take no bold action toward intervention and would not act independently of Great Britain.

Mann obtained a minor triumph in 1863 in his mission to Pope Pius IX. Catholic Ireland and Belgium had been sending thousands of young men to join the Union armies, stimulated by the huge bounties offered for recruits and by the desire of Irish youth for military training to use later in a fight for Irish freedom. Father John Bannon, chaplain of Missouri troops, and Lieutenant J. L. Capston, whom Secretary Benjamin sent to persuade Irishmen not to volunteer for Northern armies, had little success in competition with the lure of a $500 enlistment bounty. Nevertheless, Mann persuaded the Pope to discourage this enlistment of Catholics in Europe. Indeed, the Pope addressed an official letter to Jefferson Davis as "President of the Confederate States of America," which Mann unjustifiably interpreted as a recognition of the independence of the Confederacy.

Alone among the important nations of Europe, Russia was hostile to the Confederate cause. Russia emancipated her serfs during the Civil War, and the sympathies of the Czar were with the nation that was trying to destroy Southern slavery. Lucius Quintus Cincinnatus Lamar was sent in 1863 as commissioner to secure the support of the Czar with the argument that failure to recognize the Confederacy would prolong an unnecessary war. When he reached London, however, he learned that the Senate had refused to confirm his appointment.

On the other hand, Lincoln appointed as Minister to Russia the Kentucky antislavery leader Cassius Marcellus Clay, who brought back from his sojourn at the court of the Czar a collection of paintings and an illegitimate son. The Czar sent a fleet to New York harbor and another to San Francisco in the autumn of 1863— moves interpreted by Americans as a gesture of friendship to the North; but the Russian archives indicate that he was motivated by a desire to place his fleets in safe neutral territory pending a threatened war with England.[59] In 1868 we paid for the voyages of the Russian fleets when the House of Representatives influenced by a Russian lobby headed by Robert J. Walker appropriated the money for the purchase of Alaska.

The good will of Cuba was important to the Confederacy, particularly in blockade running. To this close neighbor the State Department sent Charles J. Helm, a Kentuckian, who had been United States consul at Havana. He rendered valuable service in aiding the shipment of supplies through the blockade and in dispelling fears that the Confederacy might have imperialistic designs on the West Indian islands. He pointed out that Southern efforts to acquire Cuba before 1861 were political, to obtain a balance of power in the United States Congress, but now this motive for imperialism no longer existed.[60]

The Confederacy was unfortunate in its representative in Mexico, John T. Pickett, formerly United States consul at Vera Cruz. Pickett was a soldier of fortune who frankly advocated the use of bribery, "a million or so of money judiciously applied," to secure the recognition of his government by Mexico.[61] He was discredited by participation in a brawl for which he was placed in jail, and his indiscreet correspondence with the Confederate State Department was regularly intercepted. The United States, on the other hand, was represented by the brilliant Thomas Corwin, who had a reputation as a friend of Mexico and who had plenty of money at his disposal. The swashbuckling, heavy-drinking Colonel Pickett returned from Mexico to New Orleans and entered the Confederate Army. His place was taken in 1864 by William Preston of Kentucky, minister plenipotentiary to the puppet government of Maximilian; but Maximilian, hoping to win recognition from the United States government, snubbed the Confederacy and would not even receive its envoy. Pickett, in the lean days following the Civil War, sold the whole diplomatic correspondence of the Confederacy to the United States government for approximately $75,000.[62]

In the latter part of the war the efforts of Confederate diplomacy were spurred by desperation. Jacob Thompson, James P. Holcombe, and Clement C. Clay went to Canada, from which they sent secret agents to contact disloyal elements in the North—the Copperheads, the Knights of the Golden Circle, and the Sons of Liberty. Thomas H. Hines, a Kentuckian who had fought in Morgan's cavalry, and John B. Castleman were among the boldest agents. They sought to promote a Northwestern Confederacy which they hoped would form an alliance with the Southern Confederacy.[63] Other agents tried to release Confederate prisoners in Northern camps, and some actually set fire to nineteen hotels in New York City on November 25, 1864.[64]

Finally, the secret mission of Duncan F. Kenner, who sailed from New York in disguise in February, 1865, to offer the emancipation of the slaves in exchange for European recognition and aid, represented a last forlorn gamble. When Slidell broached the subject of emancipation the French Emperor declared that he had never taken the question of slavery into consideration in determining French policy toward the Confederacy.[65] Mason also, in an interview with Palmerston on March 14, 1865, was convinced that slavery did not prevent the recognition of the Confederacy; on the other hand the Earl of Donoughmore expressed the opinion that slavery had prevented recognition of the Confederacy by Great Britain in 1863, but that now the promise of emancipation would be too late.

None of the major objectives of Confederate diplomacy was obtained: the recognition of the independence of the Confederacy; the breaking of the blockade by foreign intervention; trade treaties; important foreign loans. These failures should not be attributed to the Secretary of State, Judah P. Benjamin, but primarily to the defeats of the Confederate armies at critical moments, to the surplus of cotton in Europe at the outbreak of the war, and to the unwillingness of European nations to risk war with the United States by aiding the Confederate States. Moreover, the governments of Europe—even the strongly conservative ministry of O'Donnell in Spain—realized the new force in diplomacy, the expediency of respecting the rising liberal opinion of their peoples, which supported the North during the Civil War.[66]

The Confederate statesmen had an exaggerated opinion of the value of foreign recognition. They maintained that the failure of European governments to recognize the Confederacy gave moral support to the North and prolonged the war. Secretary Benjamin and his agents also tried to win European support by showing that the blockade was ineffective and therefore illegal. But recognition of the Confederacy was not enough to affect seriously the outcome of the war or bring about the independence of the South. The only means by which England or France could have effectively aided the Confederacy were breaking the blockade with force, sending huge supplies, and making large financial loans.

V

Soldiers in Gray

THE AMERICANS of the nineteenth century relied on the citizen militia to fight their wars. Composed of all able-bodied citizens between the ages of eighteen and forty-five, the militia held musters in the county seats at periodic intervals. The musters had their comic side, exploited by such Southern humorists as Augustus B. Longstreet (in *Georgia Scenes*); yet they did give civilians some idea of military organization and of the manual of arms, and they furnished the Southern states with such a profusion of military titles that any man of prominence in his community was usually addressed as "major," "colonel" or "general." In the War for Southern Independence, the Confederacy had to depend for its military forces entirely on its militia and on volunteers. In the spring and summer of 1861 there was a rush of volunteers in both the North and the South. Lack of guns prevented the Confederate government from taking full advantage of this martial fervor, and it therefore had to refuse numerous applications for enlistment. Secretary of War Leroy P. Walker reported in July, 1861, that the Confederate Army had thus lost the services of two hundred thousand volunteers.[1] Some governors withheld the supply of state arms in order to provide for local defense, thus retarding a quick mobilization of Southern troops.

The natural history of volunteering in the Confederacy ran as follows: a prominent citizen would raise a company of volunteers in his community; the South Carolina planter Wade Hampton, for example, organized and equipped at his own expense the Hampton Legion of 1,000 men consisting of infantry, cavalry, and artillery; after a farewell oration a banner was presented to the volunteers as they started to the front, laden with baskets of chicken, ham, and citron tarts, provided by fond mothers and wives. Some recruits brought shotguns or old-fashioned flintlocks, which were practically useless in rainy weather, or swords or sabers that had seen service in the Revolutionary War. Many were clad in vari-colored and bizarre uniforms, like the Louisiana Zouaves, who wore red fezzes and scarlet baggy trousers held up by a blue sash, so that they made superb targets.

The very superficial medical examination did not eliminate men with serious physical defects, and men past middle life were per-mitted to enroll as privates. The recruits were often thrown into battle with scarcely any training; Wade Hampton's Legion, includ-ing many society men and "gentlemen," was mobilized in early June and fought bravely in late July at Bull Run. Young aristocrats hastened to volunteer, eager for commissions and resolved not to fight on foot. Among the most effective recruiting agents were comely Southern maids who ostracized stay-at-home males of mili-tary age and sound health.

It is highly probable that the typical soldier, Northern or South-ern, had no clear idea why he was fighting. Defense of the homeland from invasion was enough of an imperative for many Southerners to volunteer. Furthermore, a strong sense of romantic honor im-pelled the upper class to fight for "Southern rights." Many volun-teers went forth to war as to an exciting adventure, cherishing the illusion that it would be short, and that one Southern soldier could "lick" at least seven Yankees—mechanics, peddlers, pasty-faced clerks, and factory hands. Actually, Northern troops proved to be as brave, dependable, and heroic in combat as Southern soldiers.

In the summer of 1862 the Northern journalist George Alfred Townsend, interviewing some Confederates from North Carolina who had been captured in the Peninsula campaign, found that many had little comprehension of the causes of the war or why they had entered the army. Some of them had enlisted for the honor of the family whose ancestors had "fit in the American Revolution"; some had joined the army to "hev a squint at the fighting," or labored under the impression that they would receive "a slice of land" and a "nigger" if the South won its independence. Some hated "Yankee institutions" and wished "to polish them off," while many expressed the sentiment that it was "dull in our deestrecks an' the niggers was runnin' away, so I thought I 'ud jine the forces."

The great majority of the defeated, miserable men whom Townsend interviewed confessed that they had never anticipated "this box," or "this fix," or "these suckemstances" in which they found themselves, and heartily wished the war to close so that they might return to their families.

The observant Northern reporter was much impressed with the contrast in appearance and manner between officers and privates in the Confederate Army. The privates wore homespun suits of gray or butternut; some were wrapped in blankets of rag carpet, some had shoes of rough, untanned hide, others were in Federal blouses, and a few sported beaver hats. They were brown, brawny, and wiry, "intense, fierce, and animal." The officers, on the other hand, were "young, athletic fellows, dressed in rich gray cassimere, trimmed with black, and wearing soft black hats adorned with black ostrich feathers. Their spurs were strapped to elegantly fitting boots, and they looked as far above the needy, seedy privates as lords above their vassals." [2] They appeared to be strongly animated by state pride.

If a majority of the Confederate troops were green country boys, there were also crack companies of the socially elite from the cities, such as the Richmond Howitzers or the Washington Artillery of New Orleans, who were smartly dressed. Furthermore, some young Southern aristocrats volunteered as privates in the ranks, notably the sons of Lee and Beauregard, and Johnny Chesnut of South Carolina, who went as a gentleman private to set an example to the sand-hill men—but Mrs. Chesnut commented, "He took his servant with him, all the same." [3] The spirit of *noblesse oblige*, the desire to place patriotic service above money, caused some volunteers to refuse to take a soldier's pay. Wrote Thomas B. Gordon, a Kentuckian, to his brother, "I understand that a few days ago the pay Master of Genl [Humphrey] Marshall's command found only five persons in the Kentucky regiments under him who would take pay." [4] This spirit of sacrifice, he predicted, would go far to balance numbers and money.

Despite a superficial hatred of Yankees, Southern soldiers often fraternized with Northern soldiers between the lines. A strong motive for fraternizing was the desire to swap tobacco for coffee or obtain newspapers. The opposing armies often would grant truces to bury the dead and collect the wounded. At times when they were bivouacked near each other they would even join together in singing nostalgic songs like "Home, Sweet Home," "The Girl I Left Behind Me," and "Lorena." The diary of John Green, a sergeant of Kentucky troops, describes an episode of chivalry that was not uncommon in both armies. While the Confederates were retreating from the battle of Jonesboro near Atlanta volunteers rushed back to bring away wounded Confederate soldiers. When the Northern soldiers saw this act of gallantry, they cheered the volunteers and withheld their fire.[5]

The impulse of volunteering began to fade early in 1862. After the reverses of Fort Donelson and Roanoke Island the Southern people gradually awakened to the bitter fact that the war was no holiday frolic. On April 16, 1862—a year earlier than the North—the Confederate Congress passed a conscription law, the first in American history. The main purposes were to prohibit the twelve-months volunteers from leaving military service and thus prevent the Confederate armies from disintegrating, and to stimulate volunteering. Most Southerners regarded being drafted as a disgrace. The act granted thirty days, therefore, in which citizens might enter the army in the honorable way by volunteering; and only volunteers had the privilege of forming new organizations and electing their own officers. The first conscription law drafted able-bodied white men between the ages of eighteen and thirty-five for a three-year period of military service.[6] Despite bitter opposition from the champions of state rights, it passed the Confederate Congress by an overwhelming majority, for it was regarded as necessary for military success.

This pioneer conscription law was marred by grave defects. Years later, when the United States Congress was considering draft legislation for World War I, it profited from experience. Both the Confederate and the Union draft laws granted the right to avoid military service by sending a substitute. This favored the rich and caused great discontent among the poorer classes. A thriving trade arose in securing substitutes, in the North more than in the South. J. Brantly Harris, a young merchant at Gold Hill, North Carolina, wrote to his sister June 3, 1862: "We are all to be enrolled on 8th July and will have to report ourselves at Salisbury on the 15th inst. I want to hire a substitute. Tell Mr. F. to try and get me one at almost any price not more than $1,000." [7]

A contract of substitution preserved in the National Archives shows the potentialities, in this system, of recruiting men of advanced age and inferior soldierly qualifications. While in camp at Coosawhatchie, South Carolina, W. C. Johnston hired John A. All, fifty-three years old, to act as his substitute. Johnston was a man of some means, who claimed to have suffered from rheumatism for many years. He paid All $2,000 and agreed to return to service if his substitute deserted or if the law was changed so as to make him again liable for duty. All was examined by the proper officers and pronounced sound and healthy, "fit for the duties of a soldier." The contract was approved by the captain of Johnston's company.[8] Under pressure from public opinion and the military authorities, Congress abolished the system of substitutes on December 28, 1863, and January 5, 1864.[9]

Another defect in Confederate conscription laws was the large list of exemptions, including schoolteachers of twenty pupils, ministers, college professors, druggists, mail carriers, postmasters, civil officers of state governments and of the Confederacy, employees of railroads, ferrymen, telegraph operators, employees in cotton and woolen mills, mines, furnaces, and foundries, shoemakers, blacksmiths, tanners, millers, saltmakers, printers, and one editor for each paper, as well as Quakers, Dunkers, and Mennonites who paid a tax of $500 or furnished a substitute. College students in general were not exempt from conscription.

The exemption which caused the greatest dissatisfaction was the release from military service by an act of October 11, 1862, of planters or their overseers supervising as many as twenty Negroes. The purpose of this exemption, according to the statute, was "to secure the proper police of the country";[10] but this provision in the draft laws caused the poorer classes to mutter that it was "a rich man's war and a poor man's fight." Actually, the number of slave owners and overseers exempted to supervise slave labor was relatively small—according to a report of the Conscript Bureau in December, 1863, only 200 in Virginia, 120 in North Carolina, 301 in South Carolina, and 201 in Georgia.

A strong feeling existed in the Confederacy that many of the exempted classes used their freedom from military service to exploit the people by speculation and extortion. Augusta J. Evans, the novelist, wrote to Representative Jabez L. M. Curry that great disaffection was rising in Alabama as a result of the exemption bill; furloughed soldiers had banded together and refused to return to the army, and desertion was appalling among Pemberton's troops. "The burden of this deplorable state of affairs," she declared, "is laid upon the Exemption Bill, which it is alleged offers premiums for extortion among all classes of artificers; instead of compelling them either to join the ranks of the army or furnish such necessities as *shoes* and *meal* at reasonable rates." [11]

So many abuses developed under the exemption provisions of the draft laws—such as the *dodge* of setting up a "drug store" at a crossroads with a few bottles of castor oil, some boxes of pills, and a soft-bottomed chair—that the Confederate Congress in 1864 reduced the number of exempted classes to less than half the original list. Although it changed the "twenty Negro law" to the "fifteen Negro law," it provided stringent safeguards against abuses, such as the requirement that the exempted overseer or planter must supervise the labor of at least fifteen Negroes between the ages of sixteen and fifty years and must give bond to produce one hundred pounds of meat per slave and sell the product of slave labor and other agricultural surplus at prices fixed by the impressment officers. Industrial exemptions also were abolished, although soldiers were detailed to vital industries.

The original draft law was followed on September 27, 1862, by a second extending the age limit to forty-five years. The desperate need for additional soldiers led to a third law in February, 1864, drafting men from seventeen to fifty years of age. The Federal government, on the other hand, kept the limits of conscription between the ages of twenty and forty-five, inclusive. It is a fallacy to conceive the Confederate Army as robbing the cradle and the grave—a charge which General Grant made late in the war. The boys of seventeen and the men between forty-five and fifty subject to the last conscription act were to be employed as home guards or reserves. Although there were boys sixteen and seventeen years old in the Confederate Army they were not numerous and were volunteers. Some of the states, such as South Carolina and Georgia, had state conscription laws enrolling white males between sixteen and sixty who were not in the army for emergency service in the state.

Conscription furnished a considerable number of soldiers both directly and indirectly to the Confederate Army. North Carolina contributed 21,343 conscripts and 8,000 volunteers forced into enlistment by the draft—the largest number of any state. The final report of John S. Preston, superintendent of the Bureau of Conscription, in February, 1865, reveals that 177,121 men had been conscripted east of the Mississippi for Confederate service. The principal benefit which the conscription laws rendered to the Confederacy was keeping the first volunteers in the ranks during the spring and summer of 1862 and thus preventing the gray-clad armies from dwindling dangerously. Although the system failed completely in the last six months of the war, it acted continuously until then as a club to force men to volunteer and thus avoid the odium of being drafted. In the North, where the draft was applied only in areas which failed to fill their quotas, only 46,000 conscripts and 118,000 substitutes, representing approximately 6 per cent of the Union forces, were obtained directly by the compulsion of the conscript system. However, the North, being far richer than the South, could stimulate volunteering by granting bounties, which frequently amounted to $800 or $1,000 per volunteer, and the states could complete their quotas with numerous immigrant recruits.

The South had desperate need of mobilizing its full strength against an enemy greatly superior in man power and economic resources. Of the 31,443,321 inhabitants of the United States in 1860 the eleven states forming the Confederacy contained approximately nine million, of whom over three and a half million were slaves. The five and a half million whites of the Confederacy confronted an enemy of twenty-two million, including about half a million slaves and more than two and a half million residents of slave states which did not secede. Superficially, the odds in white man power against the South were nearly four to one. The North was weakened by the presence in the Ohio valley and the middle states of many Copperheads or antiwar Democrats, but this disadvantage was balanced by the Unionists in the hill country and the mountains of the South. If Maryland was held in the Union by force, East Tennessee was similarly held in the Confederacy. Furthermore, the North was strengthened militarily by the immigration of young men from Europe, so that it had 4,010,000 white males between the ages of fifteen and forty at the time of the Civil War while the South had only 1,140,000 such males.[12]

The number of soldiers who fought in the Southern armies remains a subject of controversy. Thomas L. Livermore, a Northern officer, estimated in his elaborate study *Numbers and Losses in the Civil War,* on the basis of an average of three-year enlistments, that the Union armies contained 1,556,678 soldiers and the Confederate armies 1,082,119 soldiers. Southern estimates of the number of Confederate troops are much lower: between six and nine hundred thousand. The census of 1890 throws some light on the disputed matter. It records 1,034,073 Union veterans and 145,359 widows of veterans as living at that time, against 432,000 Confederate veterans and 60,564 widows of Confederate veterans—figures which indicate that the Confederate Army was less than half the size of the Union Army.[13] Albert B. Moore of the University of Alabama, in *Conscription and Conflict in the Confederacy,* estimates the number of Confederate soldiers between 850,000 and 900,000 and concludes that the conscription service was responsible directly or indirectly for the enlistment of 300,000 soldiers, or approximately a third of the total.[14]

The Confederate Army reached its peak of strength in June, 1863, just before the battle of Gettysburg, when 261,000 men through the Confederacy were reported as present for duty. Southern military power oozed away after that date, but the Northern Army gained until April, 1865, when 622,000 men were present for duty. The Northern margin of superiority over the military forces of the Confederacy increased from approximately two to one in the early part of the war to nearly three to one toward the end. The Northern Army was the invading army, so that it needed a considerable margin of strength over the defending Confederate Army.

Southerners have long maintained that the Confederate Army was beaten partly because its opponents were strengthened by a large contingent of foreigners. The assertion has been substantiated by a recent scholarly study of foreigners in the Union Army, which estimates conservatively that foreign-born soldiers formed from one-fifth to one-fourth of the strength of the Union Army.[15] The Confederate Army also had foreign-born soldiers who were resident in the South in 1861—including Irish brigades, German regiments, the European brigade from Louisiana, and even a Polish legion.[16] Furthermore, it was aided by some useful foreign officers, such as Colonel Hypolite Oladowski, a Polish officer who served as Bragg's chief of ordnance, Sir Wilfred Grenfell, and Major Heros von Borcke, the huge blond Prussian who served so exuberantly under "Jeb" Stuart.[17] The French Count de Polignac, a brigadier general leading Texan troops (who at first called him "Polecat"), contributed largely to the Confederate victory of Sabine Cross-Roads in Louisiana. Nevertheless, the proportion of foreign-born in the Confederate Army was small in comparison.

The Civil War was the first war fought in North America which was photographed. Lincoln commissioned Mathew Brady to follow the armies and make a photographic record of their life and activities. Consequently, we have realistic pictures of both Union and Confederate soldiers as well as of forts, guns, early trains, bivouacs, and battlefields, strewn with corpses.

Confederate soldiers, if they conformed to army regulations, wore a gray double-breasted coat which extended halfway between the thighs and the knees, and trousers of sky-blue. Actually, they wore a variety of uniforms, including homespun shirts, dyed a yellowish or butternut hue with walnut hulls and copperas, and often captured Federal blue uniforms. Instead of the army regulation cadet cap or kepi they frequently wore a wide-brim slouch hat. A toothbrush was carried in the buttonhole.

Southern soldiers marched light, carrying usually a rifle with bayonet, a cartridge box, a tin cup, and a blanket, totaling thirty to forty pounds. Northern soldiers were much better equipped, carrying a load of approximately fifty pounds; but they often reduced this recklessly on a long march by throwing away blankets and overcoats. The National Archives preserve a letter to the Secretary of War from a citizen of Farmville, Virginia, reporting that soldiers were in the practice of selling to speculators and sharpers large amounts of clothing and blankets that had been issued to them. He himself had recently seen an auctioneer buy an overcoat from a soldier for ten dollars and immediately sell it for twenty-five.[18]

Probably the most serious deficiency of the Confederate armies was the lack of shoes, which forced many of the men to go barefoot even in the winter.[19] There were times when numerous barefoot soldiers in both Lee's army and the Army of Tennessee would try to protect their feet from sharp stones and frozen ground by tying burlap cloth around them. Yet it must be noted that some Confederates were accustomed to going barefooted during the summer months; and they would at times remove their heavy army shoes to walk more comfortably. Although the Confederate government imported 550,000 pairs of boots and shoes from Europe, the supply did not meet the demand. Indeed, Lee may have suffered a check at Antietam because of the tremendous amount of straggling in his army, which undoubtedly was caused in part by lack of shoes.

The frequent lack of soap and of changes of clothing took away some of the glamour of a soldier's life. Alexander Donelson Coffee, an officer in Zollicoffer's army in East Tennessee, described a Confederate regiment as follows: "They were the hardest roughest looking set you ever saw, and I don't think there could have been a clean shirt in the reg. for a month." [20] The manuscript journal of the Shaker community at Pleasant Hill, Kentucky, describes the soldiers of Humphrey Marshall's Confederate brigade passing through their settlement as "ragged, greasy, and dirty and some barefoot, and looked more like the bipeds of pandemonium than beings of this earth . . . they surrounded our wells like the locusts of Egypt and struggled with each other for the water as if perishing with thirst, and they thronged our kitchen doors and windows, begging for bread like hungry wolves . . . they tore the loaves and pies into fragments and devoured them. Some even threatened to shoot others, if they did not divide with them . . . notwithstanding such a motley crew, they abstained from any violence or depredations and appeared exceedingly grateful." [21] During Longstreet's retreat from Suffolk, Virginia, Clifford Lanier (brother of Sidney) wrote to his father: "We are all well but very dirty—expect to bathe in the Nottaway river this evening tell Ma." [22] Unwashed soldiers in closed railroad passenger or box cars gave off a very annoying odor. Confederate foot soldiers did their own washing, and soap was often a luxury. Thus gray lice—"graybacks"—became the bane of both armies.

The rations of "Johnny Reb" were mainly cornbread and salt or pickled beef or pork. Army beef, pickled in brine in barrels and called "blue beef," was usually tough and unappetizing. Inefficiency of the commissariat impaired the fighting ability of the Confederate armies by failing to deliver food at the right time. Often the lack of green vegetables caused straggling when soldiers undertook to supplement the rations by digging sweet potatoes and picking apples and blackberries on the line of march. It was fatal for rabbits or chickens or pigs to stray close to a Confederate camp. The Confederates rarely enjoyed the coffee which was usual to the Federals. Marching through Maryland in the Antietam campaign of 1862, they subsisted partly on green corn plucked from the fields, which caused diarrhea and kept many away from that crucial battle. Usually messes of four to eight men engaged in cooperative cooking, handicapped often by a woeful lack of cooking utensils—especially the skillet, the chief utensil of the soldier.[23]

The common soldier grew to know intimately the weaknesses as well as the manly qualities of the men in his company. He gave most of them nicknames, such as "Sneak," "Applejack," "Hog," "Greasy," "Left Tenant," "Old Hannah," and "Buzzard." With them he enjoyed the pleasures of camp life—practical joking, snowballing, cockfighting (some of the soldiers carried gamecocks in their knapsacks), gambling, even on lice races held on tin plates, singing songs, dreaming of home, and looking at his sweetheart's picture or a keepsake such as "a braid of her beautiful hair." When the citizens of Manchester, Tennessee, gave a party for the soldiers, the boys found a violin and proposed a dance. The girls all belonged to the church and declined to indulge in this worldly pleasure; but they suggested as a substitute playing "Weevily Wheat," in which pairs lined up opposite each other and sang,

> "I will not have your weevily wheat,
>   I will not have your barley,
> I will not have your weevily wheat
>   To make a cake for Charley."

And to this music they danced the Virginia reel.[24]

Johnny Reb resented the red tape of army life, the privileges enjoyed by staff officers whom he called "yaller dogs," the corruption of commissaries who would sell extra food and luxuries to rich Johnnies, the monopoly of glory by officers, and, above all, the injustice of permitting officers to resign at will while privates were shot for desertion. Wrote Sam Watkins of "Co. Aytch," First Tennessee Regiment: "Glory is not for the private soldier, such as die in the hospitals, being eat up with the deadly gangrene, and being imperfectly waited on. Glory is for generals, colonels, majors, captains, and lieutenants." [25] Yet it is evident from the accounts of wounded and dying soldiers that they hoped to live in the memory of their comrades, their relatives, and their country as having died bravely for a patriotic cause. Asked a Kentucky youth wounded in the battle of Shiloh, "Johnnie, if a boy dies for his country the glory is his forever, isn't it?" [26] Dying that night, he was buried far from home.

In joining the army the Confederate soldier did not give up his right to vote in local elections or to run for office. Ruffin Barnes, a captain in the Forty-third North Carolina Regiment, wrote to his wife in April, 1864, to let the people of his county know that he was a candidate for sheriff. The army vote in that election, he predicted, would be small, for some North Carolina soldiers were too young to vote and others were in the hospital. The election in the army was held in July near the Potomac River, where Barnes's regiment was in camp. Barnes received nineteen votes in his company while the other candidates received only two votes. In another regiment his leading opponent, Colonel Barry Fulgrum, received twenty-one votes. It is evident from Barnes's homesick letters that his principal reason for running for sheriff was to get out of the army in an honorable manner.[27] He died as a prisoner of the Yankees, and the letters do not reveal who won the election. The candidate for civilian office had to steer a cautious course so as to win both the soldier and the civilian vote. When General Edney ran in 1863 for election to Congress from the western district of North Carolina, he sought civilian votes by claiming that he had persuaded the President to suspend the execution of the conscription law in that district; but his opponent believed the claim would cause him to lose the soldiers' vote because the soldiers wished the conscription law strictly enforced.[28]

The life of the Confederate common soldier was far from romantic. A large proportion of his service was wearisome marching, sometimes without shoes. The Southern roads were often churned into bogs by the feet of marching armies; and in the hot summer months clouds of dust marked the line of march. Other annoyances —such as guard duty, mosquitoes, sickness, and miserable food— made the soldiers long for home. In winter, campaigning usually came to an end; but the improvised winter quarters did not adequately protect the soldiers from the cold and rain.[29] The nostalgia of the uncomfortable men is reflected in the thousands of letters to mothers, sisters, fathers, and sweethearts, which, with their ignorance, crude spelling, and naïveté, are a revelation of the mind of the common people. The attitude of the common soldier to war is expressed in one of the most popular of the Confederate war songs:

Sitting by the roadside on a summer day,
Chatting with my messmates, passing time away,
Lying in the shadows underneath the trees,
Goodness, how delicious, eating goober peas!

I wish this war was over, when, free from rags and fleas,
We'd kiss our wives and sweethearts and gobble goober peas.
Peas! Peas! Peas! eating goober peas!
Goodness, how delicious, eating goober peas!

The supreme moment of a soldier's life was in battle when he faced death and saw his friends falling beside him. Alexander Donelson Coffee, the son of Andrew Jackson's friend General John Coffee, wrote to his wife in Florence, Alabama, a description of his emotions at Shiloh, April 6, 1862. As the Confederates charged through a lane of Union tents "poor Billy," only two feet away from him, fell dead; but he could not stop. He "was shocked, grieved and felt a spirit of revenge" over this killing of his friend. At night the Confederates were occupying the former camp of the enemy, and Coffee went out in the moonlight to search for the dead soldier. As he walked on the battlefield, he came upon the bodies of dead soldiers and horses; but "I had lost most of the horror of such sights from the intense excitement of the battle." [30] When he found his friend he placed "poor Billy" in the abandoned log hut of a sutler and searched for a conveyance. Finally he secured an oxcart to transport the body to the field hospital.

Most soldiers described their greatest fear of death as arising in the period just before going into battle; after the battle was engaged, the excitement of fighting restored their "nerve" and even gave them a sense of exhilaration. Coffee wrote, after leading his company into battle at Shiloh: "I went in determined to do my every duty, regardless of consequences, that I would not provoke a shot by any excited actions or undue excitement, and yet to keep my men as well up to the mark as possible. I found enough to do all the time to keep me from thinking too much of themselves and only when lying on our faces until the enemy's fire was drawn away did I have very serious thoughts." Perhaps the most nerve-racking aspect of combat experience was the noise of shrieking shells, the deep roar of cannon, and the crash of exploding shrapnel. In virtually every battle there were skulkers, who were driven back into line of battle by file closers.

The Confederate infantrymen, as well as the Northern foot soldiers, fought throughout the war with muzzle-loaders, and had to stand in order to load them. Smoothbore muskets, which were not effective beyond one hundred yards, were used at first. In the second year however, the Confederate armies were largely supplied with English-made Enfield rifles, caliber .577, or captured American-made Springfield rifles, caliber .58. Both the Enfield and the Springfield had spiral grooves inside the barrel, giving the bullet greater accuracy and force. The Springfield, weighing fourteen pounds, had a range of fifteen hundred yards. The improved muskets and rifles were fired by copper percussion caps in which the detonating agent was fulminate of mercury. The standard projectile for rifles used in the Civil War was the cone-shaped Minié ball, the concave rear end of which expanded with the explosion of the powder so that the ball fitted the spiral grooves tightly. The bullet and charge of powder were inclosed in a paper cartridge, and the soldier bit off the tip of the cartridge before inserting it in the muzzle and pushing it down the barrel with a ramrod. This practice had a curious hangover years later in army regulations that disqualified a man for service if he lacked certain teeth.

After the first year of the war the Confederate soldier fought on equal terms with his enemy as far as the equipment of guns was concerned. The Federal military authorities had a splendid opportunity to adopt the Spencer breech-loading, repeating rifle, invented in 1860. But they rejected this ultramodern invention until near the end of the war and retained the conventional muzzle-loader, particularly the .58 caliber Springfield. Some of the objections to repeating rifles seem ridiculous today, for example, that the soldiers fired too rapidly with the old rifles, thus wasting ammunition, and that the new type of rifle would only increase this extravagance. In 1864 some breech-loading and repeating rifles were introduced into the Union Army and used especially by the cavalry. The Gatling gun, invented by Richard J. Gatling of North Carolina, which could fire two hundred and fifty shots a minute, was first made at Indianapolis in 1862 but was not appreciated by the authorities; and only a few were used—by General Ben Butler. The Confederates greatly feared troops armed with the breech-loading repeating rifles. E. P. Alexander, a leading artillery officer of the Confederacy, expressed the opinion "that had the Federal infantry been armed from the first with even the breech-loaders available in 1861 the war would have been terminated within a year." [31]

Marksmanship of the common soldiers on both sides must have been remarkably inaccurate. These amateurs almost invariably aimed too high, and the use of black powder often made visibility on the battlefield bad. It was a common saying during the conflict that it took a man's weight in lead to kill an enemy soldier (estimated by Shannon to require 900 pounds of lead and 240 pounds of powder).[32] Despite the enormous number of bullets and cannon shells fired, the Confederates killed only 110,070 Yankees during the course of the war. Although the close order of fighting that was used through most of the war made bloody battles, estimates in that monumental narrative *Battles and Leaders of the Civil War* suggest that the battle deaths of the Union Army were less than a third of the total of 360,222 deaths from all causes.[33] As usual, the records of the Confederate Army are either non-existent or less complete than the reports of the Federal forces. It is estimated, however, that the total death loss in the Confederate military forces was 258,000 including 94,000 killed in battle.

Both armies changed their methods of fighting somewhat as they acquired experience. The Civil War was a transitional period in the technique of combat. Both armies marched into battle in close formation in long, thin lines, frequently double lines, preceded by skirmishers. In the battle of Missionary Ridge the Confederate line of defense was so thin that the men were two yards apart. Although the advance by rushes was adopted by some generals, a forerunner of modern techniques, close-order battle formations persisted into the last year of the war. Experience and Southern individualism led to a more natural type of fighting than the rule books specified. Soldiers lay down on the ground to avoid artillery fire much more than romantic accounts of the Civil War admit. The diary of Johnny Green, a Kentucky soldier, describes the fighting in 1863 at Jackson,

Mississippi, as follows: "Our boys would lie down and load and then rise to their knees and fire at the enemy." [34] Officers would often order their men to lie down to escape the bullets of the enemy while awaiting orders to advance.

Throughout the war a favorite tactic was the charge, the officers leading their troops. Consequently, sharpshooters of the opposing side would concentrate their fire on the officers and color-bearers. As the Southern soldiers charged the enemy, they would give the famous rebel yell. In 1862 after the battle of Shiloh General Hardee commented soberly on the proneness of Southerners to rely on the impetuous charge: "I am not so much impressed as many respecting the invincibility of our volunteers and their determination to be free—they are good for a dash but fail in tenacity. I don't think that we can yet regard ourselves as soldiers—our men are not sufficiently impressed with a sense of honor that it is better to die by fire than to run—we fail also in company officers, they want skill and instruction and lamentably neglect their duty." [35] Stories of savage combats with bayonets and bowie knives are exaggerated. The introduction of the rifle rendered the bayonet to a large degree obsolete. Although bayonets continued to be standard equipment, surgeons reported few cases of bayonet or bowie knife wounds.[36]

Before the Civil War ended, the best generals had begun to protect their men with breastworks and trenches. Lee required his soldiers to dig trenches and was accordingly dubbed "King of Spades." Josiah Gorgas, Chief of Ordnance of the Confederate Army, wrote in his journal at Richmond, June 4, 1864: "Our troops were lying behind triple lines of breastworks. They have acquired quite a respect for this sort of entrenchment, and work like beavers when they take up a new position. They began the war with a contempt for the spade, but now thoroughly believe in it. They use bayonets, tin pans, and even, I am told, split their tin canteens to get a utensil that will throw up earth." [37]

An amazing number of battles, skirmishes, engagements, bombardments and actions was fought during the four years of war. General Clement A. Evans's *Confederate Military History* lists more than fifty-five hundred, designating about ninety-five as battles.[38] The Confederate and Union soldiers must often have been skirmishing when they were not fighting big battles. Yet most of the engagements were fruitless unless constant conflict be viewed as wearing down the weaker Southern Army, which could not easily replace its losses. The opposing armies fought and departed to fight another day. Desertions, or absences without leave after battles, were no small factor in this failure to capitalize victories. The desire to plunder Federal camps for food and uniforms at times prevented Confederate armies from taking full advantage of their opportunities. Other factors in inconclusive fighting were fatigue, lack of drinking water on the battlefield, and the failure of the commissary to provide food at the right time. But perhaps the main cause of inertia in the Civil War armies after pitched battles was their imperfect understanding of logistics.

The deadliest foe that Confederate soldiers had to face was disease. The chief illnesses were measles, virulent erysipelas, malaria, pneumonia, typhoid fever, smallpox, dysentery, and diarrhea. Dysentery and diarrhea were the most prevalent. Dr. Joseph Jones, a contemporary authority on Confederate medicine, believed that disease killed three Confederate soldiers for every one killed in battle. Because the doctors knew nothing of the germ origin of disease, gangrene frequently developed in a wounded arm or leg, and they recklessly cut off these members. After the battle of Missionary Ridge, a Northern soldier saw a pile as big as a haystack of arms and legs which the surgeons had removed.[39] When the war was over, veterans with a missing leg or arm bore testimony in every community to the lack of knowledge of antisepsis. Yet the Civil War was the first American war in which anesthesia was used —a discovery made in 1842 by a Georgia doctor, Crawford W. Long. Nevertheless, many Confederate surgeons had a prejudice against the use of ether in operations because it frequently was not properly administered. Consequently anesthesia was not generally practiced in operations in the field and military hospitals. Some surgeons used chloroform, the knowledge of which as a pain-killer had been revealed in 1847 by Dr. James Y. Simpson, while others used opium and whisky.

The Medical Department of the Confederate Army was directed by Samuel Preston Moore, Surgeon General. A native of South Carolina, he had been a surgeon in the United States Army with the rank of major for many years when the Confederacy was formed. Appointed Surgeon General in June, 1861, he tried to build up the medical service on the pattern he knew. Many of the volunteer Confederate organizations elected their own surgeons as well as their field officers. Moore tried to weed out the incompetents by establishing examining boards to pass on the qualifications of the army surgeons. Also he tried to improve medical science among his staff by organizing in 1863 the Association of Army and Navy Surgeons and by encouraging the publication of the *Confederate States Medical and Surgical Journal* (January, 1862, to February, 1865). When the supply of medicines imported through the blockade began to fail, he established medical laboratories at Lincolnton (North Carolina), Charlotte, Columbia, and Macon, and imported medicines through the lines by swapping cotton for opium, calomel, and quinine. He bought two distilleries for the Confederacy at Salisbury and Columbia, which produced between 200 and 300 gallons of whisky per day.[40]

The Confederate armies had approximately thirty-four hundred doctors and surgeons, many of whom were poorly trained. Fortunately, they no longer resorted to bleeding as a favorite remedy. Instead, they relied strongly on whisky, turpentine, blisters, purgatives, opium, quinine, calomel and blue mass, a mercury preparation. In diagnosis, Dr. Joseph Jones is reported to have been the only Confederate physician to use a clinical thermometer.[41] Moreover, sanitation in camps and prisons was rudimentary. Many of the soldiers from rural districts scorned latrines and refused to be "house-broken."

The care of the sick and wounded Confederate soldiers was inefficiently organized. After battles the near-by villages or towns were crowded with wounded and dying men who were placed in makeshift hospitals that were established in hotels, churches, courthouses, and railroad stations. The wounded and dying suffered horribly as they were transported in jolting ambulances or wagons. Their wounds were often dressed with cotton and rags provided by patriotic housewives and even with tent cloth.[42] There was a serious lack of milk and appropriate food for sick men. The nurses, mostly men, were as a rule untrained. Mrs. McCord, the daughter of Langdon Cheves, who put her whole soul into hospital work in Columbia, observed that "the better born—that is, those born in the purple, the gentry—were the better patients. They endure in silence." [43] The youthful Alice Ready visited the soldiers' hospital at Murfreesboro, Tennessee, and was shocked at the conditions and at the indifference shown to dying men—"no more notice taken of them than if they had been dogs." [44]

The Confederacy had no powerful, highly centralized agency like the United States Sanitary Commission, which equipped railroad cars as field hospitals, organized women into societies for making medical supplies and holding fairs to raise money for the Union soldiers and distributed pamphlets on health and sanitation. The Confederacy did have, however, at Richmond two of the largest military hospitals in America, the Chimborazo and the Winder, each with 7,800 beds. A law of the Confederate Congress in September, 1862, recognized the strength of state pride by requiring that military hospitals should be known as hospitals of a particular state, to which wounded or sick soldiers should be allocated whenever possible.

Two private organizations rendered valuable services to Confederate soldiers. The Georgia Hospital and Relief Association acted as a central agent for collecting private contributions, money, and commodities, which it dispatched to the camps; it sent surgeons and medicines to field hospitals, organized four large hospitals in Richmond for Georgians, and sent clothing and packages to well soldiers. The South Carolina Hospital Aid Association provided similar services for South Carolinians. Both associations were active in establishing wayside homes along the main rail lines, where soldiers could get free meals and lodging. As the value of the work of these private benevolent organizations became apparent, the legislatures of Georgia and South Carolina made large appropriations to aid them.[45]

The pay of the common soldier in 1863 was $11 a month, while slaves were hired for $30 a month in Virginia. The compensation was raised to $18 in the summer of 1864, when the Union soldier received $16 a month; but the Northern soldier was paid $6.40 in gold value while the Confederate soldier was getting only 90 cents. Indeed, the low pay and tremendous inflation contributed to the large-scale desertion of soldiers in the last two years of the war, when pitiful letters from their families told about lack of food and about other hardships.

Putting on a gray uniform and following the flag of the Confederacy necessitated a new way of life for the young recruits who came mostly from farms and small villages. Many were illiterate. A large sampling of North Carolina regiments by a recent student has shown that 40 per cent of these Tarheels could not sign their names; but this percentage is certainly far higher than that of the Southern army as a whole.[46] The green country boys in the army quickly learned to gamble, curse, and drink liquor. Yet many of these essentially manly young fellows would throw away a deck of cards and refuse liquor on the eve of a great battle, not wishing to be killed with a liquor breath or with cards in their pocket. On the whole the soldiers were moral; but prostitution did occur when the armies were near cities like Richmond and Petersburg.

Although the evidence indicates that a minority of Confederate soldiers belonged to a church, many prayed and read their Bibles conscientiously. The Confederate government apportioned one chaplain for every regiment, with pay of $80 a month and the ordinary ration of a soldier. Nevertheless it was difficult to procure an adequate number of chaplains. On March 24, 1863, the Chaplains Association in the Army of Northern Virginia issued an address to the churches of the Confederacy pointing out that even in the corps of "Stonewall" Jackson, who gave great encouragement to religious services, fewer than half of the regiments had chaplains and entire brigades were without chaplains. They estimated that there were not two hundred chaplains in all the armies of the Confederacy, although there were as many as five or six thousand ministers of the Gospel within the limits of the Confederacy.[47]

Religion was brought to the army in the field not only by military chaplains but in occasional visits of missionaries, local preachers, and colporteurs. The colporteurs carried tracts and Bibles to the hospitals and to armies in the field. The most popular tract for the soldiers was *A Mother's Parting Words to Her Soldier Boy,* by J. B. Jeter, 250,000 copies of which were distributed to soldiers in the year of publication. Other favorite tracts were *Come to Jesus, Persuasiveness to Early Piety, Don't Put It Off, The Evils of Gaming,* and *Swearing,* by Hon. Jabez L. M. Curry. The British and Foreign Bible Society sent thousands of Bibles through the blockade to Confederate soldiers, and the American Bible Society of New York, rising above the passions of war, sent more than $100,000 worth of Bibles to be distributed in the Confederate Army. The cooperation of ministers of different denominations acted as a solvent of narrow sectarianism that had prevailed in the ante-bellum South.

After the chastening disasters of Vicksburg and Gettysburg tremendous revivals of religion swept the Confederate armies. A number of eminent generals—Bragg, Hood, Ewell, Hardee, and Joseph E. Johnston—joined the church. "Stonewall" Jackson, Lee, and Leonidas Polk especially set examples of Christian piety to the soldiers under their command. Christian piety, however, did not prevent them from fighting on Sunday. Even the dashing and worldly John Hunt Morgan wrote from prison in Ohio to his beautiful bride, Mattie Ready, that her Christian example had made a much better man of him, and that he read every night the prayerbook she had given him at their wedding.[48]

The Civil War has been called an infantrymen's war. Indeed, Confederate officers relied too much on infantry charges and not enough on artillery. Yet the artillery on occasions played a magnificent role, especially on Marye's Heights at Fredericksburg in mowing down the frontal attack of Burnside, and during Beauregard's defense of Charleston from the attack of the armored monitors. The chief artillery officer of Lee's army was Brigadier General William N. Pendleton, a West Point graduate, who before the war had been an Episcopal minister at Lexington, Virginia. When he was an artillery commander he alternated between preaching and shooting Yankees. The greatest artillery duel between the Union and Confederate armies occurred at Gettysburg just before Pickett's famous charge, and it was probably the Federal artillery that decided that crucial battle. Early in the war the Confederates scattered their artillery in battle; later they learned the value of massed artillery fire.

The Confederate artillery was organized into batteries, consisting of four or five guns pulled by horses and manned by forty-five to seventy-five men. The ammunition was carried in specially constructed wagons, called caissons. The favorite field guns were the bronze smoothbore Napoleons firing twelve-pound shot, Parrott rifled guns, and howitzers. Often these guns, which were loaded from the muzzle, were filled with shrapnel shells which exploded by a time fuse into many fragments of iron. Lee's army at Gettysburg had 247 guns, including 100 Napoleons, 110 rifled cannon, and 37 howitzers, opposed to Meade's 320 guns. The effectiveness of the field artillery was decreased toward the close of the war by an inadequate supply of horses (seldom more than four horses to a gun) which compelled the cannoneers to walk.[49] Also there was a heavy mortality among artillerymen because sharpshooters with long-range rifles specialized in killing them.

The heaviest guns of the Confederates, used particularly in coastal defense, were the huge Columbiads, which could send a cannonball weighing one hundred and twenty-three pounds more than two miles, the Rodman guns, and, most powerful of all, the English-made Whitworth and Blakely rifled cannon. Robert Kean noted in his diary August 23, 1863, that Federal guns on Morris Island threw two-hundred-pound shells into the city of Charleston, a distance of five and a half miles—"a range unprecedented in gunnery." [50] He was undoubtedly referring to the "Swamp Angel," which was erected on the marshy ground of an island in Charleston harbor and threw huge shells filled with Greek fire into the city.

Southern planters were trained to ride horses from their youth, and a love of fine horses was characteristic of the plantation gentry. Consequently, many young aristocrats volunteered in the cavalry. Unlike the Union cavalrymen, the Confederates had to furnish their own mounts, for which they were paid forty cents a day. When one lost his horse in battle, he received its appraised value and a thirty-day furlough to replace it. The equipment of the Southern cavalry —Colt revolver, saber, and carbine—was frequently taken from the enemy and the result was a great variety of calibers of guns with difficulty in procuring the right type of ammunition. The most important functions of the cavalry were: to serve as a reconnaissance force, the eyes of the army; to ride on the flanks of the army, in order to protect it from surprise; to destroy the communications of the enemy, particularly railroads and bridges; and to pursue the re-treating enemy. When cavalrymen fought a pitched battle they usually dismounted; but some of them had to act as horse holders.

Besides the regular branches, the Confederate Army included bands of partisan rangers; and the most notable leaders of rangers were Turner Ashby, mounted on a striking milk-white charger, and John S. Mosby, a Virginia lawyer turned cavalryman.[51] These adventurous men (much like commandos) made daring raids behind the enemy lines, acted as scouts, and captured valuable supplies. More questionable in their activities were the guerrillas, who operated chiefly in the mountainous districts.[52] Among these free-lance warriors were Sue Mundy of Kentucky and "Champ" Ferguson, who terrorized the Cumberland Mountain area of Tennessee and was credited with killing fifty-three Union men. Both Mundy and Ferguson were hanged after the war by the Federal government as war criminals. W. C. Quantrill, a Northern schoolteacher who had settled in Kansas, became a notorious Confederate guerrilla leader. His lawless band sacked and burned the town of Lawrence, Kansas, on August 20, 1863, murdering 150 citizens in cold blood. In Quantrill's band was the youthful Jesse James, who, trained in this school of crime, became America's most famous bandit.

The problem of the horse supply was one of the most critical in the Confederate logistics of defense. The horse-breeding country— Kentucky, West Virginia, Missouri, and middle Tennessee—fell early under the control of Union armies. In the summer of 1862 a stringency occurred in the horse supply of the South. There was a heavy mortality among army horses; in the artillery and transportation services, the average life of a horse was seven and one-half months, but in the cavalry the average was much shorter. Cavalrymen who had lost their mounts in battle found tremendous difficulty in replacing them, partly because of inflation and the low appraisal of their horses when mustered into the service. An equine infirmary was established at Lynchburg, Virginia, to restore sick and worn-out horses to effectiveness; but only 15 per cent were thus returned to service.[53] By the last year of the war the splendid horses of the Confederacy were used up and the poor nags which replaced them greatly reduced the efficiency of the cavalry. The result of the gradual deterioration in quality of cavalry horses was a reduction in the offensive power of Confederate armies and in the ability of the cavalry to protect railroads and communications. Meanwhile the Northern cavalry, especially under the command of Sheridan in Virginia and Wilson in the West, was growing stronger and more dangerous.

As the war progressed, discipline over the cavalry declined, and Confederate cavalrymen were feared by the country people for their plundering activities almost as much as the enemy cavalry. Bill Arp, the Confederate humorist, remarked: "I have travelled a heap of late, and had occasion to retire into some very sequestered regions, but nary hill or holler, nary mountain gorge or inaccessible ravine have I found, but what the cavalry had been there, and *just left*. And that is the reason they can't be whipped, for they have always *just left*, and took an odd horse or two with 'em." Their peculiar drill, he declared, was called damning—"they dam their eyes, they dam their ears, and they dam their guns, and their boots, and their mill-saw spurs, and they dam their horses to make 'em go faster, and they dam the fences to make 'em come down, and they dam the poor farmer to make him dry up." [54] It was no wonder that the country people began to refer to them as "the damned cavalry."

American soldiers in the Civil War were not fanatical fighters like the Japanese in World War II, who often preferred death to surrender. The Confederates captured during the war 211,000 Federals, of whom 16,000 were released on the field by parole (oath to take no further part in the war). If the paroled captives are subtracted, the Confederates had to guard in prison 195,000 Union soldiers, while the North retained approximately 215,000 Confederate prisoners. A cartel for the exchange of all prisoners, rank for rank, was ratified on July 22, 1862. If one side should acquire an excess of prisoners over the other, the cartel provided, they should be paroled until they could be exchanged. Had the cartel been kept, there would have been few prisoners left to suffer either in Southern or Northern camps. But misunderstandings and violations occurred, so that exchanges virtually ceased in the summer of 1863 after the battles of Vicksburg and Gettysburg. The North was alarmed by the encouragement that the cartel gave to their soldiers to surrender in order to be paroled. Furthermore, President Davis' violent proclamation against General Butler for his brutal acts in New Orleans and the policy announced in that proclamation (which was not actually carried out) of refusing to exchange captured Negro soldiers or white officers commanding Negro troops angered the North. Late in December, 1863, Butler, who had been transferred to command in Virginia, temporarily renewed the exchange of prisoners at City Point on the James River with the Confederate Commissioner Robert Ould. But Grant believed that the North with its superior man power and resources would profit by refusing to exchange prisoners. Accordingly, on April 17, 1863, he ordered that there should be no further exchange of prisoners—a practice which was abandoned, beginning with the exchange of sick prisoners, in February, 1865.[55]

The prison camps in the South were undoubtedly places of great suffering and death. The chief prison camps of the Confederacy were: Libby Prison, a former tobacco warehouse in Richmond which was converted into an officers' prison; Belle Isle, on an unhealthy island in the James River; Castle Thunder in Richmond, used to confine political prisoners; and the camps at Salisbury, North Carolina, Florence, South Carolina, and Andersonville, Georgia. The worst conditions prevailed at the huge prison camp at Andersonville, established early in 1864 and abandoned in September of that year as Sherman's army threatened to capture it. In July, 31,000 prisoners were crowded into the Andersonville stockade. The Confederate guards were young boys and old men who at times were afraid to go into the stockade and police it properly. Some criminals, called "raiders," from New York terrorized their fellow prisoners; but finally the Federals erected a gallows and hung six ringleaders. The food allowance was the same as that of the guards; but Northern soldiers, who came from the wheat country, were unaccustomed to a monotonous diet of cornbread. They had to cook their rations, and often the pones would be baked so hard that they were used as footballs. Furthermore, the corn meal was coarse and unsifted, resulting in widespread diarrhea. Sanitation and hospital facilities were extremely bad. A stream flowing through the stockade became a source of great pollution; nearly all the prisoners became sick, and the mortality was frightful. By the end of the war there were 12,912 prisoners' graves at Andersonville.[56]

Southerners have apologized for the Andersonville prison camp horrors by pointing out that the Confederacy did not have the proper medical supplies even for its own army, and that the policy of Secretary of War Stanton and Grant of no exchange of prisoners was partly responsible for the suffering of Northern captives. Although the mortality rate of Northerners in Southern prisons was somewhat greater than that of Confederate soldiers in Northern prisons, the difference was not striking. The atrocities of Andersonville became a bitter campaign issue of the Republican party after the Civil War, and partisan references to them were called "waving the bloody shirt." The commandant of Andersonville prison camp,

Major Henry Wirz, was convicted by a Federal court-martial after the war for atrocities and hanged—a scapegoat for Northern vengeance.

Letters from Confederate prisoners of war to their families present vivid pictures of life in a military camp and also of the psychology of the Southern soldier. The failure of Morgan's raid into Ohio in the summer of 1863 resulted in a considerable number of Confederate soldiers being imprisoned in Camp Douglas near Chicago and Camp Chase in Ohio. The letters from some of these reveal that they were humanely treated and well fed. They were permitted to write a one page letter every eighteen days and to receive boxes of food, clothing, and books from relatives and friends. The main contents of their letters were requests for food—an "old ham," for example—clothing, books, and photographs of relatives and sweethearts. The prisoners usually adjusted themselves to prison life, often becoming gay and lively playing checkers, marbles, singing songs, cheering, eating ginger cake, and running footraces. One prisoner wrote, "Eating is the principal source of happiness with me" and another, "dull hours still roll around but we keep in hopes of an exchange some day." [57] The chief discomforts of the prisons were that they were often overcrowded, and that sickness was prevalent.

Especially revealing in the prisoners' letters is their reflection of the religion of the Southern yeoman. Thee Jones of Kentucky, for example, wrote: "I am doing as well as you could expect for a prisoner. . . . I pass a great portion of my time in reading the Holy Bible. I have read it through more than twice." [58] Jasper Hunt, another Kentuckian, wrote: "I have not broke the old watch bargain yet. I have not taken a chew of tobacco nor smoked cigar or pipe since I have been in the army, nor played cards. I drank a little whiskey last winter but quit in the spring again." [59]

To some civilians it might appear humiliating to be a prisoner of war, but the average soldier did not feel that way. G. W. Logan of Shelbyville, Kentucky, one of Morgan's raiders, wrote from Camp Chase: "I expect to hold up my head before the gaze of any. Have taken prisoners on the field and have not felt that they were humiliated and treated them with more respect than I would our own men. . . . Soldiers know how to respect soldiers—citizens do not." [60]

VI

Generals and Strategy

THE SUCCESS of the South in winning its independence had to depend largely on brilliant leadership and the morale of the people, for the North had a vast preponderance of man power and economic resources. At the beginning of the conflict more than one-fourth of the officers in the United States Army were permitted to resign their commissions and join the Confederacy, a privilege that was not allowed to the enlisted men. There was an eager rush by civilians to secure commissions, and the records of both the Confederacy and the United States contain threats of officers to resign if they are not promoted as well as resignations because junior officers have been advanced in rank over them.[1]

The company officers, even the "noncoms," of volunteer units, were selected by the members, while the state governors gave commissions to majors, lieutenant colonels, and colonels. This system led to inefficiency, for stern disciplinarians were often defeated in elections. As a result, the Confederate Army set up examining boards to weed out incompetents. An unknown "Jack" wrote from McPhearsonville, South Carolina, to the schoolteacher and poet Clara Dargan of Columbia that he was "ordered before a Board of Examiners to see if I was competent to be a Second Lt. The board is a very strict one and has cashiered several old officers in this district—it made a favorable report to the General. I just being elected, the men think that they can act as they choose."[2]

A bundle of documents in the National Archives contains an excellent description of a disputed election in a Mississippi regiment on May 6 and 7, 1862. According to the brigade commander, Brigadier General L. M. Jones, the regiment was composed of admirable human material but had become mutinous and insubordinate while stationed in southern Alabama. Consequently, he had ordered a reorganization, and had appointed managers to hold an election for officers and count the votes of the 501 members of the regiment. In the race for colonel two lieutenants ran against the incumbent, D. C. Chandler. Chandler received only a plurality vote, and a runoff election was held, in which he was defeated. The brigade commander, however, declaring that the second election was unauthorized and illegal, recognized Chandler as the duly elected colonel of the regiment. The rejected candidate, Lieutenant J. C. Wilkinson, then appealed to the War Department, and Robert G. H. Kean, Chief of the Confederate Bureau of War, decided that he was the rightful commander of the regiment, basing his decision on General Order No. 30 which required soldiers' elections to conform to the laws of the states, and on the fact that the Mississippi law required a majority vote for officers. A letter from General Jones pointed out to the War Department that it was evident in this election that the regiment had determined to throw out officers who had done their duty and to elect those who had been foremost in seditious schemes. Ultimately the case reached President Davis, and one of the documents in the bundle contains his endorsement reversing Kean's decision.[3]

Most of the able officers on both sides were trained at West Point, and many had fought in the Mexican War. There were three hundred and four West Point graduates in the Confederate Army, including one hundred and forty-eight generals. The Union Army had approximately twice that number of generals who were West Point graduates. In addition to the graduates, forty-six cadets of the United States Military Academy from Southern states resigned before graduation and served in the Confederate Army; and it contained also approximately four hundred and twenty-five men trained at Virginia Military Institute and two hundred educated at South Carolina Military Academy.[4] Jefferson Davis was bitterly criticized for strong partiality to West Point officers by many Southerners, who naïvely discounted training and exalted the Southern spirit as the essential qualification for an officer.

The political generals of the South, men with little or no military training but with influential political connections, played a minor role in military operations. The most prominent of these were John C. Breckinridge, candidate for President in 1860, Congressman

Felix Zollicoffer of Tennessee, Henry A. Wise and John Floyd of Virginia, and Robert Toombs and Howell Cobb of Georgia. Toombs demonstrated a penchant for oratory before his troops and a cavalier disregard of military discipline which led to his arrest for insubordination. On one occasion he challenged General D. H. Hill to a duel for impugning his courage. A unique general in the Confederate Army was Leonidas Polk, Episcopal Bishop of Louisiana, who had been educated at West Point. A brave and noble gentleman, Polk fought in the Army of Tennessee until 1864, when he was killed in the retreat toward Atlanta.[5] Of the untrained officers who served the Confederacy, Wade Hampton, John B. Gordon, Joseph B. Kershaw, and Nathan B. Forrest overcame their inexperience and developed into effective generals.

Battle Abbey at Richmond preserves a remarkable group picture of the Confederate generals—on the whole, young men or men in the prime of their lives. Thomas Jonathan Jackson was thirty-nine when he was mortally wounded; "Jeb" Stuart was thirty-one, Patrick Cleburne was thirty-six, and A. P. Hill was thirty-nine when they were killed toward the end of the war. Joseph Wheeler was twenty-five years old when he was appointed commander of the cavalry of the Army of Mississippi. Beauregard was forty-three at the time of the battle of Bull Run; James Longstreet was forty-two and George E. Pickett was thirty-eight at Gettysburg, while Braxton Bragg was forty-five when he was placed at the head of the Army of Tennessee. The older generals of the Confederacy were Robert E. Lee, Joseph E. Johnston, both fifty-four years old at the beginning of the Civil War, and Albert Sidney Johnston, fifty-eight. Civil War officers looked older than their years to our eyes because it was the fashion of the time to wear beards. A rich assortment of these, from the long red beard of A. P. Hill to the blond beards of Stuart and Hood, decorated the faces of the generals.

A distressing and significant episode in the inner history of the Confederate command was the clash of wills and exhibition of jealousies among the officers. Two excellent generals, Pierre G. T. Beauregard and Joseph E. Johnston, quarreled with President Davis and were not utilized to the full. At the outbreak of the war Johnston of Virginia, a West Point classmate of Lee, was the ranking officer in the United States Army (brigadier general of the quartermaster department) among those who resigned to join the Confederacy. Nevertheless, the President gave higher rank to three other officers: Samuel Cooper, a native of New Jersey, who was made adjutant general, Albert Sidney Johnston, and Robert E. Lee. The high-mettled brigadier never forgave this affront. But it is highly doubtful if the Confederate Army suffered so seriously from the quarrels, jealousies, and ambitions of officers as the Union Army. Among numerous examples may be cited: McClellan's hatred of Secretary of War Stanton, and his contempt and strong dislike of General Pope; McClernand's quarrel with Grant; Hooker's efforts to undermine Burnside, the refusal of Darius Couch, Hooker's senior corps commander, to serve any longer under him; and Rosecrans's quarrel with Halleck.[6]

War was a proving ground in which some officers grew in stature and were promoted to high command while others failed. President Davis's greatest service to the Confederacy was his selection of superior officers from the very beginning, while Lincoln lost much valuable time in experimenting with incapable commanders. Some generals, like Longstreet and Hood, were excellent division and corps commanders but failed when given independent command, partly because they lacked administrative ability or tact in dealing with subordinate officers. The best commanders maintained firm discipline between battles, kept their men physically fit, and had the human touch. Luck also played an important role in the successes and failures of Civil War generals.

Douglas Southall Freeman's study of the development of generals under Lee, entitled *Lee's Lieutenants,* points out how the frequent deaths, wounds, and human failures of higher officers necessitated constant change of command and reorganization of the army.[7] Northern military leadership improved as the war progressed while the original Southern superiority in personnel declined, for the tremendous attrition of Southern officers—especially the deaths of Jackson, Albert Sidney Johnston, Stuart, and Cleburne —was more serious than the corresponding attrition in the Union Army. The development of younger officers did not fill the gap.

The first Confederate generals to attain fame were Beauregard and Joseph E. Johnston. After the reduction of Fort Sumter and the victory of Bull Run, Beauregard was acclaimed a great hero in the South.[8] A Creole from Louisiana, this short, compact soldier with curved mustaches and "big sad bloodhound eyes" was a student of Napoleon's campaigns. With a high sense of the dramatic, he gesticulated vivaciously when he talked, and liked to issue heroic proclamations. His vanity was pronounced. Suddenly during the war his raven-black hair turned gray—a phenomenon which friends attributed to his great responsibilities as a commander, but cynics attributed to his inability to get French hair dye.

An able soldier despite his foibles, Beauregard had fought in the Mexican War and was Superintendent of West Point on the eve of the Civil War. Robert Kean compared him favorably with Lee, noting that Lee's letters to the War Department were brief and jejune while "Beauregard is the only general who keeps the Department advised fully of affairs in his department—of his plans and prospects." [9] Beauregard advocated taking the offensive, especially attacking Washington early in the war, but he was overruled by President Davis. Partly on account of his quarrels with Davis and partly because of bad health, he receded into the background after the battle of Shiloh; but toward the close of the war he emerged once more as a brilliant officer in the defense of Charleston and the skillful repulse of the efforts of Butler and Grant to seize Petersburg.[10]

Joseph E. Johnston also was a general of real ability, but his performance in the field was disappointing. He was intellectual with a sense of humor. When he became bald as a result of sickness he excited the mirth of his Negro butler by wearing his hat at the dinner table. Brave and thoroughly competent, he was overcautious like McClellan and secretive about his plans, even to the President.[11] Mrs. Chesnut tells a characteristic story about Johnston on a hunting expedition in South Carolina in his younger days. He had a reputation for being a very fine shot but brought back no birds, because the situation never was right for a good shot: either the birds were flying too low, or they were too high or too far away, and he was unwilling to risk a loss of reputation through missing his aim.[12] His career was characterized by skillful retreats. Yet he was liked by his soldiers, who had confidence in him and knew that he would not sacrifice their lives needlessly.[13]

One of the most attractive and highly revered Confederate generals was Albert Sidney Johnston, who was placed in charge of the Western Department. At the beginning of the war he was regarded, both in the North and in the South, as the ablest Con-

federate general. Born at Washington, Kentucky, in 1803 and educated at Transylvania University and West Point, he had served
as a general in the Texan army and as Secretary of War of the
Lone Star Republic. When the Civil War began, he resigned his
United States commission as brigadier general and commandant
of the San Francisco Presidio and offered his services to the Confederacy. Very handsome, over six feet in height, he had a knightly
personality and displayed a noble character in adversity.[14]

Robert E. Lee did not come to the forefront until a year after the
fighting had begun. At first he was employed in supervising the
defense of West Virginia, which failed. The wounding of Joseph E.
Johnston at Seven Pines brought him appointment to the command
of the Army of Northern Virginia. The son of "Light Horse Harry"
Lee, born in the great plantation house of "Stratford" in the Potomac valley, Lee represented the finest traditions of the Virginia
aristocracy.[15] At West Point he had been second in his class; and
he had fought with distinction in the Mexican War. Although only
a colonel in the United States Army at the beginning of the Civil
War, he received an informal offer of the top command. He refused
the glittering opportunity because he placed loyalty to his native
state above allegiance to the Union, despite the fact that he was
opposed both to slavery and to secession.

Finely balanced, with magnificent self-control, Lee commanded
his officers and men through their respect and admiration for him
rather than through fear. His tact enabled him to get along well
with the irritable, thin-skinned President and with other generals.
He was remarkably thoughtful and considerate of the feelings of
other persons, and when his plans failed he blamed only himself.
He has been criticized for a lack of "thunder";[16] but it is impossible to know whether he would have been a better general if he
had displayed more sternness to his subordinate officers instead of
the grave, gentlemanly courtesy and consideration which was habit-
ual with him. The morale of his army, surely a good test, was high;
his soldiers and officers had supreme confidence in him as he led
them to battle, and he himself thought them invincible until that
sad day at Gettysburg when Pickett's charge failed. With inferior
numbers and resources he performed miracles in defeating a suc-
cession of Northern generals. He made good use of his knowledge
of many of the opposing generals, as well as of his reading of

Northern newspapers. One of his outstanding virtues was the boldness with which he took great chances to win victory, such as dividing his army before superior forces.

Although a superb general, Lee was not faultless; and the debate is still open as to who excelled as commanding officer, Lee or Grant. Lee's principal faults were his tendency to give verbal and imprecise orders, his reluctance to interfere with his officers after battle was engaged, and particularly his neglect of his supply service, which was an important factor in the failure to follow up victories. Like Grant, he took little active interest in politics and failed to put strong pressure on the government to carry out his wishes. Indeed, it was the military tradition of the professional soldier to refrain from participation in politics. His most serious failing appears to have been too great a concern with the defense of his native state. Grant had a broader and perhaps sounder conception of grand strategy; but it must be remembered that, until the end of the war, Lee did not have a comparable responsibility for planning grand strategy.

When "Stonewall" Jackson lay on his deathbed, mortally wounded at Chancellorsville, Lee wrote that he had lost his right arm. Indeed, the death of this brilliant officer broke up an invincible team. Thomas Jonathan Jackson was unquestionably the greatest of Lee's generals, but he was an enigmatic compound of contradictions. Born in a poor and humble family of western Virginia, he had been educated for war at West Point and in the Mexican War. When secession came, he was professor of mathematics and natural philosophy at Virginia Military Institute, where he was regarded as an eccentric.

One of Jackson's great passions was religion, the essence of which he conceived to be duty, and he had a firm belief in the literal word of the Bible. While he was at V.M.I., he taught a Negro Sunday school; and he enjoyed the society of preachers discussing theology. A fanatical, humorless Presbyterian, he sought to enforce the Sabbath in his army, prayed constantly before battle, and lived an austere life. Although he loved the taste of liquor, he feared it far more than the bullets of the enemy. Riding an ungainly sorrel horse, this silent man had a habit of raising his right arm on the march. He relished sucking lemons, but never used pepper on his food because, he explained, it made his left leg weak. Above average in height, he had thin compressed lips, broad forehead, calm and unflinching but often weary blue eyes, and a dark, rusty beard. Indeed, his appearance was very unimpressive, for he was notoriously careless as to clothes, had huge feet, and was awkward in his movements.[17]

In ruthlessness, aggressive fighting ability, and dedication to a cause this eccentric soldier reminds one of Cromwell. Such a stern disciplinarian was he that he arrested officers on several occasions for small offenses; and he was not loved by some of them. Nevertheless, he had the quality of a great general to inspire his men with supreme confidence. A matchless subordinate, he knew how to obey orders and to cooperate successfully with Lee; but there is some question as to his qualifications for high independent command.

Jackson's nickname indicates a steadfast fighter; actually he was far from possessing the immobility of a stone wall. He realized the value of secrecy and swiftly marched his "foot cavalry" to the weak point of the foe, meanwhile spreading false rumors to deceive the enemy. His first Shenandoah Valley campaign was a masterpiece of celerity of action, of deception, and of superb maneuver. The criticism that he was not modern in his conceptions of war and fought very much in the technique of Hannibal and Caesar over-looks his salient characteristics as a military leader. His lightning method anticipated the German blitzkrieg of World War II, and he clearly realized that the true military objective was the total destruction of the enemy army and not the conquest or occupation of territory. His death after Chancellorsville was perhaps the weightiest blow that the Confederate cause had sustained, and it may well be true that with Jackson at Gettysburg the Confederates might have won that decisive battle.

Perhaps the ablest corps commander of the Confederate Army, after Jackson, was James Longstreet. Descended from a Dutch family, he grew up on a plantation near Gainesville, Georgia. Although he was adept in horsemanship and sports, he graduated third from the bottom of his class in academic studies. Longstreet was distinguished as a soldier by his practical common sense, his bravery and coolness in battle, his blunt and outspoken speech, and his steadfastness, which caused Lee to call him his "Warhorse." A matchless corps commander with one exception—his invincible con-

fidence in the superiority of his own judgment over that of his commander—he had intuitive ability in defensive fighting to perceive
the exact moment for the counterstroke. He longed to lead an independent army; but when he was given the chance during the
autumn of 1863 in the campaign in East Tennessee he failed, and
he was glad to return to Lee's army. He deserves great praise for his
insight into the need of using the interior lines of the Confederacy
and his recognition of the vital importance of the Western front.
In these respects his concept of the grand strategy of the war was
superior to that of Robert E. Lee.[18]

Commanding the Western army was General Braxton Bragg,
whose appointment was one of the most tragic blunders of the
Davis administration.[19] Born in North Carolina in 1817, he graduated from West Point and served with credit in the Mexican War
and on the Indian frontier; and at the outbreak of the Civil War
he was commissioner of swamp lands in Louisiana. Bragg was one
of the most intelligent and experienced of the Confederate generals.
He had less sickness in his winter camps than other generals because
he moved his camp every two weeks, and he was an excellent or-
ganizer and disciplinarian. John Buie, a soldier in his army during
the invasion of Kentucky, wrote home to North Carolina: "Bragg
is beyond doubt the best disciplinarian in the South. When he took
command at Corinth, the army was little better than a mob." [20]
The men were in the habit of firing their guns indiscriminately,
but Bragg had one man shot for discharging his gun and restored
excellent discipline. Moreover, his moral character was irreproach-
able, and he was devoted to the Confederacy.

However, Bragg's good qualities were nullified by serious personality defects. This general—with a roughhewn countenance,
bushy eyebrows, and grizzled black beard that resembled, in Robert
Kean's opinion, the face of a chimpanzee—had been regarded even
in the United States Army as exceedingly quarrelsome and can-
tankerous.[21] He was a hard taskmaster, a martinet, and lacked the
magnetism of personality required for leading individualistic Southern soldiers. When he lost battles he sought scapegoats. He suffered
from dyspepsia and chronic migraine, which made him harsh and
irritable and at times almost incapacitated him for vigorous warfare.
Given independent command, he displayed vacillation and a tendency to evade responsibility—among the worst faults in a general.

He seemed to dread precipitating a great battle, and, above all, he never followed up his victories. His officers and men, consequently, lacked confidence in him and became almost openly mutinous.

Yet Davis was fatally attracted by the taciturn West Pointer and kept him in command long after his unfitness was plain. Joseph E. Johnston also had a high regard for Bragg's military ability. In the papers of Senator Wigfall is a letter from Johnston, written in March, 1863, in which he says: "In regard to Bragg, I think you underrate him. We agreed as to his Kentucky operations. I think that he has commanded extremely well in middle Tennessee—that he has exhibited great energy and discretion in his operations in that district and has done the enemy more harm than anybody else has done with the same force in the same time. . . . At Murfrees-boro', he fought double numbers and the enemy's loss was equal to about 70 per cent of his force engaged. In the great European battles of modern times there was no destruction equal to it—in proportion to the destroying force."

The Confederacy was peculiarly fortunate in developing cavalry officers. In the Western armies Nathan Bedford Forrest, John Hunt Morgan, and Joseph Wheeler were outstanding. Forrest, a tall, strongly built man with iron-gray hair and a severe countenance, volunteered as a private at the age of forty in 1861. At that time he had accumulated entirely by his own efforts a fortune which he estimated at one and one-half million dollars, part of it by slave trading in Memphis. He recruited a company of cavalry and became so successful a leader that he ended his Civil War career as a lieutenant general. Twenty-nine horses were shot from under him, but he lived to become the Grand Wizard of the Ku Klux Klan.

Forrest's stature as a cavalry leader has grown with the passing of time. Although he entered the Confederate service with practically no military training he was a natural leader of men, and exercised splendid common sense in military strategy and tactics. This self-taught soldier has been credited with a superbly simple maxim of war: "Git thar fustest with the mostest." Actually his statement was "get there first with the most," which he probably pronounced, "Git thar fust." [22] Semi-illiterate, he spelled words as they sounded, including his favorite appellation for Yankees, "suns of biches." His violent temper drove him at times to insubordination; for example, when he called his commanding officer, General Bragg, "a damned scoundrel" and threatened his life, and when he declared that he would never serve again under Wheeler. Forrest had a more modern conception of logistics than most West Point officers. He demonstrated remarkable native ability in the art of war and seems to have been without a peer in his generation in the leadership of independent cavalry commands.

In command of the cavalry of the Army of Tennessee was "Fightin' Joe" Wheeler, Georgia-born but educated in Connecticut, a major general at the astonishing age of twenty-six. Five feet, five inches in height and weighing one hundred and twenty pounds, quiet, dignified almost to the point of pomposity, he had boundless energy and courage and was described as a game bantam who "warn't afraid of nuthin' or nobody." [23] Except in deportment, Wheeler ranked almost at the bottom of his class at West Point; yet he wrote a valuable book on cavalry tactics and was a pioneer in the Confederate Army in the use of mounted riflemen, or light cavalry, who proved to be much more suited to Southern conditions than heavy cavalry. A splendid subordinate who obeyed orders, he was efficient in doing picket duty, getting information about the enemy's movements, and, particularly, covering retreats. He did not have the masterful personality and natural military genius of Forrest, who served under him. Bragg made the mistake of putting Wheeler in command of independent expeditions instead of Forrest, who was better fitted for them.

Far more spectacular than Wheeler was General John H. Morgan, a former hemp manufacturer at Lexington, Kentucky. Morgan loved to perform spectacular raiding exploits, such as his Christmas Raid of 1862–1863 into his home state, when he destroyed sixty miles of the Louisville & Nashville Railroad, the supply line of the Federal army in Tennessee, and captured nineteen hundred prisoners, numerous horses, and military stores. On his expeditions he had an expert telegraph operator who often "cut in" on Federal wires and intercepted messages that were of great value to the Confederates. Despite his usefulness as a raider, he never learned teamwork. His most sensational exploit was a raid into southern Indiana and Ohio in the summer of 1863. On his own hook, he crossed the Ohio River with twenty-five hundred men into the Copperhead country, hoping to free Southern prisoners and arm them to fight their way back to the Confederate lines. But the bold adventure resulted in the loss of most of his command and his own capture near New Lisbon, Ohio. He was placed in a Northern prison from which he escaped, according to romantic accounts, by tunneling; according to more cynical versions, it was by bribery and the use of his Masonic connections.[24]

The most celebrated Confederate cavalry leader on the Eastern front was James Ewell Brown Stuart, Lee's chief of cavalry. "Jeb" Stuart, a Virginian, liked the glitter of attractive uniforms and the pageantry of war. "Beauty" was his nickname at West Point because of his receding chin, which was later covered with a luxuriant brown beard. Mrs. Chesnut's diary, November 30, 1863, comments that some women wrote to Lee "to complain of Stuart, whose horse the girls bedecked with garlands, and said he was in the habit of kissing girls. They thought General Stuart should be forbidden to kiss one unless he could kiss all." [25] This cavalier who delighted in dancing and singing and in the music of Sweeny, his banjo player, also was deeply religious and had a noble character. Jeb Stuart's cavalry were the eyes of Lee's army, providing him with intelligence of the enemy. His greatest weakness was a propensity to daring raids.[26] After he was killed in 1864, his command was assigned to Lieutenant General Wade Hampton, a South Carolina planter and owner of thousands of slaves. Hampton had not had any formal military training before the war, but he developed into a very able cavalry officer.[27]

The organization of the Confederate Army followed the pattern of the United States Army. The Army of Northern Virginia after Antietam, for example, consisted of two corps, each commanded by a lieutenant general—Longstreet's corps numbering 38,100 men and the Second Corps under Jackson numbering 37,049. At Gettysburg Lee's army was organized into three corps. Each corps was made up of four or five divisions commanded by major generals. There was great variation in the size of Confederate divisions. The Valley army of Major General Thomas Jonathan Jackson, for example, consisted of 23,750 men, divided as follows: Jackson's own division, commanded by Winder, 3,000 men; Ewell's division, 7,550 men; A. P. Hill's "Light Division," 12,000 men, and 1,200 cavalry. Gracie's division at Petersburg in 1864 had been so reduced that it numbered only 1,200 men. The divisions were composed of four or more brigades, each under a brigadier general. The brigade commanded by General Richard Taylor contained four Louisiana regiments which averaged eight hundred men to the regiment; but many of the Confederate regiments were considerably below this strength.

As the war progressed the various organizations of the Confederate Army were greatly depleted by desertions, wounds, death, and disease. Some officers received furloughs or orders to recruit their shattered organizations, but many continued to preserve their organizations with a full complement of officers although they contained only a remnant of their former strength. After the disastrous battle of Missionary Ridge, Bragg wrote to President Davis urging that the army be drastically reorganized by "consolidating present skeleton regiments" and by abolishing "the present loose mass of commissioned officers with squads of men called regiments." [28]

In order to coordinate movements and to develop strategic plans the general of an army had a staff consisting of adjutants, chief engineer, quartermaster, commissary, ordnance officers, and various aides-de-camp. The staffs of Confederate generals were amazingly small and inexperienced in comparison with those of Northern generals. Most of Lee's staff were below the rank of colonel while the staffs of Grant and other Northern generals included major generals and brigadier generals. Consequently, Lee was often exhausted by work that experienced staff officers could have performed, and the Confederate generals lacked an organization of experts to aid them in planning battles and operating the army.

The agent in the Confederate War Department for communicating with generals in the field, for promulgating regulations and orders, and for keeping records was Samuel Cooper, as Adjutant and Inspector General. Cooper is described by Robert Kean as an old gentleman "uniformly courteous and uniformly noncommittal" and ignorant of the military legislation of the Confederacy to a marvelous degree. He failed to keep proper returns or to compel field officers to make proper returns. As a consequence, he knew little of the state of the army in the East and kept almost no account of military affairs beyond the Mississippi. According to Kean, Davis retained this incompetent in office because of "West Pointism and his desire to have accommodating, civil spoken persons of small capacity about him." [29]

At the beginning of the war no officers in the Confederate army had led even a brigade in battle or in maneuvers. The West Pointers had received instruction chiefly in engineering and had little knowledge of strategy or of planning battles. Some of the officers tried to make up for their deficiencies by reading Napoleon's *Maxims,* Jomini's treatise, and Napier's *History of the Peninsular War.* Robert Kean wrote in his diary during the siege of Vicksburg: "Seddon telegraphs Johnston to attempt relief of Vicksburg with the force he has—an error—Napoleon in Napoleon's Maxims decides that the general should not obey against his judgment. I took the book to show Seddon." [30] As to tactics, the chief textbook used by both Confederate and Union officers was Hardee's *Rifle and Light Infantry Tactics.* The author, William J. Hardee, a native of Georgia, had been commissioned by Secretary of War Jefferson Davis to draw up this manual of tactics, which followed the model of the French army. It was officially adopted by the United States Army in 1855 and later received a Confederate patent. Hardee himself became one of the ablest of the Confederate generals.[31]

A significant failure of both armies was the lack of proper intelligence services and of liaison between commanding officers and their subordinates. Both sides obtained much of their information about the movements of troops from the newspapers and deserters. McClellan relied upon civilian detectives—especially Allan Pinkerton—who misled him. The Confederacy had some spies who obtained valuable information, notably the famous female spies, Belle Boyd and Mrs. Rose O'Neal Greenhow, and "Harrison," Longstreet's spy.[32] Nancy Hart, a mountain woman of western Virginia, served not only as a spy but also as a guide for Jackson's cavalry. When she was captured in July, 1862, she seized her guard's musket, shot him dead, and escaped. Closely identified with the spies were the scouts, including Jeb Stuart's great scout Vespasian Chancellor; but they wore Confederate uniforms, which protected them from being executed when caught. The Confederates also tried to follow the example of the Union Army in the Peninsular Campaign by constructing an observation balloon, made from gay-colored silk dresses given by patriotic women; but it was captured by the Federals when the ship towing it down the James River ran aground. The main reliance of the armies for information concerning enemy movements continued to be the cavalry.

A relatively unnoticed branch of the Confederate Army was the Signal Corps, which also gave vital information to officers concerning the movements of the enemy. An effective signal system had been devised by an army surgeon, Albert J. Myer, while he was stationed on the plains of Texas. His system, known as the "wigwag," consisted of communication by the waving of flags to indicate dot and dashes of the Bain telegraphic alphabet. The army adopted Myer's signal system in 1860, and one of the army officers, youthful E. P. Alexander of Georgia, assisted him in perfecting it. When Alexander joined the Confederate Army he introduced the Myer signal code. In the first battle of Manassas he established signal stations and a signal line which gave warning to the Confederates of McDowell's turning column.[33] The Signal Corps established lookout stations on high hills or built towers from which the signalmen read the messages from the next station through powerful field glasses. At night they would signal with torches or colored rockets. Captain Alexander soon left the Signal Corps to become perhaps the greatest officer of artillery in the Confederate Army, and Colonel William Norris, a native of Baltimore, took his place as Chief Signal Officer. At first the Signal Corps was regarded as an easy berth for an unmilitary type of individual. Actually it was one of the most dangerous services in the army, and the mortality of the signalmen was much higher than that of the infantry or cavalry.[34]

One of the functions of signal officers was to accompany commanding officers in the field and send messages to distant units directing their movements in battle. Another task was to decode the enemy's signals and ciphers and to devise an undecipherable code for their own communications. The Confederate signal code used between the station on the Hawk's Nest, Lookout Mountain, and the station on Missionary Ridge in 1863 was deciphered by Union experts who thus gave the Federal officers the advantage of reading General Bragg's orders. In turn, the Confederates decoded the signals between Grant and Admiral Porter before Vicksburg, so that Pemberton was able to secure better terms of surrender. The Lanier brothers, Sidney and Clifford, were signal officers, and their letters describe the hardships, the night-guard duty, the riding for hours on horseback and delivering messages, and the constant occupation of flag waving. Near the close of the war they served on blockade runners to communicate with the shore. So essential was this service that in 1864 numerous blockade runners lay idle in Bermuda and Nassau until signal officers could be sent to them.

The field telegraph proved to be of immense value to both armies in transmitting messages and orders. Operated by electric battery wagons which accompanied the army, the telegraph lines were strung up quickly between key points. The operators in both armies were civilians. The Confederacy had great difficulty in securing "telegraphists" because the private telegraph companies paid much better salaries than the government.[35] The telegraph proved to be invaluable in operating military trains, transmitting orders of the War Department, integrating the movements of armies in the field and warning them of danger.

Throughout the war Confederate officers suffered from an amazing lack of good maps and of topographical information concerning their own territory. Lee was seriously hampered in the defense of Richmond during the Peninsula campaign by inability to secure reliable and informative maps of the region showing roads. As late as January 3, 1863, General Jeremy F. Gilmer, Chief of the Confederate Engineering Bureau, replied to an officer's request for a map of Virginia that he had no good map but would try to find one. At the same time he confessed that he did not have an adequate railroad map.[26]

Yet the providing of maps and topographical information was a direct responsibility of the Engineering Corps. In General Orders No. 90 of the Adjutant and Inspector General's Office, June 26, 1863, the duties of engineers serving with armies in the field were described as follows: (1) to make reconnaissances and surveys of the section of the country occupied by Confederate forces and as far as possible of the country held by the enemy, furnishing information of roads, bridges, fords, topographical and military features, watercourses, location of woods, etc.; (2) to select sites and make plans for military works; (3) to build forts, rifle pits, batteries, trenches, saps, mines, works of obstruction in rivers and harbors; and (4) to prepare maps for commanding generals. The necessary labor was to be provided by details of troops commanded not by engineers but by the regular officers of the troops.[37] The engineers cleared the way for advancing troops, repairing bridges and building pontoons for them to cross rivers.

The papers of General Gilmer in the Southern Collection of the

University of North Carolina throw much light on the achievements of the army engineers. In 1861 Gilmer, a West Point graduate, was stationed in San Francisco with the United States Army. A brother of John A. Gunther of North Carolina, to whom Lincoln tentatively offered a post in his cabinet, he was a conservative who deeply regretted the secession of his native state and anticipated only disaster as the outcome of the secession movement. Nevertheless, when North Carolina seceded, he resigned his commission, came East, and was appointed major of engineers in the Western army under Johnston. He was later appointed chief of the Engineer Bureau in Richmond and promoted to the rank of major general. As chief of army engineers, he supervised the construction of the defenses of Charleston and Mobile and the remarkable series of trenches for the defense of Atlanta. In addition to Gilmer, the Confederacy had in Beauregard and Lee officers of engineering ability. Lee's engineering training aided him greatly in selecting strong positions for his army, in which art he was a master.

The broad military policy which President Davis and his advisors adopted was to fight a defensive war. The wisdom of their defensive strategy will always be a subject of debate, but it seems to have been basically sound. Because the South was far weaker than the North in men and in material, it was wisdom to adopt the defensive both in grand strategy and to a lesser degree in tactics. Major General Fuller of the British Army has observed that "the supreme tactical fact of the war was that the rifle had rendered the defense the stronger form of war;[38] the rifle, ax, and spade had made defense three times as strong as offense. There were also powerful psychological advantages in fighting in one's own country against an invading force. Only on occasions during the conflict did the South abandon the strategy of defense and attempt large-scale invasions of the North: Lee's campaign in Maryland, Bragg's advance into Kentucky, the fateful Gettysburg campaign, and Early's march in 1864 to the suburbs of Washington.

The advocates of a bold policy of advance argued that the best chance of the youthful nation to win its independence was to secure a series of quick victories before the vastly superior economic resources and reserves of man power of the North could be mobilized. Major General Sir Frederick Maurice has held that the sound policy for the Confederacy was to invade the North, not straight from the field of Bull Run, but shortly afterward, for "at no period of the war was the North so vulnerable"—by a bold advance before it recovered, the Confederacy might have won some border states which were wavering.[39] Some of the wartime proponents of attack were impulsive, like ex-Governor Henry A. Wise and Robert Toombs, who relied on the supposed superiority of the Southern soldier over the Northern and the fire of the Southern spirit; but in the first year of the war the policy of attack had advocates also among Confederate officers, notably Stonewall Jackson. On September 13, 1861, seven weeks after the spectacular victory of Bull Run, President Davis met three of his major generals, Pierre G. T. Beauregard, Joseph E. Johnston, and Gustavus W. Smith at Centreville in northern Virginia to plan the military policy of the army on the northern front. The generals advocated attack on Washington; but Davis rejected a bold advance because he was unwilling to withdraw troops defending other parts of the South.

However one may evaluate the defensive policy of the South with its four notable lapses, it seems to be fairly clear today that the Confederate authorities made a serious mistake in dispersing their troops. The armies were scattered to protect a far-flung frontier with inadequate forces instead of being concentrated, with power enough to deliver crushing blows. The chief reasons for such scattering of energies were psychological and political, a yielding to the insistence of the various states that they be defended from invasion.

The grand strategy of the North for conquering the rebellious section was twofold: (1) capture of the main transportation arteries to the interior of the South; (2) destruction of Confederate armies, the primary military objective, conquest of territory being incidental. Union generals and naval officers, therefore, seized the Tennessee and Cumberland rivers, and gained control of the Mississippi by the capture of New Orleans, Vicksburg, and Port Hudson. The essential railroad lines were either captured or wrecked, and key railroad cities such as Corinth, Mississippi, Chattanooga, and Atlanta fell into the hands of the Union armies. The most powerful Confederate army, led by Lee, was in front of Richmond, and demolition of this army became the great objective of Lincoln and Grant. A secondary aim of Lincoln was to drive the Confederates out of East Tennessee because he was solicitous for its loyal Union inhabitants, and because a vital railroad line connecting Richmond and Atlanta ran through it. Some recent writers have maintained that Lincoln was a greater military strategist than any of his generals, primarily because of his tenacious insistence that the true objective of the Union armies should be the destruction of the Confederate armies, his realization of the significance of the conquering of the Mississippi valley, and his creation of a modern, unified command system.[40] But Lincoln also made serious errors, such as withdrawing McClellan from the James River in 1863, attempting prematurely to force Thomas into action at Nashville, opposing Sherman's march to the sea, and choosing incompetent generals to command the army in Virginia—making seven changes in command of the eastern army in two years.

The Confederacy was divided into three natural military sectors: an eastern one; a middle sector between the Appalachian Mountain barrier and the Mississippi River; and the region beyond the Mississippi. In the eastern sector the main effort was devoted to the protection of Richmond, an important industrial, munitions, and railroad center. Here the brilliant genius of Lee was successful until Confederate resources sank low. But the disastrous defeats in the western sector, in which incompetent leadership played a large role, probably lost the war for the South. Strangely, in comparison with the Eastern campaigns, the progress of battle in this arena has never received adequate attention from historians. The best generals of the North, Grant, Sherman, and Thomas, were early employed across the mountains, undoubtedly by accident rather than design. They won victories over the second- and third-rate Confederate commanders in this region, such as Floyd, Crittenden, Price, Pemberton, Bragg, and Hood. At the beginning of the conflict Jefferson Davis sent Albert Sidney Johnston, regarded as the ablest officer of the Confederacy, to command the Western army; but he was killed in the battle of Shiloh, April 6, 1862. Although Beauregard and Joseph E. Johnston, both able generals, also served briefly in the Western theater, the burden of Western defense was carried by Pemberton, Bragg, and Hood, particularly by Bragg. Indeed, this extremely important sector of the Confederacy beyond the Appalachian Mountains was neglected by the Davis government. While the brilliant generalship of Lee and Jackson produced a stalemate in the East, the Union armies in the West cut off one slice of the Confederacy after another, gradually reducing the area from which food and men could be drawn to bolster Lee.

The preeminent advocate in Davis's cabinet of the importance of the West in military strategy was George W. Randolph, Secretary of War from March 24 to November 15, 1862. Randolph, a grandson of Thomas Jefferson, loved society and a life of ease, and yet was scholarly and had a taste for military affairs. According to Jones the war clerk he received no votes when he ran for the Confederate Congress; but he became a brigadier general.[41] During the first few months of his tenure as Secretary of War he appeared, in his subordination to the President, to occupy the position of a mere clerk. But suddenly in the fall of 1862 he asserted himself and developed an intelligent plan for cooperation of the Western armies. On October 20 he wrote to General Theophilus Holmes, in command of the Trans-Mississippi Department with headquarters at Little Rock, Arkansas, that he had sent 25,000 arms, and that he hoped Holmes would begin offensive operations by marching on Helena and then would converge with the armies of Bragg and Pemberton to recover Tennessee and the Mississippi valley. On October 27 another letter to Holmes pointed out that his cooperation with Pemberton at Vicksburg was of the first importance and authorized him to cross the Mississippi with his forces if necessary and to take charge of combined operations on the eastern bank.[42] He sent a copy of this letter to President Davis, who was so jealous of his prerogative.

Davis countermanded Randolph's instructions and sent him a sharp note stating that the movement of armies, the stationing of officers, and the appointment of officers were functions that belonged to the President. He also observed that it was very improper for the Secretary to authorize Holmes to cross the river, for it was essential that each department commander keep in his own department. Randolph wrote asking if the President's note was to be taken literally. When Davis made only the slightest change in his original position he resigned peremptorily. To his brother Thomas Jefferson, he explained that he had resigned because of the President's unwillingness to allow the Secretary of War any discretion.[43] He declared that he would not be merely a head clerk.[44]

Although Randolph was virtually dismissed, a half-hearted attempt was made to carry out his idea of integrating the Western armies. General Joseph E. Johnston proposed to the War Department a somewhat similar plan and in late November, 1862, he was ordered to Chattanooga to take command of all the Confederate troops between the Appalachian Mountains and the Mississippi, consisting principally of Bragg's army of approximately 40,000 men in Murfreesboro, Tennessee, and Pemberton's force of approximately 30,000 men holding Vicksburg. Command over Holmes's trans-Mississippi army was not given to him, and he accomplished practically nothing in this temporary experiment of unity of command in a large region. One reason for his failure was the fact that the enemy controlled the direct rail line between Bragg's force and Pemberton's command. Johnston called his command "a nominal one," arguing that he could not do any good except by superseding either Bragg or Pemberton. He pointed out that both were too weak and too far apart to aid each other, and it would require a month to transfer 10,000 men from one army to the other.[45]

At Richmond the brilliant Robert G. H. Kean, whom Randolph had appointed chief of the Bureau of War, continued to advocate Randolph's military strategy. This young Virginian was a sound and realistic critic of Southern strategy, a proponent of greater integration and concentration of Southern forces, particularly the cooperation of the trans-Mississippi forces with those east of the river. In his remarkable diary he wrote, July 12, 1863: "The Radical vice of Mr. Davis's whole military system is the separate departmental organization, each reporting only to him. It makes each Department depend only on its *own* strength and deprives them of mutual support and combination which might else be obtained. It appears from a recent report of R. Taylor that Vicksburg might have been relieved from that side [across the river]; that the whole situation was treated with a levity incomprehensible when the vast stake is considered." [46] And he went on to tell how Randolph's resignation had resulted from the insistence of the President upon respecting rigid departmental organization.

The superior military organization of the North had great weight in the defeat of the South. All along the line, except in the Ordnance Department which was headed by a Northerner, there was a lack of strong and efficient organization in the military effort of the Confederacy. Shortly after the debacle at Chickamauga, Grant was placed in direct charge of all the Western armies, except

Nathaniel P. Banks's force in Louisiana. Having proved his ability, he was called from his notable victories in the West and made commander in chief of all the armies of the Union on March 9, 1864. Together with Sherman he put in motion the final grand strategy of the Union, a pincer or crusher operation. Sherman proceeded to capture the industrial and railroad center of Atlanta, then marched to the seacoast and turned northward to join Grant, who was holding Lee's army in a vise at Petersburg, the key to Richmond.

By this time Southern strength had oozed away. Although the Confederacy could claim that the immense superiority of the North in economic resources and in man power made the contest an unequal one, it did not use its own limited military resources to the best advantage. It failed until too late to set up an adequate command system such as the North organized in the spring of 1864.[47] Lee was not appointed commander in chief of all the Confederate armies until February 6, 1865, two months before the surrender at Appomattox. Thus the Confederacy did not properly coordinate its forces or use its advantage of interior lines to concentrate troops against the thrust of the enemy. The various units of the Confederate Army did not work as a team.

VII

The Logistics of the Gray Army

To THE genius of a Northerner, General Josiah Gorgas, Chief of Ordnance of the Confederate Army, the Confederacy owed much of its ability to maintain the gray-clad army in the field against the superior might of the North. This quiet, masterful, and devoted man was born in 1818 at Running Pumps, Pennsylvania, the son of a poor clockmaker and farmer. After graduating from West Point sixth in his class of fifty-two, Gorgas was an officer in various arsenals and served in the Mexican War. While he was stationed at Mount Vernon Arsenal, near Mobile, Alabama, he fell in love with and married Amelia Gayle, the daughter of a governor of Alabama.

On April 2, 1861, he resigned as commander of the Frankford Arsenal in Philadelphia to accept the commission of major of artillery in the Confederate Army assigned to duty as Chief of Ordnance. This surprising decision by a Northerner was motivated in part by Gorgas's detestation of abolitionists and the Republican party, in part by his strong sympathy for the Southern people, and in part by the fact that the Federal Chief of Ordnance disliked him and, out of vengeance, assigned him at the critical time to a disagreeable post.[1] For four years Gorgas worked with tremendous energy and zeal for the Confederate cause. When that cause was lost he became vice chancellor of the University of the South at Sewanee and later president of the University of Alabama. His son William Crawford Gorgas had a distinguished career as an army doctor, a hero in the fight to control yellow fever and sleeping sickness.

Josiah Gorgas developed the most successful bureau of the Confederate government. "Shrinking and modest and hardly known to the general public," he did not become a brigadier general until November 19, 1864.[2] An excellent administrator, he demonstrated strength of character, resourcefulness, and sagacity in overcoming obstacles. He obtained remarkable results partly by his wise selection of subordinate officers, to whom he gave ample authority and responsibility. Also he had a "gift of prescience" which enabled him to anticipate the movements of the Confederate armies and provide in advance for supplying them with munitions.

When Gorgas took charge of the Ordnance Bureau, he made a survey of the pathetically small supplies of guns and munitions within the Confederacy. On May 7, 1861, he reported to F. S. Bartow, chairman of the Congressional Committee on Military Affairs, that there were 159,010 small arms of all kinds in the United States arsenals seized by the several states. On the day after Virginia seceded a volunteer expedition organized by the impulsive ex-Governor Henry A. Wise captured the Federal arsenal and armory at Harpers Ferry. Although the Federal employees set fire to the buildings before escaping, some of the machinery for making rifles and muskets was saved as well as five thousand Minié muskets. Gorgas had much difficulty in persuading Virginia to hand over the machinery to the Confederate government. Another capture early in the war, the Norfolk navy yard, brought in more than five hundred cannon ranging from field howitzers to huge columbiads. Scatered along the Southern coasts in forts defending the harbors were more than four hundred cannon, mostly antiquated.

The number of rifles and smoothbore muskets in private hands and owned by the states is unknown. Only a few of the Southern states, like Virginia, with aggressive governors had secured a full quota of Federal arms before they seceded; and the Southern-born United States Secretary of War John B. Floyd was falsely accused, after he resigned, of sending huge quantities of arms into the Southern states.

In the first two years of the war the Confederacy was forced to rely upon running through the blockade munitions purchased in Europe. Indeed, only 10 per cent of the small arms distributed to the troops during those years was made in the Confederacy. Gorgas dispatched Major Caleb Huse, an able Northerner who had been teaching at the University of Alabama, to Europe as agent to purchase war materials for the Ordnance Bureau. Arriving in May,

1861, Huse found that the European market for munitions and guns had been largely "swept," or preempted, by Northern agents and by governments alarmed over the threat of a European war. Moreover, he was seriously handicapped by the lack of negotiable funds.[3] Nevertheless, he was able to send his first shipment of foreign arms on the *Fingal,* September 28, 1861. As late as February, 1862, only fifteen thousand small arms had reached the Confederacy despite strenuous exertion by its agents. After the lag described the shipments increased so that between January 1, 1862, and July 1, 1863, 185,000 small arms passed through the blockade. All told, the blockade runners brought into the Confederacy 330,000 stand of arms for the Ordnance Bureau and at least 270,000 for states and private persons.

In order to transport the ordnance which Huse bought, Gorgas purchased four blockade runners for the exclusive use of his bureau. His journal, August 2, 1863, describes their indispensable role:

> Our freight steamers continue to run to Bermuda from Wilmington. This is our chief source of supply for arms; and we get our steel, tin, zinc and various other articles in this way. We also import leather, tools, hardware, medicines, saltpetre, lead, etc., etc., in large quantities. We own four belonging to my Bureau, and there are others running in which the War Department is largely interested. Thus far none of our vessels have been captured, tho' we have now made some fifty trips out and back.[4]

In addition to bringing guns, mostly Enfield rifles, through the blockade, Gorgas established a number of armories throughout the South to manufacture rifles, revolvers, and munitions. At first he tried to centralize and standardize the manufacture of ordnance; but as the war progressed the weakness of the transportation system forced him to pursue a policy of decentralization. Gorgas found the manufacture of weapons and ammunition in the non-industrial South tremendously difficult. There was scarcely any skilled labor or suitable machinery. Moreover, the War Department often foolishly conscripted skilled workmen, and during times of alarm for the safety of Richmond his workmen were called from their jobs temporarily to serve in the home guard. During the Dahlgren raid on Richmond, March 3, 1864, an expert barrel straightener in the battalion of workers called from the armory and carbine factory was killed, and the result was a drop in production by the Richmond armory of at least 360 rifles per month.

Despite such handicaps Gorgas continued to expand the domestic manufacture of ordnance and munitions at a remarkable rate. On April 8, 1864, exactly three years after he had assumed charge of the Ordnance Bureau, he wrote in his diary that he had succeeded beyond his utmost expectations. From being the worst supplied of the bureaus of the War Department, he observed, the Ordnance Bureau had become the best. Large arsenals had been organized at Richmond, Fayetteville, Augusta, Charleston, Columbus, Macon, Atlanta, and Selma, and smaller ones at Danville, Lynchburg, and Montgomery. A superb powder mill had been built at Augusta, the credit of which was due to Colonel G. W. Rains. Lead smelting works had been established at Petersburg and turned over to the Nitre and Mining Bureau, which had been separated from the Ordnance Bureau. A cannon foundry had been established at Macon for heavy guns, and bronze foundries at Macon, Columbus, and Augusta, as well as a foundry for shot and shell at Salisbury and a large shop for leather work at Clarksville, Virginia. Besides the armories at Richmond and Fayetteville, a manufactory of carbines had been established in Richmond, a rifle factory at Asheville (transferred later to Columbia), a new and very large armory, including a pistol factory, at Macon and a second pistol factory at Columbus. "All of these," he commented, "have required incessant toil and attention, but have borne such fruit as relieves the country from fear of want in these respects. Where three years ago we were not making a gun, a pistol nor a sabre, no shot nor shell (except at the Tredegar Works)—a pound of powder—we now make all these in quantities to meet the demands of our large armies." [5] Because of Gorgas's efficiency, the Confederate armies were at times better armed than their opponents. Grant found after the surrender of Vicksburg that the defenders had sixty thousand muskets, obtained from Europe, much superior to the Federal arms, which were of many different calibers.[6]

Gorgas assigned the production of chemicals for munitions to an extremely able subordinate, Colonel John W. Mallet—a former British subject, educated as a chemist at Trinity College, Dublin, and at Göttingen. Locating his central laboratory at Macon, he made chemicals for munitions, devised substitutes, invented the polyhedral shell, which would explode in an equal number of fragments, and drew up rules of safety for the arsenals and armories.[7]

The most spectacular success of the Ordnance Bureau was in manufacturing powder. When the Civil War started, the Confederacy had only one powder factory, on the Cumberland River near Nashville. It was capable of producing five hundred pounds of powder a day provided it could procure sufficient saltpeter (niter), but it had no saltpeter. Fortunately Governor Brown of Georgia had ordered 850 tons from Philadelphia shortly before the port of Savannah was closed by the blockade. This bonanza supplied an essential for making the powder used by Albert Sidney Johnston's army. Gorgas accelerated the production of powder for the army by selecting an able North Carolinian, Colonel George Washington Rains, to supervise the manufacture.[8] Rains built a modern factory at Augusta which began operation on April 10, 1862, producing a superior type of gunpowder at one-third of the cost of powder brought through the blockade. When the Confederate powder mills stopped operation in April, 1865, they had manufactured an amount slightly larger than that imported through the blockade (2,700,000 pounds).

The supply of saltpeter, one of the essential ingredients of gunpowder (the others being sulphur and charcoal), remained precarious throughout the war. Colonel Rains secured this chemical from the limestone caves in East Tennessee, North Carolina, and northern Alabama, started niter beds, and published a pamphlet entitled *Notes on Making Saltpetre from the Earth of the Caves*. On April 11, 1862, the Confederate Congress authorized the creation of a Nitre and Mining Bureau, which was placed under the direction of Isaac M. St. John. He organized the work in the niter-bearing area of the country into districts and continued the practice of forming niter beds in which human urine was an active agent. This use of the contents of toilet chambers gave rise to some humorous and vulgar doggerel. In these ways the Nitre Bureau within the course of a year was producing half of the amount required by the Confederacy, the other half being imported through the blockade. Sulphur was obtained principally from roasting iron pyrites in small establishments operating under government contracts.

As a result of the success of the Confederate powder-making industry the gray-clad army seldom lacked sufficient powder and probably never lost a battle on account of the lack of it. Several months after Gettysburg, Gorgas wrote in his journal: "We are now in a condition to carry on the war for an indefinite period. There is breadstuff enough, and tho' the inadequacy of transportation makes prices high in some parts, there is abundance for all if the total be considered. And we have war material sufficient—men, guns, powder—the real pinch is the Treasury." [9]

The real pinch in the Ordnance Department was to come after 1863, particularly in procuring lead, copper, and mercury. The percussion caps which fired the powder in the rifles and muskets of the infantry contained fulminate of mercury. The mercury supply came from Mexico, and the Federal blockade of the Mississippi River after the fall of Vicksburg on July 4, 1863, stopped this. Mines at Wytheville in southwestern Virginia were the only large source of lead in the Confederacy, yielding 60,000 pounds per month; but snow often disrupted transportation in winter, and production was hampered by the foolish policy of army commanders who refused details of skilled miners. Gorgas said after the war that the Ordnance Bureau had to depend on window weights and unused water mains for one-third of the amount of lead consumed. Battlefields were gleaned for this indispensable material, while a major supply came from Europe through the blockade.

Mines in the extreme southeastern part of Tennessee at Ducktown furnished 90 per cent of the copper mined in the Confederacy. But the Confederacy lost control of them after Bragg was defeated at Chattanooga in November, 1863. Then the Ordnance Bureau had to depend on a trickle of shipments through the blockade and the salvaging of copper from turpentine and apple brandy stills in North Carolina and sugar-boiling kettles in Louisiana. So scarce was copper in the latter part of the war that the Confederate armories had to quit making the bronze Napoleon cannon, the favorite gun of the field artillery.

The supply of iron available to the Confederacy was never large enough to meet the needs of ordnance and also to keep the transportation system in proper repair, and a campaign to relieve the shortage by collecting scrap iron as in World War II had no great effect. With the exception of parts of Virginia, the most important producing section of the South, Maryland, Virginia, Kentucky, and Tennessee, fell into Union hands early in the war. In 1860 Tennessee, with seventeen furnaces which smelted 22,302 tons annually, was the largest producer of pig iron in the South, and Virginia led the Southern states in the manufacture of bar, sheet, and railroad iron.[10]

As the Federal Army sliced off the iron producing area of most of the upper South, it became necessary for the Confederacy to depend on the ore of the lower South, particularly of northern Georgia and Alabama. In 1860 there was only one rolling mill in Alabama: the Shelby Iron Works, founded by Horace Ware, a New Englander. During the war this company operated a charcoal blast furnace of eight tons daily capacity, a foundry and a rolling mill. After 1862 it worked mainly for the Confederate government, providing among other things the tough armor plate of the powerful Confederate ram *Tennessee*.[11] A cotton planter, Colonel Caswell C. Huckabee, started in 1861 one of the most important iron companies in the Confederacy, the Brierfield Furnace in Bibb County, Alabama. It produced such high-grade metal that the government insisted on buying the furnace in order to use its iron for naval guns. The war stimulated the pioneer development of the iron resources of the Birmingham district. At the outbreak of the war, Francis Gilmer, who had recently begun building the South & North Alabama Railroad into this iron-bearing area, secured a contract from the Confederate government granting aid to the Red Mountain Iron & Coal Company for constructing furnaces and rolling mills at Oxmoor; and, according to a list compiled by Ethel Armes, there were sixteen furnaces and six rolling mills in operation during the war period as contrasted with the existence of four furnaces and two rolling mills in 1860.[12] Practically all of these industries were destroyed by Federal armies, particularly in the devastating raid in April, 1865, of General James H. Wilson.

The mainstay of the Confederacy in producing cannon was the Tredegar Iron Works at Richmond. Until 1863, when the government acquired an iron foundry at Selma, Alabama, no other foundry could cast heavy artillery. At the beginning of the conflict Tredegar was one of the largest foundries in the United States, employing nine hundred men and doing an annual business of approximately a million dollars. During the war it expanded its force to twenty-five hundred men. Joseph R. Anderson, the president of the company, a graduate of West Point and an ardent secessionist, entered the army as a brigadier general on September 3, 1861, but was forced to resign in July, 1862, and return to the management of the company, for its policy of buying the needed pig iron had failed. Now, he wrote, "everything must stop unless we go into the mountains & purchase and operate Blast furnaces to make pig iron." [13] He proceeded to stimulate the revival of the charcoal iron furnaces of the Great Valley, which had discontinued operations during the 1850's because of sharp competition from pig iron made with the cheap anthracite coal of Pennsylvania.

Anderson's energetic management brought remarkable results. As the war progressed and supplies became scarce in Virginia he sent agents into the deep South to procure food for his men, and established a tannery to furnish leather for shoes for his employees. The flight of some of his Northern and foreign mechanics to avoid conscription and the drafting of skilled mechanics during the early years of the war seriously handicapped production. None the less, during the four years of the struggle this company made nearly eleven hundred cannon for the Confederacy. Also it manufactured the iron plate of the famous *Virginia* (the old *Merrimac*) as well as machinery for powder mills and shells and projectiles for cannon. One of the important reasons why the Confederate government was reluctant to evacuate Richmond was the realization that the abandonment of the Tredegar Works would be a crippling loss.[14]

Next to the Tredegar Works the greatest iron manufacturing center of the Confederacy was at Selma, Alabama. In 1861 Colin McRae secured a government contract and erected a foundry for casting cannon at this place. Two years later, when he was sent to Europe to coordinate Confederate purchasing, he sold his iron interests to the government. The government then developed a huge ordnance center at Selma including an arsenal and a naval foundry which was placed under the charge of Catesby ap R. Jones, the commander of the *Virginia* after the wounding of Flag Officer Buchanan. At the peak of its production the Selma plant employed three thousand workmen. Besides casting heavy cannon, it made the machinery and hull of the *Tennessee* as well as gunboats for the navy. On April 3, 1865, the Wilson raid wrecked this great ordnance center of the lower South.

The supply of ordnance was far better managed than the provision of clothing and shoes and food for the Confederate Army. The quartermaster general was Abraham C. Myers, a native of South Carolina descended from Moses Cohen, the first rabbi of Charleston, and a graduate of West Point. He was experienced in the United States Quartermaster Department, having served as chief quartermaster in the Mexican War and as quartermaster in charge of United States government stores at New Orleans in 1861. As Confederate quartermaster general he administered his department by red-tape rules and regulations, being unable to rise above the routine methods of the old army or to control his subordinates. In the non-industrial South he had a tremendous task to equip the Confederate armies with clothing and shoes. At first he obtained supplies in the open market, making contracts for the delivery of cloth, shoes, leather, tents, wagons, etc. He also had the task of buying horses, mules, and wagons, and general supervision over railroad transportation for the army. He negotiated contracts with the railroads as to rates, but was opposed to drastic government regulation.

Myers never had the money to purchase adequate supplies for the army. When he requested authorization to trade cotton for blankets at Memphis, which was in Federal hands, President Davis refused it. The Quartermaster Department came into conflict with the Ordnance Department over the hides of cattle slaughtered for food for the army. The Ordnance Department had the responsibility of providing leather harness for the artillery and leather cartridge boxes for the infantry, while the Quartermaster Department had to furnish shoes for marching soldiers and harness for 60,000 transportation animals. So the two departments fought over dwindling supplies of hides and leather. The Quartermaster General was the butt of constant criticism. Robert Kean wrote in his diary, October 25, 1863: "Our troops in Lee's army are barefooted—failure to provide shoes and blankets during all this year conclusive of mismanagement of Q.M.D. Ordnance Department is conducted with greatly more energy and so has got control of foreign transportation." President Davis disliked Myers—Kean noted the rumor that Mrs. Myers, a daughter of General David Twiggs, had "called Mrs. Davis a *squaw*, Mrs. Davis being of a very dark complexion." [15] On August 7, 1863, Davis dismissed him and appointed Brigadier General Alexander R. Lawton of Georgia in his place.

Lawton infused new vigor into the department but he faced even greater difficulties than Myers in meeting the needs of the army. The quartermasters had the invidious job of impressing manufactured goods and other articles needed by the army. Furthermore, as Lawton pointed out, the soldiers were notoriously careless and extravagant in throwing away clothing that encumbered them and often sold or bartered their surplus clothing. However, he reported on January 27, 1865, that, contrary to the impression in the country that the army had been poorly supplied, "with the exception of great coats and flannel underwear the army has been fully provided." [16] In substantiation of his contention he listed large amounts of clothing issued in the latter half of 1864, such as 104,199 jackets, 140,578 pants and 167,862 pairs of shoes for Lee's army and 45,421 jackets, 102,864 pants, and 102,558 pairs of shoes for the Army of Tennessee.

Confederate logistics and the fighting ability of the army undoubtedly suffered from the low esteem accorded to the quartermaster and commissary officers. General Bragg put the case strongly for a higher status for these officers in a recommendation to the President on November 16, 1863, urging that the best talent in the country should be secured for the posts of chief quartermaster and commissary by offering increased rank and compensation to them. "In the present condition of our country," he wrote, "the chiefs of these departments are second only in importance to the commander-in-chief, and yet they are *allowed* only by sufferance, not recognized by law, and with the paltry rank and pay of majors." [17] Near the end of the war Congress in desperation for combat troops passed a law to force all quartermasters and commissaries at posts and depots under the age of forty-five into active service in the army. President Davis vetoed this law on March 11, 1865, on the ground that it would seriously impair the war effort. He pointed out that the number of quartermasters on post duty was only 223, including officers in charge of manufacture of clothing, shoes, wagons, ambulances, harness, etc., and only 96 collecting taxes in kind, while the total number of post commissaries east of the Mississippi was only 96. Thus the drastic policy demanded by Congress would have added only two hundred men to the ranks.[18]

Feeding the Confederate armies was in the hands of the commissary general, Lucius B. Northrop, a West Pointer, who had served in the subsistence department of the United States Army but in 1861 was practicing medicine in South Carolina. President Davis described him as a man of "strong practical sense and incorruptible integrity." [19] The job of impressing food supplies in the poorly organized and individualistic Confederacy unavoidably brought friction and criticism, but Northrop's personality aggravated his difficulties and caused him to be heartily disliked throughout the Confederacy. He was a personal friend of Davis, and part of the hostility probably arose because he was one of the President's "pets." His plan of placing a commissary agent personally responsible to him in each state aroused opposition among the army officers and the people. Lee did not like Northrop and thought him inefficient. Early in 1865 in response to a request of Congress Davis removed him and appointed Isaac St. John in his place.

As early as the late autumn of 1862 the problem of feeding the army had become very grave. Lieutenant Colonel Frank G. Ruffin of the Bureau of Subsistence in Richmond explained to the Secretary of War on November 8 the great difficulties of collecting food. Contracts for large amounts of bacon and beef had been made in Tennessee, one of the great hog and cattle regions of the South, but with the falling back of the Confederate army, the warm weather, and the poor quality of salt available nothing like the expected deliveries of bacon had actually been received. Efforts to buy hogs in North Carolina were frustrated to a large extent by the unwillingness of many farmers to sell, in expectation of higher prices from the daily depreciation of the currency, and by the activity of speculators. Much meat spoiled also as a result of the slowness of transportation.[20] Northrop wrote on August 21, 1861, that the account books of the Commissary Department were on the road one month in the transfer from Montgomery to Richmond and that meats sent from Nashville to Richmond spoiled in closed cars after a delay of ten to twenty days. He declared, "There are not hogs in the Confederacy sufficient for the army and the larger force of the plantation negroes." [21]

So precarious did the situation appear to the Commissary Department on October 18, 1862, that Lieutenant Colonel Ruffin wrote: "With the whole Confederacy completely exhausted of supplies, we have only meat rations for 300,000 men for twenty-five days. As we feed by rough estimate not less than that number, including prisoners, and we cannot expect to commence on the new hog crop before the 1st Jany., the condition of the commissariat is well described by Major French as 'alarming!' " [22] In the spring of 1862 the food allowance for each soldier was reduced from the standard United States Army ration of three-fourths of a pound of salt pork or bacon, or one and one-fourth pounds of fresh or salt beef, and eighteen ounces of bread, as well as adequate amounts of peas, salt, vinegar, sugar, coffee, rice.[23] The result of this enforced economy, wrote Robert Kean on December 15, was that the "Health of the army is doubly better ever since the ration was reduced." [24]

As supplies declined after 1863 the Commissary Department relied more and more on importing meat through the blockade. Meat was bulky, and the blockade runners were averse to using cargo space for it. Ruffin noted that between August 19 and September 10, 1864, only five out of seventeen vessels brought anything for the Subsistence Department to Confederate ports.[25] Although it was terrifically expensive to bring food through the blockade at £60 a ton, plus commissions and insurance, the agricultural South imported considerable food supplies through the blockade. The cargo manifests of blockade runners from Bermuda show that importing bacon, pork, dried beef, flour, peas, sugar, and onions had become very prevalent in 1864.[26] Furthermore, despite the fact that the South was an important corn-producing section, large quantities of whisky and brandy were brought through the blockade.

In the fall of 1864 the Commissary Department was profoundly gloomy over the prospects of supplying the army with food. The daily ration for the soldier then was one-third of a pound of meat and a pound of bread. Ruffin reported that even with this reduced ration there was only nine days' supply for 100,000 men in the main supply depot at Richmond. Northrop revealed to the Secretary of War at the close of 1864 the reluctance of the farmers to sell food to the army because they could get better prices from speculators. The Confederacy had been "successful beyond expectation," however, in obtaining supplies of food by trading with enemy-held territory, exchanging a pound of cotton for a pound of bacon. Always the commissary was hampered by lack of currency with which to buy supplies.

It has long been held that the Confederacy had abundant food surpluses, but that because of the inefficiency of the railroads the army and the devastated regions came close to starvation. This view is only partly true. In the same letter of December 20, 1864, to the Secretary of War Northrop wrote: "The idea that there is *plenty for all* in the country is absurd. The efforts of the enemy have been too successful . . . people have killed whole flocks of sheep, breeding stock of cattle and young cattle." [27] Despite the abundance in some areas, the Commissary Department was tremendously handicapped by the inadequacy of the railroads. Large amounts of food awaiting shipment at railroad depots spoiled for want of transportation and of protection from the weather.

Popular opposition to the Impressment Act of March, 1863, which should have aided the Commissary Department in securing supplies for the army, prevented enforcement. When Lee protested against the scanty supplies of food for his army, Northrop wrote on December 13, 1864, that the opposition to impressment in the two Carolinas was "insurmountable," and that he lacked sterling to buy food abroad or wagons and draught animals to cart away corn and flour that were available in East Tennessee.[28] Major S. B. French, commissary officer at Richmond, wrote on September 15, 1864, that the Richmond depot lacked fifteen days subsistence of meat for Lee's army, and that the collection of meat from *all sources* during the past thirty days would not subsist the Army of Northern Virginia for one week. In all the states, he reported, impressment had been evaded "by every means which ingenuity can suggest." [29] When Lee telegraphed early in January, 1865, that his army had but two days' rations, Northrop recommended that he use his great influence to appeal to the people to sell or give food to the army.[30] One of the greatest troubles of the Commissary Department at this time was the lack of cash (the people refused to accept bonds) to pay for supplies impressed. As a result of all these difficulties the armies in the last two years of the war lived from hand to mouth, scarcely ever having more than a few days' supply of food available.

The food supplies of the Confederacy were very unevenly distributed. The armies in the trans-Mississippi district fared better than the Eastern armies. Virginia, which was the main battlefield, suffered more from insufficient food than any other large region of the South. The armies of Lee and Jackson frequently lived on a Spartan diet. In the last campaign in Virginia, from Petersburg to

Appomattox, Lee's men suffered from lack of food because of a misunderstanding which resulted in failure to send food to Amelia Court House along the route of the army, although adequate supplies were at Richmond and Danville. When Sherman marched through Georgia, on the other hand, his men lived off the country in prodigal style; and Grant found plenty of food in Mississippi during his Vicksburg campaign. In the early part of 1865 Commissary Northrop reported that two and a half million rations of meat and seven hundred thousand rations of bread had been forwarded to Richmond. Yet the failure in distribution and the inefficiency of the Commissary Department often prevented the armies in the field from being fed properly. Lack of good food, in turn, played an important part in desertion and in the spread of disease.

The Confederate Army could not have remained in the field long if the Union Navy had succeeded early in the war in enforcing a blockade of the Southern ports. The Ordnance, Commissary, and Quartermaster departments depended on access to the European markets. On April 19, 1861, President Lincoln proclaimed a blockade of the Southern coasts and thus began what has been termed "the anaconda policy" of slowly strangling the economic life of the South.

Sealing the Confederate ports to communication with Europe was difficult. When the blockade began the Union Navy consisted of only sixty-nine vessels in commission or available, and they were scattered throughout the world. All had wooden hulls, half of them were sailing vessels, and only twenty-six steamers were in commission.[31] Furthermore, the navy personnel was weakened by the loss of three hundred and twenty-one Southern officers who had resigned (three hundred and fifty officers of Southern origin elected to remain). Very few common sailors joined the Confederacy. Approximately thirty-five hundred miles of coast had to be patrolled, and the numerous sand bars, inlets, and sea islands made evasion of the blockade easy.

The attempts to evade the blockade provide some of the most thrilling chapters in the history of the Civil War. More than six hundred ships were engaged at various times in blockade running, but relatively few Southerners participated. Indeed, it was almost monopolized by Englishmen and Scotsmen, who had the capital and the ships for such hazards.[32] These British firms would dispatch goods in regular cargo ships to Bermuda, Nassau, and the Caribbean islands. At first Nassau led as a blockade-running station; but the ravages of yellow fever in summer and the close guard of Federal cruisers caused a shift to Bermuda, only six hundred miles from Wilmington. The most important port of entry was Wilmington, from which railroads ran to Richmond and Atlanta. Goods destined for the Confederacy would be transferred at Nassau or Bermuda to specially constructed blockade runners—swift, low-built ships, equipped with both sails and steam-driven propellers, that could navigate easily the shallow water of the sand banks. Painted gray and burning anthracite coal (Cardiff coal from Wales) which was relatively smokeless, they would slip into Southern ports on moonless nights or during stormy weather.

Most famous of the commanders was Lieutenant John Wilkinson of Virginia, who, after resigning from the United States Navy, commanded the Confederate-owned *Robert E. Lee*. This was one of the largest ships engaged in blockade-running, 902 tons, whereas most of the runners had a displacement of 250 tons or less; and it was capable of carrying six hundred and fifty bales of cotton. Wilkinson was a fine navigator and a master of deception. When Federal cruisers detected a blockade runner attempting to enter a port, they would send up colored rockets to indicate the location of the fugitive vessel. Wilkinson adopted the device of confusing the cruisers by sending up colored rockets similar to those of his pursuers but indicating a course at right angles to his true course. He took the *Robert E. Lee* through the blockade twenty-one times between December, 1862, and October, 1863.[33]

The British blockade runners, who were in the business solely for profit, found that luxury goods paid larger dividends than the iron rails which were desperately needed by the Confederacy. Consequently, they shipped to the Southern ports such luxuries as champagne, coffee, laces, perfumes, cosmetics, women's apparel. When Captain Hobart Pasha of the *Venus* asked a Southern woman in England what was most needed in the Confederacy, she unhesitatingly replied "corsets." So greatly were corsets in demand that his shipment of this feminine vanity netted him a profit of 100 per cent.[34] Southern ladies made heroic sacrifices for the cause of the Confederacy—they even contributed their silk skirts to make an observation balloon for the army; but they would have corsets. The blockade runners would return from the Confederate ports laden with cotton that sold for fifty to eighty cents a pound in Europe, five times its prewar value. During the war the blockade runners carried from the Confederacy approximately 1,250,000 bales of cotton.

Crenshaw Brothers of Richmond was one of the few Southern firms which had a large interest in blockade running. W. G. Crenshaw went to England in January, 1863, and contracted for six steamers to be owned in partnership with the Confederate government. The Crenshaws imported meat for the Commissary Department; but they had ill luck with their ships used for this purpose, two being lost when they tried to come into Wilmington because the government had removed the Whitworth guns that kept the blockading fleet at a distance. Lewis D. Crenshaw declared that there were so many risks in blockade running that "no one with common sense will engage in it unless with the chance of large profits if successful.[35] He observed in 1864 that of 1,000 bales of cotton shipped by the government only 396 were landed at Bermuda, and that one of the most skillful officers of the navy made five attempts to enter Wilmington and returned to "the Islands" twice before successfully entering the port.

One of the most important breaks in the blockade was through the neutral Mexican port of Matamoros near the Texas border.[36] The Confederacy had a brilliant diplomat at Monterrey, Juan A. Quinterro, who made deals with the Mexican governor of Nuevo León which were highly profitable to the governor and at the same time furnished vast supplies of lead, copper, and powder to the Confederacy. Matamoros became a thriving port of entry for goods destined for the Southern armies. Thousands of wagoners transported them into Texas, so that this state became better equipped for war than the eastern sector of the Confederacy. The United States Navy tried to stop this virtual evasion of the blockade by seizing neutral vessels bound for the Mexican port, but considerations of expediency forced it to abandon the attempt. The *Peterhoff*, engaged in this trade, was seized in 1863 and condemned in New York City, but the Supreme Court reversed this decision after the war.[37]

The Confederates failed to take full advantage of their opportunities of using the port of Matamoros. A conflict developed between the Texas Military Board which bought cotton to exchange for supplies at the Mexican port and the Confederate Cotton Bureau established by General Kirby Smith, the agents of the two bureaus competing for the cotton crop. The striking fact about this trade is that neither the Confederates nor the state authorities could get enough cotton from the planters to pay for the goods for which they had contracted.[38] The same situation also prevailed on the eastern seaboard. Caleb Huse wrote to James M. Mason, August 17, 1863, that it was so difficult to provide the government steamers with cargoes of cotton that the *Cornubia* had lately left Wilmington empty.[39]

The Confederate government failed until it was too late to organize blockade running effectively. In September, 1863, Colin J. McRae became czar of purchasing in Europe, in charge of all Confederate agents; and early in the following year Colonel Thomas L. Bayne was appointed director of shipping through the blockade. Not until February 6, 1864, did the Confederate Congress require that one-half of the cargo space of outgoing vessels should be reserved for the Confederacy. At the same time it prohibited importation of many articles of luxury, such as laces, furs, precious stones, antiques, carriages, and metal ornaments.

In contrast to the apathy of the Confederate government, the state of North Carolina under its aggressive governor "Zeb" Vance entered the blockade-running business with great success. Obtaining permission to supply its own troops with clothing and other necessary articles, it purchased an interest in three English runners, as well as the steamer *Ad-Vance,* which made eleven trips through the blockade carrying out approximately 5,000 bales of cotton and importing vast quantities of military supplies. Incidentally, Vance and some other prominent North Carolina politicians sent cotton out on the state ship for private speculation.

The papers of the captain of the *Ad-Vance,* which are preserved in the archives of North Carolina, reveal the activities of a successful blockade runner. According to Captain John Julius Guthrie's roll, this vessel had a crew of fifty-six officers and men. The crew was composed of 9 sailors from England, 4 from Scotland, 14 from Ireland, 2 each from Sweden and Portugal, 1 from Canada, 3 from the Northern states, 3 from France, and 18 from the Southern states.[40] The captain was paid exceedingly well—the regular salary of a captain in the Confederate Navy plus $1,000 in gold for each trip and the privilege of taking out four bales of cotton on his private account. A letter from a member of the crew to Captain Guthrie gives a vivid account of a trip of the *Ad-Vance,* commanded on this occasion by Captain Wyllie. The Confederate vessel went first to Nassau for coal and then to St. George, Bermuda, where it picked up a cargo of blankets, cotton cards, sugar, lead, and rope. Here five North Carolina members of the crew deserted. On the return trip forty miles from Wilmington, it was sighted by a Federal ship which gave pursuit; but it eluded the pursuer and came into the harbor at night without the slightest difficulty.[41] When the Confederate government passed the law requiring that half of the cargo space of blockade runners must be reserved for the Confederacy, Governor Vance and the private partners in the ownership of the *Ad-Vance* at first refused to send the ship out of Wilmington, causing delay at a critical time.

The effect of the Federal blockade of Southern ports has been variously estimated by historians. Some writers have represented it as one of the major causes for the defeat of the South, like a great anaconda crushing out the life of the South with its coils. On the other hand, one eminent authority has maintained that the blockade was not very important in bringing about the collapse of the Confederacy. Indeed, it was not effective in the early years of the war. Professor Frank L. Owsley estimates that the naval patrol was able to capture only one out of ten blockade runners in 1861, one out of eight in 1862, one out of four in 1863, and one out of two in 1865, making a grand average during the war of one out of six.[42] Of course this estimate of the ineffectiveness of the blockade does not take into account how many ships were deterred from even attempting to run through it.

Southerners maintained that Lincoln's blockade was a paper blockade and therefore was illegal. Secretary of State Benjamin declared that the North had only one ship to enforce the blockade for every three hundred miles of Southern coast, and that the port of Charleston in 1863 had a foreign trade of $21,000,000 while in 1858 her foreign trade had been less than $19,000,000. He also pointed out that steamers operated by the Confederate Ordnance Bureau had made 44 voyages through the blockade in the first nine months of 1863. There were, indeed, more than eight thousand violations of the blockade. The *Siren* eluded the naval patrol 64 times; the *Kate,* 44 times; and the *Robert E. Lee,* 30 times. The *Banshee No. 7* made a profit of 700 per cent before it was captured on its ninth trip through the blockade. So lucrative was blockade running that two successful trips of a vessel would compensate the owners for its capture on a third trip.

The effectiveness of the blockade, however, cannot be judged by the number of runners that reached Southern ports safely. These ships were of small tonnage. The large cargo vessels were effectively stopped, and even commerce raiders like the *Alabama* did not dare to enter Southern ports.[43] Furthermore, the tremendous rise in the price of cotton in Europe—30 pence, or 60 cents, a pound in Liverpool for cotton that had sold for 13 cents in 1860—was an indication of the effectiveness of the blockade. Even if it was not effective during the early part of the war, it prevented the shipment of iron rails and other heavy cargoes. The enormous growth of the Union Navy from 90 to 671 ships by the close of 1864 was a formidable threat. In truth, the blockade made it very difficult for the Confederate government to obtain vital military supplies and prevented it from making free use of Southern money crops in Europe.

During the Civil War railroads and telegraphs for the first time played a prominent role in strategy and in logistics. The Confederacy had an advantage over the invading army in the opportunity to use interior lines of defense, particularly railroads. In January, 1861, the Southern states had an estimated railroad mileage of 8,783 in the national total of 31,168. Virginia led the Southern states with more than 1,800 miles of tracks, Georgia came second with 1,400, and Louisiana and Florida had 328 and 327 miles respectively. Unfortunately much of the Southern trackage had been constructed to bring cotton to the seaports and therefore was roundabout for transporting troops and supplies to the main battle fronts. Furthermore, the Confederate government failed to maintain the strong control of the railroads which was required for taking full advantage of interior lines.[44]

Because the defense of Richmond and the invasion of the North through Virginia absorbed an enormous part of the military effort the Virginia railroads were of primary importance in Confederate strategy. In 1861 there were no direct rail connections between Washington and Richmond, for a railroad bridge had not yet been built across the Potomac River. The capital of the Confederacy was linked to the lower South by three railroads, one traversing the coastal plain to Wilmington and by a roundabout way to Charleston and thence to Savannah; a second running southwest to Lynchburg, Virginia, and through the mountains to Knoxville and Chattanooga; and a third penetrating the Piedmont to Atlanta except for a gap of forty-eight miles between Danville, Virginia, and Greensboro, North Carolina. The Confederate Congress appropriated $1,000,000 in February, 1862, to speed the building of this vital link, but the provincial hostility of North Carolina, whose planters were reluctant to hire their slaves for work on the project, combined with the difficulty of securing iron rails to prevent the closing of the gap until the summer of 1864. Moreover Governor Vance refused to allow the same gauge in North Carolina as in Virginia.

Among the railroads running east and west which rendered valuable military service to the Confederacy were several lines behind the battle fronts in Virginia. In the northern part of the state the Manassas Gap Railroad hooked up the Shenandoah Valley with the Orange & Alexandria Railroad, which ran southwestward from Alexandria on the Potomac to Charlottesville. South of this railroad was the Virginia Central, which ran from Richmond to Jackson's River near Clifton Forge, about two hundred miles. In the lower part of Virginia the Southside Railroad united Petersburg with Lynchburg, furnishing the Confederacy with a vital interior line for the defense of its capital and for the transportation of supplies, especially after the railroad to Wilmington had been cut by Federal forces.

The main east-and-west track of the Confederacy connected Charleston on the seacoast with Memphis on the Mississippi by way of Atlanta and Chattanooga, and one of the major objectives of the Union Army west of the Alleghenies was to disrupt it. The capture of Corinth, Mississippi, by General Henry W. Halleck in the spring of 1862 accomplished this purpose. Farther south a railroad connection existed between Savannah and Montgomery by way of Atlanta; between Montgomery and Selma there was water transportation by the Alabama River, and the laying of a track in 1862 between Selma and Meridian, Mississippi, completed the connection to Vicksburg. Very serious was the lack of railroads connecting

Texas and Arkansas with the Confederacy east of the Mississippi River, because Texas not only was a valuable food producer but gave access to the blockade-running port of Galveston and the Mexican port of Matamoros. Just before New Orleans fell in the spring of 1862, the Confederate Congress authorized a million and a half dollars in bonds to complete a line from New Orleans to Houston, but the capture of the Louisiana port stopped the work on the section from New Iberia to the Sabine River.

Railroads played a significant role not only in the concentration of troops on the northern battle fronts but in certain Confederate victories. The Manassas Gap Railroad in 1861 brought Johnston's troops to the battlefield of Bull Run and turned defeat into victory. The Virginia Central Railroad transported Jackson's troops from the Shenandoah Valley to defend Richmond during the Peninsular campaign. The largest single movement of Confederate troops by rail during the war took place in the summer of 1862 when Braxton Bragg moved at least 25,000 men by rail from Tupelo in northern Mississippi via Mobile to Chattanooga in order to head off Buell's army that was moving slowly eastward from Corinth, Mississippi. The first unit, 3,000 men, of Bragg's army arrived in Chattanooga, a distance of 776 miles, in six days. The most successful use of a railroad in shifting Confederate troops along interior lines occurred in the transportation of Longstreet's corps from Virginia to Chickamauga, which contributed greatly to the winning of that battle.

Among the lost opportunities resulting from lack of rail transportation was the inability of General Joseph Finegan to capitalize his victory at Olustee, Florida, in February, 1864. If there had been a rail connection between Georgia and Florida railroads, General Beauregard could have sent reenforcements to follow up the victory and drive the Federals from the state. Realization of this fact led the Confederate government in the spring of 1864 to begin construction of a link between the Florida railroads at Live Oak and the Georgia railroads at Lawton. In order to obtain rails for this project the government authorized the tearing up of part of the track of the Florida Railroad against the strenuous opposition of its president, David Levy Yulee, prominent secession leader and former United States Senator. When Yulee's economic interests were thus threatened, he obtained an injunction from a Florida judge to prevent this appropriation of his railroad's property. A serious conflict with state authority then arose, for the Confederate engineer officers refused to observe the injunction or submit to be arrested by the sheriff. It was fortunate that Governor Milton was an enlightened patriot and recognized the imperative necessity of suspending a fight for state rights until after the war. Accordingly, the Confederate government went ahead tearing up the rails, and on March 4, 1865, completed the connection between the Florida and Georgia railroads.[45]

VIII

Invasion of the South

AT THE outbreak of war the United States was in a condition of astonishing military weakness. According to a report of the adjutant general (April 5, 1861) there were only 17,113 officers and enlisted men in the army, of whom 3,894 were in the Department of the East.[1] General Winfield Scott, head of the Union armies, favored a period of training for his green and undisciplined troops before an invasion of the South. However, President Lincoln overruled him, yielding to popular clamor and the demands of Congress. The slogan of the North was "On to Richmond!" In addition to popular impatience an urgent reason for action was the fact that the terms of the ninety-day volunteers would soon expire.

Consequently, Brigadier General Irvin McDowell (recently promoted) was ordered to advance from Washington with approximately thirty-five thousand men and forty-nine guns to capture Richmond. Only eight hundred of the soldiers were regular army troops, the rest being raw volunteers and militia. In sultry July weather the Federal army set forth from Washington along the Warrenton pike, accompanied by newspaper reporters, Congressmen, sightseers, and ladies in crinoline skirts. Some of the motley crowd carried picnic baskets and rode in hacks and carriages. The atmosphere of the army and its civilian cortege was that of anticipation of a gay holiday or a fiesta.[2]

Twenty-five miles southwest of Washington, near Manassas, a Confederate army of twenty-three thousand men and twenty-seven guns under the command of Pierre G. T. Beauregard awaited the approaching enemy. The army was stationed north of the village, behind Bull Run, guarding the various fords and roads leading to Richmond. The Confederate position was well chosen, because it defended an important junction of the railroad from Alexandria (opposite Washington) to Gordonsville and Richmond with the Manassas Gap Railroad which ran west to the Shenandoah Valley. Besides the forces at Manassas the Confederacy had more than eight thousand men in the Shenandoah Valley under General Joseph E. Johnston opposing a Federal army of 12,000 men under General Robert Patterson, a veteran of the War of 1812. Johnston managed to slip away from Patterson, who was confused by orders of General Scott, and joined Beauregard with a large portion of his army on the eve of the battle.

The first clash took place on July 18 when Brigadier General James Longstreet guarding Blackburn's Ford sharply repulsed a feeling-out attack by a portion of McDowell's troops. The main body of the Federal army moved along the Warrenton Pike at a snail's pace on account of excessive caution and unnecessary cooking, and the delay gave the Confederate army time to concentrate its strength before the big battle.[3] Aiming to attack the left flank of the Confederates, McDowell turned off the Warrenton Pike to the right instead of following the road to the Stone Bridge over Bull Run. Beauregard, a classmate of McDowell at West Point, adopted an almost identical plan of battle, of attacking the enemy on the left flank. The Confederate left was saved from destruction only by the alertness of the Signal Corps under E. P. Alexander, who informed Major Nathan G. ("Shanks") Evans of the Federal turning movement by way of Sudley Springs Ford.[4] Evans was guarding the Stone Bridge on the Warrenton turnpike; but, surmising that the noisy demonstration in front of him was only a feint, he moved a large part of his force to meet McDowell's real attack from the Sudley Springs crossing, which was indicated by great columns of dust. General Johnston, also informed of the Federal flanking movement, dispatched reenforcements under Brigadier General Barnard E. Bee and Colonel Francis S. Bartow, and Wade Hampton's Legion of South Carolina aristocrats joined them. The Federal attack drove the Confederates back in confusion, killing Bee and Bartow; but Bee called on his men before he died to rally behind the Valley of Virginia troops commanded by Brigadier General Thomas J. Jackson who had taken position on the high point of the battlefield, the Henry House Hill. Bee's remark that Jackson's brigade was standing like a stone wall against the onward rush of the enemy gave forever to its commander the sobriquet of "Stonewall."

The battle swayed back and forth over Henry House Hill, where the residence of an eighty-five-year-old widow, Judith Henry, stood. At a crucial moment a Confederate regiment in blue uniforms captured two powerful enemy batteries because the Union commander mistook the advancing regiment for Union troops and withheld his fire. The fate of the battle was decided in favor of the Confederate army at 3:30 P.M., when twenty-three hundred fresh troops of Johnston commanded by Kirby-Smith arrived from the Shenandoah Valley by railroad and attacked the right flank of McDowell.[5]

This attack resulted in a rout of the hitherto victorious Federal army, which now retreated in a panic to Washington. The Warrenton turnpike was cluttered by a stream of frightened humanity, civilians who had come to see a great victory mingling with the beaten and terrified soldiers, many of whom threw away their guns, canteens, and knapsacks to speed their flight.[6] Nevertheless, Bull Run was not a very bloody battle, for fewer than five hundred men of the Union army were killed, while the Confederate dead were reported as three hundred and seventy-eight. Owing to a miscarriage of orders, nearly half of the Confederate army on the right flank was not engaged in the fight. General McDowell attributed his defeat to fighting a day too late, but "Stonewall" Jackson wrote to his wife, who was disappointed when the newspapers failed to play him up as a hero, attributing the victory first to God and then to the heroic stand of his brigade on Henry House Hill.[7]

The principal significance of the battle of Bull Run lay in its psychological effect on both the North and the South. It sobered the Northern people and made them realize that conquering the South would be difficult. The Confederates, on the other hand, were jubilant over the apparent proof of their illusion that the Southern soldier was the equal of seven Northern soldiers. The Confederate generals did not follow up the victory. In explanation, Joseph E. Johnston, primarily a defensive fighter, declared that the Confederate army was more demoralized and disorganized by victory than the Union army was by defeat, that the commissary had failed to provide food enough for a march on Washington, and that it was too hazardous for green troops to attempt to cross the Potomac and attack the fortifications of the Capital.[8] The Confederate pursuit was also paralyzed by the weakness of its cavalry and by a rumor of a Federal counterattack on the Confederate right. Although it is still a matter of controversy whether the Confederacy thus lost a golden opportunity by inactivity, it seems from the vantage point of today that the bold course of attempting to capture Washington should have been adopted.

After Bull Run there was a small victory at Ball's Bluff on the Potomac on October 21; otherwise the Confederate army in Virginia remained inactive through the remainder of the summer, fall, and winter of 1861–1862. Disease, homesickness, and inactivity caused low morale, and many soldiers desired to return home. Mrs. Chesnut noted on August 4 that Richmond seemed to feel that the war was over, except for Jefferson Davis and Robert Barnwell, Senator from South Carolina.[9] In the North, however, the people were chastened by the humiliating defeat; Congress authorized an increase of the regular army and strengthened the morale of the home front by passing the Johnson-Crittenden Resolutions. These resolutions, introduced by two loyal Southern members, Senator Andrew Johnson of Tennessee and Representative John J. Crittenden of Kentucky, defined the object of the war as not to interfere with slavery in the states but solely to preserve the Union.

The illusion of the martial superiority of Southerners over Northerners was strengthened by Confederate military successes in far-off Missouri. Missouri was a crucial state for the Confederacy since it outflanked Illinois and controlled the Mississippi River. In the southwestern part of the state General Sterling Price, affectionately called "Pop" or "Pap" by his men, had recruited an irregular, poorly armed body of troops numbering roughly five thousand. The commandant of the Union garrison at St. Louis, Brigadier General Nathaniel Lyon, brave, energetic, and filled with antislavery zeal, determined to rid Missouri of Southern sympathizers. Accordingly, he gathered up approximately six thousand men and advanced against the Confederate force. Among his troops was a body of German-speaking volunteers led by Franz Sigel, a German exile of 1848 who before the hostilities was director of public schools in St. Louis.

In this crisis Price appealed to General Ben McCulloch, formerly of the Texas Rangers but now commanding in northern Arkansas, to come to his support. On August 10 the opposing forces met at

Wilson Creek, near Springfield in southwestern Missouri. Lyon was killed in the battle, and his men were defeated. It was fought with bravery and ferocity and was far more sanguinary than the battle of Bull Run. A month afterwards, Price's troops, pushing bales of wet hemp ahead of them as breastworks, captured twenty-seven hundred Union troops under Colonel James A. Mulligan at Lexington, Missouri. But the Confederates failed to capitalize either of these victories.

On November 7 the Confederates defeated a Union attack on their camp at Belmont, Missouri, across the river from Columbus, Kentucky. The chief importance of this small engagement, involving only about three thousand men on each side, lies in the fact that it was Grant's first battle in the Civil War, and in the attitude toward war displayed by both sides.[10] After the battle the Confederate commander General Leonidas Polk, met Grant under a flag of truce to discuss "the principles on which I thought the war should be conducted; denounced all barbarity, vandalism, plundering, and all that, and got him to say that he would join in putting it down." [11] Indeed, much of the Civil War seems strange and romantic to moderns conditioned to the idea of total war.

The initial Confederate successes in the Missouri-Arkansas area were nullified within a year. General Earl Van Dorn, a dashing West Pointer who had been sent by the Confederate government to take charge of military operations in Missouri, developed ambitious plans of capturing St. Louis and invading Illinois. This dream, however, was destroyed on March 7 and 8, 1862, when a Federal army under General Samuel R. Curtis at Pea Ridge (or Elkhorn Tavern) in the northwest corner of Arkansas repulsed an attack by his army. Van Dorn, with 16,202 men (many of them armed only with shotguns or squirrel rifles) against Curtis's 12,000, had divided his army and attempted a wide flanking movement. A similar movement by Lyon at the battle of Wilson Creek had resulted in the defeat of the Union Army. Now the tables were turned. The two columns of the Confederate army were delayed in their schedule by obstructions in the road and were unable to communicate with each other. One of these uncoordinated forces, under Ben McCulloch, attacked the flank of the Federals but became demoralized when he was killed. The other, commanded by Van Dorn and Price, was victorious on the first day of battle but was defeated when the Federal army concentrated against it. The battle of Pea Ridge was the final disaster in the Confederate loss of Missouri.[12]

A brigade of Indians from the Five Civilized Nations under Chief Stand Watie and General Albert Pike formed a colorful part of the Confederate troops. They fought well behind trees and rocks, but they could not withstand artillery fire. Furthermore, there was such latent hostility between the various tribes and between the full-bloods and the half-bloods that Ben McCulloch advised Pike on September 27, 1861, to separate the Indian commands under Stand Watie and Colonel Drew "for fear of a collision" if they should come into contact with each other.[13] In general, the Confederate Indians played a very small part in the war, being unwilling to leave the Indian country. They were eager, however, to attack the Federal supply trains.

The first great military disaster to the Southern cause was the surrender of Fort Donelson in northwestern Tennessee, February 16, 1862. General Albert Sidney Johnston had been entrusted with defending a line four hundred miles long from the Allegheny Mountains to Columbus, Kentucky, on the Mississippi River. His headquarters was at Bowling Green in southern Kentucky, near the center of his long, thinly manned line of defense. His left flank at Columbus, "the Gibraltar of the Mississippi," was guarded by General Leonidas Polk, while his right flank was defended by George B. Crittenden of Kentucky and Felix Zollicoffer of Tennessee. Johnston was gravely handicapped by a shortage of military supplies and trained men. Many of his raw troops had only flintlock muskets, which became useless in rainy weather. Although he made earnest appeals for reenforcements to the governors of the various states as well as to Richmond the governors would not cooperate, for they thought primarily in terms of defending their own territories.

Johnston had received a tremendous ovation from the people of Tennessee when he took charge of the Western Department. They, as well as some of his officers, could not realize the internal weakness of the army which he was called to command. Johnston magnified the strength of his army to deceive the enemy but gave the true number of his forces to the War Department and the governors. Major Jeremy F. Gilmer, his chief of Engineers, advocated a bold advance to Louisville, but found Johnston to be unwilling to move until he felt confident of success.[14] The greatest weakness of the Western army proved to be its subordinate officers, who early suffered a series of humiliating defeats.

On January 19, 1862, Major General George B. Crittenden and Brigadier General Felix K. Zollicoffer, who had been assigned to defend Cumberland Gap and eastern Tennessee with the vital railroad that connected Richmond and Chattanooga, were defeated at Logan's Cross-Roads (or Mill Springs) near Somerset, Kentucky. Zollicoffer was brave, magnetic in personality, but pathetically wanting in military training, while Crittenden, the son of the famous Kentucky compromiser, was accused of drunkenness and subsequently reduced to the rank of colonel. The men in this command were miserably uncomfortable, lacking tents, adequate cooking utensils, and salt. Many of them were ill or had recently recovered from sickness. They were armed with muskets from the War of 1812 or with shotguns. Moreover, they lacked confidence in Zollicoffer. In numbers the Confederate and the Federal forces were evenly matched, each having about 4,000 men.

In violation of Johnston's plans Zollicoffer rashly advanced beyond the Cumberland River into Kentucky opposite Mill Springs. Ten miles north of his position, at Logan's Cross-Roads, was a Federal force under General George H. Thomas, a Virginian who had remained in the Union Army; and other Federal troops were advancing to strengthen him. To prevent this concentration General Crittenden ordered an attack on the main body of Thomas's force. The attack, early on a Sunday morning, was a complete surprise. During the battle Zollicoffer, wearing a white raincoat that made him stand out as a target, rode up to some enemy troops whom he had mistaken for Confederates and ordered them to cease firing. The Federals riddled him with bullets, and the news of his death caused part of his troops to retreat in a panic; a flank attack by the Federals completed the rout.[15] This defeat was the forerunner of more tragic disasters to the Western army.

The natural path for the invasion of Tennessee was along the Cumberland and Tennessee rivers. Ulysses S. Grant, at Cairo, Illinois, realized this fact and secured permission on January 30 from his superior, General Halleck, at St. Louis to undertake a joint land and naval expedition up these rivers. In the preceding September he had seized Paducah, Kentucky, controlling the mouth of the

Tennessee River, in a bloodless action. An able military historian has described the prompt decision to capture this strategic point as "one of the major decisions of the war." [16]

To guard the Tennessee and Cumberland river gateways, the Confederates had hastily constructed twin forts just below the Kentucky line at the points where the rivers approach within twelve miles of each other. Fort Henry on the east bank of the Tennessee was on low ground, so that some of its guns were subject to overflow by the river. It had eleven effective guns and a garrison of 2,734 men commanded by the Kentuckian, General Lloyd Tilghman. Fort Donelson on the southwest bank of the Cumberland near Dover, Tennessee, was on higher ground and was much stronger than Fort Henry, but was entirely too large for the size of the occupying force and could easily become a trap for its garrison.

In the morning of February 5 a flotilla of ironclad gunboats commanded by Flag Officer Andrew H. Foote appeared before Fort Henry. During the day McClernand's detachment of General Grant's army from Cairo landed below the fort and threatened investment. Before the rest of the army arrived, however, the rising water of the river and the attack of the gunboats put out of commission most of the guns of the fort and caused its surrender. Twenty-five hundred of the garrison succeeded in reaching Fort Donelson.

The defense of Fort Donelson was characterized by a series of blunders, made worse by the lack of unity of command and by the vacillation of the two ranking officers of the fort. The superior officer, John B. Floyd, was a civilian general who had served as Secretary of War in Buchanan's Cabinet and had already proved his incapacity in the campaign in western Virginia. Under him was the boastful Gideon J. Pillow, then regarded as Tennessee's ablest general. Ranking below these incompetents was Simon Bolivar Buckner of Kentucky, a West Point graduate of admirable character and an officer of ability.[17] Floyd, realizing that he had little military training, deferred to the greater experience of Pillow, a vain, dashing politician who had been something of a military hero ever since his career in the Mexican War as major general of volunteers.

It was unfortunate for the Confederacy that Pillow made the vital decisions in the Fort Donelson campaign. Besides lacking good judgment, he had a bitter grudge against Buckner, who had criticized him in a Tennessee newspaper for his boasting of his Mexican War exploits and for his ungenerous attacks on General Winfield Scott. Moreover, the generals did not arrive at the fort until shortly before the Union attack. Albert Sidney Johnston and his advisers at Bowling Green were doubtful of the ability of the Confederates to hold this fort against the combined Union army and flotilla of gunboats. Nevertheless, at the last moment Johnston ordered the concentration of 15,000 men there. When Floyd arrived on February 13, he decided to withdraw most of the forces in the fort; but Pillow persuaded him to revoke the order and to fight at Donelson.

As Grant's army was marching from the captured Fort Henry to Donelson, the Union gunboats descended the Tennessee and came up the Cumberland River. On February 14 they attacked the Confederate stronghold; but they were repulsed by the valiant Confederate gunners, who seriously wounded Flag Officer Foote. After this failure Grant invested the fort with an army of 15,000 men, which was later increased to at least 27,000. Early in the morning of February 15, while the Union commander was on a gunboat conferring with Foote, Pillow led a sortie to open a path for the beleaguered army to retire to Nashville. The Confederates were at first victorious against Grant's right wing commanded by McClernand, driving it back two miles and opening the road to Nashville.[18] Then Pillow gave an order, which is almost incomprehensible, for the victorious troops to return to their intrenchments. It may have been motivated by the bitterly cold weather and the exhaustion of the Confederate soldiers after seven and one-half hours of fighting. When Buckner, who had joined the attack, received the order to retire, he hunted up Floyd to persuade him to countermand the order. Floyd favored Buckner's policy of continuing to fight out of a trap but changed his mind after consulting the imperious Pillow and sanctioned the retrograde movement.

Meanwhile Grant had ordered General Charles F. Smith to attack the Confederate right, which had been weakened by the removal of a part of Buckner's troops in order to aid Pillow's advance. Smith penetrated the Confederate intrenchments and gained a commanding position. It was this victory in Buckner's absence that determined the Confederate surrender.[19]

At midnight of February 15 the generals debated whether to

give up the fort and garrison. Buckner advocated facing military realities and surrendering the fort, but both Pillow and Floyd declared that they would die before they would surrender. Major Jeremy F. Gilmer, who escaped from the fort, wrote to his wife on February 22 that "the generals decided that the sacrifice of human life in the attempt to cut through the superior forces would be too great, amounting in their opinion to at least one-half of the command," and consequently they decided to surrender.[20]

After this decision a disgraceful scene occurred among the commanding generals. Floyd was under unjust accusation of having sent, as President Buchanan's Secretary of War, large stocks of arms into the states that later seceded; and he had been involved in financial dishonesties in Washington and faced criminal prosecution if he were returned to the North. Fearing the consequences of capture, he turned the command of the garrison over to Pillow, who in turn "passed the buck" to Buckner, the strong advocate of surrender. Floyd and his brigade and Pillow then escaped by the river, while Nathan Bedford Forrest managed to lead his cavalry through the Union lines. General Simon Bolivar Buckner was a fitting representative of the aristocracy of the South, who unselfishly sacrificed his large property interests in Kentucky to fight for the Southern cause. On the morning of the surrender (February 16), after a rather typical Confederate breakfast of nothing but coffee and cornbread, he asked for terms of capitulation. Grant's answer was a demand for immediate and unconditional surrender, which the high-minded Buckner described as "ungenerous and unchivalric." U. S. Grant ever afterwards was called "Unconditional Surrender" Grant.

The capitulation of Fort Donelson was a severe blow to the people of the Confederacy, involving the surrender of approximately twelve thousand soldiers, twenty thousand precious stands of arms, and forty-eight pieces of artillery, and compelling withdrawal from Kentucky. While the battle at Donelson was still being fought, Johnston began the evacuation of Bowling Green. He had not come to the aid of the besieged fort, he later wrote, because he would have thereby uncovered the road to Nashville, permitting Buell at Louisville to march directly to the Tennessee capital.[20a] After the surrender of Donelson he ordered Polk to abandon his strong post at Columbus. Believing that Nashville was indefensible with his weak forces, he led his army through the city without attempting to save it or its enormous military stores.

After the debacle at Fort Donelson, Johnston was bitterly criticized by the Southern people. When a delegation arrived in Richmond demanding that he should be removed from command, President Davis replied, "If Sidney Johnston is not a general, I have none." [21] The unfortunate officer wrote a noble but pathetic letter to the President, assuming the responsibility for the disaster and refusing to blame his subordinates. He could well have defended himself by pointing to his inadequate resources and to the failure of civil and military authorities to give proper cooperation, but rather than reveal to the enemy the internal weakness of the Army of Tennessee, he chose to be silent. However, he made grave errors in scattering his forces and in not taking personal charge of the vital forts when they were threatened.

Johnston retrieved his reputation and won the veneration of the Southern people at the battle of Shiloh, April 6, 1862. After his army had passed through Nashville he succeeded in the difficult operation of uniting his force with the troops of Beauregard at Corinth in northeastern Mississippi. Braxton Bragg arrived from Pensacola to give further strength. Twenty-two miles to the northeast a strong Union force under Grant was at Pittsburg Landing on the southwestern bank of the Tennessee River. Johnston decided, despite the fact that his forty thousand men were ill trained and poorly equipped, to attack the enemy before Don Carlos Buell could arrive from Nashville with thirty-six thousand men to reenforce the Union army. Perhaps because of the storm of criticism which had assailed him after the surrender of Fort Donelson, he unselfishly offered the command to Beauregard. The Creole general refused the responsibility, but he drew up the faulty plan of attack which Johnston adopted; namely, of placing one corps behind another in three long thin lines of battle instead of advancing by columns.

In a proclamation to the soldiers Johnston described the Union army as "agrarian mercenaries sent to despoil you of your liberties, property, and honor." Appealing to his men to show themselves "worthy of the women of the South whose noble devotion in this war has never been exceeded in any time," he expressed the "trust that God is with us." [22] The Confederate advance was so delayed by rain and muddy roads that Beauregard believed all chance for a surprise had been lost and urged returning to their base; but the other corps commanders favored attack, and Johnston was so confident of victory that he said, "Tonight we will water our horses in the Tennessee River." The Confederate attack early Sunday morning April 6 on William Tecumseh Sherman's advance division proved to be a surprise, announced only by a reconnaissance force that encountered the Confederate vedettes and managed to give the alarm so that the Federals got into line of battle for the attack. Grant was at his headquarters at Savannah, Tennessee, nine miles away on the other side of the river, when the battle began. "Like an Alpine avalanche," wrote Beauregard, the gray army drove the Federal troops from their camp and occupied Sherman's headquarters at "the rude log chapel" of Shiloh.[23] Instead of following up the victory, however, many of the Confederate soldiers stopped to plunder the camp.

Johnston had been directing in person the operations on the right of his line, leaving to Beauregard the general direction of the battle and thus neglecting the role of the commander. At 2:30 o'clock in the afternoon he was hit by a Minié ball which cut an artery in his leg. The wound was not necessarily mortal, but he remained in the saddle until he bled to death. The Confederates drove the Federals, fighting bravely, nearly to the river; but, having used their reserve earlier in the day, they did not have the fresh strength to complete their victory. At six o'clock in the evening Beauregard, who was "greatly prostrated with sickness," halted the fighting. Owing to the complicated plan of battle and to the nature of the terrain, the Southern troops had become hopelessly entangled, until they were a confused mob. Moreover, Beauregard reported, his men were jaded by the previous day's march through mud and rain, and they had fought twelve hours without food. Even so, Beauregard's order stopping the battle when more than an hour of daylight remained has been severely criticized.[24] The arrival of Buell's troops late that afternoon and during the night enabled the Union armies the following day to turn the tide of battle.

General William J. Hardee, who commanded a corps at this battle, gave a lady friend an interesting account of the fighting. Curiously he did not mention the death of Johnston as a significant factor in the defeat. The Confederates, he wrote, rushed into battle with great spirit, driving the enemy before them until the gunboats on the river "opened on us a terrific fire, which tho' doing little injury, was perfectly appalling to our men." [25] When the order to fall back came it was carried out in great confusion, and divisions and brigades became separated. The Confederates renewed the fight next day; but the enemy had brought up fresh troops and Hardee's men did not fight with as much ardor as on the previous day. Although the Union lost more men at Shiloh than the Confederacy, the gray-clad army had poured out its blood on the battlefield, losing eleven thousand men, equivalent to over one-fourth its strength. It was a gallant but useless sacrifice.

After the battle the Confederate army withdrew to its base at Corinth, a strategic railroad center in northern Mississippi. Against this fortified position Major General Henry W. Halleck, who had taken command of Grant's army, a much superior force, advanced cautiously, taking a month to march twenty-one miles. Meanwhile Beauregard's army was daily losing strength through an appalling amount of sickness, and on May 30, 1862, he evacuated the town by a skillful ruse. Although the Federal army heard the rumbling of the railroad cars that carried the Confederate troops during the night to Tupelo, they were deceived into believing that Beauregard was receiving large reenforcements by the fact that the Confederates gave a rousing cheer whenever an empty train arrived. Here at Tupelo the fiery little Creole general became so ill that he asked to be relieved. In his place Jefferson Davis appointed Braxton Bragg, an old comrade of Mexican War days.

On the eastern front the Federal government was preparing for another campaign to capture Richmond. In November, 1861, General George B. McClellan, thirty-four years old, replaced the aged Winfield Scott as General in Chief of the United States armies.[26] Graduating second in his class from West Point, McClellan had served in the Mexican War and had been sent to Europe as military observer in the Crimean War. In 1857 he had resigned from the army to become chief of engineers for the Illinois Central Railroad; and he was president of the Ohio & Mississippi Railroad at the outbreak of the war.

McClellan's first military service in the Civil War was as director of operations to clear Confederate troops from western Virginia and protect the Baltimore & Ohio Railroad. Early in June, 1861, one of his subordinate officers surprised a Confederate force at

Philippi and pursued it so hotly that the retreat was called "the Philippi races." General Robert S. Garnett, a brave and able West Point graduate, was dispatched from Richmond to this wild mountainous section of Virginia to guard the western approaches and to recruit Confederate soldiers. He reported that the western Virginians were "thoroughly imbued with an ignorant and bigoted Union sentiment," and only twenty-three joined his command of 4,500 men.[27] McClellan, commanding 20,000 men, sent Rosecrans against Garnett's subordinate Colonel John Pegram at Rich Mountain. Rosecrans defeated Pegram, and Garnett was killed as he was retreating, the first loss to the Confederates of a promising general. The youthful McClellan capitalized on such glory as there was, by proclamations of victory displaying a Napoleonic flourish, and he was called to Washington.

Reorganizing and training the Federal army into a superb instrument of attack, he was ready, by the spring of 1862, for the campaign to capture Richmond. His able plan of transporting his army by ship to Fort Monroe and marching up the peninsula between the York and James rivers to his objective did not appeal to President Lincoln and to the fearful Secretary of War Edwin M. Stanton, because it left Washington precariously defended. Moreover, on March 23, just as McClellan's campaign was about to begin, they were alarmed by a bold attack of Jackson's small force in the Shenandoah Valley on Shields's division of Banks's army at Kernstown, three miles south of Winchester. Although Jackson was defeated his attack dislocated the Union plans, and Banks's troops were ordered to remain in the Valley. To insure the safety of the Capital, Lincoln ordered McDowell's corps of 37,000 men and Blenker's division, which were marching overland toward Richmond, to remain near Bull Run.

By early April, 1862, McClellan had landed a well trained army of 105,000 men at Fort Monroe to deliver the knockout blow to the Confederacy by capturing its capital. The land expedition was accompanied by a naval squadron, including the famous ironclad *Monitor,* that steamed up the James River; also McClellan had the advantage of a new military device, "Professor" T. S. C. Lowe's observation balloons. The Federal fleet, however, was held at Drewry's Bluff, eight miles from the city, by a boom across the river and by shore defenses. Opposing the invading army in the

Peninsula was a Confederate force of approximately sixty thousand men led by that masterly retreater Joseph E. Johnston. McClellan was even more cautious than Johnston, wasting valuable time in the siege of Yorktown, which was defended by "Prince John" Magruder with "Quaker guns" of wood as well as real cannon. The Confederate retreat was protected by the rear-guard action of the command of Longstreet, who at the right moment turned on the Federal army at Williamsburg and surprised it by a spirited attack.

After the stiff fight at Williamsburg the Southern army retreated to the environs of Richmond, slowly pursued by the Federal army. McClellan's headquarters and base were at White House on the Pamunkey River (an extension of the York, twenty miles from Richmond). The pickets of his advanced divisions could see the spires and hear the church bells of the city. So dangerous was the situation that the government prepared to evacuate the Capital; but the people of Richmond demanded that it be defended to the last extremity, and it was so resolved.

McClellan had advanced two of his five corps south of the Chickahominy River, a tributary of the James flowing above Richmond. The main body of the Federal army remained north of the tributary in order to establish contact with the expected reenforcement of McDowell's corps marching down from Fredericksburg. Thus, on May 31 the Federal army was dangerously astride a stream that was subject to overflow from storms, when Johnston ordered an attack on its exposed flank at Seven Pines. During the night preceding the battle a violent downpour of rain transformed the Chickahominy into a raging torrent that swept away some of the bridges. The Union troops on the south bank were in a perilous position, but they were strengthened by the promptness of General Edwin V. Sumner in transferring a part of his corps by fording and by crossing over shaky bridges to the battlefield. Notwithstanding, the gray-clad army drove the Federal troops before them, and might have delivered a crushing blow if Johnston's plan of battle had been properly executed. But the attack was not coordinated, and it resulted in only a half-victory because some of Johnston's officers were ignorant of the topography of their own region and misunderstood his verbal orders. On the following day (June 1) the Confederates again attacked at near-by Fair Oaks, but here they were severely repulsed. Moreover, Johnston was so gravely wounded that he had to relinquish command to Gustavus W. Smith. Then President Davis made his wisest decision of the war, appointing Robert E. Lee, his military adviser, to command the Army of Northern Virginia.

While McClellan's army was marching up the Peninsula to Richmond, a Confederate force under "Stonewall" Jackson was trying to clear the Shenandoah Valley of Federal troops.[28] Instead of calling these troops to strengthen the defense of the Capital, Lee pursued a more subtle plan of sending Ewell with 8,500 troops to strengthen Jackson so that he might threaten Washington and prevent large reenforcements, particularly McDowell's corps, from joining McClellan. Jackson had only 18,000 men but by brilliant tactics he was able to bring to the field at any one engagement a superior force to that of the enemy, whose scattered forces were far larger than his own. In a campaign beginning on May 8 with a victory over Milroy near Staunton, he defeated four separate commands with his famous infantry who marched so swiftly and attacked so unexpectedly that they were called "foot cavalry." On May 23 he routed a part of General Banks's army at Front Royal and drove the Federal troops through Winchester, which wildly acclaimed the Confederates as they marched in.

For a brief period the authorities in Washington were in a panic, calling on thirteen governors for fresh troops and rescinding the order for McDowell's corps, now at Fredericksburg, to join McClellan. Two civilians, Lincoln and Stanton, tried to direct by telegraph and courier the movements of the dispersed Federal forces in and near the Valley. They ordered McDowell to send a large part of his corps under Shields to converge with Frémont's troops in the southwestern part of the valley and intercept Jackson's veterans as they returned from their foray in the lower valley. In addition to his great skill, Jackson had luck in escaping the net prepared for him, for he had the advantage of the good Valley pike in the stormy weather that interfered with the movements of the enemy. Moreover, Frémont disobeyed an order to intercept him by a direct but more difficult route. Jackson defeated Frémont on June 8 at Cross Keys and Shields on the 9th at Port Republic on the other side of the Shenandoah River. After accomplishing his mission

Jackson united his forces with Lee's army on June 27 in time for a series of powerful blows that drove the Northern army in retreat from Richmond.

Meanwhile, for three weeks after Seven Pines, neither army in the Peninsula had dared to attack the other. McClellan's men were suffering terribly from "the Chickahominy fever" in the swampy environs of Richmond, and Lee was forcing his reluctant soldiers to work with pick and shovel at throwing up defenses for the Capital. During this period of preparation for attack Jeb Stuart with twelve hundred cavalry on June 15 electrified the Southern people by riding around McClellan's army. Although his exploit had little military significance it had great psychological value in increasing the confidence of the Confederate soldiers who were facing such great odds.

On June 26, instead of waiting behind the Richmond defenses, Lee took the offensive against the inert Federal army. Relying on his estimate of the extreme caution of McClellan, he boldly divided his forces. Leaving a weak force under Magruder to contain the main body of the Federal troops now south of the Chickahominy River he threw the strength of his army (56,000 out of 85,500 men) against the right wing of McClellan's army, under Fitz-John Porter, on the north bank. Jackson had been ordered to bring his men swiftly from the Shenandoah Valley by train and by forced marches through Ashland, and to attack the rear and flank of Porter's corps. Simultaneously Lee planned to send the major portion of his army across the Chickahominy for a frontal attack. Success of the plan of envelopment depended on correct timing, and Jackson upset the plan by arriving a day late. A. P. Hill, leading Lee's advance, attacked the Union army at Mechanicsville without waiting for Jackson. The Federals retired to intrenchments behind Beaver Dam Creek where they repulsed the Confederates with severe losses.

On the following day, Jackson's troops arrived, and Lee won his first victory, the battle of Gaines's Mill. The Federal army fought bravely and stubbornly until a furious charge led by Hood's Texas brigade broke the center of Porter's corps. It was a costly victory. "The list of the fallen," a Southern historian has written, "read like the roster of the Southern aristocracy." [29]

McClellan's communications with his base at White House were now dangerously threatened. He must either retreat down the Peninsula or change his base to the James River under the protection of his naval escort. Lee was in great doubt as to which course the Federal commander would take, and allowed the enemy precious time with which to begin "a transfer of base" to Harrison Landing on the James. During this operation the Federal army had to cross White Oak Swamp, where the Confederates had a splendid opportunity to rout them. Magruder attacked the retreating army at Savage Station on June 29, but unsupported, he was repulsed. Leaving their sick and wounded and destroying vast military stores, McClellan's troops continued to retreat in the night

On the following day Lee issued orders that should have brought about envelopment and destruction of the enemy; but the pursuit was slow and uncoordinated, and his officers failed to execute his plans. At Frayser's Farm (also called Glendale) the Federal army, fighting gallantly, beat off the Confederate attack and escaped. Jackson failed to show his usual promptness and vigor in the pursuit. His disappointing performance may possibly be explained by his physical exhaustion and lack of sleep. He was in "a peculiar mood" also; while the Federal guns were blazing away he sat down and wrote to his wife directing her as to the amount of money she should contribute to the Presbyterian Church.[30]

McClellan retreated to Malvern Hill, near the James River, an almost impregnable position. Lee was so disappointed at previous failure and so determined to win victory that he made the great tactical blunder on July 1 of assaulting the Federal army in its strong position. The Federal artillery mowed down the charging gray lines. The repulse was so bloody that General D. H. Hill, one of the major generals who fought at Malvern Hill, declared, "It was not war—it was murder." [31] Indeed, the Confederates during the famous Seven Days' Battles from Mechanicsville to Malvern Hill lost 20,000 soldiers, including 3,286 killed, a considerably greater loss than McClellan's army sustained.

Never afterwards did Lee have so splendid an opportunity to crush the enemy as McClellan's retreat to the James River gave him. In bitterness of soul and yet with sober truth he said, "They should have been destroyed." Why had he lost this opportunity? Aside from McClellan's admirable management of the retreat and the excellent fighting morale of his army, the Confederates made some bad mistakes. According to Douglas Southall Freeman, the expert on Lee's campaign, these errors were attributable to the Confederate officers' lack of knowledge of the terrain (poor maps and inadequate reconnaissance), the failures of Lee's subordinates, particularly Huger, Magruder, and Jackson, feeble handling of artillery, and very bad staff work, which caused the commanding general to lose touch with the various units of the army.[32]

After Lee had defeated McClellan, the Washington authorities ordered the disconsolate general to abandon the Peninsula campaign and transport his army by ship from Fort Monroe to Aquia Creek Landing on the Potomac, whence he was to reenforce General John Pope. Thus he was prevented from carrying out a campaign to attack Richmond from the south which was very promising. Grant at the end of the war returned to McClellan's plan.[33]

Pope, a native of Kentucky and a handsome, dashing soldier noted for his confidence in himself and for his aggressive qualities as a fighter, had recently won fame by capturing Island No. 10 in the Mississippi River; and the success had brought appointment to command a large concentration of troops in northern Virginia, with the duty of taking the Confederate Capital.[34] His first act was to issue to his Eastern troops a bombastic proclamation that he had come from the West, where the Union armies were in the habit of seeing the backs of their enemies.

Shortly after assuming command, Pope crossed the Rappahannock River and reached Culpeper on the Orange & Alexandria Railroad. Here his presence threatened the vital Virginia Central Railroad that connected Richmond with the Shenandoah Valley. Accordingly, Lee ordered Jackson to move northward for its defense to Gordonsville, the junction with the Orange & Alexandria, only twenty-seven miles from Culpeper. On August 9 Jackson's force of 24,000 was on the march when it was attacked by Banks's corps, vanguard of Pope's army, at Cedar Mountain, a few miles south of Culpeper. Banks drove the Confederates back until A. P. Hill's "Light Division" moved up to defeat the heavily outnumbered Federals. Jackson then withdrew to Gordonsville.

Lee now learned that McClellan's army was abandoning its base at Harrison's Landing and embarking for the Potomac River. Acting on the information, he moved rapidly to destroy Pope's army before McClellan's troops could reenforce it. It became a race as to who would reach Pope first. As Lee advanced, fording the Rapidan with 54,500 men, Pope retreated behind the Rappahannock. Then deliberately violating the orthodox rules of strategy, Lee divided his army in the face of the superior numbers of the enemy and sent Jackson and Jeb Stuart's cavalry on a wide flanking movement to the left. Jackson's force, screened behind the Bull Run Mountains, marched fifty-four miles in two days, crossed over Thoroughfare Gap, and on August 26 burned the Union army's supply depot at Manassas Junction and disrupted its communications. Following this spectacular exploit he retreated to an excellent defensive position at Groveton a few miles northwest of Manassas. Here Pope caught up with the audacious Confederate force and wasted his strength in fierce but uncoordinated attacks on its lines. During the hottest hour of the fighting General Maxcy Gregg exhorted his proud South Carolina troops not to give ground: "Let us die here, my men, let us die here!" And they bravely responded, thus saving Jackson's left flank from crumpling in defeat.[35]

The next day, August 30, 1862, was one of the glorious days of the Confederacy. Lee had followed behind Jackson with the remainder of his army, led by Longstreet, and passing through Thoroughfare Gap which was weakly defended reached the old battlefield of Bull Run. Here Longstreet stationed his troops on the right flank of Jackson. Although the first of McClellan's troops, Fitz-John Porter's corps, had joined Pope, the greater portion of the Army of the Potomac did not arrive in time to participate in the impending battle. On the morning of August 30 the Federal commander made a fresh attack on Jackson's troops but was repulsed. Then Lee launched a magnificent counterstroke against Pope's left flank with Longstreet's troops.[36] This attack overwhelmed the cumbrous Union army. Pope laid his defeat to the lack of cooperation and the disobedience of certain officers of McClellan, particularly Porter, who was subsequently tried by a court martial and unjustly cashiered. But the Union general displayed bad military judgment also and failed to utilize his superior available forces. Lee's failure to capitalize on this great victory was due partly to his lack of control over logistics, for his men were largely without food and heavy rain interfered with the pursuit. The Federal army was able to beat off an attack at Chantilly and to retreat to the defenses of Washington. During this campaign the Confederates lost 7,244 men killed and wounded while Pope's casualties were 14,462, including 4,163 prisoners.

The greatest spiritual asset of an army is the confidence of the common soldiers in their commanding officer. After the second victory at Manassas the army in gray, as well as the Southern people, believed that Lee was invincible. Disgusted with its leadership, the army of Pope, on the other hand, was whipped in spirit as well as in body. Yet only a few days later, on September 2, this same mass of dejected men, as Bruce Catton observes in *Mr. Lincoln's Army*, regained as if by magic its proud fighting spirit and became once more a great army. McClellan was restored to command.

IX

Naval Power in the Civil War

To COMBAT the Northern fleets, the Confederacy had to build a navy from the bottom. Being agricultural and unskilled in the ways of ships, the Southerners had few shipyards or industrial resources with which to build naval vessels. This weakness was displayed in the home-built Confederate ships, with inadequate engines that frequently failed at critical moments. Furthermore, the Southerners did not at first realize the tremendous significance of sea power. Indeed, in the beginning they looked upon the blockade as a blessing in disguise, which would create a cotton famine in Europe and thus cause intervention by England and France.

Privateering had been made illegal by the Declaration of Paris of 1856; but the United States, arguing against this, had refused to sign the Declaration. Consequently the Confederate government felt free to make up for its deficiency in naval vessels by issuing letters of marque and reprisal. However, privateering did not pay as well as blockade running and practically came to an end after 1861, despite the fact that the government took only one-twentieth of prize cargoes as its share of the booty.

On April 19, 1861, Lincoln proclaimed that the crews of Confederate warships and privateers were pirates—a designation which could subject them to execution if captured. Actually the United States was forced to grant to the Confederacy the rights of a belligerent despite its theory that the Confederates were organized mobs and insurrectionists. In June, the crew of the captured Confederate ship *Savannah* was tried for piracy; but the jury disagreed, and there was no conviction. President Davis threatened retaliation, if Confederate sailors were executed, by hanging some of the prisoners taken at Bull Run. When the crew of the Confederate privateer

Petrel was tried for piracy in Philadelphia in 1861, Justice Grier of the Supreme Court declared that it was foolish to treat captured Confederate sailors differently from Confederate soldiers taken in battle, and refused to try any more piracy cases.

The navy of the Confederacy was greatly overshadowed by the army. The whole number of enlisted men in the navy on October 31, 1861, was 3,674. In addition the marine corps under Colonel Lloyd J. Beall had a total strength of 539 men, and 32 recruits from the conscription camp at Raleigh were being trained in the naval station at Charleston.[1] A law of Congress of May 1, 1863, provided for the transfer of all seamen from the army to the navy; but it was entirely disregarded until May 22, 1864, when the War Department transferred 960 men. Moreover, naval construction was greatly hampered by the army's refusal, in most cases, to detail mechanics for that purpose. The navy had a training school and practice ship in the James River, the *Patrick Henry,* which instructed midshipmen between the ages of fourteen and eighteen years.[2] The Naval Rope Works at Petersburg furnished adequate cordage to the navy, as well as large amounts of rope to the army and to railroads. The Naval Powder Works at Columbia supplied the navy with an excellent grade of powder, and coal was obtained mainly from the Egypt mines of North Carolina, the mines in the vicinity of Richmond, and those near Montevallo, Alabama.[3]

The South, starting without naval traditions, had great opportunities and incentives to experiment with new types of ships. Armored steamships had been used in the Crimean War; and since then the French had built the thinly armored battleship *Gloire,* and the British, the *Warrior.*[4] Nevertheless, the Confederacy was the first nation to introduce in combat an effective warship with heavy iron armor. In the early spring of 1862 the Confederates made a spectacular attempt to break the blockade with such an experimental ship. From the bottom of Norfolk harbor they raised the warship *Merrimac,* which the Federals had sunk in abandoning the Gosport Navy Yard at the beginning of war; they repaired it and converted it into an ironclad vessel, which they rechristened *Virginia.*

The ironclad *Virginia* was designed by one of the most brilliant inventive minds of his generation, Commander John Mercer Brooke, with the aid of the naval constructor John L. Porter. Brooke was born in Maryland and had a varied training in the United States Navy, during which he invented equipment for exploring the bottom of the ocean. In 1860 he returned from an exploring trip in the waters of Japan and the South Sea islands. He resigned his commission to join the Confederate Navy and, with Porter, designed the first American ironclad warship, the *Virginia.* Another remarkable achievement was the Brooke naval gun, of cast iron strengthened by triple wrought-iron bands, seven inches across the muzzle, rifled, and using an elongated projectile, or "bolt," that could pierce the armor of the Union ironclads.

The improvised ironclad *Virginia* was 275 feet long and 38½ feet wide and weighed 3,200 tons. Her deck had an armored superstructure, consisting of iron plates four inches thick. The slanting sides extended over the wooden hull, the top was flat, and a cast-iron ram weighing 1,500 pounds was attached to the prow. Ten guns jutted out from portholes of the four sides. She carried a crew of approximately three hundred men, mostly landlubbers, as well as fifty-five marines, under the command of Flag Officer Franklin Buchanan of Maryland, who had been the first superintendent of the United States Naval Academy.[5]

On March 8, 1862, the *Virginia,* leading a squadron of five small ships, steamed slowly toward the wooden warships at Hampton Roads that blockaded the harbor of Norfolk. By ramming and by shell fire, she destroyed the largest ships of the blockading squadron and caused a third ship to run aground. Engine trouble prevented her from destroying the rest of the blockading squadron. The following day, when she came out to complete her work, another strange ironclad vessel, the *Monitor,* commanded by Lieutenant John L. Worden, confronted her. This warship, just completed, had been designed by a Swedish immigrant, John Ericsson. It was a weird-looking craft, 179 feet long and 41 feet wide, with a turret, and was humorously dubbed a cheesebox on a raft. But the revolving turret, which contained two eleven-inch guns, was to revolutionize naval warfare.

The duel between the two ironclads, fought at close quarters, was a drawn battle, neither being able to do much damage to the other. The *Monitor* with her light draft was easily maneuverable, while the heavy iron superstructure of the *Virginia* weighed her down so that she could not operate in shallow waters. Furthermore she lost her iron ram during the first day of battle, so that when she struck the Federal ship with her wooden stem she did little damage. The *Monitor,* after firing forty-one shots at the enemy in the course of three hours of fighting, retired to shoal water where she could not be followed. Faced by an adverse tide, the *Virginia* returned to Norfolk without attempting to destroy the remaining ships in the blockading fleet.[6]

The fight between the two ironclads was not renewed. Although the Confederate ship, commanded by Lieutenant Catesby ap Rogers Jones since the wounding of Buchanan, again offered battle, the *Monitor* did not take up the challenge. Nevertheless, she had destroyed the South's great hope of breaking through the blockade and quieted the fears of the coastal cities of the North, which had been thrown into a panic by news of the first victories of the Confederate warship. The *Virginia* disappeared from the spotlight of fame. She had grave defects that prevented her from continuing a career of destroying wooden vessels that blockaded Southern ports. Not only was she unseaworthy, but her defective engines prevented her from attaining more than five knots per hour. On May 11, 1862, the day after the Confederates abandoned their base at Norfolk, the *Virginia* was run ashore and burned by the crew to prevent capture by the enemy. The *Monitor,* whose deck was only eighteen inches above water, had nearly foundered on her way from New York to Hampton Roads; and during the following December she was lost in a storm off Cape Hatteras.

In addition to evading the blockade with small, swift boats, the Confederate government tried to break through the cordon of Federal vessels by securing powerful ironclad warships in Europe. In 1861 it sent Captain James D. Bulloch and Lieutenant James H. North as agents to purchase cruisers and ironclad ships.[7] A contract was made with the famous Laird firm of Birkenhead, near Liverpool, to construct two powerful ironclad rams, which were nearly completed and ready to go to sea in the fall of 1863. These warships were equipped with formidable wrought-iron rams, and, with the addition of the most destructive type of cannon, could easily have demolished the wooden ships blockading the Southern ports and could even have attacked the Northern seaports. "If the rams had put to sea," an able student of American diplomacy has written, "the South would probably have won its independence, and the North—would almost certainly have declared war on Britain." [8]

To combat this menace the United States minister, Charles Francis Adams, gathered evidence which he presented to the British ministry showing that British neutrality would be violated by allowing these warships to sail to their destination in Confederate ports. On April 5, 1863, the British government had seized the *Alexandra,* a commerce raider that was being built at Liverpool. The courts released the *Alexandra* on the ground that the Foreign Enlistment Act of Great Britain required evidence that the ship was being specifically equipped and armed for war with the intent of being employed in the service of a belligerent. The *Alexandra* seizure, however, showed a change of policy of Lord Palmerston's government in the direction of restraining the sailing of warships destined for the Confederacy. [9] On September 5, 1863, Charles Francis Adams notified Earl Russell that if the Laird rams were permitted to escape, "it would be superfluous in me to point out to your Lordship that this is war.[10] Before receiving this peremptory threat of war the Foreign Secretary had issued a secret order (September 3, 1863) to prevent the escape of the rams, and they were bought from the Lairds for the British Navy.

A similar attempt was made to purchase cruisers and ironclad ships in France.[11] Emperor Napoleon III encouraged the Confederate agents to make contracts for the building of warships in French shipyards but stipulated that the destination of such ships should be kept secret. On April 15, 1863, M. L. Arman of Bordeaux, the largest shipbuilder in France, signed contracts with the Confederacy for constructing four warships to be paid for by cotton bonds; and he began to build these ships ostensibly for the Chinese or Japanese navy. Arman sublet a part of his contract to M. Voruz, a shipbuilder of Nantes. A clerk of Voruz stole papers showing the destination of the ships and sold them to the United States.[12] After vigorous protests by the American Minister, William L. Dayton, Napoleon ordered the sale of the ships to other powers. The Confederacy also signed on July 16, 1863, a contract for building two ironclad rams light enough to enter the Mississippi. However, only one was actually delivered, the ram *Stonewall,* which had been sold at first to Denmark but was later acquired by the Confederacy.

This formidable ship sailed from Ferrol, Spain, on March 24, 1865, to break the blockade at Port Royal, South Carolina; but various delays prevented her arriving in American waters until after the war was over.[13]

The South was vastly inferior to the North in naval power, and only new types of ships and instruments of naval war could overcome its great handicaps. Stephen Mallory, the Secretary of the Navy, was alert to acquire the newest type of fighting ships, ironclads driven by screw propellers; but he was defeated by lack of ready cash and by the diplomacy of the North. He established the Confederate Torpedo Bureau, headed by Matthew Fontaine Maury, which carried on experiments to develop a powerful missile destroyer of Union warships. The torpedoes which were used were crude, frequently made of demijohns and beer kegs filled with gunpowder. Also small boats with torpedoes attached to their prows were sent against Union warships, to strike below the armor plate, since even ironclad vessels in that day had wooden hulls. Josiah Gorgas noted in his diary, March 16, 1864, that about thirty torpedo boats were being built to destroy the blockading vessels in front of Charleston. They were cigar-shaped, 60 feet long and 6 feet in diameter, propelled by steam engines submerged except for the smokestack and bearing a torpedo on a spar at the bow.[14] The Federal Secretary of the Navy, Gideon Welles, declared after the Civil War that the Union had lost more vessels by torpedoes than from all other causes whatever. Scharf, the historian of the Confederate Navy, wrote that the Confederacy was the first government to bring the torpedo into existence "as a formidable and practical weapon," and that its most valuable contributions to the implements of war were the torpedo and the steam ram.[15]

An interesting experiment of the Confederate Navy was the development of primitive submarines. One of these boats, the *H. L. Hunley*, built at Mobile, was shaped like a fish, about twenty feet long with internal dimensions of five feet, and provided with tanks that could be filled or emptied. Propelled by the muscle power of its crew of eight men, it had a speed of four miles an hour under favorable conditions. It proved to be a deathtrap for its various crews, all volunteers, sinking once in Mobile harbor and four times in Charleston harbor. On a sixth adventure, however, February 17, 1864, it sank the United States Ship *Housatonic* in the harbor of

Charleston. But the explosion also destroyed the submarine with its crew.[16]

The Federal government found that the most effective way to stop the blockade runners was to capture the leading Southern ports. A splendid naval base for the accomplishment of this task was obtained when a fleet under Samuel Francis du Pont and an army under General Thomas West Sherman captured Port Royal, South Carolina, on November 7, 1861. In the following February, General Ambrose Burnside with an army of 15,000 men defeated a pathetically weak Confederate force under General Henry A. Wise, which lacked ammunition, on Roanoke Island, North Carolina, thereby gaining command of Albemarle Sound. In March the Federal troops occupied New Bern, which was less than sixty miles from Goldsboro on the main railroad between Richmond and the southern Atlantic states.

The great prize of the Federal Navy in this year was the capture of New Orleans, the largest port of the Confederacy. The principal defense of the city was based on two forts, St. Philip and Jackson, on opposite sides of the Mississippi River seventy-five miles below the city. Also a boom of cables and hulks of ships was stretched across the river. Above the boom a Confederate fleet and fire rafts guarded the city. The inventiveness of the Southern people in this crisis was shown by the conversion of a steamship into the ironclad ram *Manassas,* that looked like a half-submerged whale with a curved iron back. Her prow contained a powerful iron ram, and to prevent boarding by the enemy, she had a device that would eject steam and scalding water from her boilers over her surface; but her engine was too weak for effective ramming. In addition the New Orleans shipbuilders were feverishly working against time to complete the formidable ironclads *Louisiana* and *Mississippi.*

The commander of the Federal fleet in the battle of New Orleans was a Southerner, Flag Officer David G. Farragut. Born near Knoxville, Tennessee, he had spent his youth in the city which he now attempted to capture. His father was a Spaniard of noble family, and his mother was Elizabeth Shine of North Carolina. Farragut had a long career in the United States Navy, characterized by stanchness and devotion to duty. When the Southern states seceded he stayed at his post. At the time of his attack on New Orleans he was sixty years old, of medium height, with plain, ruddy face, which was genial and kindly in expression, and had an alert air. He was animated by strong determination and daring.

Southerners expected the attack on New Orleans to come from the north and were unprepared for the bold enterprise of Farragut. The Washington authorities, however, had ordered Farragut to reduce Fort St. Philip and Fort Jackson, which guarded the southern approach. He first attacked the forts with his fleet of twenty-one mortar ships under Commander David D. Porter, which did great damage to Fort Jackson, setting fire to its citadel and disabling some of its guns. Then he decided to risk running by the forts. On the starlit night of April 24, 1862, his fleet of wooden vessels, consisting of eight warships and nine gunboats, with vulnerable parts protected by looped iron chains, broke the boom and passed the dreaded forts in single file.[17] The Confederates, through criminal neglect according to the commander of the forts, failed to send down fire rafts to light up the river so that the gunners in the forts could see the Federal ships. Moreover, the magnificent iron floating battery, the *Louisiana*, 4,000 tons, did not have her engine ready, and her captain refused to have her towed below the forts where she could be most effective. The Confederate defenders fought gallantly but in the disjointed manner of amateurs, using a flock of converted Mississippi steamboats, with little cooperation between the land and naval forces. During the panic occasioned by the Federal attack, the ironclad *Mississippi,* which would have been completed within ten days, was burned instead of being towed up the river.

The military force in the city, consisting of three thousand militia of ninety days' service, more than half of whom were armed with shotguns, was totally inadequate. Their commander, General Mansfield Lovell, retreated without a fight after Farragut landed the eighteen thousand troops of the political general Benjamin F. Butler. At Fort Jackson also a disgraceful scene occurred. Despite the appeal of Brigadier General J. K. Duncan, the garrison, "mostly foreign enlistments," revolted in mass, spiked the guns, and demanded the surrender of the fort, which took place on April 28.[18]

After having abandoned the city General Lovell offered to return with his troops: although such a step would be entirely indefensible from a military point of view, yet if "the people of New Orleans were desirous of signalizing their patriotism and devotion to the cause by [permitting] the bombardment and burning of their city, I would return with my troops and not leave as long as one brick remained upon another." [19] The mayor and the leading citizens declined this offer; but the women of the city were more high-spirited and, according to Julia LeGrand, were "all in favor of resistance *no matter how hopeless* that resistance might be." [20] No wonder that later Butler, as military governor of the city, had his hands full and shocked the Southerners by his notorious Order No. 28, May 15, 1862, "that when any female shall by word, gesture, or movement insult or show contempt for any officer or soldier of the United States she shall be regarded and held liable to be treated as a woman of the town plying her avocation." [21] The fall of this great port was a profound tragedy to the Confederacy, which was heightened two weeks later by the loss of Norfolk, with its naval yards and machinery.

The port of Galveston had been captured early in the war, but it was recovered by one of the most colorful exploits of the Civil War. At dawn of New Year's Day, 1863, two old river steamers and the gunboat *Bayou City* which had come down from the Confederate headquarters at Houston attacked the five Federal ships that held Galveston Bay. The steamers were protected by cotton bales (called therefore, "cotton-clads") and their crews were aided by Texas cavalry under the frontiersman Colonel Tom Green. After the *Bayou City* drove her prow into the iron wheel of the strongest Federal ship, the *Harriet Lane,* Commodore Leon Smith and his men leaped to the deck of the Federal vessel and captured her.[22] This temporary opening of the harbor, however, was followed by the reestablishment of the blockade outside the entrance. (One of the blockading warships, the *Hatteras,* was lured into pursuit of the commerce raider *Alabama,* which turned and sank her.)

Three of the most important Southern ports—Mobile, Wilmington, and Charleston—resisted capture until near the end of the war. The capture of Mobile was full of human drama. Mobile Bay was protected by forts, submerged mines, torpedoes, and a Confederate fleet commanded by Admiral Buchanan. On August 5, 1864, Admiral Farragut began to move past Fort Morgan at the entrance into the bay with his fleet, consisting of four ironclad monitors, and fourteen wooden ships tied together in pairs by cables. When the lead ship, *Brooklyn,* halted short of the submerged torpedo line, thereby throwing the rest of the fleet into confusion, Farragut, who was lashed to the rigging of the mainmast of the flagship, *Hartford,* ordered his ship to go boldly into the mined area; "Damn the torpedoes! Full steam ahead!" he is reputed to have said. Although one of his advance ships the *Tecumseh* was sunk by a torpedo, the *Hartford* avoided the mines. The powerful Confederate ironclad ram *Tennessee,* the flagship of Admiral Buchanan, attacked the whole Union fleet; but her weak engine hampered her maneuvers, and she failed to ram a single ship. The Federal ships converged on the dreaded *Tennessee* and, wounding Buchanan, finally put her out of commission by a shot that cut the rudder chain.[23] Although Mobile itself was not captured until eight months after the battle of Mobile Bay the Union victory effectively closed the harbor to blockade runners.

The most vital blockade-running port for the supply of the Virginia armies was Wilmington, which was defended by Fort Fisher at the entry of the Cape Fear River. At the very close of 1864 Admiral David D. Porter with sixty warships carrying more than six hundred guns, the most powerful group of fighting ships that had ever assembled under the Stars and Stripes, tried to capture the Confederate fort. First an attempt was made to effect a breach in its defenses by driving an old ship laden with explosives against the sea face; but this spectacular operation failed. On December 24 the fleet bombarded the fort and its garrison of 1,900 men and 44 guns under Colonel William Lamb. Although Ben Butler landed with some of the troops an assault by infantry proved to be too hazardous, and they withdrew. On January 15, 1865, Porter's fleet returned and bombarded the fort two days and nights. This time military operations were conducted by General A. H. Terry, who had eight thousand infantry, including two Negro brigades. An attack by a marine and naval force on the sea side was repulsed, but then the infantry overwhelmed the small garrison from the land side in desperate hand-to-hand fighting within the fort. The fall of Fort Fisher, which meant the closing of Wilmington to blockade runners, was a body blow to the moribund Confederacy.

Charleston resisted all of the desperate efforts of the Federal Navy to reduce it to submission. In April, 1863, a strong naval expedition which included nine ironclads, under Flag Officer Sam-

uel Francis du Pont, attempted to capture this citadel of Southern-
ism. General Pierre Beauregard, who was in charge of defense, had
trained his gunners in constant target practice so that they were
sharpshooters. Furthermore, the Confederate powder which he used,
manufactured at Augusta, Georgia, proved to be superior to the
Northern powder used by Du Pont's ships. Despite a long series
of bombardments, the Federal ships were repelled with severe
damage. In this engagement the historic superiority of forts over
ships was again demonstrated. One of the most dramatic attacks
was on Battery Wagner the night of July 18, 1863, with Negro
troops participating. General Jeremy Gilmer, who was sent to
Charleston to strengthen its fortifications, reported on September 6,
1863, the terrific bombardment of Fort Wagner by monitors; so
dangerous were the Federal long-range shells, he wrote, that "non-
combatants, especially ladies and children, have left Charleston,
and we are prepared for the most desperate defense and for the
sacrifice of the city, its monuments and houses." [24] The spirit of
Charleston was different from the spirit of New Orleans in the
spring of 1862. Not until the approach of Sherman's army did the
defiant Confederate city surrender, in February, 1865.

A prominent feature of the conquest of the South was amphibious
warfare. Notable examples of this type of warfare along Southern
rivers were Grant's use of warships in the capture of Fort Henry
and Fort Donelson, McClellan's Peninsular campaign, the Red
River expedition of Banks, and the complete conquest of the Mississippi River. The combined use of naval and military forces was
also effective in capturing certain of the principal ports of the
South, such as New Orleans and Fort Fisher. The North's use of
amphibious operations gave it the initiative and helps to explain
the wide scattering of Confederate troops to meet constant threats
to the coast at various points.

Shortly after Grant won control of the Cumberland and Tennessee rivers the United States entered upon the seizure of the
Mississippi. It used gunboats—converted river steamboats that resembled the *Virginia* with their armored decks and sloping sides.
The army also used steam rams, designed and built for speed by a
civilian engineer, Charles Ellet, Jr., with little armor at the sides
but a heavy prow. Indeed, the chief method of fighting the river
war was to ram the enemy's broadside. The Confederate gunboats

were of various sizes, the largest barely exceeding 200 feet in length and 1,000 tons. The makeshift nature of these boats is indicated by the fact that some of them, the "cotton-clads," relied on cotton bales for protection; others, "hay-plated," were protected with bales of hay; and "tin-clads" had quarter-inch iron plates and stout oak bulwarks. There was a failure of discipline on the Confederate river gunboats, which were not supervised by the navy but operated under orders from the army.[25]

After the retirement from Columbus, Kentucky, the Confederates decided to stand on the Mississippi at Island No. 10 and at New Madrid, opposite it in the extreme southeastern corner of Missouri. In the island fortress they placed a garrison of seven thousand men, effectively blocking the river. It was captured, however, on April 7, 1862, by General John Pope, aided by a flotilla of gunboats and mortarboats. A greater disaster occurred two months later when Memphis fell. Eight Confederate ironclads fought unsuccessfully in front of the city against the Union gunboats and Ellet's rams while thousands of Memphis citizens looked on.

The next defensive position of the Confederates on the river was Vicksburg on its high bluffs. One of the dramatic episodes in the river war occurred when the ironclad Confederate ram *Arkansas* came to the aid of the city, blockaded by the combined fleets of Farragut and Davis. This powerful Confederate warship had been completed at Greenwood, Mississippi, far up the Yazoo River. Its armor consisted of railroad rails and iron which had been collected in small lots from many scattered points within the Confederacy. A vivid sidelight on Confederate mismanagement is shown by the fact that General Leonidas Polk had refused to detail mechanics from his army to complete this Confederate monster.

In the middle of July, 1862, the *Arkansas,* commanded by the daring Lieutenant Isaac Brown, started down the Yazoo. Deserters had forewarned the Union commanders, and several gunboats had been sent up the river to destroy the Confederate iron ship. The *Arkansas* easily defeated these and reached Vicksburg after successfully encountering broadsides from the combined Federal fleets. Early in August it was ordered to aid General John C. Breckinridge in the recapture of Baton Rouge. Near that city its engines failed, and Lieutenant Brown set it afire with its guns loaded with powder and shot to drift toward the enemy, whom it blasted during its last moments.[26] Farragut described this event "as one of the happiest moments of my life."

The daring, resourceful Confederate fight to preserve control of the lower Mississippi is illustrated in the attack on the ironclad *Indianola* which had run by the guns of Vicksburg in February, 1863. Shortly before, the Federal gunboat *Queen of the West* had been disabled by the guns of Fort De Russy and captured up the Red River. Manned by eager volunteers from the Confederate infantry, it was now used as a ram to attack the *Indianola* in the Mississippi. The attack was made at night by the *Queen of the West* and a small but swift Confederate gunboat, the *Webb*. These rammed the larger and more powerful *Indianola,* which was protected by coal barges lashed to its sides, again and again until she sank. Thus the use of the Mississippi below Vicksburg was temporarily restored to the Confederates.

The most spectacular success of the Confederates in the river war was the defeat of General Nathaniel P. Banks's Red River expedition. In the spring of 1864 General Banks, a political general, was placed in charge of twenty-five thousand men and a fleet of gunboats (commanded by David D. Porter) for an invasion of Texas by way of the Red River. One of his principal objectives was Shreveport in western Louisiana, the center of Confederate strength beyond the Mississippi. The Union commander met a series of disasters. His army was defeated a short distance from Shreveport by General Richard Taylor, commanding 13,000 men, in the battles of Sabine Cross Roads and Pleasant Hill and had to retreat. Then the river fell rapidly and prevented his ships from descending the rapids near Alexandria. He was extricated from this dangerous situation by a Wisconsin regiment that found a way of damming the river and thus permitting the gunboats and transports to escape.

The Confederacy, according to General "Dick" Taylor, lost a magnificent opportunity of destroying Banks's army and capturing his fleet of gunboats when General Kirby-Smith, in charge of the Trans-Mississippi Department, refused to concentrate his scattered forces for a decisive blow. Thus, an army that "had been routed, and, by the incompetency of its commander, was utterly demoralized and ripe for destruction" was permitted to escape.[27] These troops later reenforced Sherman for his Georgia campaign. A sorry denouement to Banks's expedition was the collapse of the hopes of the speculators who had accompanied it to buy cotton. To foil them the Confederate troops destroyed the cotton bales accumulated near the river, worth many million dollars.

A most interesting example of Confederate employment of amphibious warfare occurred in the Albemarle Sound region. After the capture of Roanoke Island in February, 1862, the Union fleet and the army of General Ambrose Burnside obtained control of the towns on both Albemarle and Pamlico sounds, including New Bern, the terminus of an important railroad. To regain possession of the area the Southerners built the ironclad ram *Albemarle*. Launched from a cornfield on the Roanoke River, it played an effective part in the recovery of the town of Plymouth at the mouth of the river (April, 1864). Impervious to the cannon balls of the Federal ships, it rammed and sank one of them and drove another out of the river into Albemarle Sound. In the meanwhile a land expedition under R. F. Hoke, the North Carolina general, surrounded the town, which was forced to surrender to this combined attack. Six months later while the dreaded *Albemarle* was moored at Plymouth she was sunk by a young lieutenant of the United States Navy who approached at night in a small launch and drove a torpedo under her hull.[28]

The war on the sea was not entirely defensive for the beleaguered Confederacy. Its most effective use of sea power was sending commerce raiders to destroy the merchant marine of the North. The first of these was the *Sumter,* purchased in New Orleans and sent out June 30, 1861, under Raphael Semmes, who later commanded the *Alabama*. Seventeen other Confederate commerce raiders are listed by J. Thomas Scharf, the historian of the Confederate Navy.[29] Most of them were built in England, purchased by the Confederate agent Captain James D. Bulloch. His first purchase, in March, 1862, was the *Florida,* which sailed from Liverpool to the Bahama Islands for armament. Commanded by Captain J. N. Maffitt, she captured thirty-four prizes before she was seized in the autumn of 1864 in a neutral Brazilian port. Another commerce raider, the *Georgia,* purchased in Scotland, captured at least nine Union ships. Several of the cruisers were converted blockade runners, and one of these was the *Tallahassee,* which began by running the blockade between Wilmington and Bermuda, changed to a cruiser and took several prizes, then removed her guns and ended her career as a blockade runner, appropriately named the *Chameleon.*[30]

The career of the *Alabama* illustrates the remarkable effectiveness of the raiding warships. She was a ship of 1,040 tons, 220 feet long, with eight guns, and combined sails and steam power. Her crew consisted of 120 men and 24 officers. She was built in the Laird shipyards near Liverpool, where she was called "No. 290." The English Foreign Enlistment Act prohibited building or equipping warships for belligerents, but the Confederate government evaded it by contracting for cruisers as merchant vessels. These vessels, accordingly, went from port unarmed, to receive their armament later at some distant place. Charles Francis Adams, American minister to England, protested to the British government the construction of "No. 290" as a Confederate warship and demanded that it be prevented from leaving port. The British government investigated the accusation, and was on the point of seizing the ship when the Queen's Advocate in charge of the legal proceedings had a nervous breakdown and went insane. Meanwhile the *Alabama* left Liverpool, July 29, 1862, on a trial trip and never returned. At the Azores she received her guns, crew, and stores, which were brought on other ships from England.

Her captain, Raphael Semmes, was a native of Alabama and entertained a violent prejudice against Yankees. Born in 1809, he was enjoying the comfortable position of head of the Lighthouse Board at Washington when the Civil War came. Part of his life, he had been a lawyer; and he often used his legal knowledge during his career as a commerce raider to argue points of international law in neutral ports. A quiet, reserved man, he seldom spoke to his crew and officers. Nevertheless, they had unlimited confidence in their captain, whom they called "Old Beeswax" because he waxed his long black mustachios. A devout Catholic, affected at times by a nostalgia for the katydids in Alabama, he had a touch of romance in his nature.[31]

For two years Semmes ranged the seas from the Straits of Sunda to the Newfoundland banks, the Gulf of Mexico, and the coasts of Europe. Coal, water, and food could be obtained only in foreign ports; not once was he able to enter a Confederate port. His game was unarmed merchant vessels. All told he captured sixty-two

Northern ships, some of which he burned; but he treated his captives humanely. His officers were Southerners; but his crew consisted largely of foreigners recruited from a rough and reckless group (he called them "a precious set of rascals"), and he had to maintain a stern discipline.

The career of the *Alabama* ended dramatically in the harbor of Cherbourg, France, where she was caught by the United States battleship *Kearsarge*. Semmes could probably have avoided a battle, but he deliberately chose to send the commander of the *Kearsarge* a written challenge to fight. The Northern ship was more powerful than the *Alabama* and, unknown to Semmes, was protected by chain armor, while the *Alabama* was nearly worn out—her copper sheathing was in shreds, and her powder was defective. In the historic battle on June 19, 1864, the dreaded Confederate ship was at last sunk by her enemy. Semmes threw his sword into the sea and jumped overboard; but he was rescued by an English yacht and taken to England.[32]

Next to the *Alabama* the most formidable Confederate sea raider was the *Shenandoah,* which was commanded by the North Carolinian James I. Waddell. Her log, from which most of the details of this account are drawn, is preserved in the archives of North Carolina at Raleigh. The *Shenandoah* was a steam screw propeller and sailing ship of a thousand tons, carrying one hundred and thirty men and officers. She specialized in attacking the whaling fleet of New England in the Pacific and Arctic oceans. She captured more than forty ships with cargoes of sperm oil, pork, beef, tea, molasses, rope, flour, tobacco, railroad iron, soap, and beer.[33] She would frighten merchant vessels into surrender by firing blank discharges or, if necessary, would give chase. Often Confederate cruisers would parade the flags of other nations in order to trick enemy ships into disclosing their true identity. On the other hand, the officers of the *Shenandoah* would board vessels suspected of "wearing false colors" and require them to show bills of sale and other papers proving their neutral status. After the war had ended, even as late as June 28, 1865, the *Shenandoah* captured eight ships in Bering Strait. It was not until August 2 that Waddell learned from a British ship that the war was over.[34] Stopping further hostilities then, he proceeded to Liverpool, England, where the last of the Confederate flags was furled on November 6.

The Confederate cruisers did immense damage to the United States merchant marine. Not only did they capture two hundred and seventy ships, but they caused more than seven hundred ships to change to foreign registry. The *Alabama* alone was responsible for a $6,750,000 loss in American shipping. The destruction of ships and cargoes by the *Shenandoah* amounted to $887,059 according to certifications in its logbooks by a survey board of officers appointed by Waddell; but this sum seems to represent an incomplete account, and the damage done by the *Shenandoah* was probably much greater than a million dollars. After the Civil War the British government paid to the United States $15,500,000 for damages done to shipping as a result of England's allowing Confederate raiders built in England to escape.[35]

The conduct of the war on the sea and the inland rivers by the Confederacy was lacking in farsightedness and in vigor. It is true that Secretary Mallory realized the importance of ironclad ships and tried to develop this powerful weapon of war.[36] The navy received, however, very little cooperation from the administration or the military branch of the government. Skilled mechanics were absolutely essential in the building and operation of warships; but many such men volunteered or were drafted, and their unimaginative officers refused to detail them from the ranks of the army.[37] The manuscript letterbook of Admiral Franklin Buchanan (in the Southern Collection of the University of North Carolina) is filled with evidence of the lack of cooperation between the Confederate Army and Navy, suggesting the need of unity of command of all the armed forces of the struggling Confederacy. On the eve of the battle of Mobile Bay he wrote that his floating batteries and ships were only half manned, partly because of sickness, but especially on account of his inability to get men transferred from the army to the navy.[38]

The naval efforts of the Confederacy, except for the commerce raiders, were attended by misfortune. There was a heartrending destruction of warships which were being built, in order to avoid capture. The failure of the military authorities to remove obstructions in the James River so that the ironclads *Richmond* and *Fredericksburg* could go down to meet the enemy seems inexcusable. Although the Confederates were highly successful in destroying Northern merchant vessels, this type of warfare did not cause the

Union government to relax the blockade. One of the most serious mistakes which the Confederacy made was the inadequate defense of the port of New Orleans. When Farragut passed the forts below the city, the lack of resistance was pathetic. In recent times we have learned how difficult it is to capture a large city, if a determined resistance is made. But General Mansfield Lovell retreated with his small force without fighting, leaving the city to fall in Federal hands May 1, 1862. Finally, in any assessment of naval efforts, the failure of the Confederacy to avail itself to the fullest of opportunities to evade the blockade is striking. It is true that the whole economic condition of the South hampered it; yet the delusion of a short war was partly responsible for its ineffectiveness.

X

Crossing the Potomac

THE GLORIOUS victory of Second Bull Run elated the Southern people, and Lee concluded that the hour had struck to invade
the North. From one point of view this invasion was psychologi-
cally an error, for it aroused the North; but Lee hoped to free
Maryland, outfit and provision his army, gain many Maryland
recruits, and threaten Harrisburg and Washington. He thought
the defensive policy of President Davis was unwise. He wished to
retain the initiative. As Sir Frederick Maurice has pointed out,
Davis was unwilling to take great risks to gain great ends. But Lee
thought that a victory on Northern soil was the way to Southern
independence, and he was willing to take bold risks. When he
arrived in Maryland he advised the President that now was the time
to propose a peaceful settlement.[1]

On September 5, 1862, approximately fifty thousand soldiers of
the Army of Northern Virginia crossed the Potomac near Leesburg,
many of them singing "Maryland! My Maryland!" and marched
to Frederick. Proclaiming that he had come to liberate the people
of Maryland, Lee gave strict orders to his soldiers to respect the
property and rights of civilians. The Confederates were disappointed
at the cool welcome which they received, for few volunteers joined
the ranks of the invading army. Furthermore, the lack of good
marching shoes and the prevalence of diarrhea, aggravated by the
eating of green corn and apples, caused such a large number of the
men to straggle that Lee could not concentrate his forces efficiently.

Lee's generalship in this campaign has been severely criticized by
General James Longstreet as well as by the English Major General
Fuller, who observes that the Confederate general divided his com-
mand when he should have concentrated, with the special blunder

of sending Jackson and 25,000 men to capture Harpers Ferry.[2] His reason for this diversion was that he had expected the Federal garrison at Harpers Ferry to withdraw when he marched into Maryland; when it failed to do so he believed that he must capture it in order to protect his communications through the Shenandoah Valley. Furthermore had he not suffered a piece of bad luck he would have had adequate time to concentrate. A copy of his marching orders to his officers, Special Orders 191, which was wrapped around several cigars was dropped from the pocket of one of the couriers or generals at Frederick, picked up by a Union soldier, and carried to General George B. McClellan, who had been restored to the top Federal command after Pope's defeat. The document revealed that the Confederate troops were separated in four detachments, and gave him an excellent opportunity to attack before the invading army could be concentrated. When Lee learned of the loss of the orders the day after McClellan received them, he was in a desperate situation.[3]

The Federal army was twice as strong as the scattered and poorly equipped Confederate army. Marching from Washington, McClellan entered Frederick on September 12 shortly after the Confederates had departed. After the discovery of the marching orders he moved very slowly, to attack the scattered Confederate forces. Lee recalled his advance troops under Longstreet and Hill to hold the passes of South Mountain to protect the rear of his army at Maryland Heights which dominated Harpers Ferry. D. H. Hill and Longstreet fought gallantly at the passes (September 14) but were outflanked by the superior forces of the enemy and had to retire. Meanwhile Jackson had crossed to the south side of the Potomac and attacked the garrison of 13,000 men at Harpers Ferry, and it surrendered on September 15. On the evening before, Lee had made the bold decision to remain north of the river and fight at Sharpsburg, near Harpers Ferry and west of Antietam Creek.[4]

McClellan's caution gave Lee time to gather his troops at Sharpsburg. He attacked on September 16, and the battle of the 17th was the bloodiest day of fighting in the whole war. McClellan struck the Confederate left line, near the Dunker Church, in piecemeal and uncoordinated assaults.[5] An attack on the Confederate center, entrenched in a sunken road, led to terrible slaughter in the "Bloody Lane." [6] Failing to drive the Confederates from the field, he ordered

Burnside's corps to cross Antietam Creek and fall upon their right. The attack was made over a stone bridge (later called Burnside's bridge) which was held by the brigade of General Robert Toombs, who had just been released from arrest for insubordination. Toombs's men, fighting heroically against overwhelming force, yielded the bridge but held up the Federals long enough to permit the arrival of a division of 2,500 men under A. P. Hill from Harpers Ferry. Colonel D. B. Sanger, an able student of the Civil War, maintains that the brave and tenacious stand of the politician-general at the bridge prevented Lee's army from being thrust against the Potomac to destruction.[7] The Confederates retained possession of most of the battlefield. The Federal army lost approximately 12,000 men, killed and wounded, while the Confederate loss was more than 9,000.[8] Without renewing the battle the next day, McClellan permitted the Confederate army to cross the Potomac safely.

The checking of the Confederate invasion at Antietam (the Confederate name of the battle was Sharpsburg) was disastrous to the cause of Southern independence. The retreat of Lee not only gave Lincoln a favorable opportunity to issue his Emancipation Proclamation but it also chilled the enthusiasm of the British government to recognize the independence of the Confederacy.

Almost simultaneously with the invasion of Maryland, the Confederate army in Tennessee commanded by Braxton Bragg undertook to recover Kentucky. In August, 1862, General Edmund Kirby-Smith marched north from Knoxville with 12,000 men. He won a smashing victory over General William Nelson at Richmond, Kentucky, and easily occupied Lexington and the rich bluegrass country. The Confederate general had hoped that many Kentuckians would rally to his colors, but he sized up the human situation as follows: "The Kentuckians are slow and backward in rallying to our standard. Their hearts are evidently with us but their blue-grass and fat grass [cattle] are against us." [9] A detachment of his troops captured Cumberland Gap, but George W. Morgan, the Union general, and his command burned the fortifications at the Gap and escaped in one of the most dramatic episodes of the war.

With an army of nearly 28,000 men Bragg followed Kirby-Smith by a parallel route from Chattanooga to Glasgow, Kentucky. Federal troops under General Don Carlos Buell, numbering thirty-five thousand, hastened from Nashville to drive back the Confederate army. His immediate objective was Louisville on the Ohio River, from which the Louisville & Nashville Railroad ran southward providing a vital supply line for the Union armies in the West. Bragg defeated a small Union force at Munfordville, Kentucky, on Buell's route to Louisville and waited behind breastworks to be attacked; but Buell by-passed the Confederate army and raced safely to Louisville.

Chagrined, Bragg marched northward to Bardstown, but cautiously decided against advancing to Louisville when Kirby-Smith, who was trying to intercept General Morgan's retreat, failed to join him. He foolishly turned aside to honor the inauguration of Richard Hawes as the Confederate "governor" of Kentucky at Frankfort. The supposed governor was delivering his inaugural address when Federal guns interrupted the ceremony. Bragg then hastened to concentrate his scattered troops for battle against Buell, who had moved out of Louisville to clear the state of the rebel troops. The opposing armies met, October 8, 1862, by accident at Perryville in central Kentucky. Both generals were so uncertain as to the maneuvers and locations of the opposing armies that Buell employed fewer than half of his 58,000 men in battle and Bragg used only a third of his strength. In the "fog of battle," the Confederates came out victorious on the first day, and they expected to deliver a smashing blow the next day; but once more Bragg retreated after a half-victory, and his men abandoned Kentucky disconsolately. He explained the hasty return to Tennessee by saying that the Kentuckians, dominated by cupidity, had not arisen to aid the Confederates; but the real cause of the disappointing result, as General Joseph Wheeler saw it, was the neglect to concentrate and attack—a failure arising partly from the conduct of the campaign by two independent Confederate armies.[10]

The battle of Perryville has been correctly described as a "Western Antietam." Never again did the Confederacy have a chance to push its borders to the Ohio River. The withdrawal of Bragg's army from Kentucky occurred almost simultaneously with the defeat of a promising thrust by General Earl Van Dorn into northern Mississippi, which was held by Federal forces. On September 19 Sterling Price attacked the Federal garrison at Iuka, but was severely repulsed. Two weeks later the combined forces of Price and Van Dorn failed to recapture the heavily fortified rail center of Corinth in a desperate two-day assault. Thus the triple offensive of the Confederacy in the autumn of 1862 ended in frustration.

The Confederate armies again reverted to defensive strategy. On the day after Christmas, General William S. Rosecrans, who had succeeded Buell, marched from Nashville and attacked Bragg near Murfreesboro, thirty-two miles to the southeast. Before the battle the two armies faced each other at such a short distance that the Confederates could hear a Federal military band play "Yankee Doodle," and the Federals could hear a Confederate band strike up the stirring tunes of "Dixie" and "The Bonnie Blue Flag." The bloody battle of Stone's River, or Murfreesboro, began on the last day of the year. The opposing generals adopted almost identical plans of battle—a movement against the enemy's right flank. With thirty thousand men against the Union army of forty-four thousand, Bragg drove back the Federal right wing and might have won a great victory if General John C. Breckinridge had obeyed orders to lead up fresh troops for a final blow. Disappointed in his expectation of a Federal retreat on New Year's Day, he ordered an attack the following day on the left flank of the Union army, commanded by the Kentuckian, Thomas L. Crittenden. Another Kentuckian, John Breckinridge, commanding the operation on the Confederate side, protested against the attack as suicidal, for the Federal artillery was massed to command the approach. The attack of the 4th Kentucky Brigade under General Roger W. Hanson was repulsed with such fearful loss that it was later known as the Orphan Brigade.[11] Indeed, the casualties on both sides were terrific —25 per cent of the Confederate forces and 31 per cent of the Union army. It was a drawn battle—neither side knew who had won—until Bragg retreated beyond the Duck River to winter quarters at Tullahoma, Tennessee.

Counterbalancing defeats in the West, the Army of Northern Virginia was winning victories against great odds. Early in November, 1862, President Lincoln removed McClellan, who had what he called "the slows," from command of the Army of the Potomac and placed Ambrose E. Burnside in charge. Burnside, famous for his side whiskers, lacked confidence to command so large a force, but yielded to Lincoln's insistence. With a splendid army of 113,000 men, he marched from the vicinity of Warrenton southeastward to

Fredericksburg, where Lee had placed 78,000 men and 306 cannon on high ground in a line six miles long southwest of the Rappahannock River.

Federal delay in receipt of pontoons to bridge the river gave Lee time to concentrate his troops. On the other hand, the protecting screen of a heavy fog enabled Burnside's "grand divisions" under Franklin and Sumner to cross the river without serious opposition. On December 13, after laying five pontoon bridges, he ordered a frontal assault on the Confederate right at Hamilton's Crossing where Jackson was in command and on the Confederate left on Marye's Heights, which was held by Longstreet. The Union army made six heroic charges against the almost impregnable Marye's Heights, protected by a sunken road and a stone wall. The Confederate artillery and the infantry commanded by the Georgian T. R. R. Cobb repulsed them with terrible slaughter; but Cobb— noted for his fanatical devotion to secession—was mortally wounded. The fight five miles down the river at Hamilton's Crossing, the other storm center, was crucial in the Confederate victory, preventing the outflanking of the army.[12] In terms of numbers of soldiers engaged, Fredericksburg was the greatest battle ever fought in the Western Hemisphere, although a large portion of the Union army was not used in combat. Burnside was in tears over his terrible casualties— ten thousand brave men killed and wounded, while the Confederate loss was less than half that number. He explained his great reverses by lack of cooperation from his generals, and placed charges against Hooker and other general officers of his command.

Lee awaited another attack the following day, but Burnside retreated across the river during the night; thus the Confederates lost a magnificent opportunity to counterattack the Federal army with the river at its back. It is true that the Federal guns on Stafford Heights protected Burnside's troops, but the Confederates could have come so close to them that the Federal guns would have been dangerous to their own troops. Major General Fuller believed that Lee, by permitting the defeated army to recross the river, "missed his one and only opportunity of ending the war." [13]

After the Fredericksburg debacle "Fighting Joe" Hooker took command of the demoralized army (January 25, 1863). By the spring he gathered an army of 133,000 men, more than twice the size of the Confederate forces opposing him. He had boasted, on a visit by Lincoln to his army, "I have under my command the finest army on the planet." Leaving Sedgwick at Fredericksburg, Hooker with the major portion of his force crossed the Rappahannock above Fredericksburg and forded the Rapidan in an attempt to outflank and envelop Lee's army, southwest of Fredericksburg. On April 30 he established his headquarters in the plantation house of Chancellorsville, on the edge of a dense forest called "the Wilderness." Then, instead of completing his brilliant plan of envelopment, he lost his nerve and ordered his troops to intrench in the Wilderness, losing the initiative.

In this emergency Lee executed one of the boldest maneuvers in military history, which ended in dividing his army of 60,000 men into three parts. Stationing 10,000 under Early at Fredericksburg in front of Sedgwick's troops as a holding force, he marched toward the main Federal concentration at Chancellorsville plantation. Superbly audacious, he further divided his remaining troops and sent Jackson with 30,000 men across the front of Hooker's intrenched army by an obscure road through the Wilderness to attack the exposed right flank of the Union army.[14] In the meantime he himself made a demonstration against Hooker's front with a pathetically small force of 12,900 men.

The soldiers of "Stonewall" had the fanatical fervor of Cromwell's veterans; and as they attacked Hooker's rear right flank they gave the high rebel yell which they had so often used in hunting. The Federals were startled and were routed, the right flank rolling up on the main body. In the course of the battle, which lasted several days, Hooker was demoralized, and failed to bring to bear his cumbrous strength against Lee's divided forces in detail. Toward the end a pillar of the veranda of his headquarters was hit by a cannon ball and fell, knocking him unconscious. Outmaneuvered, he retreated across the Rappahannock on pontoon bridges during the night of May 5, having lost more than 17,000 men killed, wounded, and captured. Lee's casualties were 10,281 killed and wounded.[15]

The battle of Chancellorsville illustrates a striking characteristic of Civil War conflicts—their inconclusiveness, or the failure to destroy an enemy army. Although Lee won a victory he permitted the Federal army to escape. Some of his finest troops, the divisions of Pickett and Hood in Longstreet's corps, had been sent to southeastern Virginia to gather food supplies, protect the railroads, and possibly capture the Federal garrison at Suffolk. Longstreet was besieging Suffolk when he received orders to come to the aid of Lee, but he arrived after the battle was over. Had he been present, the victory might have been far more decisive.

The victory of Chancellorsville, none the less, marks "the high noon" of the Confederacy. In the eastern sector of the war the Confederates had shown that numerical superiority and industrial supremacy could not yet conquer the Confederate army commanded by Lee and Jackson. These two men gave the Confederates high élan as they fought, and to the common soldiers they seemed invincible. But Chancellorsville brought a tragic accident to the Confederacy: Jackson was fatally wounded by his own men as he was reconnoitering at twilight beyond the picket line.

After Chancellorsville the Confederate leaders were confronted with a fateful decision. Vicksburg, which controlled the Mississippi River, was in grave danger. The surrender of this strategic city and Port Hudson would cleave the Confederacy into two parts, cutting off the trans-Mississippi region with its man power and surplus food resources. The Mexican bases through which supplies for the army escaped the blockade would also be cut off. Should the Confederate command save this besieged city by dispatching troops from Lee's army to the West?

Beauregard and D. H. Hill favored such action while Longstreet, the most capable of Lee's corps commanders, advocated reenforcing Bragg's army for an invasion of Kentucky to the gates of Cincinnati.[16] Lee himself preferred another alternative—invasion of Pennsylvania and capture of some great Northern cities, Harrisburg, Philadelphia, or possibly Washington itself. He believed that success would convince the Northern people that the task of subduing the South was hopeless and cause them to demand that their government negotiate a treaty of peace. At this juncture John A. Roebuck, champion of the South in the British Parliament, introduced a resolution to recognize the Confederacy. The victory of Lee's army on Northern soil might well bring success to Southern diplomacy. In May, 1863, the Confederate cabinet considered the momentous question and consented to Lee's plan. Only Postmaster General Reagan protested, arguing that an invasion of the North would not draw Grant away from the siege of Vicksburg.

In June, Lee crossed the Potomac at Williamsport with seventy-five thousand seasoned veterans. His soldiers had a mystical faith in their leader, and many triumphs over incompetent Northern generals may have made Lee himself overconfident. Shortly before the advance Lee attended a magnificent review of Jeb Stuart's cavalry, nearly 10,000 strong, at Brandy Station, Virginia. But pride had a fall, for almost immediately after this parade of military might, the Federal cavalry under Major General Alfred Pleasonton crossed the Rappahannock River, surprised Stuart, and inflicted a near-defeat. This battle of Brandy Station (or Fleetwood) on June 9 was the greatest cavalry conflict of the war, a true equestrian battle, fought largely with outmoded sabers. Although the Federal cavalry was repulsed, it accomplished its mission by discovering that Lee's army was moving north. Robert Kean noted in his diary that the battle of Brandy Station was disgraceful. "Stuart is so conceited that he got careless—his officers were having a frolic at Col. Rosser's wedding party." [17]

Despite the apparent strength and élan of the invading army, it had serious weaknesses. Lee was suffering from rheumatism and seems to have lost temporarily his customary poise. Moreover, his staff was inadequate for formulating plans and drafting military orders. The death of Jackson had necessitated a reorganization of the army. The bald, lisping, one-legged, profane General Dick Ewell had succeeded to the command of Jackson's corps, and a new corps had been formed under A. P. Hill. Two out of three corps of Lee's army, therefore, were under officers inexperienced in high command, and there was a lack of integration and coordination between the units of the army. Furthermore, an essential part of Lee's grand strategy was that Beauregard should gather up scattered troops and make a feint at Washington. This part of the plan was not carried out. The Federal army consequently was not pinned down to protecting Washington and surprised Lee by its vigor in pursuit, catching him before he had concentrated his scattered forces.[18] On the eve of battle the Northern army received a capable commander when General George Meade succeeded Hooker. His ninety-nine thousand effective soldiers were a powerful force to oppose the Confederate invasion.

For information about the enemy Lee depended on the cavalry leader Jeb Stuart. On this critical occasion Stuart, eager to make good the reputation marred by the battle of Brandy Station, per-

suaded Lee to let him with three of his five brigades make an unwise foray around the Federal army, on which he lost touch with
his own army and failed to provide his commander with needed
information about enemy movements.[19] Neither Lee nor Meade
intended to fight a battle at Gettysburg, Pennsylvania, a short distance from Maryland. Lee planned to concentrate his army at near-
by Cashtown; but on July 1 the Confederate advance guard under
J. J. Pettigrew ran into the cavalry of Buford supported by the infantry of General John F. Reynolds at the village of Gettysburg,
precipitating the greatest battle of the Civil War.

Lee fought the battle at a great disadvantage. The Union forces,
numerically much stronger, seized strong defensive positions southeast of the town on Round Top, Little Round Top, Cemetery
Ridge, and Culp's Hill, which formed a gigantic fishhook pointed at
the town. The Confederate army formed a long thin line five miles
long on an opposite ridge, called Seminary Ridge, where the Lu-
theran Theological Seminary was located.

Lee, who was naturally combative and was concerned over the
problem of supply, determined to attack the Federal army, for the
alternative was to retreat. Longstreet, commander of the First Corps,
opposed his decision and urged, instead of an attack on the Union
army in its formidable positions behind stone walls and fences on
Cemetery Ridge, a flanking movement which would place the Confederate army between General Meade and Washington and thus
force him to attack. Lee vetoed this proposal as impractical.

On the first day of battle (July 1) the Confederate army was
temporarily victorious. After General Reynolds made the decision
to check the Confederate advance, more and more Federal troops
came to his support, while Confederate troops were marching up to
engage in fierce fighting with the enemy. In the afternoon Jubal A.
Early's division broke the resistance of the Federal troops, driving
them through Gettysburg and up the slopes of Cemetery Hill.
Early asked permission to attack the ridge, but his superior, General
Ewell, refused to take this risk.[20] It is the judgment of the English
Captain Battine that "the want of information due to the lack of cooperating cavalry lay at the root of the halting tactics of the Confederate leaders" on the first day of Gettysburg which lost them
decisive results.[21] A recent writer using Federal sources, however,

maintains that Ewell was right in not attempting to seize Cemetery Hill, because it was strongly occupied by fresh Federal troops.[22]

On the second day of battle (July 2) Longstreet's corps, which was late in arriving, was assigned to attack the Union left flank. Against this operation Longstreet argued with his commander, but finally obeyed orders. "Old Pete" was an experienced officer whom Lee described as "a very good officer when he gets in position and gets everything ready, but he is so slow." [23] The attack was intended to begin in the morning but did not take place until late in mid-afternoon, thus giving the Union army precious time to bring up reenforcements. Colonel Sanger's recent life of Longstreet absolves him from blame for slowness in launching the attack but holds him responsible for the disjointed manner in which Confederate operations on the right were carried out and finds that his personal leadership of troops in the attack caused him to lose direction of the battle as a whole.[24] Longstreet himself has pointed out that, while his 17,000 men were fighting, the other two Confederate corps remained idle, violating the supreme orders of the day for general battle and allowing Union concentration against his corps.[25]

Furiously attacking a salient held by the Union corps of Daniel Sickles, Longstreet's troops led by Hood drove the bluecoats through the Peach Orchard, across a wheat field, and over boulder-strewn Devil's Den; but the lateness of the attack gave the enemy time to concentrate strongly on Round Top and Little Round Top.[26] General Law, commanding the extreme right brigade of Longstreet's corps, found that Little Round Top was weakly held by Union troops and urged Longstreet to depart from strict adherence to orders and change the direction of the Confederate attack to seize this position which dominated the Union line; but Longstreet refused. Meanwhile Gouverneur Warren, Meade's acting chief of staff, discovered the Federal mistake and rectified it by rushing troops to hold this key to the Union left flank.

After the Confederate successes Meade called a council of war at his headquarters in the night of July 2 and proposed the question whether the army should retreat or remain at Gettysburg. The officers voted in favor of fighting it out at Gettysburg. Lee also had to make a hard decision. His supplies were low, his men were weary with marching, and reenforcements were coming to the enemy. He must make a last desperate effort to dislodge the enemy or retreat to Virginia. With great faith in the superiority of his troops, he decided to send fifteen thousand men under Generals George E. Pickett and James Johnston Pettigrew against the Union center. General Longstreet was ordered to supervise the attack, early on the following day, July 3.

To reach the Federals it was necessary to cross an undulating plain nearly a mile wide in the face of a powerful artillery and rifle fire which would enfilade the advancing troops. The Union center, commanded by able Winfield Scott Hancock and John Gibbon (reared in North Carolina and appointed to West Point from that state), was protected by stone fences and ridges. Against attacking this strong position Longstreet protested earnestly, declaring that no fifteen thousand men that had ever lived could succeed in such an undertaking. Lee held firmly to his decision.

General Pickett, who had been selected to lead the charge against the Union center, was a graduate of West Point, ranking in scholarship at the bottom of his class of fifty-nine members. Pettigrew, the second in command, had established such a distinguished academic record at the University of North Carolina that his brilliance is still a legend. Pickett represented the chivalry of the old South with its high sense of honor. He was devoted to his men, Virginians whom he thought of as gentlemen soldiers, although a few of them were "rather rough and uncouth and not, as are most of the men, to the manner born." On the day that he led the Confederate charge against Cemetery Ridge, he wrote to his betrothed, the beautiful LaSalle Corbell: "My brave Virginians are to attack in front. Oh, God in mercy help me as He never helped before! . . . Now I go; but remember always that I love you with all my heart and soul, with every fiber of my being." If Longstreet foresaw the doom that awaited Pickett's men and could hardly bring himself to give the final order, Pickett himself was cheerful; he wrote, "My brave boys were full of hope and confident of victory as I led them forth." [27]

The charge was scheduled to begin after the artillery had blasted the positions of the Federal army on Cemetery Ridge. At one o'clock the Confederate guns under E. P. Alexander began to fire, and soon the guns of the Federal army on Cemetery Ridge and Round Top replied. [28] The Confederate shells did little damage to Meade's soldiers. Furthermore, the Confederates did not have sufficient ammunition to give Pickett's men adequate artillery support after the charge began. Under the hot July sun the gray-clad troops, Virginians, North Carolinians, and men from Mississippi and Alabama, advanced across the plain toward the hills where the enemy lay, now ominously silent.

They marched as though on drill parade, with shining bayonets. At seven hundred yards, the Federal artillery began a terrific fire which mowed down the gray-clad soldiers. A handful, under the lead of General Lewis A. Armistead, penetrated the Union lines; but, unsupported, they were killed or captured. The broken remnants of Pickett's and Pettigrew's men retreated to the Confederate lines. The Union troops had a splendid opportunity for a counterstroke, but they did not follow. The battle of Gettysburg was over. Lee, sad yet serene of countenance, met Pickett and his shattered command with the words: "Your men have done all that men could do; the fault is entirely my own." [29] In the three days of fighting, the Confederate army lost 20,451 men killed, missing, and wounded; but the Union loss was 23,049.

For years afterwards, Confederate soldiers met in country stores, at courthouses, and at reunions, and argued the tantalizing question why the South lost the decisive battle of Gettysburg. Longstreet was usually the storm center of the discussions—Longstreet who after the war turned Republican. The modern expert on Lee's campaigns, Douglas Southall Freeman, has listed three fundamental reasons why the Confederates lost the battle: faulty coordination arising partly from the reorganization of Lee's army after the death of Stonewall Jackson, inadequate supply, and the Confederate extended line of battle. Contributing factors were Stuart's failure to inform Lee of the proximity of Meade; Ewell's indecisiveness on the first day in failing to capture Cemetery Hill; Longstreet's lack of cooperation, especially his conduct of the attack on the second day; and the errors of not giving Pickett an adequate force and of not supporting him properly after his troops reached the Federal positions. Lee, too, made the mistake of entrusting the carrying out of his battle plans to an officer who had no confidence in them. It was his practice not to give explicit orders to his corps commanders but allow them discretionary power. On this occasion he erred in neglecting to see that his orders were carried out.

William R. Livermore, a Union officer and a student of the Civil War, explains the Union victory at Gettysburg in terms of the superior strength of the Northern army, fighting behind entrenchments. He observes that Lee underestimated the skill of his opponent after having been uniformly successful against previous Federal commanders.[30] This analysis is supported by Kenneth P. Williams, who maintains that the real explanation of Lee's defeat was the strength of the Union army. In the Wigfall papers is a letter from Longstreet, dated August 12, 1863, before he had become embittered, which deserves careful consideration as an analysis of the Confederate defeat at Gettysburg. "Our failure in Pennsylvania," he wrote, "was due to our being under the impression that the enemy had not been able to get all his forces up. Being under this impression, General Lee thought it best to attack at once and we did attack before our forces got up and it turned out that the enemy was ready with his whole force and ours was not." War is to a great degree psychological, and the Confederate defeat can be explained in part in terms of the psychology of Lee. His mistakes, fully as much as the strength of the Federal army, were responsible.

On July 4 the Confederates began an orderly retreat in a great downpour of rain. At the Potomac River they waited for high water to subside and then crossed to Virginia. Meade had a splendid chance to attack the defeated army during the crossing and perhaps end the struggle; but he followed the advice of a council of war, at which five of his six corps commanders opposed an attack. When he thus allowed the Confederate army to escape, the Southern newspapers made light of the repulse at Gettysburg.

Most historians regard Gettysburg as the decisive battle of the war. A victory by Lee might have enabled the large number of peace advocates and antiwar Democrats in the North to swing the Federal government to a negotiated peace; or it might have led European nations to recognize the Confederacy. Lee could never again assemble such a splendid army; and the legend of his invincibility was destroyed. After this great defeat he offered his resignation as commander of the Army of Northern Virginia; but Davis refused to accept it.

On the day of the Confederate retreat from Gettysburg the strategic city of Vicksburg surrendered. It lay on a bluff two hundred feet above the Mississippi River with a corridor southward to

Port Hudson through which men and supplies could be transported from the states beyond the river and from Mexico. The city had great natural defenses, consisting of high bluffs, swamps, cane-brakes, and rivers. Grant had started a campaign against it in December, 1862, but the brilliant attack of General Earl Van Dorn on Holly Springs in northern Mississippi destroyed his depot of supplies and caused him to retire. Then Sherman at the end of the year tried to capture the city by an attack on Chickasaw Bluffs, its northern defense, but suffered a severe repulse.

In the spring of 1863 Grant returned to Vicksburg, which was defended by General John C. Pemberton, a friend of Jefferson Davis and a Northerner. Discovering that the upper defenses of the city were almost impregnable, Grant transported his army to the west bank of the Mississippi and marched his men southward. The fleet then ran past the stronghold and ferried the Union army once more to the east bank at Bruinsburg, sixty miles below Vicksburg (April 30). Thus he made a previously untried approach to Vicksburg, from the rear. In following this bold plan, he abandoned his line of communications and fed his army on the country.

In this grave crisis the Confederate War Department ordered Johnston by telegraph on May 9 to go to Jackson, the capital of Mississippi, and take charge of the armies in that area. When he arrived he ordered Pemberton to move out of Vicksburg and attack the rear of Grant's army while he engaged the front. One of the triplicate copies of the order was sent by a messenger who was a Union spy, and he promptly gave it to Grant. Pemberton delayed obeying the order, with the result that Grant was able to drive Johnston out of Jackson and then, turning westward, defeat Pemberton at Champion Hill (May 16).[31] When Johnston heard of the defeat and of Pemberton's withdrawal to the defenses of Vicksburg he ordered him to come out of the city, which he now regarded as a trap, for if Pemberton remained he would lose both Vicksburg and his army. But Pemberton, who had been strongly urged by President Davis to hold the city at all hazards, called a council of war at which it was decided to disregard Johnston's orders and remain. He was a victim of conflicting orders and his own indecision. Jefferson Davis and Johnston tried unavailingly to get the cooperation of troops west of the Mississippi under Generals Hindman, Holmes, and Kirby-Smith.

Failing in a grand assault, Grant began the historic siege of Vicksburg. Day after day he bombarded the doomed city in cooperation with the warships of Admiral David Porter on the river. The citizens dug caves in the hills as bomb shelters and lived in nervous tension. Their food supplies sank lower every day until some of the inhabitants began to eat mule meat and rats. Johnston vainly attempted to find some way for Pemberton's army to escape. Grant held on with a bulldog grip.

During this period Johnston wrote to the War Department in a profoundly pessimistic mood. He declared that he would need a force three or four times as large as he had in order to relieve Vicksburg. To obtain this force it would be necessary to withdraw troops from Bragg, which would mean the evacuation of Tennessee. The government must decide, he wrote, which state should be defended—Mississippi or Tennessee.[32]

After seven weeks of agony the doomed city was surrendered, July 4, 1863. In a long report defending himself from charges, Pemberton declared emphatically that he did not surrender on account of lack of food and supplies. He asserted that at the surrender his army had 40,000 pounds of bacon, 5,000 pounds of peas, and 51,000 pounds of rice; but his men were exhausted and emaciated by continuous service and exposure day and night for forty-seven days in the trenches, and his position had become hopeless.[33]

The garrison of approximately thirty thousand soldiers was paroled instead of being sent to Northern prisons. One hundred and seventy cannon and sixty thousand muskets of an improved make recently obtained from Europe were also surrendered. Pemberton was so disliked by the people of Vicksburg that he was mobbed as he left the city. Indeed, he was execrated throughout the South, especially because he had delivered the city to Grant on July 4. Yet this Northern-born officer, who had thirty years of honorable service at West Point and in the army of the United States, sacrificed more for the South and the cause that he thought was right than most Confederate officers who were born in the South.

The military importance of Vicksburg has probably been exaggerated, although the surrender on the day following the defeat at Gettysburg produced a psychological effect like a trauma on the Southern spirit. Port Hudson may have been more indispensable to

Confederate strategy and logistics, for it commanded the entrance to the Red River. When this Confederate fortress surrendered to General Banks a few days after the fall of Vicksburg, Lincoln rejoiced that "the Father of Waters again goes unvexed to the sea."

The fall of Vicksburg illustrated one of the weaknesses of the Confederacy; namely, its failure to use the food resources and man power of the trans-Mississippi region advantageously. Part of the failure rose from the unwillingness of Arkansas and Missouri troops to leave their states and fight east of the Mississippi. Another important cause was the incompetence of the military leaders sent west of the river, particularly Lieutenant General Theophilus Holmes, a North Carolinian who was in charge of the Trans-Mississippi Department with headquarters at Little Rock, Arkansas, and his subordinate Major General T. C. Hindman.

The Confederates constantly dreamed of recovering Missouri, using their positions in Arkansas as a base. In July, 1862, however, General Samuel Curtis captured Helena on the Mississippi River, thus obtaining for the Union army an excellent base to invade eastern Arkansas. The Confederate commander in this region, Major General Hindman, reorganized his forces and crossed into Missouri in September, establishing temporarily an outpost at Newtonia near Springfield. Forced to withdraw, he was planning another advance into the coveted territory when Holmes, prodded by the War Department, ordered him to bring his eleven thousand troops to Little Rock and proceed from there to the east bank of the Mississippi to help save Vicksburg. Hindman decided first to fight one more battle for the recovery of Missouri, and he was badly defeated on December 7, 1862, at Prairie Grove near Fayetteville, Arkansas.[34] Thus the reserve of Trans-Mississippi troops so desperately needed to defend Vicksburg was lost. After the fall of Vicksburg Major General Frederick Steele moved from Helena with approximately fourteen thousand men and fifty-seven guns to capture Little Rock. The eight thousand Confederates under Sterling Price evacuated the city on September 10, 1863.

Holmes was removed as commander of the Trans-Mississippi Department in February, 1863, and General Edmund Kirby-Smith was placed in charge with Shreveport, Louisiana, as his capital. Holmes remained, however, as a general in Arkansas and, on the day that Vicksburg surrendered, made an unsuccessful attack on

the Federal garrison at Helena. Especially after the fall of Vicksburg, Kirby-Smith ruled the vast region west of the Mississippi
almost as a Persian satrap, so that his department was humorously
called "Kirby-Smithdom." Indeed, the isolation of the region was
so great that the Confederate Treasury Department gave almost
independent powers to its agency at Marshall, Texas. The military
commander sent through the blockade huge quantities of cotton
which he purchased for three or four cents a pound and sold abroad
for fifty cents in gold, using the proceeds to import machinery and
supplies.

There was much dissension among the officers in the Trans-
Mississippi Department. General Richard Taylor, who was in
charge of western Louisiana, did not approve of the policies of his
chief. He thought that Kirby-Smith was wasting his strength in
seeking to recover lost territory to the neglect of areas that the
Confederates possessed: "the substance of Louisiana and Texas
was staked against the shadow of Missouri and northern Arkansas." [35] When Kirby-Smith tried to follow orders to send troops to
the aid of Vicksburg in the spring of 1863, Taylor thought the effort
was impractical; and so it proved. After the fall of that city individuals still could cross the Mississippi; but crossing became almost
impossible for organized bodies of troops or supplies.

XI

Society and Culture
in a War Atmosphere

THE COMING of the Civil War did not at first seriously disrupt the daily routine of the plantations and the little towns of the Confederacy. Indeed, the continuity of life in the Old South was preserved to a surprising degree especially in areas remote from battle. In the vivid diary of Catherine Ann Edmondston one may trace the effects of war on the plantation "Looking Glass" in eastern North Carolina. She continued to cultivate her garden with its tuberoses, magnificent dahlias, and sweet-smelling cape jessamines. She made blackberry wine, brandy peaches, and on one occasion put fifty hams in bags to hang up in the smokehouse. She vaccinated all the little pickaninnies, twenty-six of them, tried to prevent them from eating dirt, and taught them the catechism, which she regarded as a disagreeable task.

Childless, and commanding many servants, she had time to read widely: the poets of southern Europe from Tasso to Goldoni; Sismondi; Shakespeare's *Timon of Athens*; Milton; Macaulay's essay on Warren Hastings; Burton's *Anatomy of Melancholy*; *Morte d'Arthur*; and the diaries of Evelyn and Pepys. On May 2, 1861, Mr. Benton read poetry as she and her friends were sewing for the soldiers; but she wrote, "My mind was far away, all interest in anything but war driven away—the time for poetry is past." On May 18: "As for reading I have long given that up. I do not remember when I turn a page what was on the other side." But after the excitement of the first few months of war she took up reading again. She and her husband eagerly awaited newspapers telling of the fate of Confederate armies. Also she was interested in the gossip concerning prominent Confederate personalities, such as the report that Mrs. Jefferson Davis employed a white nurse for her baby, which Catherine Ann condemned as "disloyalty to the South." [1]

Gradually the shadows of war crept over the sunny, privileged life. On June 2, 1862, the overseer at "Looking Glass" plantation was conscripted, and Catherine Ann took over the job of weighing out the meat allowance for the eighty slaves—one-half pound of bacon a day for everyone over ten years of age. On March 25, 1862, she recorded that only forty acres of cotton had been planted whereas three hundred acres had been planted in 1861. On April 14 "Looking Glass" gave up its plantation bells for the Confederate cause and returned to the older way of calling the hands with the horn. On February 15, as Burnside invaded eastern North Carolina, she sent off her silver, brandy, and books to a place of safety. On February 17 came a requisition for one-fourth of the able-bodied men of the plantation to bring spades and axes and one week's provisions for work on military fortifications. On February 13 the Quartermaster requisitioned all the teams and wagons to move the equipment of a regiment. On May 3, 1861, she recorded: "Ladies who never worked before are hard at work making uniforms and tents." She raised flax to spin and make into cloth and knitted socks and made fatigue jackets and flannel drawers for the soldiers.

One of the most uncomfortable dislocations produced by war was "refugeeing"—civilians fleeing before invading armies. Bill Arp, the Southern humorist, remarked that the sufferings of Job were not to be compared with those of a refugee. When Burnside invaded eastern North Carolina in 1862 refugees in vehicles of every description crowded the roads to the interior. Catherine Ann Edmondston arrived at her father's plantation of "Connecanara" to find him entertaining nineteen white and seventy slave refugees. In the autumn of 1862 Federal forces captured Beaufort, South Carolina, and the planters in the neighborhood fled in panic before the invaders. Many of the Negroes ransacked and plundered the deserted homes of their fugitive masters.[2] The saddest of the refugees were the old people who had lost their homes and property. Among the uprooted persons of the Confederacy were a few de-

voted wives, like Mrs. John B. Gordon, who followed their husbands on their campaigns.[3]

The realistic history of the Confederacy cannot neglect to record
the role of the Confederate women in the rise and decline of the
morale of the people. At the beginning of the war they were as a
rule ardent rebels. Indeed, in many areas they were more defiant
than the men of the Federal government. Confident that the soldiers
of the Confederacy were far braver and more gallant than the
Northerners, they were sure that the war would be short. The
upper-class Southern women thought in romantic terms of the war
and were thrilled to see their men in colorful uniforms on caracol-
ing horses in parades. They formed sewing societies that made gay-
colored silk dresses into banners and flags, knitted socks, and sewed
shirts and underwear for the army.[4] At the railroad stations they
established canteens for soldiers. The young women were effective
recruiting agents by humiliating able-bodied men who did not
volunteer. Organizing Ladies Gunboat Societies to buy gunboats
for the Confederacy became a fad.

The war, moreover, offered an exciting outlet for the women in
dull little villages or on lonely plantations. The soldiers and officers
had to be entertained at dances, teas, picnics, etc. The war encouraged weddings, and Confederate weddings became gala affairs. The
social life of Richmond, where the brains and beauty of the Confederacy tended to gravitate, was fascinating. Here in the White
House of the Confederacy Varina Howell Davis, brimming with
zest for life, held many receptions and gay parties. The delightful
Diary from Dixie of Mary Boykin Chesnut, wife of a Senator from
South Carolina, and T. C. De Leon's *Belles, Beaux and Brains of
the Sixties* describe these aristocratic circles, where witty conversation flowed with champagne, sixty-year-old Madeira, cherry bounce,
eggnog, and mint juleps. As the war progressed, however, parties
became simpler, and women were forced to resort to various devices
to keep their wardrobes in a semblance of fashion. Nevertheless,
as late as Christmas Day, 1863, General John S. Preston entertained three generals, a Senator, and Mrs. Chesnut with a dinner
consisting of oyster soup, roast mutton, ham, boned turkey, wild
duck, partridge, plum pudding, sauterne, Burgundy, sherry, and
Madeira. "There is life in the old land yet!" Mrs. Chesnut exclaimed.[5]

The ante-bellum sentiment or sentimentality in social life was accentuated during these abnormal times. "Ladies" were liberated to some extent from the old social restraints and taboos. When the idol of the ladies, the handsome General "Jeb" Stuart, entered a Confederate town they would strew roses in his path and deck his horse with garlands. On one occasion his uniform was entirely shorn of buttons by aggressive females, and if he had given as many locks of hair as were requested he would have been entirely bald. Also, the tails of the chargers of all the military heroes were in imminent danger from hero worshippers. There was much kissing of the heroes by Southern girls. The caste system which had ruled social life in some sections of the South in peacetime tended to disintegrate in the common sacrifice of war. One of the pathetic pictures of Southern life was that of the high-born Mrs. Chesnut reading the bulletins of Confederate victory and defeat to illiterate soldiers who stood with cap in hand.

There is a strong tendency to think of Confederate women in terms of the upper class. Augusta Jane Evans of Mobile had women of the upper class primarily in mind when she expressed the belief on July 15, 1863, that slavery had adversely affected the character of Southern women. The abundance of servants inclined them to avoid systematic exercise, and although slavery gave them leisure to cultivate their intellects, they did not use it: "Thoroughly educated women are deplorably rare among us," she observed.[6] Nevertheless, planters were eager to have their daughters educated in "the ornamentals"—French, playing the piano, singing, drawing, painting, algebra, Latin.[7]

Furthermore, the diaries of Confederate women show that some of them had varied intellectual interests. Augusta Jane Evans, for example, read Buckle's *History of Civilization in England,* Mill's *Principles of Political Economy,* and Montesquieu's *Reflections on the Rise and Fall of Ancient Republics.* In November, 1862, she published an article entitled "The Mutilation of the Hermae" in the *Gulf City Home Journal.* Mrs. Chesnut read Thackeray, George Eliot, Dumas, *Uncle Tom's Cabin,* and translated French plays. Her companions, the Preston girls, translated Schiller from the German and were well versed in French. Cornelia Phillips Spencer in Chapel Hill absorbed culture from reading many books, and she could quote freely from Horace and other Latin writers. After the Civil War she was the most noted feminine intellectual in North Carolina, author of *The Last Ninety Days of the War in North Carolina*; and she was influential in reopening the University of North Carolina during the Reconstruction period.[8]

In various ways Southern women contributed to the war effort. Some of the more heroic turned to hospital work. The romantic conception of ladyhood tabooed their attending to the bodily needs of the wounded. Male nurses in the hospitals performed these disagreeable tasks. Nevertheless, energetic and practical women like Kate Cumming of Mobile, Ella King Newsom, and Captain Sallie Tompkins became hospital matrons and managers. Catherine Gibbon of Charlotte, North Carolina, established a hospital for soldiers at Yorktown and prepared herself for hospital work by reading the life of Florence Nightingale. Women served the wounded soldiers by reading the Bible to them, furnishing flowers and delicacies, writing letters for them, soothing their fevered brows and encouraging them to hope. The wives and mothers of soldiers rendered another important service by managing plantations while the masters were absent, keeping the Negroes at work and preventing them from running away to the Yankees. Many wives of farmers supported themselves and their children by plowing, planting crops, and harvesting. The frontier arts of spinning and weaving were revived in order to provide clothing for the family.

The war gave women an opportunity to enter new occupations. They entered schoolteaching, which had been monopolized by men, and were never to be expelled from it. During the last year of the war the Confederate Congress doubled the pay of the female employees of the government to compensate for the declining strength of Confederate paper money, in a law citing clerks and "cutters" in the clothing branch of the quartermaster's department, matrons in hospitals, and females engaged in preparing cartridges and other munitions in the Ordnance Department. The compensation to the women who sewed for the Confederate government was pathetically inadequate. "The government only allows us 50 cents a pr for lined pants and 75 cents for coats," wrote a North Carolina woman, "and there are few of us who can make over a dollar a day and we have upon an average from three to five helpless children to support." [9] Sherman's army destroyed a factory at Rossville, Georgia, in which four hundred girls made cloth for the Confederate government.[10]

The cult of chivalry has caused Southerners to describe the women of the Confederacy in highly romantic terms. A corrective may be found in the letters of Northern soldiers, who met chiefly the plain folk of the Confederacy. They found that the filthy practice of chewing and dipping tobacco with a sassafras brush was prevalent among the women of farm families. An Illinois captain wrote from Scottsboro, Alabama: "I went to the nearest house to camp today, to beg a little piece of tallow. . . . I sat down by a fire in company with three young women, all cleanly dressed, and powdered to death. Their ages were from 18 to 24. Each of them had a quid of tobacco in her cheek about the size of my stone inkstand, and if they didn't make the extract fly worse than I ever saw in any country grocery, shoot me." A regimental surgeon wrote that he had met on a Memphis street an attractively dressed lady with "a little stick in her mouth." "As I approached her she removed it and spit upon the pavement a great stream of *Tobacco Juice*. She then returned the little stick which I saw had a little swab on the end of it. *She* was dipping." An Illinois officer stationed in northern Mississippi wrote: "Snuff-dipping is an universal custom here, and there are only two women in all Iuka who do not practice it. . . . Sometimes girls ask their beaux to take a dip with them during a spark. I asked one if it didn't interfere with the old-fashioned habit of kissing. She assured me that it did not in the least, and I marvelled." [11] Northern soldiers commented on the number of mulatto children they saw, on the great scarcity of schoolhouses in the land of Dixie, and on the general backwardness of the South, particularly in the use of agricultural machinery and tools. Some Northern soldiers were impressed by the beauty of Southern girls and the kindness and warm-hearted nature of many Southern matrons.

Among the women of the Confederacy, as among the men, were all kinds. There were brave and patriotic women with a flair for adventure, like Belle Boyd and Mrs. Rose O'Neal Greenhow, who risked their lives to spy for the Confederacy. There were women who smuggled medicines, other products, and even military supplies through the lines beneath their voluminous crinoline skirts. There were thoughtless females whose personal vanity encouraged the blockade runners to import feminine luxuries. There were women whose letters to the soldiers at the front, as General Lee observed, weakened their morale and caused them to desert. Nevertheless, Southern women as a whole showed admirable self-sacrifice and fortitude during the long war which made many of them widows and reduced them to poverty.

One sad consequence of the conflict was its disruptive effect on schools and colleges.[12] Although teachers were exempt from conscription, a large proportion of them volunteered. Jesse R. McLean of Fayetteville voiced the feeling of many teachers when he wrote, on July 1, 1861, to Calvin H. Wiley, superintendent of common schools in North Carolina, "I have the military fever very strong"; [13] and a year after North Carolina seceded L. A. Paschall of Oxford reported to Wiley that many district schools had closed on account of lack of teachers: "We have 4 or 5 female teachers in this county but not one male." [14] The female teachers in the North Carolina common schools increased during the war from 7½ per cent to 40 per cent.[15]

Wiley strove heroically to save the state public-school system, particularly by preventing the diversion of school funds to war purposes. He received many letters from chairmen of county school boards informing him that the county courts had ordered such funds to be used for war purposes or other local needs. On May 27, 1861, D. C. McIntyre wrote from Robeson County, which had been a unit for secession, that "the Board thinks that schools would do but very little good during the crisis" and all the money from the Literary Fund, the state educational appropriation, and from local taxes should be applied to war purposes.[16] The citizen of Oxford cited above lamented further: "Our county court at the May term refused to levy any school tax, saying the Schools must stop until the war is over."

Superintendent Wiley sent out printed circulars to county officials and wrote to prominent political leaders urging the supreme importance of preserving school funds for educational purposes. The circulars brought some discouraging replies, but others that were enlightened and heartening, including that from John S. Lane of New Bern: "I think as you remark that it is perfectly suicidal to use the school funds for war purposes." [17] Fortunately the powerful influence of Governor Zebulon B. Vance supported the forces seeking to prevent the diversion of the state Literary Fund to war purposes. Although various counties appropriated local school taxes for military purposes Wiley was able to write at the close of the war, "God made me an instrument in preventing the diversion of the Literary Fund for war purposes." [18] This devoted educational statesman remained superintendent of common schools throughout the war, serving for four years on a salary "hardly worth $200 in par funds." In 1863 the state still had 875 teachers, who received an average of $25 per month for a three- or four-months school year.

One of the most serious handicaps of Confederate education was the lack of schoolbooks, which had been largely imported from the North. The need was met to some degree by the writing and publication of Confederate books free from abolition sentiments, which exalted Southern society. In 1862 the publishing house of Sterling, Campbell & Albright of Greensboro, North Carolina, began publishing "Our Own Series" of readers, grammars, and spellers as well as the much-used Latin grammar of William Bingham of the Bingham School at Mebane, North Carolina. A *Confederate Spelling Book* (published at Macon, Georgia, 1861) arose to challenge Webster's famous blue-backed speller. *The First Dixie Reader,* by Mrs. H. B. Moore, was published at Raleigh in 1863; and a *Southern Confederacy Arithmetic,* by the Reverend Charles Leverett, at Augusta, Georgia, in 1864.

The Geographical Reader for Dixie Children, published in 1863, may be taken as an example of the numerous patriotic schoolbooks published in the Confederacy. Portraying the slaves as happy, contented, and well cared for, the writer inculcated the idea that slavery was not a sin, but admonished, "Let all the little boys and girls remember that slaves are human, and God will hold them to account for treating them with justice." To him, which side would win the war depended entirely on God's favor. Obviously he believed that God was partial to the South, for there were more praying people on the Confederate side than on the Yankee side. "The Southern Confederacy," he observed, "is at present a sad country; but President Davis is a good and wise man, and many of the generals and other officers in the army are pious. Then there are many good praying people in the land; so we may hope that our cause will prosper." [19] Actually not half of the Southern people, according to estimates based on the census of 1860, were members of a church.

The impact of the Civil War on colleges and universities was perhaps even more damaging than on schools. The excitement among students at the beginning was so great that the notation of a University of Mississippi student in his diary probably represents the general attitude: "I cannot study and I wish to join a Horse Company." [20] Many of the Southern youth believed that the conflict would be short, and that unless they volunteered immediately they would miss the glamour and adventure of fighting for Southern independence.

Volunteering and conscription resulted in the closing of many Southern colleges and universities. In 1861 the University of Mississippi was closed for the duration of the war; in 1863, South Carolina College, Franklin College (the University of Georgia) and Louisiana State Seminary (predecessor of Louisiana State University); and in December, 1864, the College of Charleston. The universities of Virginia, Alabama, and North Carolina remained open through the war, but the University of North Carolina closed its doors during the Reconstruction period from 1870 to 1875. Some small church colleges, such as Davidson College (Presbyterian) in North Carolina and Wofford College (Methodist) in South Carolina, managed to survive the war by opening a preparatory department. The closing of the University of Mississippi was particularly tragic, for by 1860–1861 it was making remarkable progress under the leadership of Frederick A. P. Barnard, a Northern scientist, who returned North and became president of Columbia College. Thus the South lost its ablest leader in college education. The buildings of the University of Alabama and its library were burned near the close of the war by Federal raiders after its cadets, mere boys, had fought gallantly in its defense. Federal troops also destroyed the buildings of the Virginia Military Institute at Lexington and so damaged the buildings of William and Mary College that Congress after the war appropriated $64,000 to this institution as compensation.

Colleges and universities made strenuous efforts to secure exemption from the draft for their students. In July, 1862, when only thirty-nine students were left at the University of Georgia, Chancellor Lipscomb urged President Davis to permit students under twenty-one years of age to remain at the university until their services were needed on the battlefield; but Davis replied that he had no authority to make this concession.[21] However, when President Swain of the University of North Carolina requested in October, 1863, that the War Department exempt juniors and seniors until they were graduated, Davis consented, basing this decision on the folly of grinding up "the seed corn" of future leadership of the nation.[22] A year later, when there was "a rampant spirit" in Congress according to Senator William A. Graham "to put everybody in the ranks of the army," the Board of Trustees of the University of North Carolina ordered the president of the university to correspond with the Confederate government to prevent the withdrawal of the previous exemption of juniors and seniors from the draft.[23] When Graham presented the University's plea, President Davis gave him no encouragement, saying that Lee needed men for the army and they must be supplied from some source.[24] Accordingly "the seed corn" of the Confederate republic was cast into the hopper.

The War for Southern Independence was at first stimulating to Southern writers. Prior to the war the literary profession, with the exception of journalism, had not been highly regarded by the plantation society. William Gilmore Simms and Professor Francis Lieber at South Carolina College, author of *Civil Liberty and Self-Government,* had repeatedly complained of the low esteem in which writers were held.[25] Paul Hamilton Hayne of Charleston wrote in 1859 to James Russell Lowell, editor of the *Atlantic Monthly,* that he was living in "an uncongenial atmosphere" for a literary aspirant, and that it was discouraging "to know that his *very profession* is looked upon with contempt, or, at best a sort of half-pitying patronage." [26] Southern writers were subject to the romantic mood of the period and to the concept of chivalry which gave to their work an artificiality and sentimentality remote from actual life. The war, however, was accompanied by a surge of regional patriotism and of heroism which furnished real emotions and material for a sincere literature.

This evocation by the war of deep poetic emotion is particularly illustrated by Henry Timrod, "the poet laureate of the Confederacy." Timrod was thirty-two years old when his state seceded; and despite poverty, ill health, and a middle-class background (his grandfather had been a German merchant tailor) he had attained some literary prominence in his native Charleston. For ten years after leaving the University of Georgia he had taught school, writing romantic verse, contributing to the *Southern Literary Messenger,* and winning the friendship of the Charleston literati, particularly of Simms and Hayne, who frequented John Russell's bookshop. Too poor to buy an officer's uniform, he enlisted as a private in a South Carolina regiment and was detailed to serve as a clerk at regimental headquarters.[27] After the battle of Shiloh he went to Corinth as a war correspondent for the Charleston *Mercury.* He confessed that the object of this expedition was to earn money, $6 a day, in order that he might marry Katie.[28] Contracting tuberculosis, he was discharged from Confederate service; and in 1864 he became associate editor of the *South Carolinian* at Columbia.

In the early part of the war Timrod wrote some of his best work, notably "The Cotton Boll," in which he portrayed the fleecy staple as ruling the world, and "Ethnogenesis," hailing the rise of a glorious young republic. Perhaps the loveliest poem of this period is "Spring," which begins,

> Spring with that nameless pathos in the air
> Which dwells with all things fair,

and concludes with the thought that the season will bring military campaigns to desecrate the beauty of nature. Here Timrod reveals himself as a true artist with a spiritual love of nature. After the defeat of the South he wrote his exquisite Magnolia Cemetery Ode to the fallen Confederate Soldiers.

As the war went on, however, its hardships and discouragements adversely affected Timrod's poetic talent. On August 25, 1864, he lamented to Hayne: "I have not written a line of verse for a twelve month. All the poetry in my nature has been fagged out of me, I fear. I work very hard—besides writing the leaders of the paper I often descend into the local column, as you must have noticed by such articles as *Arsenal Hall* and the *Troubles of a Midsummer Neighbor.* My object is to show that a poet can drudge as well as duller men and therefore I don't complain. But oh Lord! for leisure enough to breathe occasionally the divine air of the Aonian Mount." [29] The physical difficulties which the deteriorating economy of the South imposed are illustrated in Timrod's apology for using a pencil in his correspondence. "Pens and inks are now so wretched in quality that I have almost entirely eschewed them."

In the summer of 1864 Timrod was in very low spirits concerning his future as a literary man. His friends had sought to publish an illustrated edition of his poems in England, but the project had evaporated in smoke, "the fate of every small poet who has no money." The buoyant hopes and dreams of the creation of a new nation expressed in "Ethnogenesis" had by this time faded. "The war, business and its troubles," he wrote to Hayne, "have fallen like a blight on that fancy which once would have found a number of subjects to touch and interest us both. I can only condole with you on the condition of the country, and ask the eternal questions, what do you think about it, and can you see the end? The end—deuce take it—I fear it will seem like the Irishman's rope, cut off." [30] The shadows grew darker for this shy idealistic and artistic young Southerner, the outstanding poet of the Confederacy, until extreme poverty forced him to sell the family furniture and "to eat" some silver forks and a huge bedstead. In 1867 he died of tuberculosis.

Paul Hamilton Hayne, like Timrod, was passionately devoted to the South. A member of an aristocratic family, he cherished an illusion that Southerners were made of finer clay than Northerners. After the disaster of Roanoke Island he wrote to John Reuben Thompson that the South must fight to the last, proudly declaring that "the blood of the Cavaliers can never succomb [sic]." [31] The defeat at Roanoke Island had a profound and melancholy effect on him. To his wife he confessed the foreboding that the fate of the Confederacy hung on Great Britain's recognition—"otherwise, a long desperate war with the scoundrel government of the Yankees" lay ahead.[32] At the beginning of the conflict he served in the garrison at Fort Sumter, where he daily looked out on the Federal blockading fleet, which enraged him. His letters to his wife reveal one reason why South Carolina took such an extreme stand in defending slavery. In Fort Sumter he heard rumors of a slave insurrection in Charleston, where she was living. He wrote to her, December 12, 1861: "I have spent a night of such agony that I wonder to find this morning my hair has not turned gray. We all thought here that an insurrection had broken out, and that the whole city was doomed." Actually, Charleston had a disastrous fire that was thought to have been started by slaves.

Hayne's absorption in military duties, particularly in artillery practice with gentlemen officers, seems to have greatly interfered with his literary life. On February 15, 1862, he remarked that he had written only one war poem; but two weeks later he exulted to his wife: "The ancient poetical 'afflatus' has strangely come over my spirit again so that I have been composing all sorts of lyrics, chiefly of a patriotic order." [33] On April 8 he declared "The poetic vein is at flood-tide." Much of his poetic work, such as "The Blockaders," appeared in the Charleston *Mercury* or in the *Southern Illustrated News* of Richmond, where on January 3, 1863, he published "Our Martyrs." Verses were inspired by the bombardment of Vicksburg, by the exploits of Stonewall Jackson's soldiers, by the glamour of John Hunt Morgan, and by the heroic defense of Charleston against the attacks of the Federals ("Charleston at the Close of 1863").

Although the war stimulated Timrod and Hayne to produce good poetry, their mentor and inspiring friend, William Gilmore Simms, suffered a decided literary decline. He was fifty-five years old when the war began, and his great romantic tales lay in the past.[34] A devoted lover of South Carolina, rewarded with neglect and ingratitude, Simms wrote ardent patriotic editorials for the *Mercury* and some heroic verse. But he was overwhelmed with a world of troubles and found composition difficult. In the summer of 1863 he wrote to Hayne: "But my head is too full of anxiety to suffer me to write and though I have a contract for some $200 worth of prose, I find myself unable to divert my thoughts from the crisis in which the country trembles in suspense. What I write is in a spasm, a single burst of passion." [35] He could not endure the drudgery of revision, and "the horrible corruptions and blunders of the press had disgusted me with every column." He did write a serial for the *Southern Illustrated News* entitled "Paddy McGann, or the Demon of the Stump," about an Irishman beset by a shrewish wife and the hallucination of a devil. During the war years his beloved plantation house, "Woodlands," with his fine library was burned and he lost by death his wife and several of his thirteen children.

These personal griefs, however, were sublimated by his sadness over the disasters to the Southern cause. The burning of Columbia aroused him to write a graphic and eloquent pamphlet entitled, "Sack and Destruction of the City of Columbia, S.C." Harassed by the task of keeping his plantation going, he expressed a feeling that comes over many men of ambition: "Life seems escaping from me —frittered away in small things and untraced details." He was a devoted Christian, and when his beloved wife died in 1863 he wrote to Hayne: "We live too much for the world, my dear Paul. It is a poor affair. This ambitious struggle after greatness is a vanity." [36]

War experiences seem to have animated youthful Confederate poets. While Sidney Lanier was in the signal corps near Bacon's Castle in Virginia, he had leisure to court the lovely Virginia Hankins and talk literature with her and to read the German authors, Novalis and Jean Paul Richter, who influenced his novel *Tiger-Lilies*, which he began at the end of 1863.[37] James Ryder Randall, a young professor at Poydras College in Louisiana, appealed to his native state to join the Confederacy in his poem, "Maryland, my Maryland." Father Abram Joseph Ryan of Norfolk, Virginia, a chaplain in the Confederate Army, wrote "The Sword of Robert Lee," one of the noblest of the war poems. Francis Orray Ticknor, a Georgia doctor in a Confederate hospital, composed "Virginians of the Valley," celebrating the Virginian soldiers as:

> The Knightliest of the Knightly race,
> That since the days of old
> Have kept the lamp of chivalry
> Alight in hearts of gold.

Perhaps the most touching narrative poem that came out of the war was Ticknor's "Little Giffen," about the death of the Tennessee drummer boy.[38]

The war letters of John Henry Boner of the little Moravian community of Salem, North Carolina, illustrate some characteristics of Confederate poets. Like Simms, Hayne, and Timrod, he had great difficulty in finding a vocation in Southern society. The others had studied and abandoned the law, the gentleman's profession in the old South. He was prevented by ill health and by devotion to his mother from joining the Confederate Army. During the war years he studied medicine, read Wistar's *Anatomy,* tried to get a teacher's position, learned the printer's trade, and briefly went into journalism in his native town. Like other Southern poets his chief publishing medium was the newspapers, which botched his poems with absurd errors. Boner described himself as a dreamer ill suited to the practical world: "Whenever my soul is *too full* of joy or sadness I write my song as a bird would warble his lay." [39] The striking characteristic which distinguishes the Confederate poets from modern poets is their deep religious feeling. To Clara Dargan in South Carolina, a graduate of Salem Female Academy and an amateur litterateur, Boner wrote a few days before his nineteenth birthday: "I desire to be a Christian. Pray for me. . . . I feel that I am a miserable wretched wilful sinner." [40]

The outstanding novelists of the Confederacy were John Esten Cooke of Virginia and Augusta Jane Evans of Mobile, Alabama. A member of an aristocratic family, Cooke was proud of the baseless tradition that Virginians were descended from Norman, Cavalier stock while the Yankees were of Anglo-Saxon, plebeian origin. Indeed, he viewed the past of his section with "rose colored goggles of enormous magnifying power." [41] Before he became a soldier he published two novels, *Leather Stocking and Silk* and *The Virginia Comedians*. As an aide-de-camp on Jeb Stuart's staff he discontinued writing novels. Instead, he kept a notebook of his war experiences (preserved in Duke University Library) and published some sketches of camp life in the *Southern Illustrated News*. But his important literary work during the war was *The Life of Stonewall Jackson,* published in 1863, which presented the great general and the Southern cause in such an appealing light that a United States Army order forbade its circulation in Kentucky. Out of the war Cooke came with a philosophy exalting self-control and the virtue of being "the considerate gentleman." [42] He had gained, too, much literary material which he later worked up into the novels *Surry of Eagle's Nest* (1866) and *The Wearing of the Gray* (1867).

Augusta Jane Evans's novels were read by soldiers and civilians with an enthusiasm that would compare with the popularity of Margaret Mitchell's *Gone with the Wind* in the twentieth century. By 1860 she was already a celebrity, having published two popular novels, *Inez: A Tale of the Alamo* (1855), and *Beulah* (1859). *Beulah* developed the theme of the victory of religious faith over skepticism. In the secession crisis she was a zealous defender of slavery and advocate of secession, scornfully rebuking the Tennessee authoress, Mrs. L. Virginia French, who asked her to sign a memorial to the Georgia legislature to forestall the secession of that state. During the war she served as a nurse in a camp hospital and published at Columbia in 1863 the novel, *Macaria; or, Altars of Sacrifice,* dedicated "To the Brave Soldiers of the Southern Army" and incorporating a report of the battle of Bull Run which General Beauregard had sent to her. *Macaria* is full of Confederate propaganda, portraying the secession movement as a revolt of conservatives and condemning both abolitionism and demagogism. Miss Evans wrote with warm sentiment and in a moralizing vein, and made her books palatable to her generation, which was hungry for culture, by interspersing commentaries upon art, literature, music, and philosophy.[43] In 1866 she published the most popular book, after *Uncle Tom's Cabin,* that had been issued in America up to that time: *St. Elmo.*

The romanticism and sentimentalism which dominated literature in the South before and during the war extended even to its humor. Charles Henry Smith, "Bill Arp," the chief humorist of the Confederacy, well illustrates this unusual blend. Born in Lawrenceville, Georgia, the son of a Yankee merchant, Smith clerked in his father's store and later practiced law in Rome, Georgia. In 1861, while he was in the Confederate Army, he began to write letters to the local newspapers addressed to "Mr. Abe Linkhorn" and signed "Bill Arp." The letters were published in book form in 1866 entitled *Bill Arp, So Called,* and later he published *The Farm and the Fireside: Sketches of Domestic Life in War and in Peace* (1892), and *Bill Arp: From the Uncivil War to Date, 1861–1903.*

These letters purporting to come from a country bumpkin and therefore full of misspellings and homely colloquialisms served a useful purpose; "the minds of the people," Smith observed, "needed relaxation from the momentous and absorbing interests of the war."[44] Bill Arp's letters and sketches are permeated with nostalgia for the simple pleasures of country life in the South, and they point up the frailties of Confederates, such as the attempt to avoid the draft (conscription "developed more rheumatics and chronics than was thought possible to exist in a limestone country"), the exactions of extortioners, the comical aspects of the Georgia militia, the scramble to leave Atlanta before Sherman occupied the city, and the egotism of Governor Joseph Brown. Bill Arp's style is often mock-heroic. Strongly patriotic, he upheld Jefferson Davis in the quarrel with Brown, Stephens, and Toombs over conscription and the suspension of the writ of habeas corpus; but he criticized the Currency Act of 1864, which seemed to him to be a violation of good faith.

The war economy of the South, very surprisingly, did not stop the publication of a considerable number of books. Confederate presses published school texts with a Southern flavor, numerous Bibles for soldiers, military manuals, as well as one hundred and five volumes of belles-lettres. West & Johnson, of Richmond, the most important press of the Confederacy, published nine volumes of belles-lettres during the war period including one edition of Augusta Jane Evans's *Macaria*, the most popular novel written by a Confederate citizen, which by 1864 had been issued in two editions of ten thousand copies each. The *Southern Illustrated News* boasted on November 2, 1862, that "the firm of West & Johnson of Richmond has issued more new books from original manuscripts during the past year than any firm in Yankee land." [45] In Mobile, Sigmund Goetzel & Company published nine volumes of belles-lettres during the Civil War. Specializing in foreign works, this firm published Bulwer-Lytton's *Strange Story*, Victor Hugo's *Les Misérables*, and a translation of the German work of Luise Mühlbach. Despite a severe paper shortage, the presses of the Confederacy published forty-two works of belles-lettres in 1864, a larger number than in any previous year of the war. [46]

The most popular foreign novel in the Confederacy by far was Victor Hugo's *Les Misérables* (which gave a nickname to the ill clad, ill fed Confederate soldiers, "Lee's Miserables"). West & Johnson published an edition of this from a Northern translation but carefully omitted the passages reflecting Hugo's abolitionism. The reviewer in the *Southern Literary Messenger* regarded it as a sublime work, marred only by "the blotch" of Hugo's antislavery views, but was confident that a short sojourn by the author in the South would have changed all this. [47] Another popular foreign novel was Dickens's *Great Expectations*. Kemp Battle, president of a small North Carolina company constructing a railroad to the Deep River coal field and later president of the University of North Carolina, read an imported copy of it on horseback during a surveying tour for his company. The ante-bellum taste for Scott in the South persisted through the war. While Johnston's army was at Dalton, Georgia, John Green of Kentucky read *The Bride of Lammermoor* as well as Dumas's *Three Musketeers* and *Les Misérables*; and he and a companion in a rifle pit during the siege of Atlanta read aloud to each other *The Heart of Midlothian*. The firing of the Federal guns so interrupted this charming story that Jim Bemis, the companion, exclaimed, "The Dag-Gone Yanks have no soul for literature." [48]

Fortunately for writers, the war came near its end before it destroyed the prominent Southern magazines or prevented the founding of new magazines. The *Southern Literary Messenger,* edited by Dr. George W. Bagby, the humorist, continued to be published at Richmond until 1864.[49] Its circulation was so small that it could afford to pay its editor a peacetime salary of only $300, which was increased in 1863 to $400 in Confederate currency, worth $20 in coin. It published romantic verse and sentimental stories, usually signed by initials or by a nom de plume. Its editorial column supported President Davis and the vigorous prosecution of the war. One of its important features was a serial history of the war by Robert R. Howison, the author of a history of Virginia.

The lower South at the outbreak of the war had two excellent periodicals: *Southern Field and Fireside* of Augusta, Georgia, and *De Bow's Review* of New Orleans. *Southern Field and Fireside,* a literary, agricultural, and horticultural weekly for farmers and planters, flourished during the war with at least 13,000 subscribers in 1864. The stringency of war conditions finally forced it to stop publication on October 29 of that year. It offered prizes for literary publications, most of which were won by women.[50] *De Bow's Review,* which had so zealously encouraged the industrial and agricultural development of the South, moved during the war from New Orleans to Richmond, where it became largely political in nature and a strong defender of the Confederacy. In August, 1862, after it had lost over half of its subscribers—in Louisiana, Texas, Arkansas, and parts of states overrun or isolated by the Union armies—it suspended publication; but a year later it revived publication briefly at Columbia, South Carolina.[51]

Three new literary publications—the *Countryman,* the *Magnolia,* and the *Southern Illustrated News*—were founded in the Confederacy in 1862. The *Countryman* was a unique weekly, published on a plantation near Eatonton, Georgia, and printed with a hand press. The editor, Joseph Addison Turner, a cultivated planter lamed from childhood and thereby prevented from entering the army, described himself as "Independent in Everything, Neutral in Nothing." He favored, for example, the unpopular policy of educating the Negroes.[52] One of his services to literature was to employ and train Joel Chandler Harris to the profession of journalism and literature.[53] The *Countryman* was self-supporting during the war, and at one time had nearly two thousand subscribers scattered through the Confederacy.

When the *Southern Illustrated News* first appeared in September, 1862, there was sunshine over the Confederacy, for McClellan's great invasion had been repulsed and Southerners were hopeful for the future. This weekly described itself as "a News and Literary Journal for Southern Families" and promised its subscribers that it would be "a high-toned Southern journal containing not a word calculated to grate harshly upon the ears of the most refined and delicate in feeling and thought." [54] It published martial poems like "The Southern Flag," by the Reverend John C. McCabe, "The Empty Sleeve," by George W. Bagby, and the anonymous "Stonewall Jackson's Way"; sketches with pictures of prominent generals; a few engravings and cartoons; and an editorial section entitled "The Times." It was very patriotic, making light of defeats and cheering its readers with optimistic predictions—as on November 24, 1864, that Grant's failures at Petersburg demonstrated the hopelessness of efforts to defeat the South. Like the *Magnolia,* it appealed to Southerners to support magazines of the Confederacy because they were free from the fanaticism of Northern periodicals. On January 3, 1863, the editors proudly announced: "We have succeeded. The demand for each weekly issue is greater than our presses will satisfy." They boasted that their magazine had the whitest paper and the best ink in the Confederacy, that they had sent agents to England to contract with Dickens, Wilkie Collins, and Thackeray for original works, and that so pressing was the demand for the *Southern Illustrated News* that it had to curtail advertising in order to save paper for larger issues.

The theater also flourished, notably in Richmond and Charleston; but most of the patrons were soldiers and transients. At the beginning of the war the casting of roles was made difficult when a majority of the actors returned to the North. In November, 1861, John Hill Hewitt, the best known Southern playwright and stage manager, opened the Richmond Theater, which—with its successor the New Richmond Theater, managed by D'Orsay Ogden of English birth, and the Varieties—entertained throngs of soldiers and civilian visitors. In Augusta, Georgia, in 1863, the Thespians had a successful run of seventy nights, presenting such plays as "King Linkum the First," "The Prisoner of Monterrey," "The Vivandière," and "Still Waters Run Deep." Besides these light and contemporary productions the stage of the Confederacy presented a large number of plays of Shakespeare.[55] Other entertainment was provided in minstrel productions, charades, and *tableaux vivants*. In the summer of 1864 the stage began to deteriorate rapidly, partly as a result of the conscription of actors.

The War for Southern Independence greatly stimulated the writing of songs and the publication of sheet music. Richard B. Harwell has found that at least 648 pieces of sheet music were published in the Confederacy.[56] The leading music publishing firm of the South was Blackmar Brothers—of New Orleans until the occupation by Ben Butler, when the main office was moved to Augusta, Georgia. Next to the Blackmars, the most successful music publishing house was Schreiner & Son of Macon and Savannah, Georgia. These companies published numerous songs about the Confederate flag and about sentimental and nostalgic subjects that would appeal to homesick Confederate soldiers. John Hill Hewitt, born in New York, a student at West Point, journalist and music teacher in various cities of the South before the war, wrote so many popular pieces of music that he has been called "the Bard of the Stars and Bars." His most popular compositions were "Southern Song of Freedom," "O! Come to Me, Love, in a Beautiful Dream," "The Stonewall Quickstep," "The Unknown Dead," "You are Going to the Wars, Willie Boy," and "The Young Volunteer." The soldiers delighted in singing "Dixie," written by the Ohio comedian Dan Emmett for the minstrel stage; "All Quiet Along the Potomac To-night," composed by a Massachusetts woman; "Richmond Is a Hard Road to Travel," written by the Southern editor John R. Thompson; "Lorena," "Home, Sweet Home," "Lily Dale," "Her Bright Smile Haunts Me Still," "Listen to the Mocking Bird," and "Just Before the Battle, Mother."

The press performed such an important function in the Confederacy that Congress exempted from military service editors and a limited number of newspaper employees. In February, 1865, the total number of editors exempted was 123, as well as 682 employees.[57] In the spring of 1863 newspapers organized the Press Association of the Confederate States with J. S. Thrasher as superintendent with office at Atlanta. This association collected the military news by maintaining telegraph reporters at the headquarters of each of the principal Confederate armies. When certain unauthorized persons sold the military news collected by this agency in the form of bulletins issued to clubs along the telegraph lines, the Press Association copyrighted its news.[58] As the war went on, newspapers found such great difficulty in securing paper that most of them by the summer of 1863 were reduced to a single sheet.

An excellent analysis of the Confederate press in 1862 was given by Henry Hotze, editor of the *Index* in London, who had been a Southern journalist before he was sent to Europe as a Confederate agent. He described the Richmond *Enquirer* as the leading journal, the oldest in the Confederate States, Democratic in background, careful in its statements, and, like the London *Times,* supporting the government. Its chief rival, the *Whig,* formerly leaning to centralization, now "watches with the utmost jealousy the powers and conduct of the Confederate government and advocates restrictions that would make the Executive powerless and useless," but adopts a fair and patriotic course on all great questions.[59] The Richmond *Examiner* is described as "the Ishmael of the Southern press, so far as it is against everybody," written with wit and smartness, but in nine cases out of ten offering virulent censure that is undeserved. The Richmond *Despatch* is described as a cheap paper, selling for two cents a copy, printed in small type, professing no political creed, "catering to the taste of the masses," and enjoying a large circulation. The Charleston *Courier,* widely distributed in South Carolina and other states, is compared to the *Enquirer* in policy and balance. The Charleston *Mercury,* Hotze regards as "almost rabid" on state rights; he notes its advocacy of such limitation of the powers of the Confederate Congress that the legislature of the central government would have less authority than the German Diet. In the lower South the two leading newspapers were the Augusta *Constitutionalist* and the Mobile *Register,* both of which in 1860 had supported Douglas for President and had opposed secession until after the election of Lincoln. The *Constitutionalist* became an independent supporter of the Confederate government. The *Register,* Hotze observes, is one of the most frequently quoted papers of the Confederacy, noted for its eminent literary quality, the extent and reliability of its news, its exceeding frankness, and "its political moderation and thorough independence." It supported the policies of the Davis administration, but not so closely as did the Richmond *Enquirer* or the Charleston *Courier.*

In the attrition of Southern morale the Confederate newspapers played a significant role. There was little criticism of the Davis administration until the late winter of 1861–1862, when the reverses of Fort Donelson and Roanoke Island gave an occasion for bitter denunciation of the President. In Richmond the *Examiner,* edited by John M. Daniel and Edward A. Pollard, and the *Whig,* edited by Robert Ridgway, and in Charleston the *Mercury,* owned by the great secessionist Robert Barnwell Rhett and edited by his son, were foremost among Southern newspapers in their strictures. Other strong critics were the Savannah *Republican,* the Lynchburg *Virginian,* the Memphis *Appeal,* and the Augusta *Chronicle & Sentinel.* The Augusta paper was purchased for $80,000 by the coterie of Davis haters—Governor Joseph E. Brown, Vice President Alexander H. Stephens, and Henry Cleveland—in order to destroy the Confederate President.[60]

The anti-Davis press attacked the President for sins of omission and commission. He was accused of being a despot, of completely disregarding public opinion, and of being incompetent. Some newspapers held him responsible for the barefoot soldiers of the Confederacy marching through the snow. Partisan editors accused him of favoritism, particularly in retaining in command such unpopular generals as Braxton Bragg, Lucius Northrop, and the Northerner John C. Pemberton. He was condemned for removing Johnston and appointing the rash and inexperienced John Hood to command the Western army. His cabinet appointments, particularly Judah P. Benjamin and Christopher Memminger, were severely criticized. The two acts of the administration most violently attacked by the newspapers were the suspension of the writ of *habeas corpus* and the alleged unfair and inquisitional enforcement of the Impressment Act.

Davis had defenders, however, in some of the most patriotic and able of the Confederate newspapers. Heading this list were the Richmond *Enquirer,* controlled by ex-Governor Henry A. Wise, and the Charleston *Courier.* Other newspapers, including the Richmond *Sentinel* and *Dispatch* and *Southern Illustrated News* and *Southern Punch* (a humorous paper started in 1863), were either mildly pro-Davis or neutral. The pro-Davis papers seem to have been motivated by the desire of preserving unity and thus aiding the cause of Southern independence. They believed that this end could best be attained by preserving confidence in the government and securing the cooperation of all citizens.

The Confederate Congress passed a law in January, 1862, by which it became a crime to publish any news of "the numbers, disposition, movements or destination of Southern land and naval forces." In this same month all newspaper correspondents were banished from the Army of Northern Virginia. Generals Earl Van Dorn and Braxton Bragg threatened to suspend the publication of newspapers that printed anything undermining confidence in a commanding officer, and Provost Marshal John H. Winder threatened to suppress the Richmond *Whig* if it did not "abandon its vicious habit of uttering unpalatable truths." [61] A sedition bill curtailing the freedom of speech and of the press was introduced into the Senate by the Judiciary Committee early in 1863 but was not passed. The infringement of civil liberties was much greater in the North than in the Confederacy. Federal records indicate that 13,535 persons were arbitrarily imprisoned, and it is estimated that well over three hundred Northern newspapers were suppressed, at least for short periods.

On the other hand, there were few actual suppressions of newspapers in the Confederacy. When "Parson" Brownlow published disloyal editorials in the Knoxville *Whig* that stirred the people of East Tennessee to burn vital railroad bridges, the supporters of the Confederacy demanded his arrest. Brownlow courted the suppression of his paper because he wished to appear as a martyr, but President Davis refused to gratify him. Finally the state authorities arrested him; but the Richmond government allowed him to go through the lines to the North, delighted to get rid of such a troublemaker.[62] The printing press of the Raleigh *Standard* was destroyed by Georgia troops passing through the city in September,

1863, because they were enraged at the peace policy of its editor, W. W. Holden. Governor Vance denounced their act, and some of Holden's followers retaliated by destroying the type of the opposition paper, the *State Journal*. He resumed the publication of the *Standard* until February 22, 1864, when he announced its suspension.

Not only did the Confederate government refrain from suppressing hostile criticism of its policies, but it did not properly censor military news.[63] The striking lack of censorship of soldiers' mail contributed to the breakdown of morale both of soldiers and of the people back home. Newspapers were permitted to publish military matter which would have been strictly suppressed during the recent war. The Southern generals were alarmed at the license allowed to the press in criticizing the generals and furnishing information valuable to the enemy. Lee once ironically remarked that all the military geniuses of the South were newspaper editors. Southern papers, however, were less flagrant offenders in publishing military news than Northern papers, probably because they did not have the large number of war correspondents that the Northern newspapers had. Lee constantly read the Northern journals, from which he acquired much significant military information. Northern officers also read Southern newspapers, and Jackson, realizing this, deliberately circulated false rumors. In general, the Southern papers cooperated with the government in concealing vital military news and tried to strengthen the morale of the people by minimizing defeats and claiming victories in drawn battles. News of the surrender of Fort Donelson and of the Roanoke Island disaster, for example, was held back for weeks. Yet the Southern press did at times publish material that should have been suppressed—for example, the sending of Longstreet's corps from Virginia in 1863 to join Bragg in Tennessee. President Davis's speech at Macon after the fall of Atlanta revealing the grave army losses by desertion and the plan of harassing Sherman's communications was reported by the press, to the detriment of the Confederate cause.

XII

Economic Disintegration

Under the abnormal strain of war the whole economy of the Confederacy virtually collapsed. An eminent student of the Civil War, Charles W. Ramsdell, concluded that "the Confederacy had begun to crumble, or to break down *within,* long before the military situation appeared to be desperate." [1] This disintegration of the home front, or of the life behind the lines, accounted in large measure for the decline in military effectiveness of the armies and for the loss of morale by the people. But so complicated is historical causation that military defeats in all probability were a cause as well as an effect of the descending spiral after 1863 of civilian morale and economic production.

The most difficult task which confronted the Confederate government was to finance the war. In the beginning the Treasury Department could procure neither bank-note paper on which to issue its bonds nor an engraver. Only after the Capital was removed to Richmond did Maryland sympathizers smuggle some bank-note paper from New York. The first cash was obtained through the seizure of $718,294.08 in the Federal customhouses and in branch mints at New Orleans, Dahlonega, and Charlotte.[2] The largest supply of gold and silver that the Treasury acquired was through the sale of bonds during the first year of the war, when patriotism flamed high and an early end of the war was expected. A military disaster, the Federal capture of New Orleans, furnished additional precious metal when the specie of six banks of that city, $4,192,-998,79, was rushed through the Confederate lines, only to be taken over by the Confederate government on the ground that the banks had fallen under the control of disloyal persons.

The Confederate Constitution prohibited a high protective tariff like that under which the Federal government collected more than $305,000,000 in gold and silver; but the Congress did levy a purely revenue tariff imposing *ad valorem* rates of 5 to 25 per cent, averaging 12½ per cent. It levied an export duty (such duties were prohibited under the United States Constitution) of ⅛ cent per pound on all cotton exported, to be paid in specie or coupons of Confederate bonds. The customs collectors turned into the Treasury a total of $3,480,617.32 from import duties, the duties being payable in specie, sterling, interest coupons of bonds, and Treasury notes, as well as $30,000 in specie from the export duty on cotton.[3] In addition to these very limited sources of revenue, the government received more than two million dollars in donations, particularly from churches, ladies' societies, and patriotic citizens. A sequestration law, seizing the funds and property of alien enemies, brought into the control of the Treasury $11,661,082.07, including the specie of the New Orleans banks appropriated after the Federal capture of that city.

The Confederate government, like the Federal, made the grave mistake in its first two years of failing to tax the people drastically to carry on the war. In August, 1861, under the Provisional Constitution, Congress imposed a direct tax of half of 1 per cent on all property, including slaves but excepting Confederate bonds and currency. (The real property of the Confederacy was assessed at $1,400,000,000, slaves at $1,500,000,000, money at interest at $94,000,000, bank stock at the same.) This had the serious flaw of permitting the states to assume the tax and paying it in a lump sum, for which they received a 10 per cent reduction. All the states except Mississippi, Texas, and South Carolina paid their quotas by borrowing, instead of collecting the money by taxation.[4] The permanent Constitution required that direct taxation of land and slaves (forming two-thirds of the property of the Confederacy) be apportioned on the basis of the free inhabitants and three-fifths of the slaves, to be determined by a census. Because of invasions the census could not be taken; but President Davis on December 7, 1863, urged Congress to interpret the Constitution according to the intent rather than the letter and levy a uniform tax on land.[5] Partly at the urging of Davis and Memminger, Congress voted on February 17, 1864, to place a direct tax on land of 5 per cent; but it was greatly weakened by a system of rebates.

The Vice President brought all his influence to bear upon members of Congress to adopt a sound and courageous system of finance. To Thomas Jenkins Semmes, who was on the finance committee of the House, Stephens wrote January 4, 1862, urging heavy taxation to bolster the finances of the Confederacy and reduce the redundant currency. At the same time he announced that he was utterly opposed to the movement for the states to guarantee the Confederate debt: the adoption of such a plan would put capital on the side of the reconstruction of the Union instead of, as it was at the time, on the side of Southern independence.[6]

The Secretary of the Treasury, Christopher B. Memminger, had so little prestige or influence with Congress that he failed to get his recommendations adopted. Gorgas commented: "Mr. Memminger treats others with rudeness, and is, besides, dogmatical, narrow-minded and slow. . . . Whenever I leave Mr. M. after an interview, I feel somehow as tho' I had been trying to do something very much out of the way, so injured and *put upon* does he represent himself."[7] Secretary of War Seddon regarded him as an ass.[8] Memminger, with the support of some state legislatures, had proposed in January, 1863, that the states guarantee the interest and principal of the Confederate debt. His failures, the attacks of Edward A. Pollard in the Richmond *Examiner,* and his unpleasant personality caused a strong movement to force his resignation to develop. But he had some good ideas, notably his advocacy of heavy taxation, and Davis doggedly supported him. Stephens wrote from Crawfordville, Georgia, to Semmes that a vote in Congress of disapproval or of want of confidence could compel the change of a head of a department; if then the President refused to remove Memminger, Congress could force his hand by withholding supplies. He cited the example of the British Parliament and declared that "Memminger ought to have resigned instantly upon his plan of finance being disapproved by Congress."[9]

The war was half over before the Confederate Congress began a realistic policy of taxation. Mounting inflation brought a strong demand from the people that they be more heavily taxed. On April 24, 1863, Congress passed a comprehensive bill placing an 8 per cent tax on naval stores, tobacco, rice, sugar, liquors, wool and flour; a heavy license tax on many occupations; a sales tax from 2½ to 10 per cent; and a tax of 1 per cent on salaries between

$1,000 and $1,500 and 2 per cent above $1,500, as well as a gradu-
ated tax on incomes from other sources than salaries ranging from
5 per cent on incomes between $500 and $1,500 to 15 per cent on
incomes over $10,000.[10]

The most irksome feature of this financial legislation was the
tithe, or levy in kind, of one-tenth of all agricultural products—
corn, wheat, tobacco, cotton, sugar, peas, and bacon. Up to the Civil
War, Southerners had paid very light taxes; consequently the individualistic farmers resented the drastic tax in kind, which was
difficult to evade. The bitter pill was rendered more unpalatable by
the method of collection by arbitrary agents, and by the fact that
much of the food, cotton, and tobacco thus acquired spoiled for lack
of transportation and of storage facilities. But the tax in kind on
agricultural produce was almost necessary because of the rapid
spiral of inflation. "The Confederacy," according to an able student,
"raised throughout its existence about one per cent of its income in
taxes!" [11]

Shrinking from heavy taxation, Congress was forced to borrow.
The only important foreign loan, however, was negotiated with a
powerful Jewish banking family of Paris, Emile Erlanger & Company, influential with the French Emperor. The remarkable fact
about this loan is that the Erlangers proposed it, and not the
Confederate agents in Europe.[12] Indeed, it turned out to be a bold
cotton speculation that brought profit chiefly to the French bankers.
Secretary Benjamin saw through the devious scheme; but after reducing the loan from twenty-five to fifteen million dollars and scal-
ing down the rate of interest he accepted their proposal because he
thought that this financial transaction might persuade the Emperor
to recognize the Confederacy. The contract provided for the sale
of fifteen million dollars of Confederate bonds, which the Erlangers
were to underwrite at 77 on the basis of 100 par value and for
which a purchaser could pay in installments. The bonds bore 7 per
cent interest and were exchangeable for cotton at six pence a pound
which was worth four times that price in Europe. Furthermore, the
Erlangers were to receive a 5 per cent commission for selling the
bonds.

When the issue was placed on sale in March, 1863, it was en-
thusiastically oversubscribed at the price of 90, chiefly by English
investors. Very soon, however, the bonds began to decline alarm-

ingly. Then the Erlangers put strong pressure on the Confederate commissioner in London, James M. Mason, to use the receipts from the first installment in payment of the bonds to bull the market. Reluctantly he and Slidell in Paris consented, and purchased more than $7,500,000 of their own bonds. At the same time Federal agents conducted a campaign to discredit the Confederate securities. The most influential of these "bears," Robert J. Walker, Secretary of the Treasury under Polk and former Senator from Mississippi, wrote a pamphlet representing the Southern states as habitually repudiating their financial obligations and President Jefferson Davis as a prewar advocate of the repudiation of Mississippi state bonds. The fall of Vicksburg in July, 1863, caused the Erlanger bonds to drop precipitously. The profits of the Erlangers from their transactions with the Confederacy were immense; but the British friends of the South who bought the bonds lost their whole investment, and the Confederate government ultimately obtained only two and a half to three million dollars of cash. In addition to this return, however, a large number of the repurchased bonds were unloaded on British firms, especially Isaac, Campbell & Co., who had cheated the Confederacy in furnishing supplies.[13]

Congress tried to shift the greater part of the burden of war upon future generations by means of bond issues. Secretary of the Treasury Memminger did not devise a method of selling bonds, such as the United States Congress employed in its National Bank Act of 1863, which gave banks a strong incentive to buy government bonds. After the sale of the first issue of bonds for fifteen million dollars in specie, the Confederate Treasury found it exceedingly difficult to dispose of later issues despite the high 8 per cent interest (compared with 2.9 per cent compound interest paid by the United States for small loans to finance the war in 1944). The government therefore had to sell bonds for agricultural produce instead of money which the people did not possess. By these produce loans the Confederacy acquired vast stores of cotton (at least 430,000 bales of 500 pounds each, of which approximately 130,000 were captured or burned by the Confederates to avoid capture), sugar, rice, tobacco, and wheat of which only a small proportion could be shipped to Europe and converted into cash or credits.[14]

The chief reliance of the Confederate government for operating expenses was on Treasury notes which bore no interest and had no metallic backing. Unlike the Federal government, the Confederate Congress refused to make its notes legal tender. This paper money promised payment in dollars "two years after the ratification of a treaty of peace between the Confederate States and the United States of America." Paper currency poured in a steady flood from the Confederate printing presses (located after the spring of 1862 in Columbia, South Carolina) until it passed a billion and a half dollars, which was over thrice the amount of greenbacks issued in the North.[15] The first Treasury notes were engraved by a firm in New York City, but later issues were lithographed and signed by clerks. Because the Confederacy was drained of specie early in the war, the states issued "shinplasters" or paper money of small denominations—fifty cents, quarters, etc. Confederate money was easy to counterfeit, and considerable amounts were printed in the North and circulated in the South to debase the currency. The supply of fiat money was increased by the fact that the individual states, which were not restrained by the Confederate Constitution, issued large quantities of paper money, and also permitted cities, railroads, and insurance companies to issue such currency. The superior value of Northern greenbacks even caused them to be used to some extent in paying Confederate soldiers.

Congress, after it was too late, tried to remedy the disastrous superfluity of paper money. Secretary Memminger reported at the close of 1863 that there was circulating in the Confederacy five times as much currency as was actually needed. In order to reduce this plethora Congress passed a law February 17, 1864, requiring the people to exchange their paper bills for long-term bonds at 4 per cent interest. Holders of $100 paper money bills were to exchange them for bonds by April 1 or suffer a reduction in value of their old currency of one-third. Thereafter such paper bills would automatically decline in value by one-tenth monthly. Bills of smaller denominations were to be converted into bonds or exchanged for a new issue of paper currency at the rate of three old dollars for two of the new money. This legislation was a form of repudiation which resulted in a considerable contraction of the currency and temporarily in a sharp drop in prices.

The last full financial statement of the Confederate government, in October, 1864, showed a debt of $1,687,000,000 represented by bonds and paper currency. A careful student, however, has estimated the total debt as $2,345,000,000 in Confederate currency, which amounted to $572,000,000 in gold content.[16] This sum represented a financial sacrifice by the Southern people over twice as great as the Northern per capita expenditure for the war.

The Confederate government operated for four years of war on about twenty-seven million dollars of hard cash. The South presented the amazing phenomenon of a nation waging a long war chiefly with fiat money, paying possibly eight hundred thousand soldiers, buying supplies of war and naval vessels in Europe, and carrying on a civil government for nine million white and Negro people. The result of the reckless printing of paper money was the greatest inflation ever seen in America with the possible exception of the Revolutionary period.[17] In April, 1863, Colonel A. J. L. Fremantle exchanged his English gold for Confederate currency at the rate of one for four; but after Gettysburg the currency fell so rapidly that in August, 1863, the dollar was equal to only eight cents in gold; in January, 1864, four and one-half cents; and in March, 1865, less than two cents.[18] The Northern greenbacks also depreciated, but at their lowest point, July, 1864, they were worth in gold more than one-third of their face value.

The dizzy inflation in the Confederacy could be illustrated by innumerable fantastic prices paid. In 1864 John S. Wise, son of ex-Governor Henry A. Wise of Virginia, paid $2,000 for a uniform coat and $100 for a black hat, while ordinary cigars were $10 each, whisky was $5 a drink, eggs $6 a dozen, butter $25 a pound.[19] J. B. Jones in *A Rebel War Clerk's Diary* listed the following prices for commodities at Richmond in May, 1864: shoes, $125; bacon, $9 a pound; turnip greens, $4 a peck; flour, $275 a barrel; potatoes, $25 per bushel; and firewood, $50 per cord. Yet these prices were not a register of the real cost of living. Although it was much higher in the overcrowded capital than elsewhere in the Confederacy, flour could be purchased for less gold in Richmond than in New York during the winter of 1864–1865. English travelers believed that living costs in the Confederacy were lower than in their country. Fremantle in June, 1863, paid $8 a day for room and board at the Charleston Hotel—the sum that was equivalent to only a little over a dollar in gold.[20]

The white-collar class of Southern society was hardest hit by inflation. Robert Kean noted in his diary October 4, 1863, that his salary of $3,000 as Chief of the Confederate Bureau of War was equal to about $300 in ordinary times. In contrast, the wages of a journeyman saddler were $10 to $12 a day, more than 30 per cent higher than the salary of a head of a bureau or an assistant secretary of one of the departments. Kean's family was reduced to eating two meals a day.[21] J. B. Jones's salary was so diminished by the inflation that he and his family wore shabby clothes and descended to eating a meal of liver, regarded then as offal, and rice.

Could the Confederate government have avoided this tremendous inflation based on irredeemable bonds and the issues of paper money without the backing of gold and silver reserves? Severe critics of the Davis administration have maintained that it made a serious blunder in not rushing as much cotton as possible to Europe at the beginning of the war before the blockade became effective. Thus, they assert, a supply of "white gold" could have been stored in European warehouses to serve both as a sound basis for currency and as a bank to pay for supplies purchased abroad. Unfortunately, the leading Confederate statesmen, except Judah P. Benjamin, were under the delusion that England and France could be coerced into recognizing the Confederacy and breaking the blockade merely by creating a "cotton famine" in Europe. Furthermore, Secretary of the Treasury Memminger asserted correctly that there was a lack of ships to carry the cotton to Europe. Although the government might have diminished the inflation by wiser tax policies, the issue of a large amount of paper currency, unsupported by gold, seems inevitable. It is well to remember also that inflation of the currency was caused by the scarcity of consumer goods as well as by the issue of fiat money. In World War II, to make a modern comparison, a prominent inflationary cause was the scarcity of goods, combined with high wages and a large surplus of cash.

The mistakes of Confederate finance can be condoned; but the failure of the agricultural South to feed its armies properly and to provide adequately for the families of poor soldiers is less forgivable. The main problem in the production of food in the Confederacy was the conversion from growing cotton to cultivating food crops. The Confederate Congress, dominated by *laissez faire* ideas, did not prohibit the raising of cotton; but the effects of the blockade, a campaign of appeal to patriotism, and state laws drastically reduced the planting of this crop. Under the voluntary system vigilance committees enforced the restriction of cotton growing. When such a committee demanded that Robert Toombs reduce his acreage of cotton he defied it, rationalizing his refusal by the claim of preserving his personal liberty. When the voluntary system failed, most of the states by law reduced the acreage of cotton and tobacco. Arkansas in March, 1862, limited the planting of cotton to two acres per field hand; Georgia, to three acres per hand; and Alabama placed a tax of ten cents a pound on all cotton grown on a farm in excess of twenty-five hundred pounds. Because of these compulsions, the effects of the owners' absences, and the restraints of the blockade, the cotton production was reduced from a bumper crop of nearly 4,500,000 bales in 1861 to 300,000 bales in 1864. Likewise, Virginia limited the production of its staple, tobacco, to 2,500 plants to each hand. Colonel Fremantle observed in the spring of 1863 that one-third of the cotton land of Texas was still planted in cotton, the rest in corn; but only in Texas was so much cotton grown.

The burning of a large quantity of cotton by the Confederates to prevent it from falling into the hands of the enemy was one of the sad consequences of Federal invasion. When the Confederates retreated from the neighborhood of Columbia, Tennessee, General Albert Sidney Johnston ordered the cavalry to burn the cotton in the region which he could not defend. A small planter of this region has described his emotions as a company of Louisiana cavalry burned his cotton: "It was a sad thing to behold a body of armed men to roll out a man's whole dependence for money and the support of his family before his eyes, and cut it open [the cotton bales] and stick fire to it and he dare not open his mouth." [22]

Another method of increasing the food supply was the adoption of wartime prohibition.[23] In 1862 the legislatures of most of the states prohibited the distilling of liquor from corn, wheat, or other grains, except for a fixed amount that was licensed for the use of the Confederate or state governments. Although these laws were completely at variance with previous Southern ideas of the authority of the state to invade private liberties, they were now demanded by the people. Huge quantities of whisky were used by the medical department of the army, while navy crews received a ration of whisky. On February 6, 1864, the Confederate Congress forbade the importation of alcoholic beverages. The Confederate government at first contracted with local distilleries for liquor supplies. It furnished the corn, which was converted into liquor at the rate of two and one-half gallons from a bushel of corn. Conflicts with state governors, especially with Governor Joseph E. Brown of Georgia, took place over the building of Confederate distilleries. Virginia, March 12, 1863, was the last of the states to pass a prohibition law; but she then forbade the manufacture of liquor even for the Confederate government. The difficulty of private individuals in obtaining whisky is indicated by the skyrocketing of the price at Richmond from 25 cents a gallon in 1861 to $35 a gallon in 1863 and $120 a gallon in 1864.

From cultivating staple crops, the agricultural energy of the Confederacy was now converted mainly to growing larger food supplies. In 1862 a protracted drought ruined the cereal crops in Virginia and the deep South; in the following year the corn crop was so large that the price in Mississippi fell to 62 cents a bushel. The government encouraged the cultivation of food crops by exempting overseers from conscription; but productivity was cut down by the impressment of necessary draft animals and vehicles for military purposes. Furthermore, the shortage of sacks, boxes, and containers was a serious factor hindering the shipment of abundant supplies of fruit, vegetables, molasses, and meat to the troops. The scarcity of salt, indispensable as a preservative, was a deterrent to the processing of meat. In the "poor-white" districts women and boys had difficulty in plowing and carrying on heavy farm work, and in plantation districts the Negroes often loafed when the strong hand of the master was removed.

In the spring of 1863 a strong impression prevailed in the Confederacy that the war would soon terminate, and planters and farmers began to cultivate cotton and tobacco instead of food crops. This caused Congress to resolve that in its judgment the war would be prolonged, and that agricultural labor should be devoted mainly to food crops. In a proclamation of April 10 President Davis warned the Confederacy not to relax in growing food crops. He observed that there should be no uneasiness in regard to a supply of bread for men, but that the cultivation of a large amount of corn and forage for livestock and for army horses and mules was needed. The supply of meat, he declared, was so deficient that some of the armies were living at times on half-rations. This serious lack he attributed primarily to transport difficulties and to the activities of speculators.[24]

The problem of feeding the families of soldiers was not solved. The pay of a private, eleven dollars a month, was a pitiful sum with which to support a family during inflation. At first the charity of neighbors furnished inadequate relief. Between November, 1861, and March, 1862, the state legislatures passed relief acts for the families of volunteers but not for the families of substitutes. These laws required each county to provide for the poor families of soldiers by a local property tax—which meant that poorer districts suffered. In the winter of 1862–1863 the legislatures appropriated large sums of money to be divided among the poor families of soldiers and bought corn as well as cotton cards which were used in preparing raw cotton for spinning to give to them—a shift from county to state control.[25] But these various expedients were difficult to administer, and much suffering occurred in some areas, resulting in loss of morale, both civilian and military.

Closely connected with the scarcity of food and of goods were the activities of speculators and hoarders. The inability of the Richmond and state governments to control the avarice of some of their people was a factor in the breakdown of morale. The planters and large farmers were accused of hoarding food and speculating in it. Governor Zebulon B. Vance of North Carolina and Governor J. J. Pettus of Mississippi received many letters from poor men and the wives of soldiers complaining bitterly that the wealthier class would not sell food for Confederate money, and that they held corn and wheat for a rise in price.[26] In order to curb speculation Governor William Smith of Virginia bought rice in the rice-growing districts in the autumn of 1864 and sold it for fifty cents a pound, in contrast to the price of two dollars and a half charged by grocers. Various states passed laws against creating monopolies, but they were not enforced. The country people fared better in regard to food than the poorer people of the cities. Bread riots led by women took place in 1863 in Richmond, Salisbury, North Carolina, and Mobile, but the rioters plundered jewelry and clothing shops as well as food stores. Farmers would not bring their agricultural products to market for fear of impressment of these valuable commodities.[27]

Of course speculation was not confined to food. There is an untold story of flagrant profiteering in the Confederacy which some future investigator may uncover. General Gorgas wrote in his journal March 25, 1863, that it was currently believed that John Frazer & Company of Charleston (later represented in the cabinet in the person of George A. Trenholm as Secretary of the Treasury) had made nine million dollars in the blockade-running business, and that the firm of Crenshaw in Richmond was reaping a golden harvest from its woolen factories and flour contracts. On July 17 he noted: "The sins of the people of Charleston may cause that city to fall; it is full of rottenness, every one being engaged in speculations." [28] Jefferson Davis in a proclamation of July 5, after the defeats of Gettysburg and Vicksburg, ordering a day of fasting, humiliation, and prayer, attributed the recent disasters to overconfidence following victories, forgetfulness of God, and the "love of lucre" which had "eaten like a gangrene into the very heart of the land, converting too many among us into worshipers of gain and rendering them unmindful of their duty to their country." [29] Yet, as a recent historian has observed: "Unlike the situation in the North, there seem to have been few dishonesties practiced or fortunes made by government contractors." [30] Indeed, government contracts had many disadvantages which deterred businessmen from seeking them. Notably the failure of the government to pay its bills.

The impact of the war on the agricultural economy of the South was felt in the serious weakening of control of the planters over the slaves. The tradition has become incorporated in American history that Southern slaves were remarkably docile and loyal to the whites during the Civil War. Some young aristocrats like W. W. Blackford in Jeb Stuart's cavalry took devoted slaves with them as valets. In the tradition of my own family there is a story of a body servant who accompanied his master from South Carolina to war. This Negro boy was taught to recite Longfellow's "Psalm of Life," and did so with great gusto in his rich Gullah pronunciation to the vast amusement of the soldiers. There are also many touching anecdotes of the loyalty of slaves, such as "Aeneas Africanus," who guarded the family silver so faithfully, and of devoted Negro servants who outwitted plundering Yankees. Most of these were house servants who held a privileged position in slave society, and had developed an affection for their masters during daily association with them.

On the other hand, the vast majority of field slaves became disloyal when the Federal armies approached.[31] Some ran away from the plantation or became insolent and, in exceptional cases, resorted to violence against their masters. The white people wondered what thoughts were concealed behind the sable countenances of their slaves or, like Louis Manigault, a South Carolina rice planter, commented bitterly on how they were deceived by their most trusted slaves. The most serious impact of the war on the slaves was their deterioration in morale as agricultural laborers when their masters had gone to war and inexperienced women or old men failed to force them to work as formerly. Numerous Negroes deserted the plantations to follow Sherman, and the redheaded general was so annoyed that he ordered them away. The slave was rare who did not wish to be free, and competent students believe that after Lincoln's proclamation of emancipation most of the slaves realized that their freedom was at stake in the outcome of the war.

It was surprising to Northern abolitionists that the slaves did not rebel and murder their masters' families while most of the able-bodied men were away in military service. At the beginning of the war some Southern communities were deeply stirred by the fear of slave uprisings. Daniel R. Hundley, author of the famous *Social Relations in Our Southern States* (1860), vividly describes in his diary the hysteria of several northern Alabama villages over reports of an insurrection plot. The scare started at Triana near Huntsville, causing the neighboring village of Mooresville to activate its patrol and to set up a Committee of Public Safety. Hundley was on patrol duty all one night and was appointed a member of the Mooresville committee. His diary records that the Vigilance Committee of Triana had "ferreted out a most hellish insurrectionary plot among the slaves." By severely whipping some suspected slaves, his committee elicited the startling testimony that the Negroes believed "Lincoln is soon going to free them all, and they are everywhere making preparations to aid him when he makes his appearance." From May 18 to June 9, 1861, Hundley's committee sat like a French Revolutionary tribunal, ignoring the regular courts and established forms of law, going to various plantations to interrogate the Negroes, beating and threatening them, conferring in joint session with the Triana committee, driving out an Englishman suspected of abolitionism, and summarily executing Negroes. Among the suspected ringleaders was the slave preacher, Peter Mud, who was caught in spite of his master's effort to save him by sending him off. Hundley recorded his sad fate as follows:

> May 30. We had an exciting time in the Committee to-day. First we tried a free negro, who was sentenced to the penitentiary for life. We then tried parson Peter Mud. Peter was proved to be one of the principal conspirators, but the influence of his master's family in his behalf was great—however, he was found guilty by the jury, and was hung about half an hour after sundown.[32]

The slaves did not attempt to gain their freedom by insurrection, except possibly in a few isolated instances, because they had long been accustomed to submitting meekly to the white master class. They also lacked means of communication to start a formidable movement, and the most intelligent among them, their natural leaders, were usually house servants, who were as a rule attached to the white people. Furthermore, Southerners prepared for revolts with "home guards" and "mounted pickets" of the older men and young boys and with vigilance committees. The Negroes therefore believed that the best thing to do was to wait for deliverance. At the same time, many slaves remained loyal because, born in the South, they loved their homeland and regarded themselves as Southerners.

Despite the insecurity of property during the fortunes of war, the value of slaves held up surprisingly well and there was a considerable traffic in them. In the Hammond Papers are receipts for the purchase of slave William in Richmond for $2,400 and Isaac in Lynchburg for $3,105 during the summer of 1863, and in the Raleigh *North-Carolina Standard* of January 6, 1864, are reports of young male adults selling for prices from $6,000 to $6,450. In 1864, field hands were estimated at $2,000 in Confederate currency in a demand for compensation for impressed slaves who had escaped to the enemy. In that summer a Negro girl eighteen years old was sold at Augusta, Georgia, for $4,250 and a man for $3,980 —values that reflected inflation.[33] Wiley's study *Southern Negroes, 1861–1865,* shows that the price of slaves increased greatly after 1862 in Confederate currency; but in terms of gold value there was a general downward trend through the war.

The life of the Southern Negro was affected in numerous ways by the war. Many masters took their slaves into the interior to escape the invading armies, thereby causing difficult problems of feeding and providing for them. At the beginning of the war the slave code was tightened, particularly by more rigorous regulations of the patrol. But as the great majority of the able-bodied white men were drawn into the army the lot of the slaves in general became easier. An important movement developed in the Confederacy to ameliorate slavery and change the laws to recognize that the slaves were primarily persons rather than soulless property. The disasters to Southern arms caused many religious Southerners to believe that God was chastising his people because they had not made slavery a more humane and Christian institution. Led by Calvin A. Wiley in North Carolina and the Reverend James Lyons in Mississippi, the humanitarians agitated for such reforms as repeal of the laws that forbade teaching slaves to read and write and new legislation to protect slave marriages, prevent the sale of young children from their mothers, and admit testimony by slaves in the courts as equivalent to circumstantial evidence, and thus protect them from cruel masters.

A serious problem of the Confederacy in utilizing slave labor was impressment for military purposes.[34] The planters were extremely reluctant to furnish their human property for building fortifications, working on the railroads, and other military purposes. They feared that their Negroes would be injured by rough treatment and would acquire bad habits or would run away. Moreover the impressment of slaves interfered with agricultural production. In the spring of 1862 General Pemberton and General Ripley demanded that planters in the Barnwell District, South Carolina, where Senator Hammond's large plantation of Redcliffe was located, send half of their labor force to construct the defenses of Charleston. Hammond bitterly protested, declaring that in all other countries the soldiers worked on the fortifications, and that if slaves were needed they should be drawn from the disturbed coastal region instead of distant parts. He believed that his slaves would be ruined if they were sent to Charleston, and he finally hired free Negroes at a dollar a day to substitute for some of his slaves.

The Confederate Congress voted in March, 1863, to authorize the Secretary of War to impress slaves for sixty days with compensation of $20 a month if voluntarily offered, or $15 if the labor was forced. In the following February Congress authorized the Secretary of War to employ twenty thousand Negroes at the pay of privates in the ranks, first using those voluntarily offered and then impressing others as they were needed, except that each slave owner was allowed to keep at least one male slave at home. Congress, however, refused to grant the request of President Davis to permit the government to buy and own slaves.

The war effort of the Confederacy was greatly handicapped by the reluctance or refusal of planters to allow their servants to work on vital military projects such as the Greensboro-Danville railroad connection and the fortification of the seacoast and of Richmond. After the fall of New Bern on the coast of North Carolina, March 26, 1862, General Branch's official report described how he had advertised in the newspapers for slave labor and for free Negroes to build defenses. His advertisements had produced only a single slave and a small party of free Negroes. "If the fate of Newbern," he wrote, "shall prevent a similar supineness on the part of the citizens and slave owners elsewhere it will be fortunate for the country." Southern planters demanded compensation for impressed slaves who escaped to the enemy, or who died while engaged in military work. The Confederate Congress honored such claims by appropriating $3,108,000 in 1864. The poor non-slaveholders felt bitter toward the wealthy planters who tried to evade the slave impressment law. Such selfishness, they regarded as additional evidence that the war was "a rich man's war and a poor man's fight." The Confederacy faced a dilemma in political economy: strong government and great material sacrifice on the part of its citizens were necessary to win independence, yet the traditions and the whole political theory of the South were against a strongly centralized government and interference with property rights.

As the war progressed the economy of the Southern people became more and more primitive, with a resort to barter instead of money. The blockade and the lack of industrial development forced the Southerners to practice an economy of substitutes.[35] Persimmon seeds were used for buttons; the juice of the pokeberry or of oak balls produced ink; and dyes were obtained from walnut hulls, indigo, and the bark of various trees. Coffee had been the universal Southern beverage, and the loss of real coffee was a cause of constant lament; but substitutes were made from parched corn, okra seed, and sweet potatoes. Sassafras root tea took the place of Oriental tea, and parched peanuts furnished a concoction that might be called "chocolate." Thorns took the place of pins; honey and molasses served for sugar; and a substitute for soda was made from the ashes of corncobs. Paper was very difficult to obtain in the latter part of the war, and the back side of colorful wallpaper was used in a few instances for newspapers.

The Confederacy was poorly supplied with wool throughout the war. In 1860 Southern flocks had produced a little more than a pound per inhabitant. Virginia had furnished a quarter of this total; but its chief wool-growing district, the western part of the state, was conquered early in the war. In wool production Texas was second to Virginia; but the lack of railroads made much of its wool unavailable.

Salt became very scarce in the beleaguered Confederacy.[36] It was needed not only as a seasoning but as a preservative. In fact, it would have been futile to slaughter large numbers of cattle and hogs without an adequate supply of salt, because artificial refrigeration did not exist. The chief source of salt was Saltville in southwestern Virginia, which was captured by a Federal army in 1864. However, other sources were developed, particularly Clarke County, Alabama, Avery Island in Louisiana, and the west coast of Florida, where huge forests provided cheap fuel for the salt furnaces.[37] Salt could be purchased at the beginning of the war for less than half a cent a pound, or 65 cents a sack; but in the same year it was selling for $20 a sack. So essential was this substance that saltmakers were exempt from military service. Private individuals and state governments entered into the manufacture of the precious commodity by boiling sea water. North Carolina created a new state office, Salt Commissioner, to which Jonathan Worth, the old Unionist, was appointed.

One of the most distressing results of the blockade was a severe shortage of drugs and medicines. The Federal government placed drugs on the contraband list, causing great suffering to Northern prisoners as well as Southern soldiers. Although the Confederacy had a plentiful supply of medicinal whisky, quinine and calomel, which were urgently needed in a region where malaria was an ever present danger, were not obtainable in sufficient quantities. Southern women grew poppies in order to furnish opium and laudanum; but the attempt to extract the drugs was unsuccessful. Children in the Confederacy must have groaned at the highly successful extraction of castor oil from palma Christi. Turpentine was also easily produced, which was not only used for blisters but as a substitute for quinine. Chloroform was hard to get and was extremely costly, so that Dr. John Julian Chisholm of Charleston invented an "inhaler" to economize it.[38]

The Southerners began to experiment with various herbs and roots that grew in their native fields and woods to obtain drugs, dyes, and medicines. Silkweed root in whisky was used as a cure for venereal disease, and arrowroot for pneumonia. The Confederate substitute for quinine (Peruvian bark) was an extract from the dogwood berry. The dandelion furnished a substitute for calomel. A professor at the Medical College of Charleston, Francis P. Porcher, published a six-hundred-page book, *Resources of the Southern Fields and Forests,* describing the native herbs, roots, and trees which were valuable for making drugs, medicines, and substitutes. Among the more useful herbs and trees he listed were wild jalap, monkshood or wolfsbane, sassafras, tulip tree, sesamum, butternut, steeplebush, blistering fly, and the castor-oil plant.

One way of obtaining drugs and manufactured goods was the trade between the lines. Women smuggled opium and quinine beneath their voluminous crinoline skirts, and funeral processions imported contraband. Memphis and New Orleans were the most flourishing centers for the illegal trade between the lines. Memphis was occupied by a Federal army in June, 1862; and according to the last Federal commanding general of the city, "Memphis has been of more value to the Southern Confederacy since it fell into Federal hands than Nassau." [39] It became a thriving center for the shipment of cotton to the North. Unscrupulous traders swarmed in it, and officers and soldiers were corrupted by bribes to connive at the sale of supplies to the Confederacy. The Congressional Committee on the Conduct of the War estimated that twenty to thirty million dollars' worth of supplies had been sold in this city to the rebels. In New Orleans the brother of the military commander of the city, Ben Butler, made a fortune out of illegal trade in cotton with Southerners. James Lusk Alcorn, a leader against secession in Mississippi and a large slave owner, remained on his plantation through the war transporting hundreds of bales of cotton at night to the Mississippi River, where he sold it for "greenbacks," gold, and manufactured goods. He made friends with Federal officers and received a pass to enter Helena, Arkansas, at will.[40]

Both the Confederate and the Union military commanders tried unavailingly to stop the trade between the lines. A Confederate law of May 21, 1861, prohibited the export of cotton except through Confederate ports or through Mexico. Trade between the lines was pernicious, because it undermined the loyalty of participants and defeated the embargo on cotton. Nevertheless, Confederate governors resorted to it at times to procure various scarce goods, such as cotton cards for the home industries of manufacturing cloth.

The Federal blockade should have stimulated the growth of Southern manufacturing plants, as the British blockade had accelerated the rise of infant industries in New England during the War of 1812. Southern industrial development profited little from the stimulus of war and of the blockade, partly because of optimism in regard to the raising of the blockade. Jefferson Davis complained bitterly that many millions of dollars of private capital had been invested in blockade running, but very little money had been devoted to manufacturing. The quartermaster department of the Confederate Army did establish tanneries, shoe shops, and clothing manufactories. Poor women were employed to sew shirts and trousers at very low wages. The state penitentiary at Jackson, Mississippi, made a valuable contribution to the war effort by operating a cotton mill. North Carolina had forty cotton mills, approximately a third of the textile mills in the Confederacy; yet the state selfishly kept the product of these mills entirely for her own troops and civilian population throughout the war. Though the Southern states had abundant iron, limestone, and coal for coke, such as the Birmingham deposits, new iron mines were only slightly developed and the vital need of iron for rails was not met. State legislatures granted numerous charters for manufacturing enterprises; but the difficulties of securing capital, a dependable labor force, machinery, and even parts for worn-out machines were so great that few new enterprises could get a successful start.[41]

The Confederate government found it necessary to invade the field of business and practice extensive regulation of economic affairs, abandoning the cherished *laissez faire* ideas of the Southern people. Yet it controlled manufacturing solely to furnish goods for the army. It could regulate manufacturers in two ways, by its command over labor through conscription and the exemption laws, and by its control of railroads essential for bringing raw materials to the factories. The act of October 11, 1862, as previously noted, authorized the Secretary of War to exempt mechanics and the superintendents and employees of cotton, woolen, and paper mills from conscription, provided that the profits of the establishments did not exceed 75 per cent of the cost of production. This limitation of profit applied not only to goods sold to the army but also to civilians, thus curbing profiteering. In August, 1863, the Quartermaster General allowed profits of only 33⅓ per cent. The contracts of the Quartermaster General with textile factories stipulated that two-thirds of the cotton goods and all of the woolen goods should be sold to the military authorities. In return, the textile factories were allowed to have exempted workers. An act of Congress of February 17, 1864, abolished exemptions for workers in factories, but authorized the President to order the detailing of soldiers from the field to work in vital industries. Consequently, the Quartermaster General by withholding labor could hold a club over manufacturers to force them to make favorable contracts. The Conscription Bureau at times used its power to compel manufacturers to charge reasonable prices not only to the army but to civilians. Often vital industrial work, such as building railroads, was interrupted by recalling military details to replenish the army.

The textile mills in the Confederacy were operated at high speed; yet the shortage of operatives prevented them from utilizing their full capacity. Because of the labor shortage the Graniteville Mill in South Carolina, for example, could not operate at night except for two hours. Although this mill made huge paper profits, its machinery was wearing out and could not be replaced. Moreover, William Gregg, the great textile promoter in the South, asserted that the Confederate government discouraged manufacturing by its policies and relaxed the efforts of manufacturers to keep costs of production down by basing the prices of impressed goods upon the cost of production. He protested to a manufacturers' convention at Augusta, Georgia, in May, 1864, that the impressment act of March 26, 1863, was unfair to manufacturers because it severely regulated manufacturers' profits but did not control the exorbitant profits of blockade runners and speculators.[42]

Tremendous inflation aroused workingmen to the need of organization and produced strikes for higher wages. The Richmond Typographical Society sought unsuccessfully to establish the closed shop in newspaper plants. The Southern Telegraphic Association struck in January, 1864, for higher wages, shorter hours, and a closed shop.[43] On August 21, 1863, Kean noted in his diary that the post-office clerks in Richmond had struck for higher wages because they were paid from $700 to $800 a year, equivalent to only $100 before the war.[44] Public opinion in the South was strongly against strikes by labor, and the Confederate government broke them by promptly drafting strikers.

Perhaps the most significant strike in the Confederacy was that of the workmen building the ironclad *Mississippi* at New Orleans shortly before the city was attacked by Farragut's fleet. The shipbuilder, Asa F. Tift, testified at a Congressional investigation that the workmen in his shipyard had struck for five days, November 6–11, 1861, to increase their wages from $3 to $4 a day. He had imported twenty Richmond mechanics who at first refused to join the strike; but the rest of the workmen forced them to quit working. The workers announced that they would go with the army or serve the government in any other way rather than work for less than their demands. Previous strikes in the shipbuilding industry at New Orleans, Tift informed the Congressional committee, had lasted as long as six weeks; but the men had returned to work, accepting the terms of their employers. In order to avoid such a delay, the Tift brothers had surrendered to the demands of the strikers; but one or two of the ringleaders had been imprisoned.[45]

One of the most serious causes of the economic collapse of the Confederacy was the breakdown of the railroads. The Southern railroads in 1860 were totally unsuited to meet the strain of war. The system consisted of a congeries of small railroads operated by at least 113 weak companies,[46] the longest line under the control of one company being the Mobile & Ohio with 469 miles of track. Practically all were owned by Southerners, the notable exceptions being the Northern-owned Brunswick & Florida in southern Georgia, which Governor Brown seized in 1861 and operated under state authority, and the Florida Railroad. These fragmentary railroads had eleven different gauges, ranging from three feet to five feet, six inches, making it impossible for the cars and locomotives of some lines to traverse the tracks of others. Fortunately, there was a continuous five-foot gauge on lines running from New Orleans, Mobile, and Memphis to Chattanooga and from there to Petersburg. All the railroads were single-track, and most of them had very inadequate sidings to permit the passage of trains going in the opposite direction. The sharp curves, the frail bridges and trestles, the waiting on sidings, the necessity of frequent stops for cordwood fuel, slowed the trains to about twelve miles an hour. The rails—some of them of the T wrought-iron type, but others merely thin iron straps on wooden stringers—were in general flimsy, and wore out under the volume of war freight. Furthermore, the railroad companies were inadequately supplied with engines and cars, the largest numbers of locomotives being owned by the South Carolina Railroad, with 62, and the Central of Georgia, with 59. The South Carolina Railroad had 849 cars as contrasted with the 4,000 owned by a single Northern company, the Delaware & Lackawanna.

At the beginning of the conflict representatives of thirty-three railroads met in convention at Montgomery, April 26, 1861, to adopt a uniform policy toward the new government. They resolved to transport troops for two cents per mile (the regular rate was three and one-half cents), and to carry government freight for half the amount charged to private business. Moreover, they agreed for their companies to accept Confederate bonds at par value in payment for services. These arrangements were later accepted by a convention of Virginia railroads. But the mood of patriotic abnegation soon passed, and the Chattanooga railroad convention of October 4, 1861, raised rates for government transportation above the charges for private individuals. Although some Confederate railroads made huge paper profits and paid prodigious dividends, the profits were illusory for rolling stock and track were steadily deteriorating without ability of replacement.

As the war progressed, the Confederate and state governments practically monopolized the use of the railroads. In the concluding year the Virginia Central Railroad, for example, transported seven-eighths of its freight and two-thirds of its passengers for "government account." Before 1861 the Virginia Central had declared a semiannual dividend of 2 per cent on its capital (nearly four million dollars); but in 1864 its president declared, "The stock holders of the railroad companies generally, are probably the only persons in the Confederacy whose capital has not been productive since the war began." [47] In evaluating war profits it is well to remember that the state governments were frequently large stockholders in Southern railroads; for example, the Virginia government owned a majority of the shares of stock of the Virginia Central and appointed three of its five directors.

The Confederacy encountered numerous difficulties in utilizing the railroads. In the first place, many Northern mechanics had returned home, and others had been turned off by the railroads during the depression that followed secession and the cotton embargo. Some of the latter had joined the army, thus depriving the railroads of valuable mechanical skill sorely needed for operation in war time. The War Department, moreover, pursued a stupid policy in regard to releasing skilled mechanics from the army for railroad repairs. The companies had great trouble in securing slaves for rough labor on their roadbeds. The Confederate authorities did not realize the imperative necessity of upkeep and repair of railroads and engines. They did not import railroad iron through the blockade, and Lieutenant Colonel Frederick W. Sims, the officer in the Quartermaster Corps directly in charge of railroads, lamented February 10, 1865, that "not a single bar of railroad iron" had been rolled since 1861.[48] Rails were torn from branch lines to repair the more essential lines. Lack of repairs of track and rolling equipment brought frequent wrecks and the loss of many days in forwarding military supplies.

Many bottlenecks developed in the flow of supplies and soldiers to the battle front. At Richmond, Augusta, Savannah, Lynchburg, Charlotte, Wilmington, and Petersburg the railroads did not connect. Thus through freight had to be hauled by wagon and dray from one side of each city to the other. Because this condition was very profitable for hotels, transfer companies, and merchants, the cities were reluctant to have the lines joined. Furthermore, railroad companies did not relish entrusting their cars to other companies, so that freight had to be transferred from the cars of one company to those of another. The result was that troops and supplies were delayed for days, and quartermaster and commissary supplies congested at the bottlenecks. The Virginia state convention authorized a connection through Petersburg, June 26, 1861; but the people of that city opposed a permanent connection, and the railroads did not wish to invest money in a flimsy temporary connection. Finally in August it was completed with Confederate funds —but with the proviso that private freight should not be transported over this link and that the tracks must be removed at the conclusion of the war. The route from Chattanooga over the mountains to Richmond was interrupted at Lynchburg by a difference of gauge. The Quartermaster General endeavored to obtain cars and engines from other roads to place on the line from Chattanooga to Lynchburg, the breadline of the Confederacy, but the jealousy of the individualistic railroads prevented this move.

The Confederate leaders did not recognize the supreme need for the government to take vigorous control over the railroads; and the laissez-faire ideas of the people and their devotion to constitutionalism militated against government seizure. Consequently, the numerous small railroads continued to operate under private management. In the first two years of the war Quartermaster General Abraham C. Myers, who had charge of transportation of the Confederate armies, was strongly opposed to government operation of the railroads. Bitterly criticized for his conduct of his department, he was replaced in August, 1863, by Brigadier General A. R. Lawton. Although these two officers had general supervision over the railroads, their control was exerted chiefly by negotiating contracts. The Confederate government did not attempt to fix passenger fares or freight rates for private individuals or businesses; but it did enforce priority of government over private freight.

Able men were placed in charge of Confederate military transportation. The first such official was a North Carolina aristocrat, William Shepperd Ashe, president of the Wilmington & Weldon Railroad, who on July 17, 1861, was appointed assistant quartermaster in charge of rail transportation for the Confederate armies in Virginia. He exerted himself to close the railroad gaps, to expedite the unloading of cars, and to procure an interchange of cars. Indeed, the use of railroad cars for storage by quartermasters and commissaries was one of the greatest evils of Confederate transportation. Another serious evil was the arbitrary interference by Confederate officers with the operation of trains. Ashe met so many frustrations in trying to secure cooperation from the railroads and quartermasters that he resigned in April, 1862.

William M. Wadley, who succeeded him, was perhaps the ablest railroad man in the South. Commissioned a colonel and appointed

Military Superintendent of Railroads, he by-passed the Quartermaster General and reported through the Adjutant General to the Secretary of War. He, too, sought to develop an efficient system of freight-car interchange and of through train schedules. In March, 1863, a Railroad Bureau was created to handle government railroad property and government freight. On April 1 of that year Kean wrote in his diary: "The railroads are worn out. Wadley says he can do nothing unless he is allowed to have mechanics—Lee has fought *against* this. Secretary of War is too deferential to officers, heeding their clamor against details." [49]

Wadley strongly advocated a railroad act that would give him adequate authority to control the railroads. On May 1, 1863, Congress responded with a railroad law introduced by Senator Louis T. Wigfall of Texas. It gave the President the authority to require the railroads to cooperate in developing through freight service, in the interchange of cars and engines, in devoting their facilities to the needs of the army, except for one passenger train within every twenty-four hours, and gave the government the right to impress railroads which were recalcitrant. But the same act relieved the able Wadley, a Yankee and former blacksmith, of his job as railroad coordinator.

President Davis failed to use the powers given him by the Railroad Act of May 1, 1863, probably because of the strength of individualism and of state rights in the Confederacy. However, he chose a capable successor to Wadley, Frederick W. Sims, placing him under the authority of the Quartermaster General. This native of Georgia, with a gift for friendliness, industriously tried to get the various railroads to work for the common cause through the Railroad Bureau. He operated a government shop at Raleigh, North Carolina, to repair broken-down rolling stock and was zealous in getting mechanics and railroad men detailed from the army and in salvaging engines and cars from railroads that had fallen into the hands of the enemy; and he rendered an indispensable service in arranging for the transportation of troops to the scene of battle.[50] In supervising the railroads he was greatly assisted by the Iron Commission, organized January 22, 1863, which determined which tracks must be torn up for use on other railroads and decided how equipment should be apportioned.

On February 28, 1865, when the war was practically lost, the

Confederate Congress authorized the Secretary of War to assume control of any railroad needed for military purposes, transfer rolling stock or equipment from one railroad to another, tear up rails on branch lines and use them on main lines, and build new railroads. Employees and officers of the railroad companies were classified as part of the armed forces of the Confederacy. This law was a belated adoption of the practice of the United States government, which had given military superintendents of railroads, such as Herman Haupt and Daniel McCallum, extraordinary war powers to seize and operate all railroads and utilize all equipment needed for military transportation.

The transportation problem in the Confederacy was much larger than the inadequacy of the railroads. Before the outbreak of war a vast amount of freight had been carried in coastal vessels and river boats; but the blockade, the lack of repair facilities for ships, and the control of important rivers by the Federal Army seriously interrupted this traffic. There was great dependence also on horses, mules, oxen, and wagons, and the impressment officers interfered by taking draft animals. Oxen which the farmers used for draft were slaughtered for food. The scarcity of horseshoes prevented efficient use of work horses and even of cavalry and artillery mounts. Wagons broke down, and parts for repair could not be secured. Impressment officers seized the substantial wagons of the farmers, leaving only rickety and infirm vehicles.

In the Wigfall Papers are copies of letters from the various bureau chiefs, dated March 10–11, 1865, to Secretary of War Breckinridge describing the prospects for supplying the Army. The Ordnance chief reported that he could supply a moderate amount of ordnance as long as the Wytheville lead mines were held. Most of the Confederate armories had been broken up so that it was necessary to import arms through Florida. The chief of the Nitre and Mining Bureau reported that the Confederacy had enough niter, lead, and sulphur for five months, but that there was a great deficiency in iron owing to lack of transportation. The Quartermaster General declared that Sherman's destruction of the rail line in South Carolina prevented transport of the abundant supplies of grain in Georgia and Alabama for the army animals, but that there was enough forage in North Carolina and Virginia to supply the army for three months to come. The manufacture of wagons and ambulances kept up with the demand, but there was a dearth of animals. He observed that "the people are clamorous for money for supplies which has been repeatedly promised and not paid." Particularly significant was his remark that "a larger supply of clothing has been issued to the armies in the last three months than in any similar period of the war." The Army was better supplied with shoes than with any other article, and he was confident that there would be no serious lack of clothing. The two essentials for continuing to supply the Army, he stated, were money and protection of the railroads from raids.

The Commissary General expressed the opinion that suitable funds and protection of the rails would make it practical to keep the Army depots full; but a lack of "funds that will be received without compulsion" would paralyze all efforts. Transportation difficulties, he pointed out, made it impossible to place more than four days' rations in reserve for the Army of Northern Virginia. J. H. Claiborne, commissary for Virginia, observed that large food supplies could be obtained from hoarders, but only in exchange for gold. S. B. French, commissary at Wilmington, reported that with acceptable money and transportation the subsistence of the troops would be easy.

The inability of the government to mobilize its resources went far to explain the economic deterioration of the Confederacy. The armies and the civilian population should have been better nourished than they were, for surplus food in some districts was made unavailable by lack of railroad transportation. The war effort of the Confederacy also would have been greatly strengthened if the government had taken control of the vital blockade-running activities early. Likewise, the government was remiss in regulating manufactures and stimulating new industries. Its currency and taxation policies proved disastrous, but reflected the lack of industrial development. All these factors lowered the morale of the people and interfered with vigorous prosecution of the war. Such errors can, of course, be extenuated by the prevailing illusion of a short war and by the people's strong laissez faire concepts of government. The evils which brought about the failure of the home front were indeed deeply rooted in history, and among them the one-sidedness of the Southern economy was perhaps the most significant.

XIII

The Loss of the Will to Fight

DISCERNING men in the South realized that the sun of the Confederacy which had reached high noon at Chancellorsville had begun to sink in midsummer of 1863. Lee and his soldiers had been regarded in the Confederacy as invincible until the defeat at Gettysburg. Kean commented in his diary, July 26, 1863, that "Gettysburg has shaken my faith in Lee as a general," and that the loss of men and material in that battle was less disastrous than the loss of prestige of the army. On November 5 he noted that the Southern people were getting tired of the war, that they lacked confidence in the President and were hopeless about Confederate leaders, and that impressment and the bankruptcy of finances were depressing their spirits. On November 9 he wrote: "The prospect is very gloomy. Men of the most hopeful temper are getting discouraged." [1]

Yet there was a chance that the Northern people would also become war-weary and willing to negotiate a peace recognizing the independence of the Confederacy. As a matter of record, the ghastly defeat at Fredericksburg, December 13, 1862, Sherman's failure to take Vicksburg, and the inconclusive fighting at Murfreesboro made Northern public opinion deeply despondent. The able historian of the Copperhead movement has entitled this period lasting until July 4, 1863, "the period of despair." [2] In April, 1863, General Ambrose Burnside ordered the arrest of the leader of the Ohio Copperheads, Clement Vallandigham, who was tried by a military court and sentenced to imprisonment for the duration of the war. This arbitrary act greatly strengthened the peace Democrats of the Ohio valley; and they captured the Democratic party convention in Ohio, which without a dissenting vote nominated Vallandigham for governor. Even the elation over the victories of Gettysburg and Vicksburg was temporary. In the summer and early fall of 1864 Northern morale seemed to have reached its lowest point. Gloomy over the news that Grant was stalled at Petersburg and Sherman was stopped before Atlanta, many Northerners envisaged the war ending in a stalemate. This was the period of fluctuating sentiment described by Wood Gray as "the period of weariness." [3]

In the Confederacy public sentiment also fluctuated between hope and despair. Many a Confederate soldier must have felt like George Woodward of Wilson, North Carolina, who wrote to his brother from camp near Orange Court House, Virginia, December 27, 1863, "I am bare footed." The dispirited soldier also mentioned that he suffered from the cold and had diarrhea. Out of this bleak prospect, he wrote, "I think the Southern Federacy is broke, for it seems so to me." [4] The poor fellow died of diarrhea a few months afterwards. J. R. P. Ellis, who had been conscripted in North Carolina, wrote to his wife from Kinston, North Carolina, June 8, 1864, that he had recently seen seven deserters hanged, that some of the boys were nearly naked, that he was dirty and "mighty tired of the war." [5] On the other hand, young Sidney Lanier wrote from his signal station at Petersburg, August 2, 1864, that he was confident of Confederate success, for the Northern people now realized that they could not defeat Lee and conquer the South.[6] Also a son of Senator William A. Graham of North Carolina wrote from Petersburg, September 25, 1864, that his men were in good spirits and confident of whipping Grant if he attacked them in the trenches.[7]

But the hopeful spirit of the Southern people which seems to have revived by midsummer of 1864 began to vanish in the autumn after the reelection of Lincoln and the defeat of McClellan, the candidate of the antiwar Democrats. In the following winter the stress and privations of war, the loss of Atlanta, disillusion over the failure of King Cotton diplomacy, and the realization of the tremendous odds accelerated the growth of dissension among Confederates, and a movement for peace arose. As Professor Edward Channing observes, the Southern people lost "the will to fight." [8]

Although the Confederate government spent much money and effort in foreign propaganda, it gave slight consideration to domestic propaganda, to buoy up the sinking spirits of the people.[9] It is true that the scattered rural population could not be reached easily through the printed word; but much more could have been done than was undertaken to keep up the morale of the civilian population. The chief methods of propaganda used in the Confederacy were proclamations by the President and the governors, editorials depicting the horrors of defeat, particularly racial amalgamation, schoolbooks—between four and five hundred different texts were published during the war—and exhortations of Southern ministers and patriotic societies of devoted women. One of the most interesting forms of propaganda was the proclaiming of days of fasting and prayer. Jefferson Davis was so engrossed with military affairs that he did not devote adequate attention to inspiring the people to heroic endeavor, and Alexander H. Stephens, although he made more than forty speeches in the first year of the war when enthusiasm for the cause was high, made hardly any during the period of reaction.

Atrocity stories have formed a staple of propaganda in almost all wars, and the history of the Confederacy conforms to the pattern. Jefferson Davis tried on occasions to inflame the Southern people to fight by atrocity stories regarding the behavior of Northern soldiers. In his proclamations and messages he accused the North of waging uncivilized warfare, of atrocities against women and children, and contrasted the conduct of the Confederate soldiers during their invasion of Pennsylvania, acting as "Christian warriors," with the ruffianly conduct of Northern soldiers.[10] His most bitter indictment of military misbehavior was reserved for his proclamation ordering the immediate hanging of Ben Butler if captured, on account of his felonious conduct as military governor of New Orleans. Lawrence Keitt, the South Carolina fire-eater, wrote to his vivacious wife Suzanna just after the battle of Bull Run that ten wagonloads of handcuffs were among the spoils of the battle. "Isn't it atrocious," he exclaimed.[11] Kean's diary, August 2, 1863, cites the cruel treatment of Southern prisoners at Fort Delaware and the episode of a smallpox Negro forced to swim across the Rappahannock River to spread the dread disease among the army.[12]

From the very beginning of the war the morale of the Southern people and the effectiveness of the Confederate government in coping with its tremendous difficulties were weakened by the disruptive effect of the state-rights doctrine. Some writers have overemphasized the importance of state rights in the defeat of the South while failing to recognize that this factor also hampered the North in its prosecution of the war. One student of the weakening effect of state rights on the Confederacy has gone to the extreme of proposing an epitaph for the Confederate cause, "Died of State Rights." [13] Most Southerners would have denied that they were fighting to preserve slavery but would have maintained that they were fighting for constitutional liberty and state rights. The doctrine of state rights was especially strong in the old states which had roots in the colonial past. The newer states of the Southwest were inclined to take a broader view of Southern nationalism, and to some extent President Davis represented this point of view.

The vigorous prosecution of the war required teamwork and a high degree of centralization. The more realistic Southerners, thinking in terms of the Confederacy as a nation fighting for survival, were willing to accept the measures necessary to win independence without scrutinizing their constitutionality too closely. But Southerners of 1860 were an individualistic people, and their agrarian economy and the defense of slavery had led them violently to oppose centralization. The stresses and strains of the Civil War caused one class of Southerners to use the doctrine of state rights to oppose the centripetal policies of the Confederate government. Consequently, serious conflicts occurred between the government of Jefferson Davis and the various state governments over conscription, suspension of the writ of habeas corpus, the control of blockade running and manufacturing, the state militia and local defense, and the impressment of supplies and slaves. [14]

When Braxton Bragg wrote a caustic letter to Secretary of War Benjamin criticizing the state governments for placing local defense above Confederate military policies, Benjamin replied on November 4, 1861: "The difficulty lies with the Governors of the States who are unwilling to trust the common defense to one common head. . . . Each Governor wants to satisfy his own people and there are not wanting politicians in each State to encourage the people to raise the cry that they will not consent to be left defenseless—The voice of reason is stilled." [15]

The first important flare-up of state-rights feeling against the Davis administration occurred over conscription. Georgia was the center of disaffection, and its governor, Joseph E. Brown, led the obstructionists. Brown had been an ardent secessionist; but during the war he was so stanch a defender of state rights that he came close to treason. The aristocrats of Georgia, like Howell Cobb, the owner of a thousand slaves, and Benjamin H. Hill, hated this plebeian whom they regarded as a demagogue. Condemning the conscription law as unconstitutional, unnecessary, and a destruction of personal liberty, Brown suspended the operation of the draft in Georgia until the legislature and ultimately the Supreme Court of his state could pass on its validity. When the Supreme Court refused to declare the conscription law unconstitutional, the obstinate governor tried to hamper the operation of the law in every possible way. He created superfluous state officers in order to evade the effect of conscription, especially by placing in the exempt class approximately two thousand justices of the peace and one thousand constables.[16]

Governor Brown acted as though the defense of the state from invasion was more important than cooperation with the Confederacy to destroy the armies of the enemy. He enrolled ten thousand men in the Georgia militia, sometimes called "Brown's Ten Thousand," whom he forbade the Confederate conscription officers to enroll or molest. Such state troops, which Governor Pettus of Mississippi and other governors also tried to establish and protect, were practically useless to the Confederate cause. When Sherman invaded Georgia, the governor condescended to place his "Ten Thousand" under nominal control of General Joseph E. Johnston; but Johnston was not allowed to appoint their officers, or incorporate them in his army. In September, 1864, during one of the most critical periods of the war, Brown granted a thirty-day furlough to the "Ten Thousand." As Sherman sarcastically reported, "Governor Brown has disbanded his militia to gather the corn and sorghum of the state." [17] After Atlanta fell the governor demanded that President Davis send reenforcements to General Hood: if the request were ignored he would recall the troops of the state from the Virginia front; he would order "all the sons of Georgia to return to their own State and within her own limits to rally around her glorious flag." [18] The masses in Georgia supported their recalcitrant executive, whom they had overwhelmingly reelected governor in 1863.

His course of obstruction was also approved by Vice President Stephens, Linton Stephens, and Robert Toombs. A. L. Alexander, a prominent planter of Washington, Georgia, wrote to his daughter, wife of the Confederate Chief of Engineers, in January, 1865, describing the disaffection of Georgia: "Toombs knows no bounds to his vituperation of the administration, and I heartily wish he would leave the country. You know how great his influence *has been* and men find it difficult now to shake that influence off. I don't think it is the purpose of these men to return to the old Govt. but to withdraw if possible this and two other States from the Confed. and set up for themselves. Such I think is the scheme now on foot—Brown is only the tool in the hands of the two others —while Toombs is in my opinion the 'primum mobile and ultimum moriens' of it all. Stephens has always been traitorous at heart, but is more wary and reticent—Toombs drinks and then it all comes out. It is sad to see the influence he has over men better than himself." [19]

Next to Brown, the most obstreperous war governor opposing the centralizing policies of the Confederacy was Zebulon Baird Vance of North Carolina. This tall, bushy-haired mountaineer from Buncombe County was extremely popular.[20] His followers regarded him as a "rough diamond" partly on account of his robust and often obscene sense of humor and his marvelous oratorical power. Although he had been a firm Union man during the crisis of secession, he later raised a volunteer company and joined the Confederate Army. In 1862, at the age of thirty-two, he was elected governor on a platform urging the prosecution of the war. As governor he was a dynamic leader of a people who had been lukewarm in the secession movement.[21] He actively cared for the North Carolina soldiers and also tried to give generous relief to the families of poor soldiers. He purchased a blockade runner, the *Ad-Vance,* as well as an interest in other blockade runners to import military and essential supplies for the North Carolina troops and the civilian population. In a lecture entitled "Last Days of the War in North Carolina" he enumerated later some of the supplies which his ships had brought through the blockade: 60,000 pairs of hand cards, 10,000 grain scythes, leather for 250,000 pairs of shoes, 50,000 blankets, gray woolen cloth for 250,000 uniforms, 12,000 over-coats, 2,000 Enfield rifles, 100,000 pounds of bacon, $50,000 worth (at gold prices) of medicine, and cotton- and woolen-mill machinery.

Yet this energetic leader was provincial in his point of view and quarreled often with the central government. He demanded that it allow conscripts the privilege of selecting the regiments to which they would go. When Secretary of War Seddon appointed a native of another state, Colonel T. P. August, as conscription officer in North Carolina, Vance vehemently protested. He declared that the pride of North Carolina was wounded by the appointment of "strangers" (citizens of other states) as officers over North Carolina troops and as collectors of the tax in kind when some of "her noblest sons" could be utilized for this purpose.[22] The masterful governor forbade the central government to distill thirty thousand bushels of grain into whisky for the Medical Department as a violation of the laws of the state. He quarreled with the central government over its attempt to regulate blockade running, especially the requirement that all ships leaving Southern ports should reserve one-half of their cargo space for the Confederacy. Also he and the legislature monopolized the product of the cotton mills of the state for North Carolina troops and civilians. While Lee's troops in Virginia were ragged and suffering from lack of shoes, Vance hoarded 92,000 uniforms and large supplies of leather and blankets for North Carolina troops.

The opposition of Vance and Brown to the centralizing policies of the Richmond government should be viewed in its true perspective. Anyone who reads the numerous letters written to Vance, preserved in his correspondence in Raleigh, will perceive the tremendous pressure exerted on him by the public opinion of his state to act as he did. Senator George Davis, for example, wrote to him from Richmond, April 16, 1863, "I have for a long time been very indignant at the appointment of persons from other states to command North Carolina troops." [23] He complained that the recommendations of the North Carolina Congressmen for military appointments were ignored and only recommendations of generals were accepted. The governor received letters from the western part of the state protesting against stationing Confederate cavalry in that area, for the horses ate up the corn necessary for the sustenance of the people; letters complaining that the textile factories at Fayetteville were charging more than 75 per cent profit, that poor soldiers' families could not buy provisions in competition with the factories, and letters describing bushwhackers terrorizing neighborhoods.[24]

Letters came also from army officers, such as D. H. Hill and Johnston J. Pettigrew, urging him to suspend the writ of habeas corpus and proclaim martial law to deal with suspected persons who were dangerous to the Confederate vedettes. D. H. Hill raved against skulkers and vile speculators, declared that the people of North Carolina did not have the unconquerable will to win, and that the North Carolina newspapers and Judge Pearson were causing men to desert.[25] Johnston J. Pettigrew declared that the soldiers felt dissatisfaction with the legislature because it gave no word of encouragement and manifested none of "that enthusiastic detestation (or hatred) of the enemy for his outrages which animates us who witness them." [26]

The opposition of some Confederate governors to the growing power of the central government was not unlike the struggle between President Lincoln and some Northern governors. Furthermore, those executives who overemphasized state rights during the conflict were in a minority among the Southern governors. Governor Thomas O. Moore of Louisiana and Governor J. J. Pettus of Mississippi had some friction with the War Department in their zealous efforts to defend their states by retaining a considerable body of militia; but Pettus rendered valuable service in strengthening the defense of Vicksburg and in other ways. Governors Francis Lubbock of Texas, Milledge Bonham of South Carolina, Henry W. Allen of Louisiana, Charles Clark of Mississippi, and John Milton of Florida cooperated well with the central government.[27]

South Carolina went through a rather drastic revolution of sentiment toward the Confederate government. During the first two years South Carolinians were zealous participants in the war. After the sea islands were captured in November, 1862, the convention that had passed the secession ordinance reassembled and appointed an executive council, consisting of the governor, the lieutenant governor, and three members, with practically unlimited war powers. The council became very unpopular when it enforced the conscription act vigorously and began a state-wide impressment of slaves. Accordingly, popular pressure forced both the dissolution of the convention and the abolition of the executive council at the close of the year. Benjamin F. Perry, the old Unionist but now loyal Confederate, observed that many of the leading movers of secession failed to volunteer to fight and were reluctant to furnish their slaves for defense projects.[28] The Impressment Act of 1863 and Confederate military reverses caused a revulsion of feeling against President Davis so that in 1864 the Charleston *Courier* alone among the newspapers of the state remained pro-Davis. Congressman William W. Boyce, in partnership with Foote of Tennessee, led a revolt against the President; and in October, 1864, Boyce publicly proposed a convention of states, North and South, to discuss peace terms, hoping thus to help the Northern Democrats elect a peace candidate for President.[29] In December of that year the anti-Davis state-rights faction elected Andrew G. Magrath governor.

After the disasters of Gettysburg and Vicksburg the peace movement developed rapidly, especially in Georgia and North Carolina. In the latter state the leader was the former Union editor W. W. Holden, whose support came largely from the western part of the state. Governor Vance, although he had been feuding with the Confederate government, strongly opposed the various peace meetings held in the state, declaring that they would cause the army to melt away by desertion, would produce civil war, encourage the enemy, and lead to the subjugation of the South. "No living man," he wrote to Senator Graham August 13, 1863, "is more anxious for peace than I am"; but it would have to be upon the basis of separation and independence.[30] He sternly opposed the movement which was then gaining momentum to take North Carolina out of the Confederacy through the calling of a convention by the legislature.[31] Nevertheless, on December 30, 1863, he suggested to President Davis that an effort to obtain peace would help the morale of the people of his state, for when they realized that only ignoble terms would be granted they would support the prosecution of the war more wholeheartedly.

The peace movement in North Carolina became involved in internal politics and personal ambitions. In 1863–1864 the scars of the fight over secession still remained, and the citizens were divided roughly into the Secessionist party (the old Democratic party) and the Conservatives (the old Whig party). Vance was a conservative, but he bitterly opposed the efforts of the turncoat Holden to seize the leadership of the Conservative party and use it to advance the peace movement. To Senator Graham he wrote: "I will see the Conservative party blown into a thousand atoms and Holden and his under-strappers in hell (if you will pardon the violence of the expression) before I will consent to a course which I think would bring dishonor and ruin upon both State and confederacy. We are already ruined almost, but are not yet dishonored. Is Holden the leader of the Conservative party? If so, I don't belong to it—a known demagogue and a man of bad character." [32] Vance spoke vehemently to the people against the movement to surrender and he was sustained by them. On April 9 he wrote to Graham that he had visited the North Carolina soldiers in camp, a journey which he regarded as very profitable, and which he hoped would not give the impression in the state that he had "gone over" to the secessionists.[33] In August, 1864, he ran for reelection against Holden, the peace candidate, and won an overwhelming victory by a majority of nearly four to one.

The hill country of Georgia, Alabama, and Mississippi was another area where the peace movement was most active. In Georgia a powerful core of leadership regarded President Davis as a "despot," and opposed many laws of Congress necessary for vigorous prosecution of the war, including conscription, the impressment act, and the suspension of the writ of habeas corpus. These leaders, who maintained that they were fighting for "Constitutional liberty," threatened by the centralizing and consolidating policies of the Davis administration, included Robert Toombs, embittered because he had not been elected President of the Confederacy and because he had failed as a general; Governor Joseph E. Brown; Vice President Alexander Stephens; and Linton Stephens. Toombs resigned his military commission and ran for Congress in 1863, but was defeated, partly as a result of the opposition of the President.

Alexander H. Stephens, also a great egotist, became the brains behind the anti-Davis movement in Georgia, the abettor of Governor Brown in his state-rights policies, and instead of attending to his duties as Vice President he spent much of his time in Georgia, agitating against the policies necessary to a vigorous prosecution of the war. His half-brother Linton, eleven years younger and Harvard-educated, faithfully cooperated with him in political policies. As a member of the Georgia legislature, Linton was in a strategic position to influence the action of the state. Governor

Brown and Alexander Stephens opposed the policies of the Davis administration so strenuously that General Sherman sent messages to them to arrange a meeting to discuss Georgia's secession from the Confederacy, which they declined.[34]

The loss of the will to fight became pronounced in the Southern people after the reelection of Lincoln in November, 1864. The conflict had entered upon a stage of attrition, wearing down the weaker military machine of the Confederacy. King Cotton diplomacy had failed miserably, and thus the South was deprived of such foreign recognition and aid as had immeasurably strengthened the American colonies in the struggle of 1776. The morale of the civilian population also must have been deeply affected after 1863 by the large number of women in mourning. The role of the anti-Davis newspapers in destroying confidence in Southern success and the will to fight cannot be measured. Economic disintegration was profoundly important in the deterioration of morale, but the most important factor seems to have been military reverses. The realization in the last year of the war of the overwhelming odds against them made the people definitely war-weary and eager to end hostilities by negotiation.

Yet the laws and resolutions of the last Congress of the Confederacy, November 7, 1864, to March 18, 1865, show scarcely a trace of defeatism. In this last year of the struggle Congress received many patriotic resolutions passed by the army, such as those of Stewart's Brigade of Virginia infantry "to dedicate themselves anew to the sacred cause of Liberty and Independence and to prosecute the struggle in which they are engaged with redoubled energy and an unfaltering purpose." Congress in reply voted its cordial thanks and declared that such examples of heroic self-sacrifice were well calculated "to revive the hopes of the despondent and to stimulate the Congress and the people at home to cultivate that spirit of harmonious and unselfish cooperation which can alone impart to our cause the irresistible strength which springs from united councils, fraternal feelings and fervent devotion to the public weal." [35]

As the shadows of war began to darken the lives of the women of the Confederacy, many of them longed for peace and meditated on the dubious value of war. Their sons, husbands, and lovers began to come back to them in coffins, causing them to put on deep black mourning, a custom rooted in old folkways that now became depressing to Southern morale. Mrs. Chesnut voiced the feeling of many of her sex when she contemplated the death of so many fine young men: "Is anything worth it—this fearful sacrifice; this awful penalty we pay for war?" [36] Another wife of a Confederate officer wrote from Richmond to Mrs. Roger A. Pryor during the dark days of the war, "I am for a tidal wave of peace—and I am not alone." [37] In contrast to these yielding women, others strongly opposed surrender. Augusta Jane Evans, the Mobile novelist, wrote July 15, 1863, that she mourned over the fall of Vicksburg like Queen Mary over the loss of Calais, and that she would rather see Mobile destroyed than polluted by the presence of Yankees.[38]

The breakdown of Southern morale in the latter years of the war was registered in the appalling amount of desertion in the Confederate armies. The official reports fixed the number of deserters at 103,400, but actually the number was greater. In addition to the loss of strength from desertion the remarkable laxity of the authorities in granting furloughs depleted the army. Modern studies indicate that there was one desertion to every nine enlistments in the Confederate armies and one to every seven in the Union armies.[39] North Carolina with 23,694 deserters and Virginia with 12,071 led the Southern states; but they also furnished the largest numbers of troops. Alabama, with 1,578 deserters, had the lowest record. The widespread absenteeism in the Confederate armies is indicated by the fact that at the beginning of the war 21 per cent of the soldiers were absent, and by December, 1864, the number had increased to 51 per cent. In a speech at Macon, Georgia, September, 1864, President Davis bluntly told the people (and Sherman also) that two-thirds of Hood's army were absent, most of them without leave. The Northern armies suffered more extensively from desertion, having more than two hundred thousand offenders; but their surplus man power made the loss less serious than the Confederate desertions.

The causes of Confederate desertion were numerous, perhaps the greatest being the decline of morale after the defeats of Gettysburg and Vicksburg. Many mountaineers and backwoodsmen who disliked slavery and the cotton aristocracy were forced into the army, and hence deserted when a chance arose. Other men absented themselves temporarily to look after wives and children who were suffering severe hardships, or were called home by pitiful letters from wives and relatives to protect them from bushwhackers and outlaws. Augusta Jane Evans wrote from Mobile in the second year of the war that courts martial condemned soldiers who pleaded "in palliation of desertion the cries of hungry wives and starving children. Officers state that they see letters from wives received by privates in which their families plead for them to come home at every hazard . . . women selling their last extra dress for food." [40] Minor causes of desertion were cowardice, shortage of rations, discomforts of camp life, tyranny of officers, and lack of money to pay the railroad fare to return after a furlough. A more important factor may have been the resentment of non-slaveholders over the exemption of owners of twenty slaves.

The relative impunity for absences without leave encouraged desertion. Although some offenders were shot, Southern courts martial generally were lenient and imposed light penalties for this dangerous crime, such as flogging with thirty-nine lashes. The Federal authorities were also merciful, executing only 121 soldiers for desertion. On August 1, 1863, following the disasters of Gettysburg and Vicksburg, President Davis issued a proclamation which portrayed the disasters that would befall the Southern people, including servile insurrection and confiscation of property, if the Federal government conquered the South, and implored absentees and deserters from the army to return to their posts. He declared that the absentees, if they returned, would "suffice to create numerical equality between our force and that of the invaders," and that their return would insure victory. He promised a general amnesty to all who would return within twenty days, and he urged the women of the country not to shelter the deserters. The Confederate government offered three general amnesties to deserters if they would return to the ranks, but the offers did not accomplish much in recouping the losses by desertion.

The story of Newton Knight of Jones County, Mississippi, is a revealing case history of a deserter. A manuscript sketch of his career by his son gives a vivid impression of a frontier individualist. Newt grew up in the piney woods of southern Mississippi, where it took six days by oxcart to make a trip to the nearest trading town, Shubuta. One of twelve brothers, he received no education until his wife taught him to read and write. He had a frontier versatility of skills which he employed in farming, making shoes for his neighbors, and building log houses. When secession came to a vote the people of Jones County voted 376 to 24 to remain in the Union. Newt was drafted, and told the authorities "that he would go with them since he had to go, but he would not fight the Union." He was made a hospital orderly in the Seventh Mississippi Battalion. After the passage of the "20 nigger law" many soldiers from his relatively slaveless home community deserted; and when a letter from Mrs. Knight told Newt that the Confederate cavalry had taken his horse and were taking other private property and mistreating women and old men he also deserted.

Returning to Jones County, he organized the Unionists and deserters into a company "to fight for their rights and the freedom of Jones County." These men bound themselves by an oath never to surrender to the Confederacy until the last man was killed. Their password was, "I am of the Red, White, and Blue." A natural leader, Knight was elected captain of the irregular Unionist company, which sustained itself partly by capturing Confederate supplies and partly by the labor of the women in the fields with hoe and plow. A company of cavalry came into the county from Louisiana to restore Confederate authority. According to Newton's son, they were "mighty ruff on the boys they caught in Jones County," hanging one of Newton's brothers. When bloodhounds were sent to track down deserters the women would poison the dogs. Newt's company attacked and defeated Lowery's Cavalry.[41] After the war the tradition arose that Jones County had seceded from the Confederacy and set up the "Free State of Jones."

The great number of absences without leave from the Confederate armies in the last two years of the war was an indication of the loss of the will to fight and had grave effects on the war effort. One serious result of desertion, which was particularly common after battles, was that the soldiers carried away precious guns and other military equipment; another was that the loss of man power prevented at times the following up of victories. Deserters hid in caves, in deep mountain fastnesses, in swampy areas, and in the debatable land between the opposing armies, often becoming plunderers and murderers.

As desertion depleted the ranks of the army and enlistments declined the Southern people in desperation began to consider the

use of Negro troops. The Union Army had set an example by recruiting Negro troops in invaded territory. The recently discovered diary of James T. Ayers, a Northern recruiter in Tennessee and
northern Alabama, illustrates the methods of recruiting Southern
Negroes for military service. This lay preacher would go to plantations behind the Union lines, announce to the slaves that they had
been freed by President Lincoln, and offer the inducements of food,
clothing, and ten dollars a month to enlist. On occasions he would
display posters and lure the Negroes to volunteer with the music
of a fiddler, the example of a detachment of Negro soldiers, and his
own fervid oratory.[42] Despite such enticements, he found the slaves
exceedingly reluctant to join and finally gave up in discouragement.
Nevertheless, 186,017 Negroes served in the Union Army, of whom
104,387 were recruited in Confederate territory.

The South could very well have profited by the example of the
North in using Negro troops. In November, 1862, Thomas Went-
worth Higginson, an ardent abolitionist and admirer of John Brown,
was placed in command of the first slave regiment employed by the
United States, the "First Regiment of South Carolina Volunteers,"
which was used in fighting in that state. Later Colonel Robert
Gould Shaw of Massachusetts commanded a regiment of Negro
troops from Massachusetts, losing his life and many of his men in a
night attack on Battery Wagner, Charleston Harbor, July 18, 1863.
Led always by white officers, the Negro recruits made brave soldiers; and they had a prominent part in the capture of Port Hudson,
the battle of Milliken's Bend on the Mississippi, and the fighting at
Petersburg, Virginia. Northern soldiers, however, were almost as bitterly hostile as Southern to Negro troops.[43]

President Davis, December 23, 1862, practically threatened death
to slave troops and their white officers, in a proclamation which
turned them over to the states to be dealt with as agents to excite
servile war. The Confederate Congress on April 30, 1863, voted
that white officers leading Negro soldiers should be "deemed as
inciting servile insurrection" and, if captured, should be put to
death. Lincoln retaliated by promising that, for every Union soldier
killed in violation of the laws of war, a Confederate prisoner would
be executed. In the spring of 1864, when Forrest recaptured Fort
Pillow on the Mississippi River in Tennessee, his men were accused
of massacring the Negro troops in the garrison, refusing to accept

their surrender. This assault became the "atrocity" of the war. A Congressional investigation headed by Senator Ben Wade branded the action as beyond the pale of civilized warfare. Actually the Confederates captured 226 of the garrison of 577, about half the Federal troops having been killed during the battle. The primary cause of so much loss of life in the assault was the havoc produced by Confederate sharpshooters before the attack and the retreat of the garrison to the protection of the gunboat *New Era* without lowering the flag of the fort. There must have been some individual atrocities, but Forrest should be acquitted of the charge of ordering a brutal murder of the Federal garrison without quarter.[44]

At Dalton, Georgia, in 1864, General Patrick Cleburne circulated among the officers under the command of Joseph E. Johnston a document advocating the recruiting of Negroes for the Confederate Army. A council of officers considered this audacious project and voted against it by a large majority. Some of them condemned the proposal as incendiary and contrary to chivalric warfare. Johnston, acting under orders from President Davis, persuaded Cleburne to suppress his memorial. After the fall of Atlanta, however, Secretary of War Seddon advocated not only employment of slaves as soldiers but emancipation as a reward for military service.

Such revolutionary proposals were debated with great excitement and vehemence in the fall and winter of 1864–1865.[45] Governor William ("Extra Billy") Smith proposed that Virginia and the other Confederate states, not the central government, should arm the slaves and later emancipate them as a necessary measure to save Southern independence. In a letter of January 11, 1865, Lee favored this plan and advised that it be adopted immediately in order to allow time for training the Negroes. However, he refused to intervene to force the issue. After a long debate the Virginia legislature voted to permit the arming of slaves without promising emancipation. Judah P. Benjamin in a speech, February 9, 1865, in the African Church at Richmond urged the enlistment of slaves with the grant of freedom, and this was one of the reasons for an attempt to drive him from the cabinet. President Davis, who had opposed the arming of the slaves, now became an ardent advocate of it, not only to fill the depleted ranks of the army but to influence European diplomacy.

The influential Richmond *Enquirer* on February 24, 1865,

strongly urged the recruiting of Negroes for the army. The fact that Lee favored the use of Negroes was sufficient reason for its adoption, according to the editor; "by all means let him have them." He pointed out that, regardless of Southern prejudice, Negroes had made respectable soldiers in Grant's army, that President Davis favored using Negroes as cooks, teamsters, servants in the hospitals, and laborers for the army, and that Lee and the army desired them; "yet the Senate deliberates, and that is all it does—deliberates, *deliberates*." [46] The editor urged the Virginia legislature to arm a large body of slaves.

On the other hand Howell Cobb, one of the largest slaveholders, opposed this measure, declaring, "If slaves will make good soldiers, our whole theory of slavery is wrong." [47] Rhett came out of retirement to write a powerful letter arguing that the proposal violated state rights by removing slavery from state control. Robert Kean of the Confederate War Bureau thought that it would be "a colossal blunder" because it would dislocate society and for every Negro recruit the Confederacy got the enemy would get four.[48]

On February 10, 1865, bills to arm the slaves were introduced both in the Senate and the House of Representatives. After much debate a compromise bill was passed and signed by the President one month before the surrender at Appomattox. It gave him the power to ask slave owners for Negroes to serve in the army and, if enough were not offered, to call on each state for its quota of 300,000 troops "irrespective of color." This reluctant decision to use Negro troops was tremendously weakened by a proviso in the law that emancipation of slave soldiers should take place only with the consent of the owners and of the states which furnished them. A consideration that was urged against Negro troops was the strong aversion of white troops to fighting side by side with Negroes. Several companies of Negroes were organized in Richmond as decoys to encourage volunteering by other members of the race; but they were ridiculed, and their gaudy uniforms were pelted by small boys.

In World War I the German people lost the will to fight after four years of deprivation with the prospect of military defeat. Somewhat similarly the Southern people became war-weary after three years of fighting for independence, and a peace movement developed. One of the most popular songs in the South at this time was "When This Cruel War Is Over." John Dimitry, chief clerk in the

Post Office Department, attributed the loss of enthusiasm among Southerners to fight for independence to a lack of moral principle. "Want of Moral Principle in the People," he wrote, "has done more to injure the Cause than either Grant or Sherman. . . . I am, honestly speaking, disappointed in our people. They are not up to the mark of the times. They have failed to rise to the grandeur of the War. . . . If we lose, the Posterity of the actors in this war . . . will decide that while the President did his full duty honestly and conscientiously, the cause was lost because there was no Wisdom in Congress and no Public Virtue among the People." Senator Clement C. Clay likewise wrote to Wigfall that he was "sick of the selfishness, demagogism and bigotry that characterize a large portion of those in office," and when he saw "how many are growing rich in the Commissary and Qr. Masters Departs. by defrauding the Government and the people and yet are unchecked," and how many "cheating impressing agents" there were, he wished to retire from public life.

Throughout the great Allegheny peninsula which jutted far into the South, the Unionists began to make trouble for the Confederacy.[49] They formed secret organizations such as the Heroes of America, peace societies, and constitutional societies, with rituals, grips, and passwords. Kean noted in his diary, June 20, 1864, that there was a curious secret society in North Carolina which extended into Alabama and the army, whose principles were the second and sixth chapters of Joshua; namely, to obtain peace and preserve their property by betraying their country.[50] The commissary stationed at Dublin in southwestern Virginia wrote to Bragg, September 21, 1864, that he was amazed at the extent of disloyalty in that part of the state—he was informed that in Montgomery County there were no fewer than eight hundred "Heroes of America," who had elected the sheriffs and the justices of the peace, and there had been a meeting in Floyd County of fifty-one deserters armed with Enfield rifles who planned to destroy a section of the Virginia & Tennessee Railroad.[51]

These revolutionary associations protected deserters and engaged in "fifth column" activities. Some of the members were bushwhackers who plundered and murdered loyal Confederates. The illegal trade in cotton between the lines contributed to the growth of disloyal sentiment, and the mountain vendettas and private feuds, intensified by the Civil War, led some clans to side with the Union forces. But the main cause of disaffection in North Carolina, Georgia, and Tennessee stemmed from Unionism in 1860–1861.

The passing of the Impressment Act in March, 1863, aroused a storm of opposition that injured the morale of the people. The purpose was to legalize a practice of military officials and to protect the people from impostors. According to the law, if the impressment officer and the producer could not agree on a price, the price was to be decided by local arbitrators, with an appeal by the Confederate officer to a board of impressment commissioners in the state appointed jointly by the President and the governor. This board was required to fix, every two months, a schedule of prices for goods taken within the states by the Confederate government. In addition to impressment by the Confederate authorities, there was impressment by state governments for public defense or poor relief. Indeed, the depreciation of the currency made such practices almost imperative.

The enforcement of the impressment law contributed much toward turning loyal sections into Unionist districts. The Confederate cavalry would often stir hatred and dread by their seizure of food and horses under the law. The people bitterly resented the fact that corn and other agricultural produce were impressed at about half the market price. The law was carried out by agents who could not be closely supervised, who were susceptible to bribery, and who followed the line of least resistance; and, according to an able student of the Civil War, "No other one thing, not even conscription, caused so much discontent and produced so much resentment toward the Confederacy." [52]

The suspension of the writ of habeas corpus at intervals by the Confederate Congress was another important factor that lowered the morale of the people. Although President Davis used it conservatively, chiefly to rid Richmond and other cities of spies, traitors, and deserters, he was violently attacked as a despot. In the spring of 1864 the Georgia legislature adopted resolutions introduced by Linton Stephens declaring the suspension of the writ to be "a dangerous assault upon the Constitution" and recommending peace offers after every Confederate victory.[53] When the last suspension expired in August, 1864, a long and bitter struggle took place in Congress over its renewal. Finally a bill restoring the suspension passed in the House but received a tie vote in the Senate. Vice President Stephens cast the deciding vote against the bill, and took advantage of the occasion to deliver a diatribe against the Davis administration.

In North Carolina the opposition to the suspension of the writ was perhaps more disastrous to morale than in Georgia. On February 9, 1864, Governor Vance wrote to Davis earnestly urging him to refrain from suspending the writ in that state, because it would accelerate the growth of the peace sentiment. The Chief Justice of the North Carolina Supreme Court, Richmond M. Pearson, discharged many men arrested by conscript officers by granting them writs of habeas corpus. Vance supported him in resisting the arbitrary arrest of citizens by the military officers. Kean noted in his diary, May 3, 1863, that General W. D. Pender, a commander of North Carolina troops, revealed "disgraceful desertion of North Carolina troops as a result of Judge Pearson's decision on conscription." [54] However, when Pearson held that the Confederate Congress could not change the terms of exemption, he was overruled by his Associate Justices. In various other parts of the South, suspension of the writ of habeas corpus was violently attacked as an infringement on constitutional liberty.

The initiative for peace negotiations, however, came from the North through an unofficial visit of Francis P. Blair, Sr., to Richmond. Blair advocated reunion on the basis of a joint war against the French in Mexico to enforce the Monroe Doctrine. A conference between the two governments was finally arranged for February 3, 1865, on the *River Queen* at Hampton Roads. Here Lincoln and Secretary of State Seward met Vice President Stephens, Senator R. M. T. Hunter, and former Justice of the Supreme Court John A. Campbell, representing the Confederate government. Stephens urged the wisdom of the two nations concluding a peace treaty and then together enforcing the Monroe Doctrine. He pointed out that history showed examples of nations at war laying aside a quarrel and cooperating in matters of mutual interest. Lincoln replied that he knew nothing of history: "You must talk history to Seward." [55] Brushing aside protocol, he insisted on the restoration of the Union of all the states and the abolition of slavery as indispensable peace terms. Such proposals, the Confederates refused to consider; and peace negotiations thus ended in failure.

XIV

Sunset of the Confederacy

THREE MONTHS after the surrender of Vicksburg, Bragg lost Chattanooga, a vital railroad center and the back door of the Confederacy. General William S. Rosecrans ("Old Rosy") was menacing this key to the Cotton Kingdom with an army of sixty thousand men. From his base at Murfreesboro in September, 1863, he marched toward Chattanooga, threatening to seize the railroad to Atlanta, an indispensable supply line of the Confederate army. To prevent this catastrophe Bragg abandoned the city without a fight, continuing his old habit of falling back, which had weakened the confidence of his soldiers and officers in his leadership. Rosecrans followed the retreating army through the mountainous country in a series of detached divisions. Bragg lost a splendid opportunity to turn on the enemy and destroy him in detail. He was handicapped, however, by lack of information concerning the movements of the Federal army and by the failure of General Leonidas Polk to obey orders to attack. Rosecrans thus had time to concentrate his troops before a general engagement.

On September 19–20, 1863, the two armies engaged in mortal combat a short distance south of Chattanooga near the Georgia line at Chickamauga Creek—called by the Indians, "River of Death." [1] Bragg had the advantage of superior numbers. He had received reenforcements from Johnston's troops, released from the Vicksburg campaign. Also for the first time the Confederate government had decided to take advantage of its interior lines and transfer a corps to the Western sector. General Longstreet had urged sending reenforcements across the mountains to strengthen the Army of Tennessee, so that it could strike a decisive blow. In September, 1863, he received permission to take his whole corps of 12,000 men to the aid of Bragg. His soldiers and equipment were transported over crazy and worn-out railroads around the mountains via Wilmington, Augusta, and Atlanta, and a part of them reached Chickamauga just in time to turn the tide of battle. It was the attack of Longstreet's troops through a gap in the Federal line that defeated the Union army.

Rosecrans was still in pursuit of Bragg's army on September 19 when it turned on him and attacked him in echelon formation. After the hard first day's fighting Bragg ordered an attack at sunrise of Sunday, September 20, upon the Federal left flank, commanded by Thomas. General Leonidas Polk was placed in charge of this operation—intended to be a turning movement with Longstreet's command, the left wing, as a pivot. Longstreet was ordered to attack as soon as he heard the sound of Polk's guns. But the sun arose, and when for some time thereafter there was still no sound of attack Bragg sent an officer to learn the cause of this inaction. The Bishop-General was "two miles from his troops sitting in a rocking chair at a house waiting for his breakfast, and did not know why the action was not commenced" as he had ordered it.[2] The tardiness of the attack gave Rosecrans the opportunity of massing troops on his left to repel it.

The Union commander was bent on preserving his communications with Chattanooga and unnecessarily weakened his right flank to strengthen his left. He also gave a blundering order which opened a gap in the center of his line. The Confederate army poured through the gap, demolishing his right flank, and in the rout he and his staff were swept to Chattanooga. Charles A. Dana, Assistant Secretary of War, who was at army headquarters when the rout occurred, was awakened from an afternoon nap by the most infernal noise he had ever heard and saw General Rosecrans, a devout Catholic, crossing himself: " 'Hello!' I said to myself, 'if the general is crossing himself, we are in a desperate situation.' "[3] On the left flank the corps of General George H. Thomas, the imperturbable Virginian who had remained loyal to the Union, fought so bravely and stanchly that it stemmed the Confederate onslaught. His corps was saved by General Gordon Granger, commander of the reserve corps, who violated orders and went to his aid. Moreover, Thomas's men had the great advantage of being strongly protected by abatis. For his valor and steadfastness in this battle he was called the "Rock of Chickamauga"; but his soldiers called him "Slow Trot." [4]

Chickamauga has been evaluated by the Confederate general D. H. Hill as "the great battle of the West." [5] Certainly it was one of the bloodiest conflicts of the Civil War. Longstreet's corps lost 44 per cent of its strength in the first two hours of fighting, and both armies were reduced approximately a third by the battle. Thomas Wolfe's short story of "Chickamauga" portrays the desperate valor, the blood and sweat, of that battle. A ninety-five-year-old Confederate veteran told him: "But the biggest fight that I was ever in— the bloodiest battle anyone has ever fought—was at Chickamauga in that cedar thicket—at Chickamauga Creek in that great war." [6] Bragg, accustomed to defeat, did not recognize that he had won an overwhelming victory. Despite the pleas of Longstreet and Forrest he refused to follow up his advantage and demolish the Federal army. This glorious triumph in which Southern blood flowed so profusely was fruitless because the leader of the Army of Tennessee had not the spirit to follow up his opportunities. "What does he fight battles for?" asked the blunt and realistic Forrest. His failure to use fresh troops, particularly Cheatham's division and Wheeler's cavalry, to block Thomas's retreat to Chattanooga was a great blunder. [7]

Bragg now began a siege of Rosecrans' army penned up in Chattanooga and suffering from lack of food. While the Confederate army was encamped before Chattanooga, a group of officers led by Longstreet and Buckner sent a round robin to President Davis (dated October 4, 1863), asking for the removal of Bragg, whose ill health, they stated, unfitted him for the command of an army in the field. The President came to Chattanooga and held a conference with the generals. In spite of Bragg's presence his officers gave an adverse opinion on his fitness. Nevertheless Davis retained the discredited general in command.

Although Bragg had thrown away his opportunities after Chickamauga, the Confederates still had an excellent chance to capture the entrapped Union army in Chattanooga. So dangerous was its position that Grant rose from a hospital bed and went to Chattanooga. Hooker's corps of 23,000 men was sent by rail from Alexandria, Virginia, via Cincinnati, Louisville, and Nashville to Bridgeport, across the Alabama line, arriving in less than six days—the most spectacular use of railroads for military movements during the Civil War. Also, reenforcements under Sherman came from Mississippi to break the siege. Replacing Rosecrans with Thomas in command at Chattanooga, Grant managed to establish a supply line into that city by means of an expedition from Chattanooga under General William F. ("Baldy") Smith which floated pontoons to Brown's Ferry, where a bridge was laid over the Tennessee with only slight resistance from the Confederates. The Confederate sharpshooters, who had made the wagon road along the Tennessee unusable, were driven away, and Hooker marched up from Bridgeport to the base of Lookout Mountain. Too late, Bragg tried on October 28 to close the trap thus opened by ordering a night attack on Hooker's rear. Hooker's mules became frightened and stampeded with whiffletrees and trace chains rattling so that the Confederates thought the enemy was charging against them. They fled, and the battle was lost.[8] The way was now opened for the Federals to supply their army in Chattanooga.

While the Federal leaders were gathering reenforcements to relieve Chattanooga, Bragg was fatuously dispersing his troops. On the eve of battle he sent away his ablest subordinate, Longstreet, with 20,000 troops—one third of his strength—in a fruitless effort to capture Burnside's army at Knoxville. In the meanwhile (November 23–25) the Union army, increased to 61,000, attacked the passive gray army of 40,000 which was holding strong strategic positions around Chattanooga. In the ensuing battle of Lookout Mountain, south of Chattanooga, Hooker's men, 10,000 strong, charged up through fog and mist to drive a weak Confederate skirmish line of 2,000 men from the top. This engagement has been romanticized as the "Battle Above the Clouds."

Then occurred one of the greatest disasters to the Confederacy: the defeat of Bragg's army in the battle of Missionary Ridge, which ranked next to Gettysburg and Vicksburg. The main part of the Confederate army held Missionary Ridge, reaching southeast from Chattanooga. Very unwisely Bragg had placed approximately half of the defending forces at the bottom of the ridge in rifle pits, while the remainder held the narrow crest. On November 25 Grant sent Sherman against the Confederate right wing, commanded by Cleburne and Hardee; but this assault was repulsed. Then he ordered General Thomas, commanding the center, to send troops to take the rifle pits at the foot of Missionary Ridge. The Federal soldiers not only carried the rifle pits but, without orders, charged up the mountain and drove the Confederates from their strong position. Bragg described this precipitate retreat as follows: "A panic which I had never before witnessed seemed to have seized upon officers and men, and each seemed to be struggling for his personal safety, regardless of his duty or character." [9] He thought that they had become demoralized because they could plainly see the mobilizing of the great numerical superiority of soldiers to be hurled at them. Also the Confederate artillery on the crest could not be sufficiently depressed to blast the charging blue lines as they came up the slope. After this shameful defeat, which might have been reversed if Longstreet and his troops had been present, Bragg retreated to Dalton in northern Georgia.

The colossal failure of the Confederates at Chattanooga led to a change of commanders. Bragg had completely lost the confidence and respect of his soldiers. Private Watkins described this demoralization as follows: "The army was routed and Bragg looked so scared. Poor fellow, he looked so hacked and whipped and mortified and chagrinned at defeat, and all along the line, when Bragg would pass, the soldiers would raise the yell, 'Here is your mule'; 'Bully for Bragg, he's h——l on retreat.' " [10] On December 1 Bragg asked to be relieved, accusing some of his officers, particularly John C. Breckinridge and Frank Cheatham, of being drunk and unfit for duty during the great trials of the Army of Tennessee. Davis recalled the unsuccessful general to Richmond to act as his military adviser and appointed Joseph E. Johnston to command the Western army.

During the winter of 1863–1864 active campaigning was suspended in the East, except for an invasion of northern Florida by six thousand Union troops under Major General Truman Seymour. By the fall of 1863 Florida had become the main source of beef and bacon for the Confederate armies. The object of the Federal expedition was to cut off this important source of food, to aid the Unionists of the state in reconstructing a loyal state government, to obtain cotton and naval stores, and to recruit Negro soldiers. On February 20, 1864, when Seymour's troops, including a Negro regiment, reached the Olustee River in the interior, they were decisively defeated by approximately 5,000 Confederates under Brigadier General Joseph Finegan, with a loss of one-third of the number.[11] The battle of Olustee gave the people of the Confederacy a gleam of hope in the dark gloom following the disaster of Missionary Ridge.

On March 9, 1864, Grant was called from the West where he had won important victories—mostly over second-rate Confederate generals, however—and appointed Lieutenant General over all the armies of the Union. Thus the North obtained unity of planning and action which the South never achieved. The new commander proved to be a master of grand strategy. He planned his spring campaign of 1864 to encircle the two main Southern armies: Sherman was to move from Chattanooga against Johnston's army and Atlanta and thereby threaten the rear of Lee's army; Banks was to finish his Red River campaign and move against Mobile; George Crook, commanding in West Virginia, was to move from Gauley Bridge to cut the Virginia & Tennessee Railroad connecting Richmond and Knoxville; Sigel was to advance up the Shenandoah Valley, covering Washington and depriving Lee of provisions; Ben Butler was to advance from Fort Monroe up the James River with Richmond and Petersburg as objectives; Grant himself proposed to accompany Meade's army in a frontal advance on Richmond, with the destruction of Lee's army as the main objective.[12]

Grant had almost every advantage over Lee except the important one that the Confederates would be fighting defensively west of Fredericksburg in the region of tangled forest and undergrowth called the Wilderness. Not only did he have a superiority in soldiers of two to one, but he could continually get replacements. In contrast to the poorly clad, ill fed gray army, the Union soldiers were comfortably dressed, well fed, and had abundant ammunition and military stores. With an early superstition about retracing his steps, Grant was determined not to retreat and was willing to sacrifice large numbers of his men in order to destroy Lee's army and take the Confederate Capital.

On May 4, the Federal army crossed the Rapidan River, a tributary of the Rappahannock, at Germanna Ford and entered the Wilderness. Lee sent his three corps from Orange Court House along the Orange Turnpike and the parallel Orange Plank Road to strike the enemy in this terrain, which largely offset the superior numbers and artillery. On May 6 Longstreet led his troops against the left flank of the Federal army and was driving it toward the Rapidan when he was accidentally wounded by his own men and had to be carried from the field. On that day the Confederates had their greatest chance for victory when General Gordon discovered that the right flank of the enemy was exposed and very vulnerable. He asked permission to attack; but his corps commander, General Ewell, refused because he believed that Grant could not have committed such an error,[13] and it was late in the afternoon when Lee arrived on the left and issued the order. Then Gordon boldly advanced, routing the enemy's right wing. Grant was deeply agitated by this grave crisis which threatened disaster; but night intervened, and he was able to restore order in Sedgwick's corps.

Lee made the most of his slender resources, checking Grant's every move with brilliant maneuver and with defensive works and inflicting tremendous losses on the Northern army. Grant did not retreat, but advanced by a flanking movement. Divining that he would move southeastward to Spotsylvania Court House, about a dozen miles southwest of Fredericksburg, Lee quickly transferred his army and was waiting behind strong field fortifications on May 12 when the Federal army arrived. There Hancock's corps attacked a salient and broke through the Confederate line. In this ominous situation Lee himself prepared to lead a counterattack to plug the gap; but his soldiers and officers, with a cry, "Lee to the rear," refused to let him risk his life. In desperate fighting at the "Bloody Angle" troops under General John B. Gordon finally checked the victorious blue army as it was pouring through and restored the Confederate line.

The most violent fighting of the campaign occurred June 3, 1864, ten miles northeast of Richmond at Cold Harbor, where Grant ordered a charge against entrenchments which led to a horrible slaughter. In the campaign from the Wilderness to Cold Harbor the Federal army lost fifty-five thousand men by deaths, wounds, disease, and desertion—a number nearly equal to the battle deaths of the United States in World War I, and also to the whole of the opposing Confederate army. Grant had begun a war of relentless attrition. Moving stubbornly toward Richmond, he sought to envelop Lee's right flank and get between the Confederate army and the city. Lee anticipated the tactics, however, and always extended his right flank in time to avert disaster. Finally Grant changed his strategy, slipped by Lee's army, crossed the James on June 12–16, and marched south toward Petersburg. This city, twenty-three miles below Richmond, was the key to the Capital, for it commanded vital railroad lines of supply and communication with the rest of the Confederacy.

In May a Federal army of 36,000 men under Ben Butler had come up the James and established a base at Bermuda Hundred in an angle between the James and Appomattox rivers. From this point Butler succeeded in destroying part of the railroad between Petersburg and Richmond; and he attacked the defenses of Richmond at Drewrys Bluff, where Beauregard struck the Federal army with great vigor and might have demolished it had General W. H. C. Whiting obeyed orders and arrived in time from Petersburg to attack the Federal rear and flank.[14] Nevertheless Beauregard drove the Federal army back to its base at Bermuda Hundred, where it remained "corked in as in a bottle" by his engineering skill and strategy.

Whiting's failure in this campaign underlines one of the most tragic personal careers of any of the Confederate officers. A native of Mississippi and the son of an army officer, he had a brilliant career at West Point, ranking No. 1 in the same class with "Stonewall" Jackson, who had a mediocre record. He was handsome and aristocratic in manner although of short stature. Early in the war he antagonized President Davis, who wished to brigade the Mississippi troops together, by brusquely declining to accept such a brigade and declaring that to regiment troops by states was "as suicidal as foolish." [15] Brooding over his failure to play a role in the war commensurate with his talents, he drank heavily and became morose. He atoned for the failure to cooperate at Drewrys Bluff, however, by serving as a volunteer in the defense of Fort Fisher, where he was mortally wounded.

Beauregard, on the other hand, grew in stature as the war progressed. When Grant began crossing the James on June 14 and advancing toward Petersburg, Beauregard sent repeated messages informing Lee of the dangerous movement; but Lee discounted them. At this time the Confederate forces, under Brigadier General Henry A. Wise, holding Petersburg numbered only 2,200; but they responded heroically to Beauregard's order "to hold the line at all hazards" against the repeated assaults of 18,000 men. Beauregard brought up reenforcements increasing the number to 15,000 men against the whole of Grant's army of 90,000 men; he shortened his line around Petersburg and held the position against overwhelming odds until Lee arrived with his army on June 18. Robert Kean noted in his diary, June 20, that the President's circle criticized Beauregard for abandoning his line in front of Butler at Bermuda Hundred and throwing all his forces into Petersburg, but that it was "one of the finest movements of the war," showing the mark of genius: it alone saved the city of Petersburg, the key to Richmond.[16] In the heroic defense Wise's brigade, which up to this engagement was known as "The Life Insurance Co.," never having accomplished anything and being given to spreading sensational rumors, redeemed itself.[17] Nevertheless, its commander, the great talker ex-Governor Wise, remained a brigadier general until the surrender at Appomattox.

When the arrival of Lee's army made it impossible to capture Petersburg by assault, Grant began siege operations that lasted nine months. A notable trench warfare resulted, a precursor to the trench warfare of World War I. During the early part of the siege the Union soldiers dug a tunnel 510 feet in length and placed a mine of 8,000 pounds of powder under the Confederate fortifications. It was exploded on July 30, forming a crater 30 feet deep, 60 feet wide, and 170 feet long. Federal attacking troops then made the mistake of descending into the crater rather than marching around it and, once they were in the crater, refused to move from its shelter. A division of 4,300 Negro troops under Brigadier General Edward Ferrero was ordered to support the original attacking force, and displayed greater bravery in assaulting the Confederate lines than the white troops. The Confederates, under the command of Bushrod Johnson and "Billy" Mahone, repulsed the attack through the crater, inflicting a loss of nearly four thousand men.[18]

While Grant was bludgeoning his way through the Wilderness toward Richmond, Sherman was advancing steadily toward the railroad center of Atlanta. With an army of a hundred thousand men he started from Chattanooga in early May, using the Western & Atlantic Railroad as his line of supply. The conquest of Atlanta, he declared later, would have been impossible if he had not preserved his line of supply stretching 473 miles to the Ohio River, which provided for the needs of his huge army and 35,000 animals for 196 days.[19] To protect his communications from Forrest's cavalry he sent Major General Samuel D. Sturgis with a force of cavalry and infantry. In Sturgis's command was a division of 1,200 Negro troops under General Edward Bouton, who had vowed to avenge the Fort Pillow "massacre." Although Forrest's command was only half the size of the Federal force, he defeated Sturgis in a brilliantly fought battle at Brice's Cross Roads in northeastern Mississippi on June 10 and drove the demoralized force back to Memphis. But Sturgis's invasion caused General Stephen D. Lee, departmental commander, to recall Forrest from going to Tennessee to attack Sherman's communications. A month later Lee and Forrest suffered a defeat at Harrisburg near Tupelo when they rashly attacked the much superior force of General Andrew J. Smith waiting for them behind breastworks and entrenchments.[20]

In the march to Atlanta, Sherman did not have to fight as hard as Grant against Lee in Virginia. With a superiority of two to one, he advanced by constantly flanking the Confederate army. Johnston conducted a skillful retreat, making effective use of breastworks, abatis, and redoubts to save his men, many of whom were barefooted.[21] His soldiers, numbering about 53,000 men, had such great confidence in their leader that they did not grumble at the constant retreating and the use of spade and ax for entrenchments. It was Johnston's plan to attack at an advantageous place after Sherman had extended his line of communications. He was deceived, however, in thinking that Sherman would become vulnerable by leaving his base so far behind. The Northern general was well supplied by a railroad, which was defended by blockhouses and kept constantly in repair by the railroad genius, Daniel McCallum. At Kennesaw Mountain, Johnston made a valiant stand, and Sherman lost three thousand men by hurling them against entrenched Confederate troops.

In the meanwhile, President Davis had become alarmed at the constant retreating of Johnston. This peppery Virginian, although very competent, seems to have suffered from "a nervous dread of losing a battle," which made him excessively cautious and averse to offensive and aggressive action. When Sherman's army got close to Atlanta, Davis sought to find out what Johnston's plans were; but Johnston, who deeply disliked his commander-in-chief, refused to confide in him. The people of Georgia strongly urged the dismissal of Johnston, and Davis with the concurrence of his Cabinet suddenly removed the retreating general July 17, 1864, and appointed the thirty-three-year-old John B. Hood to the command.

The new commander, born near Mount Sterling, Kentucky, had graduated from West Point, where he ranked forty-fourth in a class of fifty-five.[22] A striking individual, six feet, two inches in height, with the long blond beard of a crusader and with the light of battle in his eyes, he had lost the use of an arm at Gettysburg; and one of his legs had been amputated on the battlefield of Chickamauga. Leading Texan troops, he had won a fine reputation as an aggressive fighter, and had become a favorite of President Davis. Sherman was delighted at news of the change of the Confederate leadership, noting that two of his corps commanders, McPherson and Schofield, had far outranked Hood at West Point, McPherson being the No. 1 man of the class and Schofield No. 7. The appointment on the eve of battle proved to be a fatal mistake. Hood had never exercised independent command, and he felt a fearful responsibility in taking charge of the Confederate army on the eve of a crucial battle. Unfortunately, his subordinate officers distrusted his ability; and both Joe Johnston and General Hardee, the second in command, lacked the noble virtue of self-effacement and failed to cooperate wholeheartedly with the rash young general.

While Sherman's army was crossing Peachtree Creek, a few miles above Atlanta, it was dangerously divided into three parts, presenting a splendid opportunity for the Confederates to attack. Accordingly, Hood ordered an attack July 20 on Thomas's corps, the right flank of the Union army. Although his plans and orders were excellent they were not properly executed, because Cheatham on his right had shifted his division two miles beyond Hardee's troops which held the center, and Hardee was greatly delayed in closing the gap. Thus the opening engagement resulted in a Confederate defeat. Then on July 22 Hood ordered a brilliant maneuver in which Hardee led his men by a night march to attack the Federal rear and flank; but an unlucky accident prevented this second battle of Atlanta from resulting in a smashing victory. On the 28th, when Sherman began to move his army around Atlanta, Hood attacked him fiercely at Ezra Church, four miles to the west; but his able plan was poorly executed. The Federals, protected by breastworks and armed with repeating rifles, mowed down the indomitable Confederates. After this defeat the gray-clad army retired behind its fortifications, and the siege of Atlanta began, lasting a month.[23]

On August 10 Hood committed his first major blunder by sending "Fightin' Joe" Wheeler with 4,000 cavalry to destroy Sherman's communications. Thus, having lost the eyes of his army, he was deceived in thinking that the Federal army was leaving its entrenchments north of the city to retire on account of a shortage of food. Actually Sherman was shifting around Atlanta to cut its vital railroad supply line to Macon. When Hood finally learned the real state of affairs on August 31 he sent Hardee to drive back the vastly superior flanking force of the enemy. Hardee and Stephen D. Lee attempted to smash the Federal flank attack at Jonesboro, south of the city on the Macon railroad.[24] When this effort failed, Hood began evacuating Atlanta on September 1, moving south to Lovejoy's station on the line to Macon.

Hood blamed his troops for lack of courage and fight, comparing their spirit unfavorably with that of the Eastern army. To General Bragg he wrote on September 4: "It seems the troops had been so long confined to trenches and had been taught to believe that entrenchments cannot be taken that they attacked without spirit and retired without proper effort. . . . I am officially informed that there is a tacit if not expressed determination among the men of this army extending to officers as high in some instances as Colonels that they will not attack breastworks." [25] Yet the gray and butternut-clad troops of the West often attacked gallantly in the battles to save Atlanta. Although Hood had some unlucky breaks in the execution of his plans, the great reasons for his defeat were the skill of Sherman and the strength of Sherman's army which had at least twice the number of men that Hood commanded.

On September 2 Sherman's troops marched into Atlanta, which in 1860 was a town of only 12,000 inhabitants. The victorious commander shocked Southerners when he ordered the complete evacuation of the town by the civilian population, saying that he needed all the houses for his army. Grimly he announced: "If the people raise a howl against my barbarity and cruelty, I will answer that war is war, and not popularity seeking." [26] On another occasion he declared, "War is cruelty and you can not refine it." The capture of Atlanta restored the will of the North to subdue the South and probably won many votes for Lincoln in the election of that fall in which he was opposed by McClellan, widely regarded as the "peace candidate."

The siege of Atlanta had lasted thirty days, during which screaming shells and cannon balls devastated the city and drove the citizens into cellars and underground bombproof shelters. In the great emergency, the militia of Georgia—mostly old men and young boys, known as "Joe Brown's Pets" because some were able-bodied shirkers whom Governor Brown had protected—was called into action. Some of the old gentlemen carried umbrellas or walking sticks as well as shotguns and flintlock rifles, adding a touch of comedy to the grim tragedy of defeat. Before Hood evacuated the town, seventy freight cars of ordnance stores and ammunition were burned to avoid capture by the Federals. Margaret Mitchell's famous novel *Gone with the Wind* skillfully portrays the human drama of this historic siege and the flight of the citizens.

After the evacuation of Atlanta, President Davis went to Palmetto, Georgia, to which the gray army had retreated, to confer with Hood. The Confederate general presented his plan of a campaign into Tennessee to cut Sherman's communications with Nashville, defeat Thomas at that Union bastion, and march to the Ohio River. Davis gave his consent, for both he and Hood believed that Sherman would follow the Confederate army in order to preserve his communications. Beauregard, whom Davis placed in charge of the Military Division of the West, including the departments commanded by Hood and Richard Taylor, also consented to the risky plan but urged Hood to execute it with the greatest speed.

With approximately 40,000 troops Hood moved north toward the Tennessee River. Sherman followed him briefly but, unable to force the Confederates into battle, returned to Atlanta. From there he put into execution a bold plan of abandoning his line of communications and marching to the sea at Savannah. He determined to make the civilian population of the lower South suffer the horrors of an invasion—in his own picturesque language, "to make Georgia howl." Before he left the ruined city of Atlanta, however, he detached 30,000 of his troops under Schofield and sent them to strengthen Thomas.

Instead of following Beauregard's advice of the imperative necessity of speed, Hood was dilatory and moved toward his objective in a roundabout way, crossing the Tennessee at Tuscumbia, Alabama. He was delayed by rainy weather, by the fact that the railroad from Corinth upon which he depended for accumulating supplies was not repaired as soon as he expected, and by his uncertainty as to whether Sherman would follow him. Accordingly, although he arrived at Tuscumbia on October 30, his army did not complete the crossing of the river by pontoon bridge until November 15. Over this delay Thomas Robson Hay comments, "The paralysis of Hood's decision cost him many lives, the campaign, and finally his command." [27]

While Schofield was on his way, Hood had a splendid chance to destroy the Yankee army at Spring Hill, Tennessee, on November 29; but the opportunity was lost through inaction and misunderstandings. Late at night Hood was informed that the Federals were passing on the turnpike to Nashville; but he delegated the task of investigating to subordinate officers and went back to bed and to sleep. Thus Schofield escaped in the night and marched on toward his destination. The Confederate army pursued the retreating Federal army and caught up with it the next day shortly before sunset at Franklin, eighteen miles south of Nashville. Here the Union troops were strongly protected by breastworks and entrenchments. Chagrined by the escape of Schofield at Spring Hill, Hood rashly ordered an attack without waiting for his artillery. The Confederates bravely charged over a distance of about two miles against the intrenched enemy. The result was an appalling loss of life, partly owing to the fact that one of the Federal brigades was armed with Spencer's breech-loading rifle. "Casement's brigade with these arms," wrote General E. P. Alexander, "decided that battle with terrific slaughter." [28] At Franklin the South lost twelve generals and fifty-three regimental commanders by death, wounds, or capture. Among them Pat Cleburne, "the Stonewall Jackson of the West," died leading his troops. The charge of the Army of Tennessee at Franklin was as brave and tragic as Pickett's charge at Gettysburg.

After this repulse Hood marched to the environs of Nashville and besieged Thomas, who had 60,000 men against his own 25,000. It was foolish for Hood to advance to Nashville, but he believed that his army would disintegrate as a result of desertion if he did not put on a bold front. During this period Grant urged Thomas to attack. When he refused to move until he was ready, Grant sent an officer to relieve him; but, too soon for that, Thomas struck the weak, starving, and shivering Confederate army on December 15 and shattered it in the most complete victory by a Union army during the war. An interesting feature of this battle was the participation of Negro troops in a fierce assault on the Confederate lines.

The forlorn remnant of the Confederate army, many of them barefoot in the icy weather, retreated from Tennessee singing a paraphrase of a new song entitled "The Yellow Rose of Texas":

> And now I'm going southward,
>   For my heart is full of woe,
> I'm going back to Georgia
>   To find my "Uncle Joe." *
>
> You may talk about your Beauregard
>   And sing of General Lee,
> But the gallant Hood of Texas
>   Played hell in Tennessee.

Following this great disaster, Hood resigned, and the remnant of the Army of Tennessee was placed under General Richard Taylor, son of "Old Rough and Ready."

Sherman's march from Atlanta to Savannah and north through the Carolinas was one of the most important and spectacular campaigns of the Civil War. This redheaded general had a modern conception of war, that success in military affairs was to be obtained not merely by defeating hostile armies but by breaking the morale of the civilian population. He declared: "We are not only fighting hostile armies, but a hostile people, and must make old and young, rich and poor, feel the hand of war, as well as their organized armies." [29] War was not a gallant and chivalric play, as some of the Southerners thought, but might be summed up in the phrase "War is hell," which he is reputed to have used in conversation. He determined to disillusion the civilian population of the lower South who had been deceived by "their lying newspapers" into believing that the South was victorious. Sherman demonstrated his audacity also in breaking away from his communications and depending on the food resources of Georgia to feed his army. He had observed the ease with which Grant had abandoned his line of communications during the Vicksburg campaign and had lived off the country.

* Johnston.

In early November, 1864, Sherman left Atlanta, shrouded with a great pall of black smoke. His sixty-two thousand men, seasoned veterans, had unlimited confidence in "Uncle Billy." [30] They moved in four parallel columns, carrying pontoon bridges in sections to cross the numerous rivers ahead of them. He was able to deceive the Confederate generals as to his objective, whether it was Macon or Augusta, so that he was practically unopposed. Beauregard, in general command of the Southern troops opposing Sherman's army, issued bombastic proclamations urging the Southern people to arise and destroy the roads and communications of the Federal army. Jefferson Davis predicted in a speech at Macon that the Yankee invasion would result in a Moscow disaster.

Sherman's orders to his troops were more moderate than his violent threats had indicated. "The army will forage liberally on the country during the march," he announced. Each brigade was to send out a foraging party to gather food supplies and to secure horses and mules. They would go out on foot and return on captured horses and mules, frequently driving wagons and family carriages and coaches loaded with turkeys, chickens, pigs, hams, corn, etc. Although they were ordered not to enter the homes of the people, the order was disregarded, and the soldiers would laugh heartily as they obeyed the injunction to "forage liberally"! Sherman estimated when he arrived at Savannah on December 10 that he had deprived the state of Georgia of fifteen thousand first-rate mules as well as many horses. He had started from Atlanta driving five thousand head of cattle and arrived at Savannah with ten thousand beeves.

One of Sherman's principal objects was to destroy Southern railroads. His men tore up the iron rails, made bonfires of the wooden ties, heated the rails, and twisted them in spirals around trees and telegraph poles. The twisted rails were facetiously called "Sherman's neckties." The invaders demolished more than two hundred miles of railroad during the forty days' march to the sea. By such destruction and interference with the food supplies of the lower South he believed that he would starve Lee's army in Virginia into submission.

The army had a great lark marching through Georgia. The weather was fine and the band played "John Brown's soul goes marching on!" Feasting royally on the fat of the land, they were in superb physical condition, so that they marched fifteen miles a day. When they reached Milledgeville, the capital of Georgia, some of the officers held a mock assembly of the legislature and repealed the ordinance of secession. Large numbers of Negroes followed the army, to the disgust of Sherman, who stubbornly refused to use Negro troops, desiring to keep the war a white man's war.

From Savannah the Federal army turned north through South Carolina.[31] The Yankees entered the cradle of secession with vindictive feelings. "The truth is," wrote Sherman, "the whole army is burning with an insatiable desire to wreak vengeance upon South Carolina. I almost tremble at her fate, but feel that she deserves all that seems in store for her." [32] There will always be a difference of opinion as to the conduct of Sherman's soldiers—especially the individual raiders sometimes called "bummers." Southern sources indicate that they entered private homes, destroyed furniture, ordered the mistresses to prepare meals for them, and stole silver, jewels, and any valuables they could find. According to Mrs. Elizabeth W. Pringle, author of the *Chronicles of Chicora Wood,* their unvarying cry as they burst into the homes of the planters was "We Want Whiskey!" Despite wanton destruction of property and plundering, they did not murder or rape the defenseless women. None the less, they destroyed many beautiful old plantation homes along the Cooper, Ashley, and Combahee rivers in South Carolina. "Drayton Hall," one of the most magnificent, was saved by the ruse of a slave who told the Northern soldiers that it was being used as a smallpox hospital. The capital of South Carolina, Columbia, was burned while Sherman's army was marching in. Sherman maintained that Wade Hampton's cavalry before they retreated, had set fire to cotton bales piled in the streets and that a high wind fanned the flames. Southerners, on the other hand, believed that drunken soldiers of the Federal army deliberately set fire to the city. Sherman's cavalry leader, Judson Kilpatrick, who led the advance into the city, has been described as a ruffian who set a bad example to his troops.

From Columbia, Sherman marched to Fayetteville, North Carolina, and thence to the railroad junction town of Goldsboro in the eastern part of the state. At this desperate moment President Davis restored Joe Johnston to the command of the scattered Confederate forces opposing Sherman. But Johnston had no hope of stopping the victorious Northern army, of which he declared, "there has been no such army since the days of Julius Caesar." [33] Nevertheless on March 19–20 he attacked Sherman's army, 60,000 strong, at Bentonville, near Goldsboro, in a hard-fought battle in which an amazing number of Confederate generals commanded only 15,000 men. Hardee led a charge in which his sixteen-year-old son, a volunteer cavalryman, was killed. After this last-ditch fight the forlorn gray army began a retreat which ended in surrender near Durham, North Carolina.

Sherman's march through Georgia and the Carolinas effectively demonstrated to the people of the lower South the hopelessness of continuing the fight for independence. [34] Yet the destruction of civilian property and nonmilitary objectives by his army is highly questionable from a psychological point of view. A bitter feeling toward the North, a belief that Yankees were barbarians, an utter detestation of Sherman, lived long in the minds of Southerners. This tradition was a real factor in delaying the reconciliation of the North and the South.

While Grant was grappling with Lee in the Wilderness, the Federal campaign in western Virginia started with a series of failures. From the Kanawha valley Major Generals George Crook and William W. Averell set out to disrupt the Virginia & Central Railroad and destroy the lead mines at Wytheville and the salt mines at Saltville. Opposing them was a small cavalry and infantry force under Morgan, who after his spectacular escape from prison in Ohio had been placed in command in western Virginia. On May 11 near Wytheville, Morgan defeated the Federal troops and saved the vital lead mines. Subsequently he invaded Kentucky and captured Lexington but was disastrously defeated at Cynthiana by a Kentuckian in Union service, Major General Stephen G. Burbridge, and driven from the state.

In the Shenandoah Valley General Franz Sigel was defeated on May 15 at New Market by John C. Breckinridge with a makeshift army which included 225 cadets of the Virginia Military Institute. [35] This minor victory gave the Confederates control over the valley long enough to gather the harvest needed to feed Lee's army. Sigel's failure led to his replacement by General David Hunter, who was hated by Southerners for his proclamation early in the war freeing the slaves within the lines of his command in South Carolina.

As Grant advanced toward Richmond on the right flank of Lee's army, he sent the Union cavalry commanded by Major General Philip H. Sheridan around the Confederate left flank to cut its communications with the "rebel" Capital. At this time the Federal cavalry was far stronger and in much better physical condition than the worn-out Confederate cavalry. Despite the fact, Jeb Stuart succeeded in stopping Sheridan's raid at Yellow Tavern, only six miles north of the city, and thus "saved" Richmond (May 11-12); but in so doing he was mortally wounded.

In an attempt to relieve the pressure on Richmond Lee dispatched Lieutenant General Jubal A. Early to the Shenandoah Valley to threaten Washington. "Old Jube," a West Point graduate and a Virginia lawyer, had strongly opposed the secession of his state. He was somewhat of an eccentric, an old bachelor of biting and sarcastic tongue who acquired the reputation of outcursing any man in the Confederate army, even exceeding the remarkable powers of Colonel Hypolite Oladowski, Bragg's chief of ordnance. An aggressive fighter, he was an exponent of celerity of action, of audacity, of what later became known as "blitzkrieg." A modern military writer has aptly described him as "an unlucky Jackson." [36] On July 12, 1864, Early led eight thousand ragged men, nearly half of whom were barefoot, past Silver Spring, Maryland, into sight of the recently constructed dome of the United States Capitol. [37] Although he wisely retreated without attempting to capture the city, his raid gave a great fright to Lincoln and his fearful Secretary of War, Edwin M. Stanton. Recrossing the Potomac, his cavalry burned Chambersburg, Pennsylvania—an act which contrasted with Lee's human policy of protecting enemy civilian property and lives.

In order to free Washington from further menace from this direction, Grant sent Sheridan's cavalry to clear the Shenandoah Valley of Confederate troops. Sheridan was only thirty-three years old, but he was the ablest of the Federal cavalry leaders. With a numerical superiority of approximately fifty thousand men to twenty thousand, he defeated Early on September 19 at Winchester and shortly afterward at Fisher's Hill. But while the Union army was resting in fancied security at Cedar Creek with its left flank protected by Massanutten Mountain, Early sent a force under General John B. Gordon in the night along the top of the mountain which attacked its left flank and rear. Two of the three corps of Sheridan's army were routed. But Early failed to complete his victory. Why the "fatal halt" occurred is a controversial subject.[38] Early attributed the failure to pursue the fleeing Federals vigorously and to attack the Sixth Corps, which had retained its formation, to the demoralization of his men in stopping to plunder the Federal camp.

This battle has been romanticized in legend because of a famous ride that the youthful Sheridan made. He was absent from his army at the time of the rout at Cedar Creek. Returning to Winchester from a quick visit to Washington, he heard the noise of distant cannon down the Valley pike. Jumping on his black horse, he rode madly for twenty miles until he met his fleeing troops. Quickly he rallied them, to turn a disgraceful defeat into victory over the Confederates. Sheridan then completed the ravaging of the Shenandoah Valley, which General Hunter had begun, so thoroughly that it was said "a crow flying over the valley would have to carry his own provisions."

All through the winter of 1864–1865 the siege of Petersburg continued. On March 25 Lee attempted a last gamble to break through the Federal lines by capturing Fort Stedman. He selected Major General John B. Gordon, only thirty-three years old, to lead the hazardous mission. Gordon made a night attack, using fifty axmen to clear the obstructions of chevaux-de-frise in front of the Confederate fortifications and those protecting Fort Stedman. The attack was a complete surprise, and the Confederates occupied the fort; but they failed to capture near-by Fort Haskell and a Federal counterattack recaptured Fort Stedman the same day.[39]

Then Grant determined to cut the life line of the besieged city and of Richmond by sending Sheridan to seize control of the South Side Railroad which ran west from Petersburg to Burkeville on the Richmond & Danville Railroad. On April 1 Sheridan attacked Pickett at Five Forks so unexpectedly that Pickett and the leader of his cavalry, Fitzhugh Lee, were away from the scene enjoying a shad feast. Although Sheridan won a spectacular victory, the Confederates fought with great bravery and tenacity, demonstrating that their morale remained high. Among those killed was the Confederate "boy" colonel of artillery, William Pegram, twenty-three years old, described by one of his officers as "the truest Christian, the most faithful friend, and the most superb soldier in all the world." [40]

On April 2 while Jefferson Davis was in his pew at St. Paul's Episcopal Church, he received a note from Lee that Richmond must be evacuated. That night the army marched out of Petersburg southwest toward Lynchburg with the object of using the Richmond & Danville Railroad to effect a junction with Johnston's army in North Carolina. Davis and his cabinet left Richmond at midnight for Danville, taking $500,000 of gold belonging to the government and the banks of the city. As the Confederate authorities were leaving the doomed city, they gave orders to distribute the commissary stores to the mob, pour the liquor stores into the gutter, and burn the tobacco warehouses. This last order led to the burning of a large part of Richmond, for the wind spread the fires before the Federal army marched in.

Grant vigorously pursued the forlorn Confederate army and on April 6 captured Ewell's corps at Sailor's Creek. Although there were four million rations of meat and two and a half million rations of bread at Richmond or near by, the Confederate supply train failed to bring food, and Lee's army had little to eat except parched corn. On April 9 at Appomattox Court House, near Lynchburg, Lee surrendered his tattered and half-starved army of approximately eight thousand infantry and five thousand cavalry and artillery, all that was left in arms of the twenty-eight thousand men that had set out from Petersburg.

The meeting in the McLean House at Appomattox on the day of the surrender is one of the unforgettable pictures of American history. Lee, in the immaculate dress uniform of a Confederate general, carrying a sword of exquisite workmanship, was the embodiment of the Southern gentleman. The Northern conqueror, the son of a tanner, on the other hand, wore the crumpled and shabby uniform of a private with the shoulder straps of a lieutenant general. Present at the surrender was General Eli Parker, a full-blooded Iroquois Indian. Grant gave magnanimous terms: the defeated Confederate officers and men were paroled, not arrested as prisoners of war; the officers were permitted to retain their sidearms, and soldiers as well as officers were allowed to keep their horses to do the spring plowing.

Lee had refused to resort to guerrilla warfare that could only lead to the sacrifice of many gallant young Southerners; but Jefferson Davis was unwilling to capitulate. After holding a Cabinet meeting at Danville, he and the Confederate cabinet fled southward to

Greensboro, North Carolina, where he had a conference with General Johnston. Johnston opposed Davis's foolish plan of continuing the war and surrendered his forces to Sherman at the Bennett House near Durham on April 18. Sherman's terms were so generous, including promises as to reconstruction, that the Washington authorities revoked them and substituted conditions similar to Grant's terms to Lee. On May 4 General Richard Taylor surrendered the largest remaining Confederate army at Citronelle, Alabama; and three weeks later the Trans-Mississippi forces under Kirby-Smith capitulated to the Union commander at New Orleans. A total of 175,000 Confederate soldiers surrendered. Following a final cabinet meeting at the little village of Washington, Georgia, Davis tried to escape; but he was captured May 10 at Irwinville, Georgia, and brought to prison at Fort Monroe, Virginia, where he was put in chains. The last flag of the Confederacy was furled when the cruiser *Shenandoah* surrendered in Liverpool, England, on November 6, 1865. The dying Confederacy passed into the emotional realm of the "lost cause." Wrote the South Carolina poet, Henry Timrod (1867):

> Sleep sweetly in your humble graves,
> Sleep, martyrs of a fallen cause.

The "martyrs of a fallen cause" were principally young men, representing a large proportion of the natural leaders of the South who had volunteered early from chivalric honor and patriotism. An even greater tragedy than the death of vigorous young men (the "seed corn" of the future) was the traumatic effect of the Civil War upon the mind and spirit of the South. Like the French Revolution, the Civil War destroyed the society of the old regime. The corrosive memory of the defeat of the Confederacy continued long in the rural South. Walter Hines Page, a North Carolinian, recognized this fact when he observed that one of the three ghosts which troubled the life of the New South was the ghost of the Confederate Dead.

Notes

CHAPTER I

1. Richmond *Semi-Weekly Enquirer*, Dec. 23, 1859. Va. State Library.
2. Richmond *Daily Dispatch*, Dec. 23, 1859. Va. State Library. See Clement Eaton, "The Resistance of the South to Northern Radicalism," *New England Quarterly*, VIII, 215–216 (June, 1935).
3. Clement Eaton, "Mob Violence in the Old South," *Mississippi Valley Historical Review*, XXIX, 351–370 (Dec., 1942).
4. See Allan Nevins, *The Emergence of Lincoln* (2 vols., New York, 1950), II, 58–68.
5. Robert Toombs expressed such a demand in a letter to Alexander H. Stephens, Feb. 10, 1860, opposing the Davis Resolutions in Congress. U. B. Phillips, *The Life of Robert Toombs* (New York, 1913), 184.
6. Clement Eaton, *Freedom of Thought in the Old South* (new ed., New York, 1952), chap. iv.
7. J. M. McCue to J. L. Imboden, Dec. 26, 1860. James Blythe Anderson Papers, MSS, University of Kentucky Library.
8. *Ibid.* See also letters of McCue to Imboden, July 23, Nov. 22, and Dec. 4, 1860, and Imboden to McCue, Dec. 4 and 7, 1860.
9. MS Diary of Catherine Ann Edmondston, June 6 and July 16, 1860, in North Carolina State Department of Archives and History.
10. New Orleans *Bee*, Nov. 8, 1860, and Lexington *Kentucky Statesman*, Nov. 20, 1860, quoted in Dwight L. Dumond, ed., *Southern Editorials on Secession* (New York, 1931), 221–223, 253–255.
11. F. G. Murphey to George, Sept. 26, 1860. B. F. Buckner Papers, MSS in University of Kentucky Library.
12. W. B. Rogers to his wife, Feb. 6, 1861. W. B. Rogers Papers, MSS in University of Kentucky Library.
13. These letters are published in John G. Nicolay and John Hay, *Abraham Lincoln: A History* (10 vols., New York, 1904 ed.), II, 306–314.
14. Raleigh *Register,* Nov. 20, 1860.
15. W. H. T. to Miles, Nov. 8, 1860. William Porcher Miles Papers, MSS, Southern Collection, University of North Carolina.
16. Lawrence Keitt to Miles, Oct. 3, 1860. *Ibid.* In the Lawrence Keitt Papers at Duke University is a letter from Keitt to Mrs. Frederick Brown, Mar. 4, 1861, which describes the Republicans as "a motley throng of Sans Culottes and Dames des Halles, infidels, and free lovers, interspersed by Bloomer women, fugitive slaves, and amalgamists."

17. Ollinger Crenshaw, "Christopher G. Memminger's Mission to Virginia, 1860," *Journal of Southern History*, VIII, 334–349 (Aug., 1942).
18. A recent scholarly monograph, H. S. Schultz, *Nationalism and Sectionalism in South Carolina, 1852–1860* (Durham, 1950), 233, concludes: "The movement for Southern independence in South Carolina during the period 1852–1860 was primarily a process by which the conciliatory group in the state became convinced that the antislavery party must eventually gain the ascendancy in the federal government."
19. John Berkley Grimball Diaries, 1832–1883, MSS in University of North Carolina Library; Charleston *Daily Courier*, Nov. 3, 8, 9, Dec. 21, 1860.
20. Lillian A. Kibler, *Benjamin F. Perry, South Carolina Unionist* (Durham, 1946), 325, 336–346; O'Neall wrote to J. H. Hammond Sept. 22, 1860, "If Lincoln is elected, *I would say wait,* let us see fully developed his course of action." James H. Hammond Papers, Vol. 28, MSS in Library of Congress.
20a. MS Diary of Jacob F. Schirmer, Dec. 20 and 31, 1860, in South Carolina Historical Society archives.
21. Mary Boykin Chesnut, *A Diary from Dixie,* ed. Ben Ames Williams (Boston, 1949), 218.
22. MS Diary of Catherine Ann Edmondston, Nov. 16, 1860.
23. Chesnut, *A Diary from Dixie,* 244.
24. Laura A. White, *Robert Barnwell Rhett: Father of Secession* (New York, 1931), 179–181; Charles E. Cauthen, "South Carolina's Decision to Lead the Secession Movement," *North Carolina Historical Review*, XVIII, 360–372 (Oct., 1941). Prof. Cauthen thinks that Georgia's actions largely explained the advancing by the South Carolina Legislature of the date for the assembly of a convention.
25. Chesnut, *A Diary from Dixie,* 3.
25a. Hammond to the committee, Nov. 8, and to J. W. Hayne, Sept. 19, and to Major M. C. M. Hammond, Nov. 12, 1860. James H. Hammond Papers, Vol. 28, MSS in Library of Congress.
26. Roy F. Nichols, *The Disruption of American Democracy* (New York, 1948), 372–373.
27. William Gilmore Simms to W. P. Miles, Nov. 12, 1860, Miles Papers.
28. John D. Ashmore to Miles, Nov. 13, 1860, Miles Papers.
29. Ashmore to Miles, Nov. 20, 1860, *ibid.*
30. See Clement Eaton, *Freedom of Thought in the Old South,* chaps. ii, xii.
31. Carl Russell Fish, *The American Civil War: An Interpretation* (New York, 1937), 11.
32. David Clopton to C. C. Clay, Junior, Dec. 13, 1860. Clement C. Clay, Junior, Papers. MSS in Duke University Library.
33. Howell Cobb to W. P. Miles, Jan. 10, 1860. Miles Papers.
34. *Journal of the Senate of the United States,* 36th Cong., 2nd Sess. (Washington, 1860–1861), Vol. 78, p. 76.
35. Clinton E. Knox, "The Possibilities of Compromise in the Senate Committee of Thirteen and the Responsibility for Failure," *Journal of Negro*

History, XVII, 457–458 (Oct., 1932). *Journal of the Senate,* Vol. 78, p. 107.

36. For general studies of the secession movement in the lower South, see Clement Eaton, *A History of the Old South* (New York, 1949); Dwight L. Dumond, *The Secession Movement, 1860–1861* (New York, 1931); and J. G. Randall, *The Civil War and Reconstruction* (Boston, 1937).

37. W. R. Smith, *History and Debates of the Convention of the People of Alabama* (Montgomery, 1861), 445–447.

38. Hugh Lawson Clay to Senator Clement C. Clay, Huntsville, Ala., Jan. 11, 1861. Clement C. Clay Papers. MSS in Duke University Library.

39. Speech before the Georgia House of Representatives, Nov. 14, 1860. See Frank Moore, ed., *The Rebellion Record* (New York, 1861), I, 220, Doc. 147½.

40. R. G. Osterweis, *Romanticism and Nationalism in the Old South* (New Haven, 1949), 7. Lawrence Keitt wrote to his wife from Montgomery, Feb. 19, 1861, of his delight over the vision of a great new nation coming into existence. Lawrence Keitt Papers, MSS, Duke University Library.

41. See Avery O. Craven, *The Coming of the Civil War* (New York, 1942) and *The Growth of Southern Nationalism, 1848–1861* (Baton Rouge, 1953), and J. G. Randall, "The Blundering Generation," *Mississippi Valley Historical Review,* XXVII, 3–29 (June, 1940).

42. Nichols, *The Disruption of American Democracy,* 6–7.

43. Chesnut, *A Diary from Dixie,* 20.

44. Charles A. and Mary R. Beard, *The Rise of American Civilization* (2 vols., New York, 1927), II, chap. xviii.

45. See U. B. Phillips, "The Central Theme of Southern History," *American Historical Review,* XXXII, 30–43 (Oct., 1928).

46. P. S. Foner, *Business and Slavery: The New York Merchants and the Irrepressible Conflict* (Chapel Hill, 1941), 218, 302.

47. Kenneth M. Stampp, *And the War Came* (Baton Rouge, 1950), 159–165.

48. See Harvey Wish, *George Fitzhugh: Propagandist of the Old South* (Baton Rouge, 1943).

49. Charles W. Ramsdell, "The Natural Limits of Slavery Expansion," *Mississippi Valley Historical Review,* XVI, 151–171 (Sept., 1929).

50. Clement Eaton, "Censorship of the Southern Mails," *American Historical Review,* XLVIII, 266–280 (Jan., 1943), and *Freedom of Thought in the Old South,* chaps. v, vii.

51. J. G. de Roulhac Hamilton, "Lincoln's Election an Immediate Menace to Slavery in the States," *American Historical Review,* XXXVII, 700–711 (July, 1932).

52. Allan Nevins, *The Emergence of Lincoln,* I, chap. v.

53. Abraham Lincoln, *Complete Works,* ed. Nicolay and Hay (New York, 1905), III, 2.

54. See Howard K. Beale, "What Historians Have Said About the Causes of the Civil War," in Social Science Research Council Committee on Historiography, *Theory and Practice in Historical Study: A Report* (New York, 1946).

CHAPTER II

1. Judicious discussions of the Fort Sumter crisis are found in J. G. Randall, *Lincoln, the Liberal Statesman* (New York, 1947), chap. iv, and C. R. Fish, *The American Civil War: An Interpretation* (New York, 1937), chap. iv.
2. K. M. Stampp, *And the War Came,* 99–100.
3. J. D. Richardson, ed., *Messages and Papers of the Confederacy* (2 vols., Nashville, 1905), I, 93–96.
4. Burton J. Hendrick, *Lincoln's War Cabinet* (Boston, 1946), chaps. iii–v.
5. Neal Dow to A. Lincoln, Mar. 13, 1861. Robert Todd Lincoln Papers, Vol. 37. MSS in Library of Congress.
6. Carl Schurz to A. Lincoln, Apr. 5, 1861. R. T. Lincoln Papers, Vol. 40.
7. Abner Doubleday to Mrs. Mary Doubleday, Fort Sumter, Apr. 2, 1861. R. T. Lincoln Papers, Vol. 40.
8. John Tyler to his wife, March 24, 1861. Tyler Papers, Vol. IV. MSS in Library of Congress.
9. George Plummer Smith to John Hay, Jan. 7, 9, 20, 1863, R. T. Lincoln Papers. I was directed to these letters by Benjamin Thomas, who has an account of this episode in his *Abraham Lincoln* (New York, 1952).
10. Abraham Lincoln, *Complete Works*, ed. Nicolay and Hay, VI 300–302, Message of July 4, 1861, to Congress.
10a. D. M. Potter, *Lincoln and His Party in the Secession Crisis* (New Haven, 1942), 361–363.
11. Anderson's reply is quoted in Jefferson Davis, *The Rise and Fall of the Confederate Government* (New York, 1881), II, 247–248.
12. A. R. Chisolm, Journal of Events Before and During the Firing on Fort Sumter, Apr., 1861. MS in private possession.
13. K. M. Stampp, "Lincoln and the Strategy of Defense in the Crisis of 1861," *Journal of Southern History,* XI, 297–323 (Aug., 1945).
14. See C. W. Ramsdell, "Lincoln and Fort Sumter," *Journal of Southern History,* III, 259–288 (Aug., 1937).
15. Jonathan Worth, *Correspondence,* ed. J. G. de R. Hamilton (2 vols., Raleigh, 1909), I, 143.
16. Frederick S. Daniel, *The Richmond Examiner During the War; or, The Writings of John M. Daniel* (New York, 1868), 7–13.
17. Maximilian Schele de Vere to Frederick Seward, Mar. 13, 1861. R. T. Lincoln Papers, Vol. 37.
18. See Henry T. Shanks, *The Secession Movement in Virginia, 1847–1861* (Richmond, 1934), chaps. viii–xi.
19. George E. Pickett, *Soldier of the South: General Pickett's War Letters to His Wife,* ed. A. C. Inman (Boston, 1928), 2.
20. W. C. Rives to W. C. Rives, Jr., Feb. 11, 1861. W. C. Rives Papers, MSS in Library of Congress.
21. Letters of John Tyler, Apr. 16 and May 17, 1861. W. C. Rives Papers, MSS in Library of Congress.

22. John B. Jones, *A Rebel War Clerk's Diary at the Confederate States Capital,* ed. Howard Swiggett (new and enlarged ed., 2 vols., New York, 1935), I, 20.

23. George W. Randolph to a young man, 1861. Edgehill-Randolph Papers, MSS in the University of Virginia Library.

24. See Avery Craven, *Edmund Ruffin, Southerner: A Study in Secession* (New York, 1932).

25. W. C. Rives to George W. Summers, Apr. 15, 1861. W. C. Rives Papers.

26. Barton H. Wise, *The Life of Henry A. Wise of Virginia* (New York, 1899), chap. xv. J. B. Jones, *A Rebel War Clerk's Diary,* I, 20–21.

27. C. H. Ambler, *Sectionalism in Virginia from 1776 to 1861* (Chicago, 1910).

28. See C. H. Ambler, *West Virginia, the Mountain State* (New York, 1940), and J. C. McGregor, *The Disruption of Virginia* (New York, 1922).

29. J. G. Randall, *The Civil War and Reconstruction* (Boston, 1937), 330–339. C. H. Ambler, *Francis H. Pierpont, Union War Governor of Virginia and Father of West Virginia* (Chapel Hill, 1937).

30. See E. M. Coulter, *William G. Brownlow, Fighting Parson of the Southern Highlands* (Chapel Hill, 1937); W. G. Brownlow, *Sketches of the Rise, Progress, and Decline of Secession, with a Narrative of Personal Adventures Among the Rebels* (Philadelphia, 1862); and J. W. Patton, *Unionism and Reconstruction in Tennessee, 1860–1869* (Chapel Hill, 1934).

31. U.S. War Department, *War of the Rebellion: The Official Records of the Union and Confederate Armies* (Washington, 1880–1901), Series I, Vol. 52, Part 1, pp. 172–173. Hereafter cited as *O.R.*

32. Letter of Apr. 15, 1861. B. F. Moore Papers, MSS in North Carolina State Department of Archives and History.

33. J. C. Sitterson, *The Secession Movement in North Carolina* (Chapel Hill, 1939).

34. William K. Boyd, *William W. Holden* (Durham, N.C., 1899).

35. MS Diary of Catherine Ann Edmondston, May 22, 1861.

36. Lewis Collins and R. H. Collins, *History of Kentucky* (Covington, 1874), I, 90–91. The lower house of the legislature adopted the neutrality resolution by a vote of 89 to 4.

37. E. Merton Coulter, *The Civil War and Readjustment in Kentucky* (Chapel Hill, 1926), 82–91.

38. Kenneth P. Williams, *Lincoln Finds a General,* III (New York, 1952), 5.

39. *Journal of the Congress of the Confederate States of America* (Washington, 1904), I, 536–543.

40. Ben Hardin Helm to his wife, Bowling Green, Oct. 10, 1861. B. H. Helm Papers. MSS in Confederate Room, University of Kentucky Library.

41. J. G. Randall, *Lincoln and the South* (Baton Rouge, 1946), 69.

42. M. P. Andrews, *Tercentenary History of Maryland,* I (Chicago, 1925), 826–853. W. B. Hesseltine, *Lincoln and the War Governors* (New York, 1948), 213–215, 154–156.

43. Rhodes, *History of the United States from the Compromise of 1850 to the McKinley-Bryan Campaign of 1896* (8 vols., 1920), III, 277.

44. E. C. Smith, *The Borderland in the Civil War* (New York, 1927), 3–6, 219.

45. Jonas Viles, "Sections and Sectionalism in a Border State," *Mississippi Valley Historical Review*, XXI, 3–22 (June, 1934).

46. See W. H. Ryle, *Missouri: Union or Secession* (Nashville, 1931).

47. J. H. Browne, *Four Years in Secessia* (Hartford, Conn., 1865), 115.

48. Elsie M. Lewis, in "From Nationalism to Disunion: a Study of the Secession Movement in Arkansas, 1850–1861," shows that, despite the influence of secessionist agitators like T. C. Hindman and the Johnson family, Arkansas was Unionist in sentiment until Lincoln's decision to send the Fort Sumter expedition upset the delicate balance. Ph.D. Thesis, University of Chicago, 1946, chap. ix. See also D. Y. Thomas, *Arkansas in War and Reconstruction, 1861–1874* (Little Rock, 1926).

49. A. W. Bishop, *Loyalty on the Frontier; or, Sketches of the Union Men in the Southwest* (St. Louis, 1863), 15–28.

50. A. H. Abel, *The American Indian as a Participant in the Civil War* (Cleveland, 1919).

51. L. M. Ganaway, *New Mexico and the Sectional Controversy, 1846–1861* (Albuquerque, 1944), chap. vi.

52. Both Kentucky and Missouri maintained governments in exile in the Confederacy, with governors and full delegations in Congress. The letterbook and papers of Thomas C. Reynolds, Confederate governor of Missouri, illustrate the problems of a government in exile. As governor of the fifteen or twenty thousand Missourians within the Confederate lines (his estimate), he sought to recruit soldiers in Missouri for the Confederacy, to prevent guerrilla warfare in the state, for it alienated the people from the Confederate cause, to alleviate the jealousies of Missouri officers and politicians, and loyally to support President Davis. Papers and Letterbook of Thomas C. Reynolds, 1862–1865, MSS in Library of Congress.

CHAPTER III

1. For a study of the Confederate Convention see Albert N. Fitts, "The Confederate Convention" and "The Confederate Convention: The Constitutional Debate," *Alabama Review*, II, 83–101, 189–210 (Apr. and July, 1949); Hammond Papers, Nov. 8, 1861, Vol. 28.

2. The Confederate Constitution is printed in the *Journal of the Congress of the Confederate States of America* (Washington, 1904), I, Appendix, 899–924.

3. William Gilmore Simms to William Porcher Miles, Nov. 12, 1860, W. P. Miles Papers, MSS in Southern Collection, University of North Carolina Library.

4. Henry T. Shanks, "Conservative Constitutional Tendencies of the Virginia Secession," in Fletcher M. Green, ed., *Essays in Southern History,*

Presented to Joseph Grégoire de Roulhac Hamilton by His Former Students at the University of North Carolina (Chapel Hill, 1949), 28–48.

5. Augusta J. Evans to J. L. M. Curry, July 15, 1863. Jabez L. M. Curry Papers, MSS in Library of Congress.

6. Augusta J. Evans to J. L. M. Curry, Oct. 16, 1863. Curry Papers.

7. C. W. Ramsdell, ed., *Laws and Joint Resolutions of the Last Session of the Confederate Congress, Nov. 7, 1864, to Mar. 18, 1865* (Durham, 1941), 79.

8. E. Merton Coulter, *The Confederate States of America, 1861–1865* (Baton Rouge, 1950), 23–26, 31.

9. Rudolph R. von Abele, *Alexander H. Stephens* (New York, 1946), 173. See also R. M. Johnston and W. H. Browne, *Life of Alexander H. Stephens* (Philadelphia, 1878).

10. Alexander H. Stephens to Thomas J. Semmes, Mar. 29, 1863. Thomas Jenkins Semmes Papers, MSS in Duke University Library.

11. See James Z. Rabun, "Alexander H. Stephens and Jefferson Davis," *American Historical Review,* LVIII, 290–321 (Jan., 1953).

12. Conflicting evaluations of the Confederate President are presented in W. E. Dodd, *Jefferson Davis* (Philadelphia, 1907), Allen Tate, *Jefferson Davis: His Rise and Fall* (New York, 1929), H. J. Eckenrode, *Jefferson Davis, President of the South* (New York, 1923), and Varina H. Davis, *Jefferson Davis: Ex-President of the Confederate States of America* (New York, 1890).

13. Diary of Robert H. G. Kean, MS in University of Virginia Library, courtesy of Edward E. Younger, who is editing it for publication. Vol. I covers period Sept. 17, 1861, to Aug. 13, 1863; Vol. II, Aug. 13 to Oct. 23, 1865. Kean, born in 1828 in Caroline County, Virginia, was appointed chief of the Confederate Bureau of War, Apr. 1, 1862, by Secretary of War George W. Randolph. His diary is more intelligent and penetrating than the *Rebel War Clerk's Diary* of J. B. Jones, and is more valuable than Jones's daily chronicle as a source for Confederate history. Jones did not like Kean and thought of him as a young man who should be in the field, a very ambitious young fellow intriguing to become Assistant Secretary of War, and a bureau chief who was very critical of older bureaucrats. See *A Rebel War Clerk's Diary at the Confederate States Capital* (New York, 1935), I, 119, 173, II, 52, 142–143, 184, 412.

14. See E. W. Knight, ed., *A Documentary History of Education in the South Before 1860,* III (Chapel Hill, 1952), 447–452.

15. Kean MS Diary, II, Aug. 23, 1863.

16. George W. Randolph to Col. T. J. Randolph, Nov. 25, 1862, Edgehill-Randolph Collection, MSS in University of Virginia Library.

17. Varina Howell Davis to Clement C. Clay, Jr., May 10, 1861. C. C. Clay, Jr., Papers, MSS in Duke University Library.

18. Jefferson Davis, *Jefferson Davis, Constitutionalist: His Letters, Papers and Speeches,* ed. Dunbar Rowland (10 vols., Jackson, Miss., 1923), VI, 76–77.

19. Diary of Stephen Mallory, II. MS in Southern Collection, University of North Carolina Library.
20. H. S. Commager, ed., *The Blue and the Gray: The Story of the Civil War as Told by Participants* (2 vols., Indianapolis, 1950), I, 27.
21. R. W. Patrick, *Jefferson Davis and His Cabinet* (Baton Rouge, 1944), is an admirable defense. For a contrast between the cabinets of Davis and Lincoln see B. J. Hendrick, *Statesmen of the Lost Cause* (Boston, 1939) and *Lincoln's War Cabinet* (Boston, 1946).
22. Pictures of wartime Richmond are found in T. C. De Leon, *Four Years in Rebel Capitals* (Mobile, 1892); A. H. Bill, *The Beleaguered City: Richmond, 1861–1865* (New York, 1946); and Jones, *A Rebel War Clerk's Diary at the Confederate States Capital.*
23. Elizabeth L. Van Lew, Personal Narrative of the Civil War; Letter of Gen. George M. Sharpe, head of Secret Service of the Army of the Potomac, to Gen. C. B. Comstock, Jan., 1867 (copy). MSS in New York Public Library.
24. J. D. Richardson, ed., *Messages and Papers of the Confederacy* (2 vols., Nashville, 1905), I, 184–185.
25. See J. W. DuBose, *The Life and Times of William Lowndes Yancey* (Birmingham, 1892); and Laura A. White, *Robert Barnwell Rhett: Father of Secession,* chap. xi.
26. Varina Howell Davis to Clement C. Clay, May 10, 1861. Clement C. Clay, Junior, Papers.
27. Alexander H. Stephens to Thomas Jenkins Semmes, Mar. 29, 1863. T. J. Semmes Papers.
28. Kean MS Diary, Vol. I, Mar. 15, Vol. II, Oct. 4, 1863.
29. James H. Hammond to R. M. T. Hunter, Apr. 9, 1863. R. M. T. Hunter Papers, MSS in University of Virginia Library.
30. Kean MS Diary, Vol. II, Nov. 2, 1863.
31. Yancey and Clay to Davis, April 21, 1862; Yancey to Davis, May 6, July 11, 1863; Davis to Yancey, June 20, 1863. William L. Yancey Papers, MSS in Alabama State Department of Archives and History.
32. See Nathaniel W. Stephenson, *The Day of the Confederacy* (New Haven, 1920), chap. iv. Coulter, *The Confederate States of America,* 135–136, and Henry S. Foote, *War of the Rebellion; or, Scylla and Charybdis* (New York, 1866).
33. H. W. Bruce to Robert McKee, spring, 1863; W. B. Machen to Robert McKee, April 21, 1863; and W. E. Simms to Robert McKee, Nov. 16, 1863. Robert McKee Papers, MSS in Alabama State Department of Archives and History; Clement C. Clay, Jr., to William L. Yancey, June 30, 1863. Yancey Papers.
34. James M. Matthews, ed., *Public Laws of the Confederate States of America, 1863–4* (Richmond, 1864), 187–189.
35. W. M. Robinson, *Justice in Grey: A History of the Judicial System of the Confederate States of America* (Cambridge, Mass., 1941).
36. W. B. Hesseltine, *Confederate Leaders in the New South* (Baton Rouge,

1950), 16–20. See also Allan Nevins, *The Statesmanship of the Civil War* (New York, 1953).

CHAPTER IV

1. A basic book in the study of Confederate diplomacy is F. L. Owsley, *King Cotton Diplomacy* (Chicago, 1931). Other valuable works are E. D. Adams, *Great Britain and the American Civil War* (2 vols., London, 1925); J. M. Callahan, *The Diplomatic History of the Southern Confederacy* (Baltimore, 1901); and D. Jordan and E. J. Pratt, *Europe and the American Civil War* (Boston, 1931).
2. Edward Channing, *A History of the United States,* VI (New York, 1935), 340–341.
3. See note, "Wheat Versus Cotton," in S. F. Bemis, *A Diplomatic History of the United States* (New York, 1950), 383.
4. Jones, *A Rebel War Clerk's Diary,* I, 38–39.
5. See R. D. Meade, *Judah P. Benjamin, Confederate Statesman* (New York, 1943); Pierce Butler, *Judah P. Benjamin* (Philadelphia, 1907); and Gamaliel Bradford, *Confederate Portraits* (Boston, 1914), chap. v.
6. Kean MS Diary, II, Aug. 13, 1863.
7. W. L. Yancey to R. M. T. Hunter, Dec. 31, 1861. Pickett Papers (Confederate State Department, A: Great Britain), MSS in Library of Congress.
8. E. J. Simpson (Evan John), *Atlantic Impact, 1861* (New York, 1952), contains reactions of fifteen prominent persons in Great Britain and the U.S. to the Trent affair.
9. Chesnut, *A Diary from Dixie,* 123–124, 131.
10. Benjamin Moran, *Journal, 1857–1865,* ed. S. A. Wallace and F. E. Gillespie (2 vols., Chicago, 1949), II, 963–964, 1040–1041.
11. Yancey, Rost, and Mann to Earl Russell Nov. 29, 1861. Pickett Papers (Confederate State Department, A: Great Britain, Nos. 1–4).
12. Richardson, ed., *Messages and Papers of the Confederacy,* II, 128.
13. For accounts of Hotze, see Owsley, *King Cotton Diplomacy,* 166–175; and Richard B. Harwell's Introduction to *Three Months in the Confederate Army,* by Henry Hotze (University, Ala., 1952).
14. Henry Hotze to R. M. T. Hunter, Feb. 23, 1862, Apr. 25, 1862. Commercial Agency, C.S.A., London, Letterbook, pp. 15, 48. Papers of Henry Hotze and others, Oct. 1, 1862, to Aug. 13, 1865, MSS in Library of Congress.
15. Hotze to Hunter, Feb. 28, 1862. Commercial Agency, C.S.A. Letterbook, pp. 24–25, no. 4. Hotze Papers.
16. Hotze to Judah P. Benjamin, Aug. 4, 1862. *Ibid.,* No. 9.
17. A complete file of this publication, 5 vols., is to be found in the Rare Book Room, Library of Congress.
18. Hotze to S. Ricker of Frankfurt, Germany, June 18, 1864. Letterbook of Henry Hotze, May 28, 1864, to June 16, 1865. MS in Library of Congress.

19. Hotze to Benjamin, Sept. 26, 1862. Commercial Agency, C.S.A. Letter-book, pp. 88–94. No. 11.
20. Yancey to Hunter, July 15, 1861. Pickett Papers, Dispatch, No. 3.
21. *The Index,* II (June 11, 1863), 109.
22. W. C. Ford, ed., *A Cycle of Adams Letters, 1861–1865* (2 vols., Boston, 1920), I, 220–221.
23. *Ibid.,* II, 65.
24. *Ibid.,* II, 58–63.
25. *Ibid.,* I, 14.
26. *Ibid.,* I, 243.
27. Jordan and Pratt, *Europe and the American Civil War,* 72–79.
28. Hotze to Benjamin, Sept. 26, 1862. Commercial Agency C.S.A. Letter-book, p. 81. Hotze Papers.
29. See W. O. Henderson, *The Lancashire Cotton Famine, 1861–1865* (Manchester, England, 1934), and M. B. Hammond, *The Cotton Industry: An Essay in American Economic History* (New York, 1897).
30. E. D. Adams, *Great Britain and the American Civil War,* II, 11, 21.
31. Lord Lyons to Earl Russell, Jan. 9, 1863. Lord John Russell Papers. P.R.O. 30/22: United States, 1863. MSS in Public Record Office, London.
32. Lord Lyons to Earl Russell, Mar. 2, 1863. *Ibid.*
33. Benjamin Moran, *Journal,* II, 962–964, gives an interesting but preju-diced account of this debate.
34. *Hansard's Parliamentary Debates* (London, 1862), 3rd Ser. CLXV, 189–190.
35. *Ibid.* CLXV, Gregory's speech, 1158–1174; Fergusson, 1197; Lord Rob-ert Cecil also spoke in favor of the South, 1228.
36. Slidell to Mason, July 16 and 20, 1862. James M. Mason Papers, II, MSS in Library of Congress.
37. *Hansard's Parliamentary Debates,* 3rd Ser., CLXVIII, 511–522, 527–529. Moran, *op. cit.,* 1038–1040.
38. Hansard, 538–549.
39. Henry Hotze to Benjamin, Feb. 14, 1863. Richardson, ed., *Messages and Papers of the Confederacy,* II, 432–433.
40. W. D. Jones, "The British Conservatives and the American Civil War," *American Historical Review,* LVIII, 527–543 (Apr., 1953).
41. Owsley, *King Cotton Diplomacy,* 365–366.
42. For a discussion of this episode, see J. G. Randall, *Lincoln, the Presi-dent* (New York, 1952), III, 342–344.
43. E. D. Adams, *Great Britain and the American Civil War,* II, 54–55.
44. *Ibid.,* II, 74.
45. *Hansard's Parliamentary Debates,* 3rd Ser., CLXXI, 1771–1780. After a sarcastic reference to "those who deem themselves the salt of the earth"—namely, the opponents of Confederate recognition—he pledged his veracity that the French Emperor had stated to him in an interview that France would act with England in recognizing the Confederacy.

The men of the South, he declared, were Englishmen, and those of the North came from "the scum of Europe."

46. Benjamin to Mason, Aug. 4, 1863. James M. Mason Papers, VI.
47. Ford, ed., *A Cycle of Adams Letters,* II, 85–86. See also Richardson, ed., *Messages and Papers of the Confederacy,* II, 538.
48. See M. L. Bonham, *The British Consuls in the Confederacy* (New York, 1911), chap. xii.
49. Hotze to Judah P. Benjamin, Apr. 25, 1862. Dispatch No. 7. Commercial Agency C.S.A., London, Letterbook, p. 45.
50. W. L. Yancey and A. D. Mann to Robert Toombs, London, June 1, 1861, Dispatch No. 2. Pickett Papers.
51. Yancey and P. A. Rost to R. M. T. Hunter, Paris, Oct. 5, 1861, Dispatch No. 8. Pickett Papers.
52. For an account of De Leon's activities as Confederate agent, see Owsley *King Cotton Diplomacy,* 175–182.
53. Henry Hotze to A. Havas, July 2, 1864, announces he is sending Havas 720 francs for *abonnements.* Owsley maintains that Havas published news which Hotze supplied without compensation.
54. Judah P. Benjamin to James M. Mason, July 19, 1862. J. M. Mason Papers, II.
55. John Slidell to James M. Mason, July 16 and 20, 1862. J. M. Mason Papers, II.
56. L. M. Case, ed., *French Opinion on the United States and Mexico, 1860–1867* (New York, 1936), 257. There seems to have been little prejudice against the South in France because of the existence of Southern slavery.
57. Slidell reported to Benjamin his interview with Napoleon III at St. Cloud, October 24, 1862, in which the Emperor expressed his entire sympathy with the South and suggested that the Confederacy build ships in France, concealing their destination. He stated to the Confederate commissioner the danger of France moving for mediation and recognition without the cooperation of England. See Richardson, ed., *Messages and Papers of the Confederacy,* II, 345–351, and L. M. Sears, "A Confederate Diplomat at the Court of Napoleon III," *American Historical Review,* XXVI, 255–281 (Jan., 1921).
58. Hotze to S. Ricker, June 18, 1864. Letterbook of Henry Hotze, May 28, 1864 to June 16, 1865.
59. See F. A. Golder, "The Russian Fleet and the Civil War," *American Historical Review,* XX, 801–812 (July, 1915), and T. A. Bailey, "The Russian Fleet Myth Re-examined." *Mississippi Valley Historical Review,* XXXVIII, 81–90 (June, 1951).
60. Richardson, ed., *Messages and Papers of the Confederacy,* II, 46–48.
61. Hendrick, *Statesmen of the Lost Cause,* 132.
62. J. M. Callahan, *The Diplomatic History of the Southern Confederacy* chap. i, "The Confederate Diplomatic Archives," gives an interesting account of this deal.

63. See Thomas Henry Hines Papers. MSS in University of Kentucky Library.
64. Wood, Gray, *The Hidden Civil War: The Story of the Copperheads* (New York, 1942), 217.
65. Richardson, ed., *Messages and Papers of the Confederacy*, II, 709–718.
66. Jordan and Pratt, *Europe and the American Civil War*, chap. xi.

CHAPTER V

1. F. L. Owsley, *State Rights in the Confederacy* (Chicago, 1925), 22.
2. George Alfred Townsend, *Rustics in Rebellion* (Chapel Hill, 1950), 83–87. For descriptions of army life, see the regimental histories cited in E. M. Coulter, comp., *Travels in the Confederate States: A Bibliography* (Norman, Okla., 1948).
3. Chesnut, *A Diary from Dixie*, 54.
4. Thomas B. Gordon to "Brother Neal," Feb. 11, 1862. Gordon Family Letters, 1860–1924, MSS in University of Kentucky Library.
5. Diary and Memoir of John W. Green, Aug. 31, 1864, p. 207. MS in the possession of Miss Marian Green, Louisville, Ky.
6. *Journal of the Congress of the Confederate States of America* (Washington, 1904), 767.
7. J. Brantly Harris, Gold Hill, N.C., June 3, 1862, to his sister. J. P. Clark Papers, MSS in North Carolina State Department of Archives and History.
8. Office of the Adjutant and Inspector General, C.S.A. Letters received, 1863. Box 128, MS in National Archives, Washington, D.C.
9. J. M. Matthews, ed., *Public Laws of the Confederate States of America Passed at the Fourth Session of the First Congress, 1863–4* (Richmond, 1864), 172.
10. J. M. Matthews, ed., *Public Laws of the Confederate States of America Passed at the Second Session of the First Congress, 1862* (Richmond, 1862), 79.
11. Augusta J. Evans to Jabez L. M. Curry, Dec. 20, 1862. J. L. M. Curry Papers.
12. Fish, *The American Civil War*, 161.
13. Robert P. Porter, Supt., *Compendium of the Eleventh Census: 1890* (Washington, 1897), Part II, 572.
14. A. B. Moore, *Conscription and Conflict in the Confederacy* (New York, 1924), 356–358; see also summation of evidence in J. G. Randall, *The Civil War and Reconstruction*, 685–687.
15. Ella Lonn, *Foreigners in the Union Army and Navy* (Baton Rouge, 1952), 581-582.
16. Ella Lonn, *Foreigners in the Confederacy* (Chapel Hill, 1940).
17. See Heros von Borcke, *Memoirs of the Confederate War for Independence* (New York, 1938).
18. John Jones to James A. Seddon, Sept. 4, 1863, Office of the Adjutant and Inspector General, C.S.A., Letters Received, 1863. J. 1045, Box 28.

19. The superiority of the Union over the Confederate Army in equipment, food, sanitation of camps, and discipline is well portrayed by a Tennesseean, H. V. Redfield, in Otto Eisenshiml and Ralph G. Newman, *The American Iliad* (Indianapolis, 1947), 78–81.

20. Alexander Donelson Coffee to his wife, Nov. 3, 1861. A. D. Coffee Papers, MSS in Southern Collection, University of North Carolina Library.

21. Family Journal, Book A, East House, United Society of Believers (Shakers), Pleasant Hill, Ky. MSS in Filson Club, Louisville, Ky.

22. Clifford Lanier to his father in Macon, Ga., May 5, 1863. In Sidney Lanier, *Letters, 1857–1868,* ed. C. R. Anderson and A. H. Starke, 92— Vol. VII of Lanier, *Works,* Centennial ed., general ed. C. R. Anderson (10 vols., Baltimore, 1945).

23. See Bell I. Wiley, *The Life of Johnny Reb, the Common Soldier of the Confederacy* (Indianapolis, 1943).

24. Diary and Memoir of John W. Green, pp. 87–88.

25. Sam R. Watkins, *"Co. Aytch," Maury Grays, First Tennessee Regiment; or, A Side Show of the Big Show,* with an Introduction by Bell I. Wiley (Jackson, Tenn., 1952), 194.

26. Diary and Memoir of John W. Green, p. 46.

27. Ruffin Barnes to Mary A. Barnes, Apr. 5 and July 28, 1864, MSS in possession of Hugh Buckner Johnston, Wilson, N.C.

28. J. D. Hyman, Asheville, Apr. 30, 1863, to Governor Zebulon Vance. MS in Zebulon Vance Papers, II.

29. Carlton McCarthy, *Detailed Minutiae of Soldier Life in the Army of Northern Virginia, 1861–1865* (Richmond, 1899), chap. vi.

30. Alexander Donelson Coffee to his wife from camp near Corinth, Miss., Apr. 10, 1862. A. D. Coffee Papers.

31. E. P. Alexander, *Military Memoirs of a Confederate* (New York, 1918), 53.

32. Fred A. Shannon, *The Organization and Administration of the Union Army, 1861–1865* (2 vols., Cleveland, 1928), I, 139.

33. Robert V. Johnson and C. C. Buel, eds., *Battles and Leaders of the Civil War* (4 vols., New York, 1887–1888), IV, 767.

34. Diary and Memoir of John W. Green, pp. 32, 103, 115–116.

35. William J. Hardee to Mrs. Felicia L. Shover, Corinth, Apr. 9, 1862; also letters from Corinth, Miss., May 19 and 26, 1862. William J. Hardee Papers, MSS in Library of Congress.

36. G. W. Adams, *Doctors in Blue: The Medical History of the Union Army in the Civil War* (New York, 1952), 113–114.

37. Josiah Gorgas, *Civil War Diary,* ed. Frank E. Vandiver (University, Ala., 1947), 68.

38. Clement A. Evans, ed., *Confederate Military History* (12 vols., Atlanta, 1899), XII, 389–498.

39. Theodore F. Upson, *With Sherman to the Sea,* ed. Oscar O. Winther (Baton Rouge, 1943), 86.

40. Samuel P. Moore, Surgeon General of the Confederate Army, to John C. Breckinridge, *O.R.,* Ser. IV, Vol. 3, p. 1074.

41. G. W. Adams, "Confederate Medicine," *Journal of Southern History,* VI, 151–166 (May, 1940).

42. Kate Cumming, *Gleanings from Southland* (Birmingham, 1895), chap. iii.

43. Chesnut, *A Diary from Dixie,* 245.

44. Journal of Alice Ready, Mar. 3, 1862. MS in Southern Collection, University of North Carolina.

45. E. B. Coddington, "Soldiers' Relief in the Seaboard States of the Southern Confederacy," *Mississippi Valley Historical Review,* XXXVII, 17–38 (June, 1950).

46. Wiley, *The Life of Johnny Reb,* 386–387.

47. John W. Jones, *Christ in the Camp* (Richmond, 1887), 233.

48. John Hunt Morgan to "darling Mattie," Columbus, Ohio, Penitentiary, Aug. 10, 1863. John Hunt Morgan Papers, MSS in Southern Collection, University of North Carolina.

49. J. W. Mallet and O. E. Hunt, "The Ordnance of the Confederacy," in F. T. Miller, ed. *The Photographic History of the Civil War* (10 vols., New York, 1911–1912), V, 156–170; and O. E. Hunt, "The Ammunition Used in the War," in Miller, *op. cit.,* 171–192.

50. Kean MS Diary, II, Aug. 23, 1863.

51. See V. C. Jones, *Ranger Mosby* (Chapel Hill, 1944).

52. After the war numerous suits against Confederate soldiers and guerrillas were prosecuted to collect damages for property, particularly horses, taken away during the Civil War. See Pike County Circuit Court Records, 1866, in University of Kentucky Library.

53. C. W. Ramsdell, "General Robert E. Lee's Horse Supply, 1862–1865," *American Historical Review,* XXV, 758–777 (July, 1930).

54. Charles H. Smith, *Bill Arp, So Called* (New York, 1866), 75–76, 116.

55. A good account of this controversy is given in Coulter, *Confederate States of America,* 475–481.

56. See W. B. Hesseltine, *Civil War Prisons* (Columbus, O., 1930), chaps. vi-viii.

57. G. W. Logan to his mother, Aug. 8, 1863. Logan Letters, microfilm in University of Kentucky Library.

58. Thee Jones to his sister, Dec. 31, 1864, from Camp Douglas, Chicago. MS in University of Kentucky Library.

59. Jasper Hunt to ———, Aug. 21, 1863, from Camp Chase, Ohio, Prison No. 3. MS in University of Kentucky Library.

60. G. W. Logan to his mother, Aug. 12, 1863. Logan Letters.

CHAPTER VI

1. Jeremy F. Gilmer to Loulie, his wife, Mar. 12, 1862: "If not given rank of colonel soon I will quit the service." J. F. Gilmer Papers, MSS in Southern Collection, University of North Carolina. Gilmer was eventually promoted to the rank of major general and appointed chief of the Engineer Bureau.

2. Jack to Clara V. Dargan, Aug. 13, 1863. Clara Dargan McLean Papers, MSS in Duke University Library.

3. Brig. Gen. L. M. Jones to Secretary of War, June 9, 1862, and Robert G. H. Kean to G. W. Randolph, July 17, 1862. Confederate War Department Papers, Letters Received, 1862, Box 10. MSS in the National Archives.

4. Ellsworth Eliot, *West Point in the Confederacy* (New York, 1941), xv, xvii–xix, 31–32. William Couper, *One Hundred Years at V.M.I.* (4 vols., Richmond, 1939), IV, 115, cites 607 Confederate Army officers from V.M.I. above the rank of first lieutenant.

5. See W. M. Polk, *Leonidas Polk, Bishop and General* (New York, 1894), II.

6. T. Harry Williams, *Lincoln and His Generals* (New York, 1952), 230–231, 243.

7. Douglas S. Freeman, *Lee's Lieutenants: A Study in Command* (3 vols., New York, 1942–1944).

8. Alfred Roman, *The Military Operations of General Beauregard in the War Between the States* (New York, 1884); Hamilton Basso, *Beauregard, the Great Creole* (New York, 1933), and a vivid portrait of Beauregard's personality in Bradford, *Confederate Portraits,* Chap. iv.

9. Kean MS Diary, I, July 26, 1863. Kean had a great admiration for Beauregard and repeatedly commented on President Davis's bitter prejudice against the Creole general.

10. In *Grant and Lee: A Study in Personality and Generalship* (New York, 1933), Maj. Gen. J. F. C. Fuller of the British army ranks Beauregard as one of the greatest Confederate generals, with a sense of strategy superior to that of Lee.

11. Kean MS Diary, I, Mar. 22, 1863: "Johnston never treats the government with confidence." Apr. 16, 1863: "General Johnston has written another sharp captious letter. He treats the Dept. as an enemy—holds no communication with it which he can avoid . . . full of himself . . . eaten up with morbid jealousy of Lee."

12. Chesnut, *A Diary from Dixie,* 175.

13. See Joseph E. Johnston, *Narrative of Military Operations Directed During the War Between the States* (New York, 1874); Thomas Robson Hay, *Davis, Bragg, and Johnston in the Atlanta Campaign* (Savannah, 1924); and Alfred P. James, "General Joseph Eggleston Johnston, Storm Center of the Confederate Army," *Mississippi Valley Historical Review,* XIV, 342–349 (Dec. 1927).

14. See William Preston Johnston, *Life of General Albert Sidney Johnston* (New York, 1878).

15. The classic study of Lee and his campaigns is Douglas Southall Freeman, *R. E. Lee: A Biography* (4 vols., New York, 1934–1935). Other valuable studies are: Capt. Robert E. Lee, *Recollections and Letters of General Robert E. Lee* (New York, 1904); Walter H. Taylor, *Four Years with Lee* (New York, 1871), and *General Lee: His Campaigns in Virginia, 1861–1865* (Richmond, 1906); Gamaliel Bradford, *Lee the American*

(Boston, 1912); and Maj. Gen. Frederick B. Maurice, *Robert E. Lee the Soldier* (Boston, 1925).

16. J. F. C. Fuller, *Grant and Lee.*

17. The outstanding study of Jackson is G. F. R. Henderson, *Stonewall Jackson and the American Civil War* (2 vols., New York, 1936). Also valuable are: Robert L. Dabney, *Life and Campaigns of Lieutenant-General Thomas J. Jackson* (Richmond, 1866); Mary Anna Jackson, *Life and Letters of General Thomas J. Jackson* (New York, 1892); Allen Tate, *Stonewall Jackson, the Good Soldier* (New York, 1928); and Henry Kyd Douglas, *I Rode with Stonewall; being chiefly the War Experience of the Youngest Member of Jackson's Staff,* ed. Fletcher M. Green (Chapel Hill, 1940).

18. D. B. Sanger and T. R. Hay, *James Longstreet: Soldier, Politician, Office Holder, and Writer* (Baton Rouge, 1952); H. J. Eckenrode and B. Conrad, *James Longstreet: Lee's War Horse* (Chapel Hill, 1936).

19. See Don C. Seitz, *Braxton Bragg, General of the Confederacy* (New York, 1924).

20. John Buie—in Camp near Bardstown, Ky., Sept. 30, 1862—to J. C. Buie. John Buie Papers. MSS, Duke University Library.

21. U. S. Grant, *Personal Memoirs,* ed. E. B. Long (Cleveland, 1952), 343.

22. Robert S. Henry, *"First with the Most" Forrest* (Indianapolis, 1944), 18–19, and J. A. Wyeth, *Life of General Nathan Bedford Forrest* (New York, 1899), are excellent accounts of Forrest.

23. John P. Dyer, *Fightin' Joe Wheeler* (Baton Rouge, 1941), presents a vivid and reliable account of this general.

24. See Howard Swiggett, *The Rebel Raider: A Life of John Hunt Morgan* (Indianapolis, 1934) and Basil Duke, *Reminiscences of General Basil W. Duke, C.S.A.* (New York, 1911).

25. Chesnut, *A Diary from Dixie,* 328.

26. See W. W. Blackford, *War Years with Jeb Stuart* (New York, 1945), and J. W. Thomason, *Jeb Stuart* (New York, 1930).

27. M. W. Wellman, *Giant in Gray: A Biography of Wade Hampton* (New York, 1949), gives a colorful portrait of this South Carolina aristocrat.

28. Braxton Bragg, Missionary Ridge, Nov. 16, 1863, to Jefferson Davis. Jefferson Davis Papers. MSS, Duke University Library.

29. Kean MS Diary, I, June 15, July 27, and Aug. 9, 1863.

30. *Ibid.,* June 15, 1863.

31. T. Conn Bryan, "General William J. Hardee and Confederate Publication Rights," *Journal of Southern History,* XII, 263–274 (May, 1946).

32. John W. Headley, "The Confederate Secret Service," in F. T. Miller, ed., *The Photographic History of the Confederacy,* VIII, 285–304.

33. Alexander, *Military Memoirs of a Confederate,* chaps. i, ii.

34. A. W. Greely, "The Signal Corps," in Miller, *op. cit.,* 312–340. Sidney Lanier, *Works,* Centennial ed., Vol. VII, *passim.*

35. Douglas S. Freeman, ed., *A Calendar of Confederate Papers* (Richmond, 1908), 431–433.

36. Gilmer to ———, Jan. 4, 1863. Jeremy F. Gilmer Papers, MSS in Southern Collection, University of North Carolina.
37. MS in Gilmer Papers.
38. Fuller, *Grant and Lee,* 45.
39. Sir Frederick B. Maurice, *Statesmen and Soldiers of the Civil War: A Study of the Conduct of War* (Boston, 1926), 25.
40. T. Harry Williams, *Lincoln and His Generals,* and Colin R. Ballard, *The Military Genius of Abraham Lincoln* (London, 1926).
41. John B. Jones, *A Rebel War Clerk's Diary,* I, 117.
42. George W. Randolph to Gen. Theophilus Holmes, Oct. 20 (copy) and 27, 1862. Edgehill-Randolph Collection, MSS in University of Virginia Library.
43. George W. Randolph to Col. T. J. Randolph, Nov. 25, 1862. Edgehill-Randolph Collection.
44. Kean (MS Diary, I, Nov. 15, 1862) gives a vigorous account of the resignation of Randolph and observes: "My own belief is Davis became jealous as to the independent character of the Secy. . . . General R. had not been treated with confidence and consideration by the Pres. for some time."
45. Johnston to Senator Louis T. Wigfall, Dec. 4 and 15, 1862, and Jan. 8 and 26, 1863, quoted in Mrs. D. Giraud Wright (Louise Wigfall), *A Southern Girl in '61* (New York, 1905), 98–100, 121–123.
46. Kean MS Diary, II, July 12, 1863.
47. Congress on Mar. 14, 1862, passed a bill creating the office of commanding general, having authority to take command in the field at his own discretion of any army or armies of the Confederacy. Davis vetoed this bill. Richardson, *Messages and Papers of the Confederacy,* I, 215–216.

CHAPTER VII

1. A good biography of Gorgas has recently been written by Frank E. Vandiver, *Ploughshares into Swords: Josiah Gorgas and Confederate Ordnance* (Austin, 1952).
2. A succinct account of the life of Gorgas by Thomas L. Bayne, a brother-in-law and Confederate ordnance officer, is to be found in *Southern Historical Society Papers,* XIII (1885), 216–228.
3. Caleb Huse, *The Supplies of the Confederate Army: How They Were Obtained in Europe and How Paid For* (Boston, 1904). See also William Diamond, "Imports of the Confederate Government from Europe and Mexico," *Journal of Southern History,* VI, 470–503 (Nov., 1940).
4. Josiah Gorgas, *Civil War Diary,* ed. Frank E. Vandiver (University, Ala., 1947), 57.
5. *Ibid.,* 90–91.
6. U. S. Grant, *Personal Memoirs* (2 vols., New York, 1885–1886), I, 572.
7. J. W. Mallet, Memorandum of My Life for My Children, MS in University of Virginia Library.

8. George W. Rains, *History of the Confederate Powder Works* (Newburgh, N.Y., 1882).
9. Gorgas, *op. cit.*, 68 (Oct. 29, 1863).
10. *The Eighth Census of the United States: Manufactures* (Washington, 1864), clxxix-clxxxiii.
11. Frank E. Vandiver, "The Shelby Iron Company in the Civil War," *Alabama Review*, I (1948), 13–26, 111–127, 203–217.
12. Ethel Armes, *The Story of Coal and Iron in Alabama* (Birmingham, 1910), 186.
13. Joseph R. Anderson to Gen. Lawrence O'Brien Branch, July 23, 1862. Lawrence O'Brien Branch Papers, MSS in North Carolina State Department of Archives and History.
14. Kathleen Bruce, *Virginia Iron Manufacture in the Slave Era* (New York, 1931), chap. x.
15. Kean MS Diary, II, Oct. 25 and Aug. 13, 1863.
16. *O. R.*, Ser. IV, Vol. 3, pp. 1039–1041.
17. Braxton Bragg to Jefferson Davis, Nov. 16, 1863. Jefferson Davis Papers.
18. *O.R.*, Ser. IV, Vol. 3, pp. 1126–1127.
19. Davis, *Rise and Fall of the Confederate Government*, II, 263.
20. Frank G. Ruffin to Secretary of War George W. Randolph, Nov. 8, 1862. Frank G. Ruffin Papers, MSS in Virginia Historical Society, Richmond.
21. L. B. Northrop to President Davis, Aug. 21, 1861. Frank G. Ruffin Papers.
22. Frank G. Ruffin to Col. L. B. Northrop, Oct. 18, 1862. Frank G. Ruffin Papers.
23. The standard U.S. ration was three-fourths of a pound of pork or bacon, or one and one-fourth pounds of fresh or salt beef, eighteen ounces of bread, peas, salt, vinegar, sugar, coffee, rice. *O.R.* Ser. IX, Part 2, p. 571. For reduction of ration, see *O.R.* Ser. I, Vol. XIX, Part 2, p. 716.
24. Kean MS Diary, I, Dec. 15, 1862.
25. Frank G. Ruffin to L. B. Northrop, Richmond, Nov. 28, 1864. Frank G. Ruffin Papers.
26. Between Nov. 1, 1863, and Dec. 8, 1864, there were imported into the Confederacy through the blockade 8,632,000 pounds of meat as well as 520,000 pounds of coffee on government account. F. E. Vandiver, ed., *Confederate Blockade Running Through Bermuda, 1861–1865* (Austin, 1947), 109–148 and xxxix. See also S. B. Thompson, *Confederate Purchasing Operations Abroad* (Chapel Hill, 1935).
27. L. B. Northrop to Secretary of War Seddon, Dec. 20, 1864. Ruffin Papers.
28. L. B. Northrop to Gen. Robert E. Lee, Dec. 13, 1864. *Ibid.*
29. S. B. French to Lieut. Col. Frank G. Ruffin, Sept. 15, 1864. *Ibid.*
30. L. B. Northrop to James A. Seddon, Jan. 11, 1865. *Ibid.*
31. J. R. Soley, *The Blockade and the Cruisers* (New York, 1883), 243. List of U.S. vessels in commission, March 4, 1861.

32. For one of the exceptions, see E. B. Coddington, "The Activities and Attitudes of a Confederate Business Man: Gazaway B. Lamar," *Journal of Southern History,* IX, 3–26 (Feb., 1943).
33. J. D. Hill, *Sea Dogs of the Sixties* (Minneapolis, 1935), especially chap. iv, "John Wilkinson, Phantom of the Blockade"; and John Wilkinson, *The Narrative of a Blockade Runner* (New York, 1877).
34. F. B. C. Bradlee, *Blockade Running During the Civil War* (Salem, Mass., 1925).
35. Memorandum by Crenshaw, MS in Frank G. Ruffin Papers.
36. *The Diary of Gideon Welles* (3 vols., Boston, 1911), I, 283, records, Apr. 22, 1863, a report from Admiral Bailey that an immense trade has developed on the Rio Grande, employing 180 to 200 vessels as compared with 6 or 8 before the war.
37. K. T. Abbey, "Incidents of the Confederate Blockade," *Journal of Southern History,* XI, 214–229 (May, 1949).
38. Mitchell Smith, "The 'Neutral' Matamoros Trade, 1861–65," *Southwest Review,* XXXVII, 319–324 (Autumn, 1952).
39. Caleb Huse to J. M. Mason, Aug. 17, 1863. Mason Papers, VI.
40. List of officers and crew of the steamer *Ad-Vance.* John Julius Guthrie Papers, MS in North Carolina State Department of Archives and History.
41. Frank Wilson to Capt. J. J. Guthrie, Apr. 6, 1864. John Julius Guthrie Papers.
42. Owsley, *King Cotton Diplomacy,* chap. viii. See also Thomas E. Taylor, *Running the Blockade* (London, 1912), 85. Taylor, as supercargo, made 28 trips through the blockade.
43. Randall, *Civil War and Reconstruction,* 651. Also French consuls in Confederacy report blockade to be stifling and partly responsible for tremendous inflation, Gordon Wright, "Economic Conditions in the Confederacy as Seen by the French Consuls," *Journal of Southern History,* VII, 195–214 (May, 1941).
44. For an able study of the Confederate railroads, see Robert C. Black 3rd, *The Railroads of the Confederacy* (Chapel Hill, 1952). For comparison with Northern railroads, see Thomas Weber, *The Northern Railroads in the Civil War, 1861–1865* (New York, 1952).
45. Letter Book of Governor John Milton, 105–127. MS in Florida State Library.

CHAPTER VIII

1. Report of Adjutant General Lorenzo Thomas to the Secretary of War, Apr. 5, 1861. Robert Todd Lincoln Papers, Vol. 40.
2. For the military history of the Confederacy, consult D. S. Freeman, *The South to Posterity: An Introduction to the Writing of Confederate History* (New York, 1939); U.S. War Dept. Library, *Bibliography of State Participation in the Civil War* (3rd ed., Washington, 1913). For maps

and pictures, see U.S. War Dept. Library, *Atlas to Accompany the Official Records of the Union and Confederate Armies* (3 vols., Washington, 1891–1895); Lamont Buchanan, ed., *A Pictorial History of the Confederacy* (New York, 1951); D. H. Donald, H. D. Milhollen, and M. Kaplan, eds., *Divided We Fought: A Pictorial History of the War, 1861–1865* (New York, 1952).

3. Williams, *Lincoln Finds a General*, Vol. I, chap. iii.

4. Alexander, *Military Memoirs of a Confederate*, 29–34.

5. "Report of General Beauregard of the Battle of Manassas, August 26, 1861, in Confederate States of America, *Official Reports of Battles, as Published by Order of the Confederate Congress at Richmond* (New York, 1864), 5–31.

6. W. H. Russell, correspondent of the London *Times*, vividly describes the rout in *My Diary, North and South* (Boston, 1863), chap. i. His account in the *Times* was much resented in the North, and he was called "Bull Run" Russell.

7. D. S. Freeman, *Lee's Lieutenants*, I, 82–83.

8. Gen. Joseph E. Johnston, "Responsibilities of the First Bull Run," in Johnson and Buel, *Battles and Leaders of the Civil War*, I, 240–259.

9. Chesnut, *A Diary from Dixie*, 102–103.

10. Grant, *Personal Memoirs*, ed. E. B. Long (Cleveland, 1952), chap. xx.

11. In Johnson and Buel, *Battles and Leaders of the Civil War*, I, 356–357.

12. Accounts of the battles of Wilson Creek and Pea Ridge in Arkansas by participants are to be found in Johnson and Buel, *Battles and Leaders of the Civil War*, I, 289–334.

13. James McIntosh, Col., to Gen. Albert Pike, Jan. 10, 1862. Thomas Henry Hines Papers, MSS in University of Kentucky Library.

14. Jeremy F. Gilmer, Bowling Green, Oct. 23, 1861, to his wife, Loulie. J. F. Gilmer Papers.

15. Vivid descriptions of the personality of Zollicoffer and of the condition of his troops are found in the Papers of Alexander Donelson Coffee, who was an officer in his army. MSS in Southern Collection, University of North Carolina.

16. Williams, *Lincoln Finds a General*, III, 56.

17. See A. M. Stickles, *Simon Bolivar Buckner, Borderland Knight* (Chapel Hill, 1940).

18. Buckner gave lucid reports of this battle from Dover, Tenn., Feb. 18, 1862, and from Richmond after his return from prison Aug. 11, 1862: O.R. Ser. I, Vol. 7, pp. 327–336. The Union side of the story is told by Gen. Lew Wallace in Johnson and Buel, *Battles and Leaders of the Civil War*, I, 398–428.

19. Reports on the battles at Fort Henry and Fort Donelson are given by Tilghman, Floyd, Pillow, Buckner, Forrest, and Gilmer in Confederate States, *Official Reports of Battle*, 36–176. Secondary accounts of the battle are to be found in Williams, *Lincoln Finds a General*, Vol. III, chaps. ix–x; Stanley F. Horn, *The Army of Tennessee* (Indianapolis,

1941); and Robert S. Henry, *The Story of the Confederacy* (Indianapolis, 1931), chap. vi.

20. Jeremy F. Gilmer, Murfreesborough, Feb. 22, 1862, to his wife, Loulie. J. F. Gilmer Papers.

20a. Albert Sidney Johnston to "My dear General" [President Davis], Mar. 18, 1862. William Preston Johnston Papers. MSS in Tulane University Library.

21. W. P. Johnston, *Life of General Albert Sidney Johnston* (New York, 1878), 497.

22. *O.R.* Ser. I, Vol. 10, part 2, p. 389.

23. P. G. T. Beauregard, "Preliminary Report of the Battle of Shiloh, Corinth, April 11, 1862." Letterbook of P. G. T. Beauregard Jan. 2 to Sept. 9, 1862. MS, Library of Congress. The Beauregard Papers are a huge collection.

24. Maj. Gen. Leonidas Polk gave a report, Sept., 1862, in which he observed that on Apr. 6 the Confederate army had an hour or more of daylight in which to fight the enemy, "nothing seemed wanting to complete the most brilliant victory of the War, but to press forward and make a vigorous assault on the demoralized remnant of his forces." *O.R.,* Ser. I, Vol. 10, Pt. 1, p. 410.

25. William J. Hardee to Mrs. Felicia Lee Shover, Corinth, Apr. 9, 1862. W. J. Hardee Papers, MSS in Library of Congress.

26. H. J. Eckenrode and B. Conrad, *George B. McClellan: The Man Who Saved the Union* (Chapel Hill, 1941); Randall, *Lincoln, the President,* II, chaps xviii–xx; and George B. McClellan, *McClellan's Own Story* (New York, 1887), chaps. xv–xxii; and Williams, *Lincoln Finds a General,* Vols. I, II.

27. In Johnson and Buel, *Battles and Leaders of the Civil War,* I, 129.

28. G. F. R. Henderson, *Stonewall Jackson and the American Civil War,* is the classic study of Jackson's campaigns.

29. Freeman, *R. E. Lee: A Biography,* II, 157. See also Henry, *The Story of the Confederacy,* chap. xiii.

30. Freeman, *R. E. Lee,* II, 197–198 and 579–580, suggests that Jackson was not physically fit for battle partly because he sacrificed sleep in long hours of prayer.

31. Johnson and Buel, *Battles and Leaders of the Civil War,* II, 394.

32. Freeman, *R. E. Lee,* Vol. II, chap. xviii, particularly p. 241.

33. J. G. Randall in review of Williams, *Lincoln Finds a General,* in *American Historical Review,* LV, (Apr., 1950), 627.

34. Williams, *Lincoln Finds a General,* I, chaps. ix–xii, gives a much more favorable view of Pope's generalship than most students and blames McClellan for lack of cooperation.

35. H. S. Commager, ed., *The Blue and the Gray,* I, 182 (*O.R.,* Ser. I, Vol. 12, Pt. 2, p. 262).

36. Report of Lee to Adj. Gen. Cooper, June 8, 1863, *O.R.* Ser. I, Vol. 12, Pt. 2, pp. 551–560; Longstreet's report, No. 130, *ibid.,* pp. 563–568.

CHAPTER IX

1. *Official Records of the Union and Confederate Navies in the War of the Rebellion* (Washington, 1894–1922), Ser. II, Vol. 2, pp. 749–750.
2. William H. Parker, *Recollections of a Naval Officer, 1841–1865* (New York, 1883), chap. xxix.
3. *Official Records of the Union and Confederate Navies,* Ser. II, Vol. 2, pp. 753–754.
4. J. P. Baxter III, *The Introduction of the Ironclad Warship* (Cambridge, 1933), chaps. vi–vii.
5. H. A. Trexler, *The Confederate Ironclad Virginia (Merrimac)* (Chicago, 1938); Johnson and Buel, *Battles and Leaders of the Civil War,* I, 692–748.
6. Reports by Flag Officer Buchanan and Lieut. Jones in Ben La Bree, ed., *The Confederate Soldier in the Civil War, 1861–1865* (Louisville, 1897), 393–398; and Parker, *Recollections of a Naval Officer,* chaps. xxii–xxv. An excellent critical account of this battle is given by Baxter, *op. cit.,* chap. xiii.
7. J. D. Bulloch, *The Secret Service of the Confederate States in Europe* (2 vols., London, 1883), and J. D. Hill, *Sea Dogs of the Sixties,* chap. ii.
8. T. A. Bailey, *A Diplomatic History of the American People* (New York, 1940), 373.
9. See debate in Parliament on the seizure of the *Alexandra* in *Hansard's Parliamentary Debates,* 3rd Ser., CLXX, 702–759.
10. E. D. Adams, *Great Britain and the American Civil War,* II, 144.
11. See Owsley, *King Cotton Diplomacy,* chap. xiii.
12. Bulloch, *op. cit.,* Vol. II, chap. i.
13. John Bigelow, *France and the Confederate Navy, 1862–1868* (New York, 1888), chaps. vi, vii.
14. Josiah Gorgas, *Civil War Diary,* 86–87.
15. J. T. Scharf, *History of the Confederate States Navy* (New York, 1887), 768.
16. *Official Records of the Union and Confederate Navies,* Ser. II, Vol. 1, p. 256.
17. Reports of Commander Jno. K. Mitchell, Aug. 13; Maj. Gen. Lovell Mansfield, May 22; and Commander David D. Porter, Apr. 30, 1862. *O.R.,* Ser. I, Vol. 18, pp. 289–301, 253–259, 361–374.
18. Reports of Gen. J. K. Duncan, Apr. 30, and Gen. Benjamin F. Butler, Apr. 29, 1862. *O.R.* Ser. I, Vol. VI, pp. 521–535, 503–506.
19. *Official Reports of Battles, as Published by Order of the Confederate Congress at Richmond* (New York, 1864), 362–363.
20. *The Journal of Julia Le Grand, New Orleans, 1862–1863* (Richmond, 1911), 40.
21. *O.R.,* Ser. I, Vol. 15, p. 426.
22. See account by Gen. Magruder, commander of Confederate forces at Galveston, in La Bree, *The Confederate Soldier,* 408–411.

23. Reports of Admiral Buchanan and of the commander of the *Tennessee*, J. D. Johnston, Aug. 26 and 13, 1864, *O.R.*, Vol. 39, Part 1, pp. 443–448.
24. Jeremy F. Gilmer to Loulie, Sept. 6 and 9, 1862. J. F. Gilmer Papers.
25. H. A. Gosnell, *Guns on the Western Waters* (Baton Rouge, 1949), chap. i.
26. Captain Isaac N. Brown, "The Confederate Gun-Boat Arkansas," in Johnson and Buel, *Battles and Leaders of the Civil War*, III, 572–580.
27. Richard Taylor, *Destruction and Reconstruction* (New York, 1879).
28. Capt. W. H. Parker, "The Confederate States Navy," in Evans, *Confederate Military History*, Vol. XII, chap. xi.
29. Scharf, *History of the Confederate States Navy*, 761.
30. Soley, *The Blockade and the Cruisers*, 227–229.
31. See Gamaliel Bradford, *Confederate Portraits*, chap. viii.
32. Raphael Semmes, *Service Afloat* (New York, 1903), and Arthur Sinclair, *Two Years in the C.S.S. Alabama* (Boston, 1896).
33. Log Book of the *Shenandoah*, 1864. MS in North Carolina State Department of Archives and History.
34. "Journal of Chas. E. Lining, C.S.S. Shenandoah," in D. S. Freeman, ed., *A Calendar of Confederate Papers* (Richmond, 1908), 152.
35. G. W. Dalzell, *The Flight from the Flag* (Chapel Hill, 1940), describes the careers of some of the cruisers.
36. Philip Melvin, "Stephen Russell Mallory, Southern Naval Statesman," *Journal of Southern History*, X, 137–160 (May, 1944).
37. Augusta J. Evans wrote, Jan. 27, 1864, to J. L. M. Curry of a conversation with Buchanan in which he described his difficulties in securing a crew for the *Tennessee*. He said he had made 650 applications to the War Department for sailors in the army to be detailed for naval service but had received only 20 men. J. L. M. Curry Papers.
38. Letterbook of Admiral Franklin Buchanan. MS in Southern Collection, University of North Carolina.

CHAPTER X

1. Sir Frederick B. Maurice, *Statesmen and Soldiers of the Civil War* (Boston, 1926), 40–42.
2. James Longstreet, *From Manassas to Appomattox* (Philadelphia, 1896), chap. xx.
3. General D. H. Hill was blamed for the loss of the orders; but he denied that he had received them, and furthermore maintained that "the loss of the orders was a benefit and not an injury to the Confederate arms." Hill, "The Lost Dispatch," *The Land We Love*, IV, 278 (Feb., 1868).
4. E. P. Alexander, *Military Memoirs of a Confederate*, chaps. xii and xiii, contains an excellent account of this battle which criticizes Lee for fighting the battle and risking the life of the Confederacy when he could have retired behind the Potomac and concentrated his army. For a defense of Lee's Maryland campaign see Robert E. Lee, *Lee's Dispatches . . . to*

Jefferson Davis and the War Department of the C.S.A., 1862–65, ed. Douglas S. Freeman (New York, 1915), 61–64.

5. Report of Lee on the capture of Harpers Ferry and the battle of Sharpsburg, Aug. 19, 1862. *O.R.*, Ser. I, Vol. 19, Pt. I, pp. 144–153.

6. In *The Story of the Civil War* (3 vols. in 4, New York, 1933) J. C. Ropes, a Federal officer and historian, gives an intelligent account of the battle.

7. Sanger and Hay, *James Longstreet*, 102.

8. E. P. Alexander, *op. cit.*, 274–275, lists the casualties of the Confederate army as 13,609 and of the Federal army as 27,767; Johnson and Buel, eds., *Battles and Leaders of the Civil War*, II, 600–603, gives 15,203 for the Union army and 13,964, or over one-third, for the Confederate army.

9. Johnson and Buel, *op. cit.*, III, 13.

10. *Ibid.*, 1–61. E. P. Alexander, *op. cit.*, 220–222, observes that the Confederates should have used their interior lines to strengthen either Bragg for the invasion of Kentucky or Lee for the invasion of Maryland.

11. Edward Porter Thompson, *History of the Orphan Brigade* (Louisville, 1898).

12. Lee's Report to Seddon, Dec. 14, 1862; Longstreet's report, Dec. 20, 1862; Jackson's report, Jan. 31, 1863. *O.R.*, Ser. I, Vol. XXI, pp. 545–556, 568–572, 630–635.

13. Fuller, *Grant and Lee*, 174. On the other hand Sir Frederick Maurice points out that Lee fought at Fredericksburg only because of the insistence of President Davis since he realized that the higher hills on the north side of the Rappahannock, dominated by the heavy guns of the Federals, would make pursuit after victory extremely dangerous. Maurice, *op. cit.*, 42–44.

14. Report of Lee to Adj. Gen. Samuel Cooper, Sept. 21, 1863. *O.R.*, Ser. I, Vol. 25, Pt. I, pp. 795–805.

15. *Ibid.*, 809.

16. Longstreet, *From Manassas to Appomattox*, 327.

17. Kean MS Diary, I, June 14, 1863.

18. Sanger and Hay, *James Longstreet*, 159–160; Longstreet, *op. cit.*, 336.

19. G. Moxley Sorrel, Longstreet's chief of staff, believed that Stuart's critical absence from Lee's army caused the loss of the battle at Gettysburg, *Recollections of a Confederate Staff Officer* (2nd ed., New York, 1917), 158–160, 164.

20. Report of Jubal Early to Major A. S. Pendleton, A.A., Aug. 22, 1863. Jubal H. Early Papers, IV. MSS in Library of Congress.

21. Capt. Cecil W. Battine, *The Crisis of the Confederacy: A History of Gettysburg and the Wilderness* (New York, 1905), 195.

22. Williams, *Lincoln Finds a General*, II, 689–690, maintains that Ewell's decision on this occasion was sound.

23. Freeman, *R. E. Lee*, III, 80.

24. Sanger and Hay, *James Longstreet*, chap. xiii, and Longstreet, *op. cit.*, chap. xxvii.

25. Longstreet, *op. cit.*, 373–374.
26. The battle is vividly portrayed by participants in Commager, *The Blue and the Gray*, Vol. II, and in E. S. Miers and R. A. Brown, eds., *Gettysburg* (New Brunswick, N.J., 1948).
27. George E. Pickett, *Soldier of the South: General Pickett's War Letters to His Wife*, ed. A. C. Inman (Boston, 1928), 57–58, 68.
28. Alexander, *Military Memoirs of a Confederate,* chap. xviii.
29. Freeman, *R. E. Lee*, III, 130.
30. W. R. Livermore in Pt. III, Bk. II, pp. 488–499, of Ropes, *The Story of the Civil War.*
31. See J. C. Pemberton, *Pemberton, Defender of Vicksburg* (Chapel Hill, 1942), and an opposing point of view: Joseph E. Johnston, *Narrative of Military Operations, Directed During the Late War Between the States by Joseph E. Johnston* (New York, 1874).
32. Kean MS Diary, II, June 14, 1863.
33. Report of Maj. Gen. John C. Pemberton, Aug. 2, 1863, *O.R.*, Ser. I, Vol. 24, Pt. I, 249–330.
34. Samuel Jones (formerly major general, C.S.A.), "The Battle of Prairie Grove, Dec. 7, 1862," *The Southern Bivouac*, new ser., I, 203–211 (Sept., 1885).
35. Richard Taylor, *Destruction and Reconstruction*, 126.

CHAPTER XI

1. Diary of Catherine Ann Edmondston, May 2 and 18, 1861, and May 8, 1862.
2. Loulie Gilmer to her father A. L. Alexander, autumn, 1861. Jeremy F. Gilmer Papers.
3. John B. Gordon, *Reminiscences of the Civil War* (New York, 1903), 91, 319. Mrs. Gordon intrepidly followed her husband on his campaigns in a carriage and nursed him after he was wounded at Antietam.
4. See F. B. Simkins and J. W. Patton, *The Women of the Confederacy* (Richmond, 1936); Matthew Page Andrews, comp., *Women of the South in War Times* (Baltimore, 1920); and Freeman, *The South to Posterity,* chap. vi.
5. Chesnut, *A Diary from Dixie*, 341. For insights into the social life of the Confederacy, see Coulter, *Travels in the Confederate States.*
6. Augusta Jane Evans to Jabez L. M. Curry, July 15, 1863. J. L. M. Curry Papers.
7. S. L. J. (i.e., Catherine C. Hopley), *Life in the South; from the Commencement of the War, by a Blockaded British Subject* (2 vols., London, 1863), I, 46, 205, II, 62–64.
8. See Phillips Russell, *The Woman Who Rang the Bell: The Story of Cornelia Phillips Spencer* (Chapel Hill, 1949), 20, 90–96.
9. Ramsdell, *Behind the Lines in the Southern Confederacy*, 49.

10. T. F. Upson, *With Sherman to the Sea*, 118–119.
11. Bell I. Wiley, *The Life of Billy Yank, the Common Soldier of the Union* (Indianapolis, 1952), 101–102.
12. Eaton, *Freedom of Thought in the Old South*, chap. iii, and C. W. Dabney, *Universal Education in the South* (Chapel Hill, 1936), I.
13. Jesse R. McLean, to Calvin H. Wiley, July 1, 1861. C. H. Wiley Papers, MSS in North Carolina State Department of Archives and History.
14. L. A. Paschall to Wiley, May 22, 1862. Wiley Papers.
15. M. C. S. Noble, *A History of the Public Schools of North Carolina* (Chapel Hill, 1930), 245.
16. D. C. McIntyre to Calvin H. Wiley, May 27, 1861. Wiley Papers.
17. John S. Lane to Calvin H. Wiley, May 11, 1861. Wiley Papers.
18. Calvin H. Wiley to W. J. Yates, Mar. 31, 1865. Wiley Papers.
19. M. B. Moore, *The Geographical Reader for Dixie Children* (Raleigh, 1863), 5, 14.
20. John K. Bettersworth, *Confederate Mississippi: The People and Policies of a Cotton State in Wartime* (Baton Rouge, 1943).
21. E. M. Coulter, *College Life in the Old South* (New York, 1928).
22. Minutes of the Board of Trustees of the University of North Carolina, Oct. 8, 1863. MSS in University of North Carolina Library. See also Kemp P. Battle, *History of the University of North Carolina* (Raleigh, 1907), I, 732.
23. Minutes of the Board of Trustees of the University of North Carolina, Oct. 31, 1864.
24. William A. Graham to David L. Swain, Nov. 26 and Dec. 17, 1864. William A. Graham Papers.
25. See Clement Eaton, *Freedom of Thought in the Old South*, chap. ii.
26. Paul Hamilton Hayne to James Russell Lowell, Dec. 28, 1859. Paul Hamilton Hayne Papers, MSS in Duke University Library.
27. G. P. Voigt, "Timrod in the Light of Newly Revealed Letters," *South Atlantic Quarterly*, XXXVII, 263–269 (July, 1938).
28. Henry Timrod to his sister Emily, Apr. 11, 1862. Hayne Papers.
29. Timrod to Hayne, Aug. 25, 1864. Hayne Papers.
30. Timrod to Hayne, July 10, 1864. Hayne Papers.
31. Paul Hamilton Hayne to John Reuben Thompson, Feb. 15, 1862. Copy in Stauffer Collection, New York Public Library.
32. Hayne to his wife, Mary Michel Hayne, Feb. 10, 1862. Hayne Papers.
33. Hayne to his wife, Feb. 28, 1862. Hayne Papers.
34. See William P. Trent, *William Gilmore Simms* (Boston, 1892).
35. William Gilmore Simms to Paul Hamilton Hayne, July 29, 1863. Hayne Papers.
36. Simms to Hayne, Sept. 3, 1863. Hayne Papers.
37. See Sidney Lanier, *Letters, 1857–1868*, and *Tiger-Lilies*—respectively Vols. VII and V of Lanier, *Works*, Centennial ed., ed. Charles R. Anderson. In *Tiger-Lilies* one of the characters is Lanier's signal officer in the Confederate Army, Maj. Milligan.

38. A collection of papers of Francis Orray Ticknor is in the Duke University Library.
39. John Henry Boner to Clara V. Dargan, Oct. 29, 1863. Clara Dargan McLean Papers, MSS in Duke University Library.
40. John Henry Boner to Clara V. Dargan, Jan. 12, 1864. C. D. McLean Papers.
41. Richard B. Harwell, "John Esten Cooke, Confederate War Correspondent," *Journal of Southern History*, XIX, 501–516 (Nov., 1953).
42. Jay B. Hubbell, ed., "The War Diary of John Esten Cooke," *Journal of Southern History*, VII, 540 (Nov., 1941).
43. See W. P. Fidler, *Augusta Evans Wilson, 1835–1909*, (University, Ala., 1951).
44. C. H. Smith, *Bill Arp, So Called* (Atlanta, 1866), Preface.
45. Editorial, "The Literary World," in *Southern Illustrated News*, Nov. 2, 1862. Scattered file in University of North Carolina Library.
46. See Richard B. Harwell, *Confederate Belles-Lettres: A Bibliography and a Finding List* (Hattiesburg, Miss., 1941). C. N. Baxter and J. M. Dearborn, *Confederate Literature: A List of Books and Newspapers, Maps, Music, and Miscellaneous Matter Printed in the South During the Confederacy, Now in the Boston Athenaeum* (Boston, 1917).
47. *Southern Literary Messenger*, XXXVII, 434–446 (July, 1863).
48. Diary and Memoir of John W. Green, pp. 149, 194.
49. See B. B. Minor, *The Southern Literary Messenger, 1834–1864* (New York, 1905).
50. See B. H. Flanders, *Early Georgia Magazines: Literary Periodicals to 1865* (Athens, Ga., 1944).
51. Frank Luther Mott, *A History of American Magazines* (3 vols., Cambridge, 1938), Vol. II.
52. *The Countryman*, Turnwold, Putnam County, Ga., Nov. 17 and Dec. 1, 1862.
53. Joel Chandler Harris, *On the Plantation* (New York, 1892), chap. ii.
54. *Southern Illustrated News*, Sept. 6, 1862.
55. W. S. Hoole, "Charleston Theatricals During the Tragic Decade, 1860–1869," *Journal of Southern History*, XI, 438–547 (Nov., 1945).
56. Richard B. Harwell, *Confederate Music* (Chapel Hill, 1950), 22.
57. Richmond *Enquirer*, Feb. 24, 1865.
58. Mobile *Advertiser and Register*, Aug. 11, 1863: see also J. S. Thrasher to Robert McKee, Sept. 5, 1863. McKee Papers.
59. *The Index*, Nov. 27, 1862.
60. Coulter, *Confederate States*, 501.
61. See Harrison A. Trexler, "The Davis Administration and the Richmond Press, 1861–1865," *Journal of Southern History*, XVI, 177–195 (May, 1950).
62. Coulter, *William G. Brownlow, Fighting Parson of the Southern Highlands*, chap. ix.
63. J. G. Randall, "The Newspaper Problem in Its Bearing upon Military

Secrecy During the Civil War," *American Historical Review*, XXIII, 313–316 (Jan., 1918).

CHAPTER XII

1. Ramsdell, *Behind the Lines in the Southern Confederacy*, vii. Ramsdell thought that the greatest single weakness of the Confederacy was its handling of finances.
2. Richard C. Todd, "A History of Confederate Finance"—Ph.D. thesis, Duke University, 1950—pp. 341–347, 380. Of this sum $510,248 was taken from the mints, and $208,046.08 from the customs.
3. Table compiled from Confederate Treasury Reports by Richard C. Todd, *op. cit.*, 271, 272.
4. J. C. Schwab, *The Confederate States of America, 1861–1865: A Financial and Industrial History of the South During the Civil War* (New York, 1901), chap. xiii.
5. Richardson, ed., *Messages and Papers of the Confederacy*, I, 363–366.
6. Alexander H. Stephens to Thomas Jenkins Semmes, Jan. 4, 1862, and Jan. 17, 1863. T. J. Semmes Papers, MSS in Duke University Library.
7. Josiah Gorgas, *Civil War Diary*, 92.
8. Kean MS Diary, II, Aug. 21, 1863.
9. Stephens to Semmes, Jan. 27, 1864. Semmes Papers.
10. James M. Matthews, ed., *The Statutes at Large of the Confederate States of America Passed at the Third Session of the First Congress: 1863* (Richmond, 1863), 115–126.
11. Coulter, *The Confederate States*, 182.
12. Richardson, ed., *Messages and Papers of the Confederacy*, II, 339–340, 399–400.
13. Owsley, *King Cotton Diplomacy*, chap. xii.
14. Todd, *op. cit.*, 141.
15. *Ibid.*, 261.
16. J. L. Sellers, "An Interpretation of Civil War Finance," *American Historical Review*, XXX, 282, 287, 294 (Jan., 1925).
17. Todd, *op. cit.*, 427 (Appendix C), contains a table showing gold value of Confederate Treasury notes, May, 1861, to April, 1865, compiled by Wm. B. Isaacs & Co., Bankers, of Richmond, found in James H. Hammond Papers, Library of Congress.
18. A. J. L. Fremantle, *Three Months in the Confederate States, April–June, 1863* (Edinburgh, 1863), 29. Todd, *op. cit.*
19. John S. Wise, *The End of the Era* (Boston, 1899), 393–394.
20. Fremantle, *op. cit.*, 62.
21. Kean MS Diary, II, Oct. 4, 1863.
22. Henry Harris to Rev. George Gordon, May 12, 1862. Gordon Family Letters.
23. W. M. Robinson, Jr., "Prohibition in the Confederacy," *American Historical Review*, XXVII, 50–58 (Oct., 1931).
24. Richardson, ed., *Messages and Papers of the Confederacy*, I, 331–335.

25. E. B. Coddington, "Soldiers' Relief in the Seaboard States of the Southern Confederacy," *Mississippi Valley Historical Review*, XXXVII, 17–38 (June, 1950).
26. Bell I. Wiley, *The Plain People of the Confederacy* (Baton Rouge, 1943), 43–49.
27. Nathaniel W. Stephenson, *The Day of the Confederacy* (New Haven, 1919), chap. v.
28. Gorgas, *Civil War Diary*, 51.
29. Richardson, ed., *Messages and Papers of the Confederacy*, I, 328.
30. Coulter, *The Confederate States*, 204.
31. B. I. Wiley, *Southern Negroes, 1861–1865* (New Haven, 1938).
32. MS Diary of Daniel R. Hundley, May 18–June 9, 1861. Southern Collection, University of North Carolina. There were vigilance committees that tried and executed slaves for plotting insurrection during the war period. See Eaton, *Freedom of Thought in the Old South*, 105–107.
33. T. C. Bryan, *Confederate Georgia* (Athens, Ga., 1953), 130–131, 125.
34. H. A. Trexler, "The Opposition of Planters to the Employment of Slaves as Laborers by the Confederacy," *Mississippi Valley Historical Review*, XXVII, 211–244 (Sept., 1940).
35. See Mary Elizabeth Massey, *Ersatz in the Confederacy* (Columbia, 1952).
36. Ella Lonn, *Salt as a Factor in the Confederacy* (Baltimore, 1933).
37. Kathryn T. Abbey, *Florida, Land of Change* (Chapel Hill, 1941), 276–277.
38. C. W. Adams, "Confederate Medicine," *Journal of Southern History*, VI, 151–166 (May, 1940).
39. J. H. Parks, "A Confederate Trade Center Under Federal Occupation: Memphis, 1862–1865," *Journal of Southern History*, VII, 289 (Aug., 1951).
40. "Letters of James Lusk Alcorn," ed. P. L. Rainwater, *Journal of Southern History*, III, 196–209 (May, 1937).
41. For discussions of manufacturing in the Confederacy, see Schwab, *op. cit.*, chap. xii and Ramsdell, *Behind the Lines in the Southern Confederacy*, chap. ii.
42. Broadus Mitchell, *William Gregg, Factory Master of the Old South* (Chapel Hill, 1928), chap. x.
43. See Roger W. Shugg, *Origins of Class Struggle in Louisiana: A Social History of White Farmers and Laborers During Slavery and After, 1840–1875* (Baton Rouge, La., 1939).
44. Kean MS Diary, II, Aug. 21, 1864.
45. *Official Records of the Union and Confederate Navies*, Ser. II, Vol. 1, Pts. 1–4, 552–553.
46. See Black, *The Railroads of the Confederacy*, chaps. i, ii.
47. C. W. Turner, "The Virginia Central Railroad at War, 1861–1865," *Journal of Southern History*, XII, 518 (Nov., 1946).
48. C. W. Ramsdell, "The Confederate Government and the Railroads," *American Historical Review*, XII, 805 (July, 1917).
49. Kean MS Diary, I, Apr. 1, 1863.

50. See Robert S. Henry, "Railroads of the Confederacy," *Alabama Review,* VI, 3–13 (Jan., 1953).

CHAPTER XIII

1. Kean MS Diary, I, July 26, 1863; II, Nov. 5 and 9, 1863.
2. Gray, *The Hidden Civil War: The Story of the Copperheads,* chap. vi.
3. *Ibid.,* chap. viii.
4. George Woodward to his brother, Dec. 27, 1863. MS in possession of Hugh Buckner Johnston, North Carolina.
5. J. R. P. Ellis to his wife, Feb. 15 and June 8, 1864. MSS in possession of Hugh Buckner Johnston.
6. Sidney Lanier, *Works,* Centennial ed., VII, 162.
7. Robert D. Graham to Senator William A. Graham, Sept. 15, 1864. William A. Graham Papers, MSS in North Carolina State Department of Archives and History, Raleigh; for other evidence of high morale in 1864, see Freeman, *Calendar of Confederate Papers,* 181–184, 388.
8. Channing, *History of the United States,* VI, 612–616.
9. See J. W. Silver, "Propaganda in the Confederacy, " *Journal of Southern History,* XI, 487–503 (Nov., 1945).
10. Richardson, ed., *Messages and Papers of the Confederacy,* I, 232.
11. Lawrence Keitt to his wife, 1861. Lawrence Keitt Papers.
12. Kean MS Diary, II, Aug. 2, 1863.
13. Owsley, *State Rights in the Confederacy,* 1.
14. See Stephenson, *The Day of the Confederacy,* chaps. iv, x, xi.
15. Judah P. Benjamin to Braxton Bragg, Nov. 4, 1861. MS in University of Rochester Library. Photostat in North Carolina State Department of Archives and History.
16. Burton J. Hendrick gives a vivid description of Brown's recalcitrance in *Statesmen of the Lost Cause* (Boston, 1939). See also Louise B. Hill, *Joseph E. Brown and the Confederacy* (Chapel Hill, 1939) and Bryan, *Confederate Georgia,* chap. vi.
17. Gen. William T. Sherman, *Memoirs* (2 vols., New York, 1891), II, 138.
18. H. A. Fielder, *A Sketch of the Life and Times and Speeches of Joseph E. Brown* (Springfield, Mass., 1883), 324.
19. A. L. Alexander to Mrs. Jeremy F. Gilmer, Jan. 20, 1865. Jeremy F. Gilmer Papers.
20. See Clement Dowd, *Life of Zebulon B. Vance* (Charlotte, N.C., 1897).
21. See R. E. Yates, "Zebulon Vance as War Governor of North Carolina," *Journal of Southern History,* III, 43–76 (Feb., 1937).
22. Dowd, *op. cit.,* 489.
23. George Davis, Richmond, Apr. 16, 1863, to Vance. Zebulon B. Vance Papers, II, MSS in North Carolina Dept. of Archives and History.
24. Letters to Vance from A. S. Merrimon, Asheville, July 31, 1863; Samuel Wilkinson, Rutherfordton, Mar. 16, 1863; W. M. Poisson, Fayetteville, Feb. 23, 1863; and A. C. Cowles, Feb. 24, 1863. Vance Papers, II, 4, 22, 25.

25. Gen. D. H. Hill to Vance, June 4, 22, and 25, 1863. *Ibid.*
26. Johnston J. Pettigrew to Vance, Feb. 5, 1863. *Ibid.*
27. See J. K. Bettersworth, *Confederate Mississippi* (Baton Rouge, 1943); K. T. Abbey, *Florida, Land of Change* (Chapel Hill, 1941); J. D. Bragg, *Louisiana in the Confederacy* (Baton Rouge, 1941), and Francis R. Lubbock, *Six Decades in Texas* (Austin, 1900).
28. Kibler, *Benjamin F. Perry*, 362
29. White, *Robert Barnwell Rhett*, 225, 237–238.
30. Vance to William A. Graham, Aug. 13, 1863. William A. Graham Papers.
31. John H. Houghton was advocating a speedy peace. On Aug. 17, 1863, Vance made an eloquent and moving appeal to him and the people of the state. His letter referred to the recent failure of Alexander Stephens's efforts to negotiate with the enemy, and pointed out the results of the conquest of the South by the North, confiscation of estates, hanging of the principal leaders—a ruinous tariff, and four million Negroes let loose on society. He declared that the Northern people were weary of fighting also, and that it was impossible to restore the Union after all the hate generated by the war. The people of the South could not be conquered if they had the will to resist, and he declared that he himself would never submit on the basis of the restoration of the Union. Rather than peace meetings, meetings should be held to aid the poor and persuade deserters to return. Vance Papers, II.
32. Vance to Graham, Jan. 1, 1864. Graham Papers.
33. Vance to Graham, Apr. 9, 1864. *Ibid.*
34. Rabun, "Alexander H. Stephens and Jefferson Davis," *American Historical Review*, LVIII, 290–321 (Jan., 1953).
35. Ramsdell, ed., *Laws and Joint Resolutions of the Last Session of the Confederate Congress*, 37–38, 43.
36. Chesnut, *A Diary from Dixie*, 422.
37. Mrs. Roger A. Pryor, *Reminiscences of Peace and War* (New York, 1905), 293.
38. Augusta J. Evans to J. L. M. Curry, July 15, 1862. J. L. M. Curry Papers.
39. See Ella Lonn, *Desertion During the Civil War* (New York, 1928) and Bessie L. Martin, *Desertion of Alabama Troops from the Confederate Army: A Study in Sectionalism* (New York, 1932).
40. Augusta J. Evans to J. L. M. Curry, Dec. 20, 1862. Curry Papers.
41. Short Sketch of Life of Newton Knight Told by His Son, T. J. Knight. MS in Louisiana State University Library, Manuscript Division.
42. *The Diary of James T. Ayers, Civil War Recruiter*, ed. J. H. Franklin (Illinois State Historical Society, Springfield, Ill., 1947).
43. Even Charles Francis Adams, Jr., while stationed at Hilton Head, S.C., opposed using Negro troops; he wrote to his father that the white troops were very anti-Negro and hailed with joy the breaking up of Hunter's Negro regiment. He revised his views later and even commanded Negro troops. Ford, ed., *A Cycle of Adams Letters*, II, 170–174, 212–219.

44. Henry, *"First with the Most" Forrest,* chap. xvii.
45. See T. R. Hay, "The South and the Arming of Slaves," *Mississippi Valley Historical Review,* VI, 34–73 (June, 1919), and N. W. Stephenson, "The Question of Arming the Slaves," *American Historical Review,* XVIII, 295–308 (Jan., 1913).
46. Clipping in the Jeremy F. Gilmer Papers.
47. Hay, *op. cit.,* 63.
48. Kean MS Diary, II, Dec. 25, 1864, and Jan. 1, 1865.
49. See Georgia L. Tatum, *Disloyalty in the Confederacy* (Chapel Hill, 1934); Martin, *Desertion of Alabama Troops from the Confederate Army;* and Bryan, *Confederate Georgia,* chap. ix.
50. Kean MS Diary, II, June 20, 1864.
51. Henry J. Leroy to Gen. Braxton Bragg, Sept. 21, 1864. Jefferson Davis Papers, MSS in Duke University Library.
52. Ramsdell, *Behind the Lines in the Confederacy,* 93, 117.
53. Rabun, *op. cit.,* 300–321.
54. Kean MS Diary, II, May 3, 1863.
55. *Ibid.,* II, Feb. 5, 1865.

CHAPTER XIV

1. See T. R. Hay, "Campaign and Battle of Chickamauga," *Georgia Historical Quarterly,* 213–250, VII (Sept., 1923); Seitz, *Braxton Bragg,* chaps. ix, x; and Horn, *The Army of Tennessee,* chap. xiv.
2. Seitz, *op. cit.,* 359, quoting Bragg's letter to his wife, Sept. 22, 1863.
3. Charles A. Dana, *Recollections of the Civil War* (New York, 1899), 115. His work, as well as John Beatty, *Memoirs of a Volunteer, 1861–1863* (New York, 1946), gives a valuable insight into the Western campaigns from the Northern side.
4. See Freeman Cleaves, *Rock of Chickamauga: The Life of General George H. Thomas* (Norman, 1948), chap. x.
5. D. H. Hill, "Chickamauga—the Great Battle of the West," in Johnson and Buel, eds., *Battles and Leaders of the Civil War,* III, 638.
6. Thomas Wolfe, *The Hills Beyond* (New York, 1941), 107.
7. Sanger and Hay, *James Longstreet,* 210.
8. Johnson and Buel, *op. cit.,* 690. Longstreet, *From Manassas to Appomattox,* 472–478.
9. Johnson and Buel, *op. cit.,* 727.
10. Sam R. Watkins, *"Co. Aytch," Maury Grays, First Tennessee Regiment,* 126.
11. See W. W. Davis, *Civil War and Reconstruction in Florida* (New York, 1913), chap. xi.
12. T. Harry Williams, *Lincoln and His Generals,* chap. xii.
13. Freeman, *R. E. Lee,* III, chaps. xvi, xvii, xxiv. For a vivid account by participants in the fighting in the Wilderness, see *The American Iliad,* chap. xviii.

14. Report of the Battle of Drewry's Bluff, fought May 16, 1864: Letterbook of P. G. T. Beauregard, May 30 to July 9, 1864. MS, Library of Congress.
15. Freeman, *Lee's Lieutenants*, I, 119.
16. Kean MS Diary, II, June 20, 1864.
17. *Ibid.*, Aug. 30, 1863.
18. A vivid account of the explosion of the mine and the Battle of the Crater was given by Maj. Gen. Bushrod R. Johnson, Aug. 20, 1864, *O.R.* Ser. I, Vol. 40, Pt. I, pp. 787–793. See also Nelson Blake, *William Mahone of Virginia, Soldier and Political Insurgent* (Richmond, 1935).
19. Black, *The Railroads of the Confederacy*, xxx.
20. See Henry, *"First with the Most" Forrest*, chaps. xix, xx.
21. See Joseph E. Johnston, *Narrative of Military Operations Directed During the Late War Between the States* (New York, 1874), chaps. ix–xi.
22. See John P. Dyer, *The Gallant Hood* (Indianapolis, 1950).
23. For Hood's own reply to Johnston's criticisms, see John B. Hood, *Advance and Retreat* (New Orleans, 1880), especially chaps. vii–xiii.
24. A vivid account of the battle of Jonesboro from the point of view of the soldiers may be found in the MS Diary and Memoir of John W. Green, pp. 199–219.
25. Hood to Bragg, Sept. 4, 1864. MS in the Jefferson Davis Papers, Duke University Library.
26. William T. Sherman, *Memoirs* (2 vols., 1875), II, 111, 126.
27. See T. R. Hay, *Hood's Tennessee Campaign* (New York, 1929), 66.
28. Alexander, *Military Memoirs of a Confederate*, 53.
29. Sherman, *Memoirs*, II, 227.
30. See J. D. Cox, *The March to the Sea* (New York, 1882), and Henry Hitchcock, *Marching with Sherman* (New Haven, 1927).
31. Clement Eaton, ed., "Diary of an Officer in Sherman's Army Marching Through the Carolinas," *Journal of Southern History*, IX, 238–254 (May, 1943).
32. Sherman, *Memoirs*, II, 227–228.
33. Lloyd Lewis, *Sherman, Fighting Prophet* (New York, 1932), 490.
34. See J. B. Walters, "General William T. Sherman and Total War," *Journal of Southern History*, XIV, 447–480 (Nov., 1948).
35. See a vivid account by one of the cadets, John S. Wise, *The End of an Era*, chap. xix.
36. R. E. Dupuy, *Men of West Point* (New York, 1951).
37. See Jubal A. Early, *Autobiographical Sketch and Narrative of the War Between the States* (Philadelphia, 1912).
38. See Gordon, *Reminiscences of the Civil War*, chaps. xxiv, xxv.
39. *Ibid.*, chap. xxvii.
40. Commager, *The Blue and the Gray*, Vol. II, 1126.

Index